Obstruction

Obstruction

Nick Salvato DUKE UNIVERSITY PRESS Durham and London 2016

© 2016 Duke University Press
All rights reserved
Printed in the United States of America
on acid-free paper ∞
Designed by Amy Ruth Buchanan
Typeset in Quadraat and Helvetica Neue
by Graphic Composition, Inc.

Library of Congress Cataloging-in-Publication Data
Salvato, Nick, [date] author.
Obstruction / Nick Salvato.
pages cm
Includes bibliographical references and index.
ISBN 978-0-8223-6084-1 (hardcover : alk. paper)
ISBN 978-0-8223-6098-8 (pbk. : alk. paper)
ISBN 978-0-8223-7447-3 (e-book)
1. Affect (Psychology) 2. Doctrine of the affections.
3. Popular culture. 4. Culture. I. Title.
BF175.5.A35S25 2016
152.4—dc23
2015033382

Cover art: Liliana Porter, *Untitled with Fallen
Chair II*, detail. Courtesy of the artist and
Espacio Minimo, Madrid.

Contents

Acknowledgments

If it is with irony, then it is also with real gratitude that I begin these acknowledgments for a book called *Obstruction* by saluting two people, Robert and Helen Appel, who helped to dislodge a signal, potential blockage to my sustained work on the project: the loss of time to other obligations. Receiving an Appel Fellowship for Humanists and Social Scientists in 2012, I used the leave time in 2013 that the fellowship afforded to accomplish a great deal of the research, thinking, and writing expressed in the pages that follow.

Though time away from Cornell proved useful in a late-ish phase of the book's construction, so, too, did the conversations at Cornell that helped me to figure out *that* I was writing this book, and how and why it might matter, in a much earlier, more porous stage of *Obstruction*'s percolation. Amy Villarejo demonstrated typical, and typically beatific, patience as I came up with—and, through many conversations with her, came to discard—dozens of ideas that had to be both entertained and jettisoned as I set to work in a form that, well, works. Sara Warner inspired and encouraged me to take the particular kinds of risks that tenure ought to afford, as well as to trust that my feminist and queer commitments would remain evident despite the riskier, weirder aims to which I fastened them and in the service of which I contorted and recontorted them. Masha Raskolnikov reminded me more vividly and poignantly than anyone else (could) how "the nineties" felt when we were inside that formation and how to think about that feeling now. Sabine Haenni helped me to let go of the nagging worry that coming "late" to writing professionally about cinema would harm the effort. Jeremy Braddock supplied some thrilling book recommendations and sanguine beverage time to accompany them. Tim Murray made possible a strange, fun Shanghai trip that taught me, in less than a week, a lifetime's worth about *obstruction, work, value, (non)contemporaneity*, and any number of the other keywords that animate this book. And literally scores of other colleagues and students, especially those in my seminars "Television's Theatres" and "Theorizing Media and Performance," buoyed me in this work as they committed themselves to provocative and engaged conversation, sustained critical inquiry, sober self-assessment, yet at the same time the self-permission to indulge genuine flights of fancy.

Within and beyond Cornell, public occasions to share work in progress challenged and also encouraged me. Earliest of all, Samuel Dwinell invited me to speak on embarrassment and pop at a Cornell Department of Music colloquium, on the heels of which Lily Cui helped me to understand better anecdotal theory, unease, and why I was dragging Henry James into conversation with Tori Amos—and Liz Blake showed me the necessity of going once more into the breach with camp. Anthony Reed and a group of wonderful graduate students working in twentieth-century studies brought me to Yale and gave me clarity about how to put more valuable pressure on terms like *leisure* and *lounge*. At meetings of both the American Society for Theatre Research and the Society for Cinema and Media Studies, giving presentations on Kelly Reichardt's slowness proved fruitful, particularly because of the conversations that those presentations spurred with Jason Fitzgerald, John Muse, Lindsay Reckson, and Phil Maciak. Lindsay was also present to an American Comparative Literature Association forum on "Flatness," where she and a number of others, including Alan Ackerman, pushed me further in my thinking on cynicism, animation, and MTV.

Alongside Anthony's collegiality, I want to highlight the conversations I had with Joseph Roach when I traveled to Yale in fall 2012; and alongside Lindsay and Alan's insights, I want to underline the efforts of Maria Fackler, who helped to organize the "Flatness" seminar at ACLA. Yet Joe and Maria deserve thanks for so much more. When Joe told me, many years ago, that advising was forever, I had no idea how committed to that proposition and promise he would remain, or how effective his cheerleading would prove in helping me stay the course while writing *Obstruction*. Joe also had the most perverse, which is to say delightful, investment in the meanings and implications of bodily obstructions for this project—and, over the years, kept trying to gross me out with his vivid invocations of them. I hope that he finds a suitable payoff in the words herein that salute his brilliant hijinks. As for Maria, there are not enough words—or, rather, there have been too many words, as she has, in her singularly loving and lovingly singular way, let me talk to her for hours and hours about the ideas and objects (especially *fourfour*) that make up the fabric of this book. Without her telephonic effervescence-cum-divinity, my life and work would be mightily impoverished.

In a further embarrassment of riches, many other friends have helped me along by talking with me about *Obstruction* when I needed to, talking about anything else when that was required, and in any event offering affection and good humor in spades. I can't name all of them here, but a partial list must include Carlynn Houghton, Simon Pratt, Jane Carr, Tristan Snell, Megan Quigley, Rebecca Berne, Kamran Javadizadeh (Wordsworth!), Jennifer Tennant, Brian Herrera, Aaron Thomas, Joseph Cermatori, Kate Bredeson, Josh Chafetz, and Kate Roach.

Family supports have been likewise strong and grounding; and, while I remain most grateful in this regard for the ongoing love and generosity of Annette and Nicholas Salvato and Lee Drappi, I have been touched in the years of this book's progress to find so much ballast, affirmation, and intimacy in the relationships forged with my new family, the Buggelns and Corletts. Cathy was game and sweet enough to let me drag her to the Chocolate Factory to see *The Dream Express* (and for so much more, from Scrabble in Michigan to hiking in Peru), and Richard deserves a special mention for the appetite and stamina with which he kept talking with me about obstructions and reading pages of this book and a slew of others. I treasure our conversations.

At Duke University Press, I couldn't have asked for more. Two anonymous readers were incredibly generous yet also rigorous in assessing the manuscript, and they disclosed new and exciting potential dimensions of the work to me, of which I hope to have captured some sliver or flavor in revision. Ken Wissoker and Elizabeth Ault are a dream to work with, and I appreciate so keenly the care and cheer with which they encouraged me to think clearly and sharply about matters big, small, and at a variety of scales in between. Likewise, all of the other personnel at the press have been peaches as they have paid exacting and gorgeous attention to the verbal, visual, and related elements of the book. Any errors are solely mine to acknowledge.

Samuel Buggeln, who always has the most interesting ideas for adventures, was particularly inspired to suggest that we spend half a year in Buenos Aires—which we did, and where my work flourished as I learned unexpected and shimmering lessons from a new desk, a new view from the window under which that desk was perched, a new regular walk through San Telmo and Puerto Madero, and the countless other sensorial impressions and experiences that have shaped *Obstruction* in ways I am still endeavoring to understand. For this reason, my dear pal Jean Graham-Jones has suggested that I dedicate the book to BsAs. (And certainly a special nod must be made to

Porteña and fellow New Yorker Liliana Porter, who has permitted the use of her stunning work to grace the cover of this book.) Jean almost has it right. With gratitude for the perspective that Argentine times and spaces gifted to me, I dedicate the book rather to Sam, who is always the biggest champion, the best helpmeet, and the most beautiful partner in crime. In a turn of fortune for which I try every day to be as grateful and as nurturing as I can be, there is nothing obstructive or obstructed in my love for him, or his for me, and that love makes all the difference.

Introduction. Trafficking in Five Obstructions

Object Lessons

This book proceeds from and elaborates on an argumentative framework whose central lineament is deceptively simple: certain experiential phenomena prevalent at the turn of the twenty-first century, of which I highlight five—embarrassment, laziness, slowness, cynicism, and digressiveness—are almost always taken to be incompatible with and detrimentally obstructive to scholarly inquiry, but they may, if properly directed, be conducive to critical work and valuable, more broadly, for intellectual life. If embarrassment, cynicism, and the like obstructions are routinely identified as detriments, then that is because they really are, or at any rate, really can be and probably most often are, damaging to the critical inquiry and to the intellectual life that I have just invoked and in whose advocacy I write. That these obstructions need not, however, be felt and understood merely as detriments to intellection, especially to intellection's cultivation in writing—that the obstructive may, rather, and rather paradoxically, form the basis for and sustain material manifestations of generative thinking—is the key claim for which the book *Obstruction* itself is offered as a kind of token, emblem, or proof. In order to give that claim texture, weight, color, and force; in order to determine how, exactly, the obstructive, properly regarded, inflected, and deployed, may have value; and in order to announce the delimitation of obstruction, in a special sense of critical blockage that I have in mind, from other kinds of obstacle or blockade, I have had to work both locally and globally: at once to consider particular objects that could teach me in a fine-grained way about digressiveness, slowness, and so forth, and to meditate at a more abstract level about particular qualities, available for theoretical privileging, in which the potential benefits of obstruction inhere. Where the local is concerned, each of the five obstructions named here is theorized through and illuminated by a consideration of an exemplary, contemporary "case study" (circa 1990 to 2010) whose artistic contours are instructive for related critical enterprise. Thus I limn an account of embarrassment's richness by meditating on the corpus of a paradigmatically embarrassed and embarrassing popular musician, Tori Amos; redeem laziness and lounging through a confrontation with the performances of a lazing, lovingly parodic neo-lounge act, The Dream Express; uptake slowness as it has been likewise taken up in recent, magisterial—and slow—films directed and cowritten by Kelly Reichardt; challenge cynicism to be usefully mobilized as I ruminate on the cynically fashioned MTV animated series *Daria*; and encounter the merits of digressiveness in the digressively styled yet strangely encyclopedic blog of journalist and cultural commentator Rich Juzwiak.

Why do I begin with the assertion that the constitutive argumentative scaffolding on which these more discrete assays build is a deceptively simple one? First, there is nothing simple or straightforward about the use and valuation of terms like *generative, directed, work*, and even *value* itself, begun in this book's opening gambit and extended and refined over the course of its pages. To be sure, no determination of value is separable from the coordinating movements of capital through which all value gets routed at one point or another; yet to observe only as much is to absorb at best half of the lesson articulated in a well-established critical tradition—one in sympathy with which I write—that alights on the constitutive indeterminacies in any chains of value.[1] Among other effects, these indeterminacies complicate the very notion of value's determination as strictly answerable to or captured by capital and make provisions, however fleeting or fragile, for eccentric, sometimes nonce forms of value whose uses may accord with an equally fleeting or fragile *extrinsicalness* to capital's seizures, one echoed lightly in *eccentricity*. (Certainly, no one who has read even casually about the ostensible "crisis" in academic publishing—a condition perhaps better understood as a chronic response to the ongoing fabrication, no less real for the fabricating, of crisis rhetorico-logic and attendant production strategies and distribution platforms—would be likely to nominate *exchange value* as the primary analytic through which to understand the rendering and circulation of often overpriced, under-purchased scholarly monographs.)[2] Likewise, another critical tradition with which I write in sympathy and solidarity has advocated not simply or easily for the repudiation, abolition, or supersession of work but rather for the renovations of work in its various forms, because of or en route to which careful affirmations of work may be entailed, sometimes (but not only or best) under the rhetorical banner of *post-work*.[3] So to remark, as I do here, that I stand for locating value in intellective work is to make an assertion as slippery as Portia's when she declares her standing for justice[4] or as Tammy Wynette's when she advocates standing by your man.[5] Like the participation in a recursive masquerade that thickens the former and the cracking of plaintive voice that cuts through the latter, this stand has layers, some of whose edges are also fault lines, measuring, again, the eccentricity whose capacities home my project.[6] Such eccentricity is akin (in the distantly intimate—which is to say, queer—manner that kissing cousins are kin) to the sort that Judith Jack Halberstam enacts in his performance of "fail[ing] spectacularly";[7] where that performance makes a success, indicated for instance in blurbs and reviews, of failure's in every sense winning embrace, this not quite obverse one aims to pressurize its substance beyond the terms or forms described in the binary suturing of success with failure.

Returning to the question of deceptive simplicity, I must also mark that to value work in the funny way that I suggest in the preceding paragraph means to wield or render each of my obstructions in ways neither straightforward nor transparent. How, for instance (and to invoke and restage performance elements of the sort used in classic psychology experiments), to be neither the subject who runs from the room in extreme embarrassment—nor the one who coolly designs an experiment in which a simulation of that scenario unfolds—but, strangely, both? How to "do" real laziness or cynicism yet not thereby capitulate, merely and banally, to the norms connoted in the worn phrases *goofing off* and *selling out*, respectively (and how, in the process, to answer for not *dropping out*)? How to slow down without also sliding into what Lauren Berlant calls, in an evocative phrase, a dance with "slow death" or related versions of immobility?[8] And how to digress in a fashion that avoids distraction (of oneself, of one's interlocutors), a source of no small amount of recent critical despair, by rather manifesting attention (to twinkling details, to the larger constellations that they may star)? Ensuing chapters provide answers to these and related questions; and, as the manner and matter of their posing here begins to intimate, the project that they animate does not endorse getting over—or sidestepping—obstructions but instead champions taking them up *as* complexly comprehended obstructions and, in the process, activating their potential, often surprising energies.

This insistence raises the further question of what, exactly, and for the present purposes, defines an obstruction that has the particular valence(s) I prize. Far afield as its object may be from the contemporary archive in which this book invests, Paul Fry's writing on Wordsworth, among the very few scholarly efforts to deploy the word *obstruction* with precision, may for this reason offer an inroad to the question's answering and model a version of the different but closely related precision with which the term becomes a keyword here. Tracing the way in which Wordsworth routinely "replaces" an "epiphanic sense of 'clearing'" with "a blockage or obstruction," Fry accounts for what (else) this sort of obstruction does as it "throw[s] a barrier across the path" of the poet: "In many cases, at least, that is what it does; but what it does yet more notably in nearly all cases . . . is simply to intensify the experience of being on the path itself, radically undermining the before-and-after structure on which epiphany had traditionally depended."[9] An obstruction "experience[d]" in the full, "intensif[ied]," and nonteleological way that Fry, following Wordsworth, conceives might be further theorized not through an emphasis "on the path" but rather through a redirection to "the barrier [thrown] across the path" that Fry describes more briefly: the barrier whose encountering we understand well—via a cliché that merits its exhaustion because of its exhaustive usefulness—when we metaphorize it as hitting the wall. One response to hitting the wall is to climb over it, constituting relatively uncomplicated achievement and perhaps an epiphany (depending on what is more or less Romantic—but not, in this way, Wordsworthian—about the experience). Another response is, with equally uncomplicated cleverness or facility, to circumvent it: to refuse to stay "on the path" by finding another that rounds the wall. Yet a third is to hang—dwelling, prolonging, and thereby suspending—in the impasse that the path, no longer a path, has become and that this word, *impasse*, has conjured so vividly in the recent writing on affect that discloses with appropriate ambivalence the simultaneous promise and peril occasioned by hanging (out) in the impasse.[10] Distinct from all three of these modes—and perhaps most crucially distinct, in our current critical climate, from the complex impassivity shading into impassion that affect studies has imagined in the impasse—is the embrace of obstruction that I affirm and anatomize. To embrace obstruction is to scale the wall not in order to surmount it but *to cling to it*, in such a way that the subject of this "intensif[ied]" obstruction and the obstructive wall itself change, perhaps move, precisely because of the clinging and the more granularly textured feeling of, up, and against the wall that the clinging enables. In the process, the moving wall might become a dance floor. And, as this torquing of a common metaphor suggests, the character of such an obstructive phenomenon is not only spatial but also temporal, given the (decidedly nonepiphanic, but also nonimpassive) interval that it would take to cling thus.

To think of these spatial and temporal qualities together, less metaphorically, and in a more prosaically definitional way, I would add that an obstruction or blockage is both durable and durational—and, in these ways, different from a mere obstacle or blockade, which is passing and passable. Turning to a literally more concrete example of an obstruction than the Wordsworthian barrier—one also more directly consonant with this book's focus on the contemporary—may help to clarify further the distinction drawn here between such obstruction and related obstacle. The example comes from Matthew May's *In Pursuit of Elegance: Why the Best Ideas Have Something Missing*, which alights briefly and celebratorily on a design experiment that Dutch traffic engineer Hans Monderman implemented at a busy intersection in the village Drachten (formerly troubled by a high number of accidents for a crossing of its size). Guided by a vision of "shared space" and a speculation that drivers, cyclists, and pedestrians will be more mindful in the absence of traffic's ruling and regulation, Monderman removed all lights and signs from the hazardous intersection—with the following results, as described and interpreted by May:

> There are no road divisions, no white lines, no curbs to separate cars, bikes, or people. Finally it dawns on you that what is missing is the conventional prescription for order at a traffic crossing: right-of-way.
>
> If you were to observe the action for a few hours, you would soon see that something else associated with most intersections is also missing: obstruction. The wheeled and walking traffic through [the four-way intersection] Laweiplein flows continuously in all directions across an equally shared space.[11]

In his interest to locate and praise examples of elegant simplicity, May asserts that "obstruction" is signally "missing" from the intersection in Drachten—but it takes only a slight, albeit crucial, semantic recalibration to interpret the traffic phenomenon along different lines. In the terms that I have established here, we could say instead that Monderman has capitalized on the difference between an *obstacle* (any given, particular traffic jam) and an *obstruction* (the ongoing existence of traffic as such) in a way that exploits the obstructive "problem" of traffic and calls into question traffic's very status as a problem. In other words, the "problem" of traffic is not exactly, elegantly solved: "wheeled and walking traffic," as May calls it, still abounds in Drachten. Rather, this traffic itself is accepted as a constitutive condition of intersectionality; no longer construed as a phenomenon to eliminate, it may alternatively be taken up as a useful and usable obstruction, one whose adjusted embrace enables the "continuous" "flow" of subjects who, together, make the space a valuably, "equally shared" one.

I.1 and I.2 Drivers, cyclists, and pedestrians cross through heavily trafficked intersections designed by Hans Monderman.

A similar example of obstruction's difference from obstacle could emerge from a reading of the 2003 film *The Five Obstructions* (an artifact veritably begging for a gloss in a project fashioned as this one is and whose introduction is titled and styled in this one's way). Conceived by *auteur terrible* Lars von Trier, the film documents a series of five agonistic challenges in which von Trier invites mentor Jørgen Leth to remake his 1967 short *The Perfect Human* within various sets of constraints that are, in von Trier's estimation and language, "perverse" and even "sadistic."[12] On his own, initial (and predictably Oedipal) understanding of the contest, the sadism will have a therapeutic value and force a shattering of the cool, calculated methods with which Leth approaches filmmaking—and with that shattering, a like one of what von Trier takes to be the cool, calculated performance of persona beneath which Leth supposedly hides his deep "depression" and rage. For his part, Leth rejects von Trier's model of surface and depth and dismisses the cathartic goal toward which von Trier aims to drive the project as "pure romanticism"—yet, all the same, he accepts the challenges for the "sophistic game" he understands them to comprise, one whose playing yields pleasure and the besting of whose obstacles allows him to render thoughtful, indeed beautiful remakes of *The Perfect Human* (a feat that makes von Trier "furious" rather than producing the intended effect of unleashing the fury that he supposes unflappable Leth to conceal). Characterizing von Trier's challenges as *obstacles* rather than, as in his own estimation, *obstructions*, I not only look to develop further the premise established above but also attend to Leth's interpretation of the first challenge as consisting in "quite a few obstacles for an obstruction": that is to say, with only minor tweaking, quite a few obstacles that simply make for a multifaceted obstacle. When von Trier responds impatiently to the gamesmanship and artistry with which Leth greets the second challenge—"You always try to be too good: this is therapy, not a film competition with yourself"—what von Trier fails to grasp is that the "competition with yourself" is all too available a way for Leth to embrace the challenges as a series of discrete obstacles, not as an overriding obstruction.

The embrace, rather, of "therapy" might have landed Leth in the space of the impasse, as discussed above and as theorized in affect studies; but to direct Leth thus is an outcome over which von Trier has no "control," a key term animating a pivotal conversation between Leth and von Trier (in what may at first blush seem like an obversion of their expected positions, "pure romantic," von Trier admits to panic in the face of filmmaking conditions that he cannot control, whereas Leth revels in the paradoxically "out of control" effects that carefully arranged and manipulated filmic inputs can yield). Indeed, alongside the obstacles that Leth navigates deftly and the therapeutic impasse that fails to obtain, *The Five Obstructions'* actual obstruction turns out to be von Trier himself: that is, his fantasy of hypercontrol as manifested in his obduracy, which creates precisely the conditions for the circumvention of the impasse and the gaming of the obstacles that Leth performs. Von Trier is at once too controlling, too obsessed with the details of the game, and too sure of his ability to break down Leth to produce an actual theater or laboratory of cruelty. Instead, the great, initially unintended gift of *The Five Obstructions* is the array of *Perfect Humans* that von Trier's obstruction to his own agenda positions Leth to create.[13] It is an obstruction, moreover, that

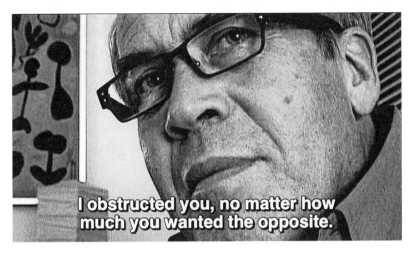

I obstructed you, no matter how much you wanted the opposite.

I.3 In *The Five Obstructions*, Jørgen Leth's face is imaged in close-up as we hear "his" words (penned by Lars von Trier) in voiceover.

von Trier belatedly and complexly positions himself to accept, when, for the final challenge, he asks Leth to read in voiceover a letter from "Leth" to "von Trier" hinging on "Leth's" line, "I obstructed you": von Trier's reflexive translation of the admission, *I obstructed myself*, where *myself*, multiply "constructed" and "mediated" and thus highly contingent,[14] may nonetheless be the (non) feeler of a pathos central to a final short "film that leaves a mark on [that self]"—and perhaps also on otherwise "unmarked" Leth and on the film's audiences.[15] In ceding control by accepting obstruction, von Trier draws, finally, nearer than we might expect to Monderman, who forgoes the more usually engineered forms of traffic regulation in order to reanimate the subjects of the intersection, no longer also the wearied subjects of congestion but instead the nimbler ones of possibility. Similar modes of control's relinquishment will animate this book.

So much, then, for theoretical and material differences between obstacles and obstructions: what unites rather than distinguishes *obstacle* and *obstruction* (as well as words like *obversion*, *obtain*, *obduracy*, and *obsessed* that I deployed with deliberation in the preceding paragraph) is their shared prefix; and the special force with which that *ob-* combines with its stem in the case of *obstruction*—indeed, the special force of *ob-* as such—draws me to privilege *obstruction*, here and throughout, over the *blockage* that Fry, for instance, reasonably understands *obstruction* as synonymizing. Retaining "classical Latin . . . senses" and "reflect[ing] [them] in English use," the prefix *ob-* may mark the paradoxical conjuncture of seemingly opposed meanings: an *ob-*position can be oriented both "toward" and "against" an object; likewise, an *ob-* movement may obtain as a "fall down" (not incidentally, the final physical act in *The Five Obstructions*) or as a "complet[ion]" in intensification (ditto, a final physical act that, repeating and reframing footage from earlier in the film, also spikes it).[16] *Obstruction* emerges as the most apt descriptor for the experiential phenomena that I investigate, in no small part because it carries within it these countervailing connotations. To dispose, to face a subjectivity toward that which would seem to run against or even deface it—or, more processually, to collapse into a heightening—is to work the aslant value of ostensive impedition that I have otherwise been tracking in this introduction. As for *obstruction*'s stem, derived from the Latin *struere* (to build, to assemble), we may well build on this account itself by asking, with the paradox of obstruction's embrace in mind: What is the "manner of building" opened in obstruction's grip?[17] How does an ob-structed building or assemblage differ from a more typical con-struction, and how does it relate to pedagogical in-struction?

In framing a couple of key questions in this way, I owe a debt to Martin Heidegger's *Being and Time*, the most careful English translation of which lingers emphatically, as I do here, over words prefixed by *ob-* as it also unfolds ideas about making and teaching. In a passage concerned with the "conspicuousness," "obtrusiveness," and "obstinacy" of things, Heidegger uses these three concepts to delineate when, how, and why (otherwise) useful things become no longer (merely) useful things: that is, when, in a "breach" or "disruption," they announce themselves as impedimental to or unavailable for use. This interval or gap marks a time for learning, insofar as it measures a moment in which "noticing" may happen and at which the abeyance of typical makings allows worldliness to "make . . . itself known."[18] In other words, *ob-*like inutility is the condition for insight, for the apprehension of the worldliness of the world—with the implication that so-called inutile things have an intellective use value, precisely in their blockage of "use," that we could call *obstructive* in a philosophically positive sense. Following this logic, I see the kind of instruction entailed by obstruction as fundamentally reorienting the phenomenal—and with it the intellective—perspective of the subject of both the obstruction and its implantation of instruction. If a more concrete construction (for instance, a writing) proceeds and develops from this instruction, then it, too, will be marked by the trace of reorientation, as an effort of, in, and through redoubling: call it, if you're Lars von Trier, and to (re)name one example of such a redoubled effort already invoked, *The Five Obstructions*.

Contre Temps

Circling back to *The Five Obstructions* has a further purchase because of the way in which continued interpretation of the film is uniquely well poised to launch us toward some claims about the contemporary, a term that I have already used here to describe the archive—and, indeed, the impetus—to which *Obstruction* owes its fabrication. More specifically, the film enjoins us to consider and differentiate a recently passed "present"—captured in the times and spaces of the film's making (and in the repeated remaking of *The Perfect Human*)—from an older postmodernity, which is residually aligned with that more recent past and of which the original *The Perfect Human*, with its coolly devastating indictment of the white bourgeois subject's claim to transcendent being and mastery, offers an exemplary chronicle. Contradistinct from that quintessentially postmodern 1967 film, *The Five Obstructions* announces its difference, its contemporaneity, in meditations on globalized manipulations of capital and the brutal, racialized inequities that those manipulations produce; in a reflexively marked reliance on digital technologies; in a turn to and wrestling with overtly ethical questions; and in a dissonant collision of von Trier's new—which is to say, old and renewed—articles of (Romantic, Freudian, religious) faith with Leth's abiding skepticism.[19] At the level of form, another dissonant collision irrupts in the juxtaposition of Leth's sleek, crisp, exquisite, and comparatively expensive short films with the footage of conversational encounters between Leth and von Trier and with behind-the-scenes footage of Leth's shoots, both of which are noteworthy for shaky shots from handheld cameras, confessionally oriented close-ups, and crude wipes between shots—in short, elements we would find at play in almost any example of slapdash reality television. Despite the juxtaposition of these reality television–styled portions of the film with Leth's variegated shorts, each of which is rendered in a different, referential style (including expressionist split-screen, surrealist animated, and hyperrealist travelogue works), *The Five Obstructions* is not a pastiche of the sort that Fredric Jameson famously identified as one of postmodernism's signatures.[20] Rather, the deliberately labored, repetitively contrasted movements between these respective portions of the film position it, as a whole, to do a different kind of cultural work, neither pointedly parodic nor catholically pastiche but exhaustively—and exhaustedly—eclectic. As for the reality TV–like scenes, the weird, winking *rigor* with which the film refuses to deviate from an "unvarnished" (that is, elaborately citational), populist-documentary approach to their making renders these scenes candidates for what José López and Garry Potter call "critical realism" in their introduction to an assertively periodizing anthology, *After Postmodernism*.[21]

In itemizing what features *The Five Obstructions* asks us to recognize as constitutive of contemporaneity, I draw near to a list of keywords generated by Terry Smith when he argues that *multeity, adventitiousness*, and *inequity* are the "three antinomies that have come to dominate contemporary life."[22] This list forms Smith's partial answer to a question italicized and made a refrain both in his introduction to the anthology *Antinomies of Art and Culture* and in a shorter preface cowritten by Smith with Okwui Enwezor and Nancy Condee: "*In the aftermath of modernity, and the passing of the postmodern, how are we to know and show what it is to live in the conditions of contemporaneity?*"[23] Sympathetic as I am to what both von Trier and Smith show us about "globalization's thirst for hegemony in the face of increasing cultural differentiation, . . . accelerating inequity among peoples, classes, and individuals," and "a regime of representation . . . capable of . . . potentially instant yet always thoroughly mediated communication," I wonder at the same time whether Smith's catalogue of distinctly contemporary antinomies runs the risk of defining an era, even as he argues elsewhere in the same essay that he wants to resist both the definitional and periodizing impulses of modernity.[24] To remain open in the face of the difficult, refrained question about contemporaneity that Smith and his collaborators pose is an effort that he models more closely when he deemphasizes his three master antinomies and pauses instead over "*the actual coincidence of asynchronous temporalities*," oscillating before and behind the political and aesthetic ossifications that antinomously limn the contemporary for him.[25] Moreover, that pausing over the untimeliness of time itself—in and as the contemporary—aligns Smith with other thoughtful commentators on the temporal textures that make and mark the contemporariness of contemporaneity. In a comparatist framework, Natalie Melas conceptualizes such untimeliness—to borrow her words, "a contemporaneity that would not be premised on the exclusion of the non-contemporaneous, but that would instead take critical account of non-contemporaneity"—precisely as an antidote to the "terminal presentism" that haunts so many (and such worn) arguments about the end of history.[26] Similarly concerned with how to attend to historicity without sliding into a mode of positivist historiography tethered to epochal thinking, Paul Rabinow affirms of the contemporary (which is to say, of its temporal slipperiness and the perhaps estranging curiosity that we need to attend with precision and care to that slipperiness) that it is "*a moving ratio of modernity, moving through the recent past and near future in a (nonlinear) space that gauges modernity as an ethos already becoming historical*"; in the face of this

ratio, critics must "find . . . means to remain close to diverse current practices producing knowledge, ethics, and politics, while adopting an attitude
of discernment and adjacency in regard to them."[27]

Concurrent and recurrent times out of joint with themselves (and each
other), historicity without certain epochality or proscribed telos, responsiveness to these conditions through methods animated by simultaneous dwelling in and dwelling apart or aside from them: these common motifs, uniting work by Melas, Rabinow, Smith, and others,[28] come arguably into most
acute focus in Giorgio Agamben's meditation on what is noteworthy about
the contemporary (as a temporal phenomenon of ostensible presentness riven
by "disjunction" and "anachronism") and about *a* contemporary (that "rare"
and "courage[ous]" subject who forges "a singular relationship with [her]
own time, which adheres to it and, at the same time, keeps a distance from it"
precisely in order to comprehend what is anachronistic or disjunct about it).[29]
Agamben's compelling theorization of contemporariness pivots, without finally depending, on an invocation of Osip Mandelstam's 1923 poem, "The
Century" (or, as it is more typically rendered in English, "The Age"), whose
speaker—in Agamben's argument, closely identified with the poet himself—
accomplishes what Agamben takes to be a "singular," if also temporally
disorienting and self-splitting, act of becoming contemporary through his
"ability" to "hold . . . his gaze [firmly] on his own time": a prelude to the
yet more active achievement of "weld[ing] with his own blood the shattered
backbone of [that] time."[30] Yet to understand "The Age"—and its stakes for
thinking the contemporary—in this fashion means to predicate the poem's
interpretation on two yoked assumptions about its opening question, "My
age, my beast, who will ever / Look into your eyes / And with his own blood
glue together / The backbones of two centuries?":[31] first, that the question is
a rhetorical one; and second, that by asking it, the poet has also answered it,
and the answer is ipso facto none other than himself.

Yet a counter-reading of the poem (again, with implications for thinking
about the contemporary) is palpably available. After the introduction of what
would appear to be a bounded subjectivity in the poem's first line ("My century, my beast"), that subjectivity, already indirect ("my," not I), is immediately decentered or diffracted: "who" will do the work that the question asks?
What if this question is not rhetorical but uneasily open-ended, and what if
that which makes the poet contemporary is that he asks the question rather
than that he is its answer? Regarding the question's open-endedness, one
possibility is that the answer is *nobody*, as the final lines of the poem suggest
strongly: "Cool indifference pours, pours down / On your [the age's] mortal

injury." On this understanding, the movement of the poem is almost a non-movement, stuckness, perhaps an obstruction: the beastly age, an animized monster looking backward with a "cruel and weak" "smile" and a "broken" "backbone," is neither ocularly engaged nor haptically, viscerally "glue[d] together" with curative blood; instead, it is met passively with "cool indifference." The alternative posited in the third stanza—"To wrest the age from captivity, / To begin a new world, / The knees of gnarled and knotted days / Must fit together like a flute"—is imagined but unperformed and, for that reason, appropriately conceived in a sentence without an explicit subject: a syntactical move (inherent to Mandelstam's Russian as well as to this English translation) matched by the other figural ways in which the poem brackets, almost entirely, agential human endeavor and highlights instead the motility of nonhuman actants: the blood of "things," not people, "gushes" and "build[s]"; "buds" (a word whose Russian equivalent evokes semantically, only then to deny the copresence of, lungs) will "swell," not breathe; and the sea's "cartilage," replacing that of a now-bygone infant whose similar, "tender" cartilage is also imaged, "splashes ashore."

Agamben is correct that the poem's proposed, hopeful measure—knotting together the gnarled bones of the age like a flute—is an "impossible," or at least "paradoxical," task; far less certain is his conjoint claim that the poet accomplishes this gesture, paradoxically.[32] What he accomplishes instead is (at least) twofold: the asking of his age a question that has as yet no definite answer, and the making of a poem that can lyrically fit together ("like a flute") words that point to the age's "gnarled and knotted" bones, not the fitting together of the bones themselves. If this poet is indeed, as Agamben asserts of his relationship to the broken time that he inhabits, likewise a "fracture," then he remains one; he is not the healer of his age, he is not a prophetic seer and a welder, and he is not merely or simply possessed of what Agamben calls "capacity"; instead, he may be thought as an analyst of his age, as a suffering searcher and a maker of secondary or second-order things (that is, poems), and as endowed with the capacity to embrace an *incapacity* of a piece with—yet also apart from—the age's own.[33] The analysis constitutes his movement with the age, the making of the poem its apartness, a critical mark, a meta-language; for that making, he is legible, in Agambenian terms, as "a" contemporary, if in his minor, modest activity and unmitigated misery not quite as heroic a contemporary as Agamben would portray him. Yet to the side of that more or less plausible (when tweaked) reading, and in keeping with the disbursal of subjectivity toward which the first stanza of the poem gestures—a disbursal shored up by the third—the contemporariness on offer here could be comprehended not as the poet's but the *poem's*. To be sure, some of its magnetic attraction to contemporary readers, like Agamben, stems from its strange imagining of a century that is sutured to the one that precedes it and that must, brutally and intractably, carry that other century forward with it (in Russian, a portion of that brutality and intractability is conjured acoustically in the relentless repetitions of harsh, guttural sounds).[34] Yet, just as Agamben de-privileges the idea of century in favor of age—and thereby moves away from strictly epochal or flatly chronological thinking—so, too, may we de-privilege the conceit of "the poet" and take up instead the untimely timeliness of the artifact left behind him (as Melas does, for instance, with *The Black Jacobins* rather than with its author, C. L. R. James): an assemblage of words at once poised on the modern "threshold of new days" and sutured to the archaic "age of the earth's infancy,"[35] possessed of or endowed with "a multidirectional aspect in which there is a complex interplay between contemporaneity and noncontemporaneity."[36]

Without aspiring to the agonized beauty of Mandelstam's poem or pretending to the longevity of its contemporariness, *Obstruction* does, in a few key ways, move in (perhaps gnarled and knotted) sync with its timely, untimely rhythms. The book's attention is lavished on now-contemporaneous objects that it aims to understand both tenderly, on their own terms, and pointedly aslant from them. Those objects include the five obstructive phenomena themselves, which saturate the politics and aesthetics of the present; with and simultaneously against their saturation in those spheres, *Obstruction* works by torquing the phenomena toward the project of rethinking thinking itself. From time to time, the book collides its contemporaneous objects, phenomena and artifacts alike, with noncontemporaneous ones whose traffic with the former affirms the principles of multidirectionality and complexity that Melas advocates. And, as the next section of this introduction explores in greater detail, it foregrounds the shaping eye and hand of its author precisely as the basis (to repurpose a generative term of Agamben's) for his "fracture" or fraying.

Homing (I)

By anatomizing the manner in which von Trier himself becomes the signal obstruction of his film—but in such a way that the self in question is contingently, even phantasmatically, rendered—and then turning to Mandelstam's poetic giving of subjectivity, which is also its taking away, I have endeavored to lay some groundwork for a more explicit accounting of the role that the author's inscription, or "I," plays in this book. Embarrassment, laziness, cynicism, slowness, and digressiveness are the more discrete obstructions that I examine in the following chapters, but the principal obstruction whose blockages—which is also to say, in the context of this book's argument, whose conditions of possibility and value—prompt the five reckonings to come is just this authorial I. Indeed, it is an I that, for a contemporary critic writing after the poststructuralisms of the mid- and late twentieth century, must occupy the status of a problematic—a status for which I ask you to take my warrant that I have thought carefully about how it must be implied in every deployment of I in these pages, even when the status and the thinking are not explicitly marked as such. At the same time, such explicit marking, in the forms for instance of reflexive meditation and metacommentary, will also emerge over the course of the ensuing pages. Mostly located in the introductory sections of each of the book's five chapters, these anecdotal— in Jane Gallop's precise sense of "anecdotal" as eminently theoretical[37]— exfoliations provide keen evidence; without it, the fleshly, reflexive (and thereby, if it works) refreshing phenomenology of obstruction to which I aspire would not have its constitutively propre subject, however impeded and improper a prop that propre constitutes. After a fashion, then, the authorial I also becomes a "case study" here, an obstruction not dodged but embraced in order to enable alertness to the loopy significance of language and the ruses of intentionality and to demonstrate the continued generativity of a criticism whose archive is thickly experienced, powerfully lived. In short, risking the I makes for a valuable working with obstruction, insofar as it highlights that which we cannot, finally, dislodge—but out of which and in which we can make our lodgings. On the question of this risk, I can think of no better assessor than Amy Villarejo when she writes of the sharp difficulty we encounter in rising to the level of "engaged intellectual work, linking the self to the process of study, linking one's own political and intellectual investments to the writing-work of cultural criticism":

> While I happen to be of the opinion that very few authors of academic monographs successfully sustain that fragile balance between autobiography and critical argument, I do find useful those deictic gestures that disclose the production of the value of a given work. . . . The more clearly one lays out the stakes of a given inquiry—the value of the study undertaken— the more one might avoid the twin dangers of taking the self as an adequate measure of the readership and, more perilously, of the topic at hand.[38]

To attempt to "sustain [the] fragile balance" that Villarejo describes is, then, not to indulge in I for I's sake but to frame that I with regard for you and with a like regard and affection for the objects of contemplation to which that I will sometimes be hitched or stitched.

It is also, as Villarejo makes plain, to return to and redouble the question of value with which this introduction began. Perhaps one value of obstruction (and in *Obstruction*)—whether or not the precise obstruction in question is the I and the body that it cannot help but conjure, ephemerally—is indeed a value inseparable from the question of embodiment, one to which the word *obstruction* makes a "deictic gesture" in its medical sense as "blockage of a body passage, esp[ecially] the gastrointestinal, urinary, biliary, or respiratory tract; an instance of this."[39] One such "instance of this" sort of bodily obstruction, transformed metaphorically in its brief yet potent invocation in the queer theoretical tradition in which both Villarejo and I have worked, comes from the pen of the late, great Eve Kosofsky Sedgwick in collaboration with Michael Moon. They write of the "fat female body," which has historically been "visible on the one hand . . . as a disruptive *embolism* in the flow of economic circulation," that it has, on the other hand, "function[ed] . . . more durably" as that flow's "very *emblem*."[40] Doing the inside/out work so central to some practices of queer theory,[41] Sedgwick and Moon make *out of* the body an embolism that we would more ordinarily expect to find *in* the body in order to demonstrate, via a rhetorically performative enactment, how one kind of body in particular, the unpredictably unruly and/or ruling "fat female body," has itself flip-flopped between its status as a signifier *out of* and *in* sync with the flows of capital. Enlivened by this gesture and the argumentative work that it supports, I perform a modified version thereof and ask you not to think consecutively about *Obstruction* that it is "here and now" an "embolism" and "there and then" an "emblem" but rather to identify one aspect of its value in its simultaneous and coconstitutive figuring as emblematic and embolistic: emblematic of the "engaged intellectual work" that Villarejo salutes— precisely because I have engaged and twisted five obstructions supposed to be embolistic to "the writing-work of cultural criticism"; embolistic "in the flow of economic circulation" that Sedgwick and Moon describe—precisely as a monograph emblematizing densely felt intellective endeavor, activity that has a number of potent opponents, to be sure, but also an oppositional potency of its own to value and to fight for.

When, in the prior paragraphs of this introduction, I emphasize (and will now redouble an emphasis on) what is "thickly experienced," "powerfully lived," "densely felt" work, I make those moves in part to pave the way for an ampler explanation of my archive's shaping. The objects under close consideration here may strike some readers as minor, eccentric, and eclectic (and to a certain, limited extent, they may be construed as such), but they also appear here out of necessity—albeit a cleaved, ambivalent necessity. On the one hand, these objects grabbed me, durably, as much as I fastened onto them, and thus became obstructions demanding that I grapple with them. On the other hand, I only chose to meet that demand, after great care and deliberation, because of the special and highly specific pedagogical purposes in whose service the objects are enlisted. To be sure, they form just one cluster among a range of fascinating contemporary artifacts, which likewise hail me and which offer their own lessons about embarrassment, laziness, cynicism, and so forth; but these other, related artifacts do not model the *exact* lessons about the book's five obstructions in which I could find the most compelling value for myself and for the colleagues whom I seek to address. At the most general and abstract level, I would say about the process of homing in on the music of Tori Amos, the films of Kelly Reichardt, and the like that, to make my obstructions work in the paradoxical ways that they do, I needed to learn about them by moving in sync with texts, broadly construed (and the creators of those texts), as they are animated by precise admixtures of privilege and precarity, fragility and force: blockages not so wholly blocked that they could not also become building blocks. Yet to submit this global proposition for meaningful consideration demands in turn a closer, local set of investigations of where the precarious may intersect with the privileged, how the fragile may exhibit force, why the blockage builds. In order to explain more fully, then, what my case studies offer—and en route to likewise offering a fuller and more shimmering context in which to appreciate them alongside contemporaneous objects that I have also contemplated with curiosity and regard—I use this moment to break down the arguments and (re)introduce the key players of the chapters that follow *Obstruction*'s introduction (or, roadmap time!).

(1) Though a rich tradition of American cultural studies has worked to dislodge the embarrassment that may attend work on such elements of mass culture as pop music (for instance), an Adornian countertradition reveals the value in continuing to privilege intellective sophistication. Aligning chapter 1, "Embarrassment," with this countertradition, I highlight a further complication: sophistication may now, itself, constitute a source of embarrassment, placing in a double bind any critic who would set aside neither the objects producing embarrassment (for the critic as sophisticate) nor the sophistication that is in its turn embarrassing (for the critic as champion of

the popular). That obstructive double bind bespeaks a failure—perhaps, if positively embraced, a refusal—to engage in precise role segregation, an (in)ability that has been conceptualized by thinkers like Erving Goffman as central to the production of embarrassment.

Building on sociological ideas about role segregation, as well as drawing on work from a variety of other disciplines, I offer a provisional definition of embarrassment: one that begins by distinguishing embarrassment, a strong feeling, both from the affects that Sianne Ngai theorizes as weak in *Ugly Feelings* and from another strong feeling, shame, with which it has been all too often confused or to which it has been errantly attached as a subspecies. Unlike singularizing shame, embarrassment has a collectivizing potential and is fundamentally relational, figuring the place of the other as one that could be or become the place of the factitiously produced self. Factitiously produced in its own right (as, for instance, adolescent "in nature"), embarrassment's exposure of the environmentally situated, divided self—as divided—manifests in such somatic markers as the blush and cringe, the latter of which has had more cultural traction and visibility in recent years than in earlier historical periods. Alighting on the cringe in (or as) criticism alongside its recent artistic mobilizations, I see this gestural sign as in fact more helpful than the blush (so indelibly associated with transparent ideas about subjectivity and the interiority on which such subjectivity is supposed to be predicated) for a project that would comprehend the dance of self and other in embarrassment's manufacture, given the cringe's movement of a self from another or from a part of the self as other. Situating the cringe in this way inaugurates a movement en route to a more robust, poststructuralist-informed account of subjectivity and feeling (foreshadowed in this introduction), which, like Rei Terada's work, affirms pathos as the paradigmatic emotion constituting the split or even nonself—and embarrassment as the corollary, paradigmatic emotion experienced by that split self in the field of relationality.

In turn, I consider what distinguishes a specifically critical version of embarrassment from this more generally relational form of the feeling. Via an engagement with Henry James's "Figure in the Carpet," as well as recent critical work on Rousseau's *Dialogues*, I identify critical embarrassment as undergirded by and bound to a sense of stupidity—moreover, a basically inchoate sense that does not direct the senser to a strict categorization of stupidity as either a thought or a feeling. The critical embarrassment founded on category-upsetting stupidity is itself turbulent, offering the critic no safe ground from which to work but rather a moving terrain in which what can be counted stable is precisely the endurance of the stupidity that confounds the critic's thinking self with her or his feeling self. To embrace this critical embarrassment means then to share, carefully and caringly, such confounding and the curious kinds of insight to which it may lead critics and their interlocutors. Understanding as much emerges, in this case, not just from a reckoning with Goffman, James, and Rousseau, for instance, but also and more fundamentally from pressing on and pressing through my embarrassed experience of Tori Amos's music: Amos, long recognized as a cultivator of shame in her work, is just as much if not more a purveyor of embarrassed feeling, corresponding thinking, and the blurring of the two. Indeed, the sometimes shrewd management of this blurring or coextensivity makes Amos herself a critic as well as an artist of embarrassment, who capitalizes instructively—because reflexively—on the proliferation of "conflicting" roles and their oddly desirable nonsegregation. The instruction is particularly apt for the critic who would keep generatively in tension and at play a paranoid mode of engagement, its reparative obverse, and (in the process) a reparation of paranoid criticism itself.

(2) Chapter 2, "Laziness," begins with an anecdotal meditation on the obstructive experience of finding oneself unable to bring a critical project to fruition—yet just as unable, or unwilling (or unable to embrace willingness), to relinquish the project. Befitting the assay on laziness that the anecdote inaugurates, the realization of what to do with such a stymied critical project—how to (re)do it—comes not epiphanically but in a gradual, trickling way: that is to say, liquid and lazing. Conceiving an active form of lazing, distinguished from a more passive or even ossified state of laziness, as also crucially fluid in its active movements is one key to finding value in such a mode of intellection.

Indeed, for a long and varied line of writers working in a still underrecognized tradition of lazing thus (one inviting us to read its players' efforts as constituting a genealogy of "laziness studies"), what unites their historically, politically, and aesthetically diverse projects is the liquid set of styles that they all embrace, as well as the liquidification of the contingent norms governing work and value that all of their liquidly expressed writings affirm. Far from "doing nothing"—permutations and contestations of which phrase illuminate many of these writers' works—their cumulative, abundant pages constitute precisely the proof that slacking, in the sense of un-tautening thought, is not coeval with thought's abandonment or, less dramatically, with the abandonment of its concretion. For the contemporary scholar aiming to work in such a lazing mode, to do so responsibly means, as I endeavor here, to situate such work in both the narrower context of critical university studies and the broader context of postwork studies that constitute the necessary horizons for contemporary academic work and value. More far-reaching, any contemporary thinker angling toward lazing writing does well to address Hannah Arendt's still-timely concern that the concretion of thought constitutes its instrumentalization and, in the process, its deadening. In fact, it is the very loosening of the lazing writer's grip on her or his product, the liquid or light emphases on process that she or he is uniquely poised to generate, that offer such writing the potential to align with Arendtian ethics and politics.

Less obvious yet just as compelling, such projects in writerly lazing may also align with a superficially, often quite different tradition of artistic lounging. Within a longer history and broader geography, *lounge*'s various forms—adjectival, verbal, and nominal—converge with special potency on a set of postwar, American performance practices (lounge musics) enacted in a lazing manner (loungily) in a series of spaces marked by their disruptions of normative time and work (hotel and motel lounges). Though critics like Sigfried Kracauer read such spaces and related ones, like lobbies, as sites of perniciously wayward, (self-)indulgent contemplation, the vivid attraction with which Kracauer alights on such sites in order to condemn them suggests the value of reading his attraction against the grain and, per Villém Flusser's celebration of (a slightly misnamed) leisure, as indicating the value in the idling thought and related expressive behavior that the lounge, or lounging, conduces.

Because the politics of some of the preeminent practitioners of such lounging, like the paradigmatically "lazy" Dean Martin, are inhospitable to progressively committed scholars, the genuinely if trickily instructive lessons inhering in performances like Martin's have been critically underattended. More palatable and arguably more relevant to the twenty-first century are a set of pointed, contemporary reckonings with the lounge idiom, parodically reincarnated precisely so that the idiom may initiate progressive movement. Among such reincarnators of lounge, the playwright/actors performing as The Dream Express (and performing a set of meta-lounge pieces likewise called *The Dream Express*) generate work with particular pedagogical value for their lazing critical allies. Championing an anti-neoliberal restructuring of work and value within the diegeses of their performance pieces, they are also lazing developers and archivists of those pieces, and these efforts model an eccentrically apt way of making and maintaining work that relinquishes the toxic pretension to mastery and that embraces instead the boons that come from relaxation.

(3) To approach the topic of the book's third chapter, "Slowness," re-

quires at the outset a clarification of what its title indexes. Though sometimes used interchangeably in both everyday and critical contexts, two different meanings of *slowness* or *slow time* may be profitably distinguished from each other: the long (slow) experience that takes time, and the stretched or dilated experience that makes time feel slowed. Following a theoretical tradition that has directed much more attention to the former phenomenon, chapter 3 fastens on the latter as it asks: When encountering the obstacle that there is not (enough) long time to take, how best to make what time there is arresting? That is, how to embrace the obstruction of arresting time in such a way that time is not impassively and impoverishingly arrested but pleasurable and full? In the process of answering these questions, I also investigate what further articulation may obtain between acts of taking (long) time and making time (slow).

To begin that investigation requires an engagement both with a prominent critical literature of speed, in which a pervasive worry over contemporaneity's accelerations has been powerfully expressed, and with a more minor literature of slowness, in which some forms of slowness (in food preparation and consumption or travel, for instance) are—ironically—harnessed too quickly to the agendas of neoliberal capitalism. Nonetheless, key texts in the two literatures suggest commonly that an ethically and politically viable mode of slowness—one that could imbricate taking slow time *and* making time (of whatever duration) slowed—may be imagined. As yet, that mode has been imagined imprecisely, raising the question of the exact nature of the relationship between the two kinds of slowness. Engaging in a metacritical act of bifurcating time, I propose that answering this question requires, for a spell, its deferral in a non-Agambenian open: a space not for potential inoperativity but for an alternative operativity, one that keeps implicitly clocking, as it were, the passing of taken time as it makes more explicit time for other addresses and attentions.

Chiefly, that attention is given to two strikingly, if weirdly, overlapping discourses in which the otherwise bracketed phenomenon of slowed time has been intermittently considered: a strand of cognitive psychology, focused on optimal experience and "flow," and interwoven strands of Eastern and popularizing Western Buddhist philosophy, focused on the dimensionality of time (with an eye trained particularly on its fourth dimension). In the end, neither discourse provides a model for the scholar who would wish to make time feel intensively, valuably slowed: the latter rejects explicitly such a mode of critical intellection as it advocates instead disengagement from the worldliness of the world, a reach beyond speculative inquiry; while the former's method admits only descriptions of, not prescriptions for, slowing (flowing) time. Tellingly, though, both discourses disclose an attraction to the cinema, some of whose artists do, by contrast, enact a mode of stretching time that may inspire a corresponding critical movement.

One such artist is writer and director Kelly Reichardt, who routes her techniques for the exemplary, pleasurable slowing of time through the *stillness* of her camera. That still camera is at the center of a cinematic practice defined by long(ish) takes, making time slow even when only a few minutes may be taken for a shot; considerable depth of field, providing compositions with arresting clarity and detail; likewise arresting figure behavior, as actors move pointedly within or across the borders of the still, "static" frame; occasional movements of the otherwise still camera whose very smallness is striking; and recurrent motifs that spike the scenes and sequences of Reichardt's films. Once time has been slowed through these aspects of production, so, too, may it be slowed in reception for the thinking viewer, who is indeed poised to think further and better in the slowed (though not long) time spent with Reichardt's films. Likewise, these production strategies provide a model for scholarly thinking and writing, which may develop homologous strategies for time's slowing. A further lesson emerges from Reichardt's typically long preproduction periods: taking long time may be the precondition and ground for making time slowed; and, in a further wrinkle, pleasurable experiences of slowed time may (re)fuel and replenish some subsequent endurances of long time's duration.

(4) Writing in sympathy with those who wish to move flexibly beyond the cynicism in which so many contemporary subjects, especially in academe, have been mired, I nonetheless ask a harder and, to a certain extent, more initially distasteful question in chapter 4, "Cynicism": Can value be located in some version(s) of cynicism, whose wholesale relinquishment may not, after all, be desirable or even possible? To pose this question of and in academe works well in tandem with an exploration of television, a field that has likewise been thick with and thickly accused of cynicism. Yet in both cases, at least some of that saturating cynicism is multifaceted, and this chapter advocates in its turn just such a multifaceted version of cynicism's embrace, one animated by three interpenetrating attitudes: cynical accommodation to systems and structures whose navigation is inevitable, but in navigating which tactical accommodation need not become accommodationist strategy; a critical cynicism that works precisely to identify and defend against such accommodationism; and, following yet renovating classical models, a Cyn-

icism (as such classical precedents are orthographically designated) that is defined by risky acts of truth-telling and related, theatrical expressivity.

For all of its dimensionality, the version of tripartite cynicism that I advocate does not confuse cynicism (as some other accounts do) with nihilism or pessimism or, more mundanely, with banally dishonest or evil behavior. Nor does it ignore the trenchant critiques of "merely" accommodational cynicism—or of accommodational cynicism that overwhelmingly compromises the critical cynicism to which it would be hitched—that have emerged recently (for instance, in Alan Liu's work) and that may be genealogically situated alongside similar postmodern critiques (most famously, in Peter Sloterdijk's work). Nonetheless, a look yet further backward to antiquity and to modern (alongside postmodern or contemporary) commentators on antiquity discloses a staggeringly longstanding, albeit diverse, effort to understand the relationships among Cynicism and what we may call critical and accommodational cynicisms as not simply or only damaged by transactions with the latter form of cynicism's experience. Inspired by, yet also wary of, those scholars who would avoid such damage by yoking cynicism(s) to optimism— and so wary because of Lauren Berlant's stirring account of optimism's likely cruelty today—I look instead, yet in a related manner, to the perverse and eccentric uptake of classical Cynicism (one that has generative implications for its relationship to other cynicism[s]) in Foucault's late work. Following his account of how one may responsibly care for other and self, speaking risky truth to power—and just as riskily accommodating oneself to power in nimble, provisional ways—I treat that account as consonant in its aims with projects guided by sanely and sanguinely radical incrementalism (or incremental radicalism).

Arguably, one such project is configured by the MTV series *Daria*, "cynically" fashioned in the tripartite way that the chapter otherwise delineates. Indeed, the cynical-cum-Cynical creators of the series endow its eponymous protagonist with a related version of their cynicisms and Cynicism as she engages in Foucauldian (also Chekhovian) acts of *parrēsia* and related forms of protest and display. At the same time, the mobilization of cynicisms, plural, is registered not just in the diegetic content of *Daria* but also in the very form of the series' limited cel animation and the movements that it arranges, as well as those that precede it at the level of production. Accommodating some exigencies of global capitalism yet wishing at the same time to espouse a critical, global cosmopolitanism—and, I argue, fulfilling that wish—the series instructs the scholar, working within yet against the baleful features of the corporatized university, how to embody the gingerliness required to make radical gains incrementally and to ensure that incrementalism retains its radical complexion.

(5) Predicated on the act and idea of stepping aside, digressiveness may inform both a working style and a working strategy—such as those informing chapter 5. Indeed, though veering away from a project (as I did during the writing of this chapter to complete a "side" effort) may appear as an obstruction to the project's sustenance, the embrace of such obstructive digressing is situated, in turn, to allow a reengagement with the project that benefits from the differently contoured and textured forms of attention that can then be lavished on that project. Nor is *attention* a casually chosen word to describe the renewed activity in question, because digressiveness must, as a valuable obstruction, be distinguished from the distraction that has been the source of so much critical concern, bordering on consternation, in recent years, particularly among literary critics predicting the end of print reading and related interlocutors worrying more broadly over the means and modes of contemporary subjects' engagements with "new" media.

Taking up key texts from these annals in "distraction studies"—no mere distraction from digressiveness—is rather a generative digression from digressiveness. Not only revealing that distraction may not be as corrosive or pervasive as many commentators would claim and that certain forms of distraction may even lead to insight, some of distraction studies' dissenters have also aimed, in a more far-reaching way, to redefine distraction: a redefinition, in fact, that draws *distraction* nearer to what I have identified here as *digressiveness*—and that, as a consequence, helps to limn a further and fuller definition of the renovated distraction or, more properly, digressiveness in question. Drawing likewise from the small body of work on digressive practices in early modern and modern literary production, I conceptualize digressiveness as an art of *strolling*, a word whose capacity to echo both *trolling* and *scrolling* begins to index the combinations of pleasure and ambition, waywardness and direction, curiosity and concentration that mark digressiveness as an ongoing practice—and to gesture toward its dialectical interplay with an encyclopedic impulse.

The version of encyclopedism that I advocate is far from the one made objectionable by its rigidly teleological orientation, its fascist insistence on hierarchical ordering, and its morbid fantasy of completism. Looking to Diderot, his contributions to the *Encyclopédie*, and his most insightful critics to pinpoint this alternative encyclopedism, I find that such encyclopedism may instead be inseparable in its constitution—and in its appeal—from its stroll with digressiveness. And though it would be tempting to "link" the *renvois* of the *Encyclopédie* to the hyperlink as a version thereof avant la lettre (as one contemporary critic has plausibly done), the broader Diderotian choreography of digressiveness with encyclopedism has more explanatory purchase when we turn to new media ecologies because of the ways in which that choreography's combination of movement, modesty, and uncertainty provides a model for how to think of related Web forays at the level of production and at the level of reception: forays, like those of the *Encyclopédie* (itself now translated, with important consequences, into a Web artifact), that are simultaneously freeing and constraining—and, indeed, paradoxically defined by limited freedom's manufacture through constraint.

Turning to one such Web foray, Rich Juzwiak's blog *fourfour*—celebrated chiefly for its recaps of the television series *America's Next Top Model*—I ask how Juzwiak may help us, like Diderot, understand not only the traffic between digressiveness and encyclopedism but also the traffic between "newness" and "oldness": a traffic that prompts Wendy Hui Kyong Chun to wonder (and me to wonder with her) how the ephemeral endures and what forms of endurance that ephemerality may take. Asking as much means also and inevitably, in this context, to digress from both questions. That digressive swerve leads me instead to take up *remixing*, a term deployed more or less literally by Juzwiak, and to locate in the word's multivalent, metaphorical meanings its value as an umbrella concept through which to understand Juzwiak's cross-medial and cross-generic work—and its specifically haptic portions. Indeed, the commerce between the haptic and the optic in *fourfour* helps to coordinate its simultaneous courting of digressiveness and encyclopedism—*and* to account for part of its ongoing interest as a "touching" object. At the same time, the blog has a different kind of ongoing interest and instruction to offer the scholar who would, like and with Juzwiak, find in dispersion a special form of collection and in meandering an eccentric mechanism for staying an intellective course.

To stay an intellective course begun earlier in this section of the introduction, I circle back now, with more information on array, to the question of how and why I dwell with my objects yet also how to understand them as just one part of a larger archive of contemporary culture marked pervasively by embarrassment, laziness, cynicism, slowness, and digressiveness. Where the last is concerned, I am touched by and learn a great deal from work in live performance like *The Provenance of Beauty*, poet Claudia Rankine's collaboration with The Foundry Theatre to produce a meandering bus ride through—and to use a metatour guide to tell the meandering histories of—the streets of the South Bronx; as well as from work in television like *Veronica Mars*, which both embraced and eschewed the logic of the procedural as it digressed away from crimes-of-the-week toward baroquely serial, intricately multiseasonal narratives. But in the end, Juzwiak's *fourfour* tells me more about the particular, valuable interplay of digressiveness and encyclopedism, identified above, than could for instance *Provenance* (whose painstakingly calibrated bus route was not wholly digressive, though its catalogue of South Bronx tales approximated neighborhood encyclopedism) or *Veronica* (which "digressed" away from the encyclopedism of its accretive, ongoing storytelling after a network smack-down forced it to comply to more rigidly episodic norms). Likewise, a range of limited cel animations—I think here especially of *The Boondocks*—could help one to understand the uncomfortable marriage of what I am calling accommodational and critical cynicisms; yet that series, for all its wicked satire *and* pliability to the expectations of cable network programming, does not disclose a pedagogy of renovated Cynicism in the fashion that obtains in *Daria*, rarer for this quality. As for slowness, a weird magic of slowed—yet not very long—time is locatable in a series of YouTube videos in which pop hits by the likes of Aaliyah, Beyoncé Knowles, and Justin Bieber are played eight hundred times more slowly than in their original recordings; but the trancelike upshots may tend more in the direction of the consciousness-effects associated with Buddhist pedagogy than toward the pedagogy of focused thinking to which I turn in moving to the side of Buddhist teachings. Similarly, Occupy protesters performing as zombies have a great deal to teach us about the critical and purposive uptake of laziness—and its stakes in the face of the twenty-first-century capitalism that Rebecca Schneider, following Chris Harman, has called its "zombie" mode[42]—if less to demonstrate about the cognitive lazing that marks projects like *The Dream Express*. And while I admit (cue the tune, "It Had to Be You") that I have been on a collision course with Tori Amos since I was thirteen, chapter 1's argument about embarrassment's role in subject-formation and relationality pushes through what is merely personal or privatized in order to consider the collective forces and social meanings of cringing, critical and otherwise. What's more, I may—may—have been able to exercise the volition to consider closely other "embarrassing" artists (though the dozens of interlocutors who have sought me out to agree that Amos is distinctively embarrassing and to share their own awkward relationships to her music since the appearance, in essay form, of a version of chapter 1 testifies both to Amos's value in a project like this one and to what is relational, collective, and social about embarrassment), I'm not certain that, say, Paula Abdul or George Michael is all that embarrassing on close inspection. They are cheesy, yes, and even subject to occasional public mortification, but in ways that conform easily to the machinery of the entertainment industry (which is perfectly happy to sell bathroom sex to the tabloids, as Michael well knows and shruggingly accepts); whereas Amos's insistence on her activating of a politics and artistry more laudable than usually found in the pop arena is embarrassingly at odds with the relationship to pop norms and successes that she nonetheless enjoys, one made uneasy by her insistence on exceptionalism. In a further turn of the screw, her sometimes awareness of tensions like this very one, manifest in her marking of them for her audiences, is thus idiosyncratically instructive.

To understand Amos relative to Michael, or Juzwiak in conversation with Rankine, provides a way to ensure that the archive of Obstruction, while focused for the sake of detail and clarity, does not emerge as a hermetically sealed one. In part for that reason, other subjects and objects make guest appearances over the course of the five chapters to come (that is, get ready for a parade capacious enough to include Janet Jackson, Split Britches, and Silk Stalkings) and continue the work, begun in this introduction, of situating the book's most closely attended items alongside others. As that effort unfolds— and as will already have been noticeable in a nascent way, here—we will encounter differential ways in which obstructions can and can't, are and aren't, made to work. Recall my mention earlier of obstructions' deployments hinging on "precise admixtures of privilege and precarity, fragility and force." When, how, and why a cultural scene does or does not yield these admixtures is telling, and one of the many things it tells us is how complexly markers of identity—like (but not only) class, ethnicity, gender, race, and sexuality—are set in motion in my case studies and the others in juxtaposition with which they demand to be understood. In other words, meditating on privilege and precarity requires attention to the markers of identity with which they are often in close, though not saturating, correspondence: that is, to the (various) differences that (various) differences make, especially with regard to the inequitable possibilities—or foreclosures of possibility—structured by obstructions in general and by this book's five obstructions in particular.

To start to think along these lines, again a matter for revisitation in the rest of the book, I find helpful a turn to a longish, provocative moment in Hortense Spillers's now-canonical essay on race and psychoanalysis, in which the notion of unease plays a crucial, if only implicit and therefore underattended, role—prompting me to reconsider my own uses of the word unease or its cognates in the course of this introduction and later in the book and, indeed, my conceptualization of obstruction:

There is much insistence, at least in our customary way of viewing things, that the professional has little in common with the majority of the population. True enough as far as it goes, this truism is tinged with animus toward activity perceived to be esoteric, elitist, uncommon. But this simplified reading of the social map, sealing off entire regions and territories of experience from the reciprocal contagion proper to them, offers us a slim opportunity to understand how the social fabric, like an intricate tweed, is sewn across fibers and textures of meaning. There is the discourse in which the professional, as de Certeau observes, dares and labors, the discourse of *travail*; but there is also the mark of the professional's human striving in terms of the everyday world of the citizen-person—coming to grips with the pain of loss and loneliness; getting from point *a* to *b*; the inexorable passing of time, change, and money; the agonies of friendship and love, and so on. . . . In that regard, the professional's relationship to discourse is tiered, but it is also imbricated by forms of dialects through which she lives her human and professional calling, as work is rent through with the trace of the uncommon and the more common. On this level, speaking is democratically impoverished for a range of subjects, insofar as it is not sufficient to the greedy urge to revelation of motives that the social both impedes and permits, nor is it adequate to the gaps in kinetic and emotional continuity that the subject experiences as discomfort. Psychoanalytic literature might suggest the word *desire* here to designate the slit through which consciousness falls according to the laws of unpredictability. In that sense, the subject lives with desire as intrusive, as the estranged, irrational, burdensome illfit that alights between where she "is at" and would/wanna be. On this level of the everyday, the professional discourser, if we could say so, and the women commandeering the butcher's stand at the A&P have in common a mutually scandalous secret about which they feel they must remain silent, but which speaking, more emphatically, *talking*, about appeases, compensates, deflects, disguises, and translates into usable, recognizable social energy.[43]

In what appears at first blush to be the key takeaway from this passage, Spillers makes her provisional rapprochement with psychoanalysis through the figure of desire and the process or project—if not exactly the cure—of talking. Yet for those of us who, Bartleby-like, would prefer not to (fill in any number of blanks) with psychoanalysis, we might fasten our attention not on desire as "the slit through which consciousness falls" but rather on what I nominate as unease and Spillers labels "discomfort," the "gaps in kinetic and emotional continuity" that play just as foundational a role in the forming and deforming of a split, or "slit," subjectivity (again, comprehended as such after poststructuralisms) as may the "estranged, irrational" vectors of desire. Neither as totalizing as anxiety nor even as locally determinate as worry (about both of which I will say more in this book's conclusion), unease may designate the low, nagging hum within and conditioning of consciousness as such: a hum intense enough to constitute noise in the circumstances—that is, the encounters with obstruction—in which all kinds of subjects, from the "professional discourser" to "the women commandeering the butcher's stand at the A&P," confront the disjunctures "between where [they] '[are] at' and would/wanna be." Spillers's generous, delicate effort to imagine what such superficially yet meaningfully disparate subjects may "have in common," beyond what is "perceived to be esoteric, elitist, uncommon" in the work of the professional discourser—let us call her the scholar—suggests a related imagining that I share, as an invitation, to whatever more and less expected readers may come to *Obstruction*. This book lands squarely in "the discourse of *travail*" at the same time that it takes up such mundanities as "the inexorable passing of time" and "getting from point a to b." I cannot know precisely in advance, nor would I presume to predict, how the value that I find in strategic embraces of obstruction, enabling the management of time's passage, the movement from a to b, and the like, will or will not emphasize for each reader what is "uncommon" or what is "more common" about our "everyday world[s]"—especially when at least some of those readers also approach the question of commonness or uncommonness from the perspective of what Stefano Harney and Fred Moten have called *the undercommons*.[44] In common, then, with their searching work, I ask you, whoever you are, to steal what "translates into usable, recognizable . . . energy" for you, to put aside what does not, and in these ways to test the possibilities and the limits of "reciprocal contagion" that the reading experience may produce.

Coda: Homing (II)

With continued reference to the "everyday world" that I just invoked, and by way of modeling a version of the value to be found in the anecdotal that I affirmed yet earlier in this introduction, I pause here to reflect briefly on a complicated business that demanded my attention and engagement during the years of *Obstruction*'s percolation: the effort to carry on and maintain the integrity of my department's work after the department's annual operating budget was slashed by university administrators, part of their multipronged response to financial precarities engendered by investment losses and endowment attrition amidst the Great Recession. Among other serious consequences of this budget cut, most painful was the departure of wonderful colleagues who lost their jobs in the process of the department's shrinkage. And though, unsurprisingly, the ongoing employment of the department's tenure-track and tenured professors was much more secure compared to the uncertainty—or, again, and more direly, the actual job loss—confronted by lecturers and staff members, the relativity of that security was nonetheless clear: one distinct possibility that my colleagues and I faced was the shuttering of the entire department if we, as its stewards, could not develop a financial, pedagogical, and intellectual strategy for reimagining our work whose coherence and sustainability (and affordability) satisfied our administrators. Mournful a complexion as our response sometimes, inevitably took, we had either to find what value we could in this obstruction or face the wholesale erosion of our collective endeavor. Choosing the former way with as much care for each other and dignity as we could muster, we initiated widespread curricular reform, still in the process of implementation and signaled in part by our name change from a Department of Theater, Film, and Dance to one of Performing and Media Arts: a change meant to index the fuller integration of the study and practice of live performance and of cinema and media that the curricular renovations would entail.

I share this institutional narrative not for the basically personal reason that I would have been less likely to gravitate to *Obstruction*'s topics and arguments had my professional lifeworld not been powerfully reoriented in the manner toward which I gesture, but rather en route to making two claims, one political and historical and the other methodological, about the book's artifactual status. First, even under less (and of course under more) extreme circumstances than the ones that I describe, scholarly research and concomitant writing are always inseparable from teaching and administrative labor, as well as from the larger institutional structures and imperatives that coordinate such research and writing (but do not, in my view, simply or strictly contain these efforts so long as academic freedom is a meaningful, activated concept), ones that likewise participate in coordinating the broader "state of the humanities" within whose sphere we operate and circulate our work. *Obstruction* comes aslant at this nexus of issues and concerns, in part because of my desire not redundantly to retread ground covered by other, lucid commentators on contemporary humanities work in the corporatized university (including Louis Menand and Cary Nelson);[45] and in part because of my hope and warrant that those commentators' efforts may be valuably complemented by a book that offers a reflexively marked, phenomenal view—from avowedly privileged, even if also shifting, ground—of what research and writing look like as they are "transformed" by (which is just to say, made in) circumstances in which obstruction is a constitutive condition of the work and of the life shaping and shaped by that work.

Second, and as I have argued on other occasions and in different ways (including in my advocacy for the curricular reform and corresponding departmental name change mentioned above), works on and in live performance and media arts *belong* together, however small, still—though growing—the number of researchers and writers whose scholarship moves across the disciplinary boundaries that distinguish performance studies and media studies from one another. To be sure, those disciplinary distinctions have meaning and use, but so, too, and at the same time may have an insistence on what media and performance have in common and thus what may be reckoned by an intellective approach that draws on the methods that bind the two disciplines as consonant versions of (once more, in Villarejo's words) "cultural criticism": commonalities that include the embodiment of expressive behavior (or its proximation), the presentational or representational framing of this behavior, and the likewise embodied effects of this framed behavior on the audience subjects who engage it. As one such audient subject, I traffic, over the course of *Obstruction*'s chapters, with live and recorded popular music, theatrical performance, cinema, television, and new media practices, constituting an archive whose specific uptake here provides one measure of the more general ways in which, over the course of my career, I have moved from earlier training in performance studies to more recent, effortful development of deep competency in media studies. Indebted as one part of my thinking about obstruction has been to Heidegger's *Being and Time*, as elaborated in this introduction's first section, I reject that work's condemnation of curiosity as merely "*not-staying*," "*never dwelling anywhere*."[46] My own curiosity to interpret objects different from live performances—and thus my commitment to cultivate the skills necessary for such interpretation—is, by contrast, precisely what enables me to keep dwelling, too, with live performance forms in ways that are enriched, not compromised, by that dwelling's location in a many-roomed house.

That house may be conceived not only as many-roomed but also as multi-storied—which is to say, I have, for *Obstruction*, been propelled toward a set of objects that (in addition to the other qualities that I highlight in the previous section of this introduction) are distinguishable as respectively "higher" and "lower" than one another according to certain standards of cultural value.

Whatever postmodernity accomplished toward chiseling away at such hierarchizing distinctions, and for all the ways in which much formerly stable categories of taste have been subject to long-standing contestation and fracture, snobberies of various sorts have nonetheless persisted with a weird contemporary vengeance—and in equally weird, untimely, even afterlife-like guises. The promise of nobrow may never have properly or fully obtained, yet it is in part because so much cultural production has for so long flirted (cynically?) with nobrowing promiscuities and volatilities that contemporary subjects respond with desire and need to the call to distinguish themselves from one another along ever more obsessive, particularized, idiosyncratic, and minutiose axes of taste. Some of these subjects have responded with glee when I have told them, for instance, that *Obstruction* takes up *Old Joy* and *Daria*—and (quite opposed to those closet fans who come out to me) with awkwardness or barely concealed disdain at the mention of Tori Amos, thereby exposing the potential for disruption latent in even well-lubricated social dynamics: an issue to be explored further in the ensuing chapter on "Embarrassment."

At the same time, and from one compelling perspective on capital and its global flows, what I am calling these "afterlife-like" persistences of taste speciation may not be as "weird" as I also call them but rather make perfect, and perfectly morbid, sense. Confronting what Mark Fisher calls "capitalist realism," a "'system of equivalence' which can assign all cultural objects, whether they are religious iconography, pornography, or *Das Kapital*, a monetary value," subjects snobbishly cultivating more nonce systems of taste, which endeavor to make equivalences and account for value along nonmonetary lines, find one weak, minor way to make the endurance of capitalist realism more bearable.[47] In the face of this regime, as well as of the contemporary efflorescence of snobbisms that it incites, genuine (if complicatedly arrived at) nobrow deserves a reinvigoration—resistant to the valuative norms both of neoliberalism and of its taste-making "resistors"—in which my archive's activation participates. This tactic is just one element of the overall strategy, sketched here and elaborated in the pages that follow, whereby *Obstruction* transvalues obstructions as a way to conceive alternatives to the critical routines that capitalist realism tends to produce, encourage, and reward.

1. Embarrassment

A Catalogue of Embarrassment

In a highly lauded essay for the journal n+1, "Radiohead, or the Philosophy of Pop," Mark Greif frames a series of guiding questions—"Does pop music support revolution? . . . Is pop truly of its time. . . . Does it really influence my beliefs or actions in my deep life"—as often left unasked "because of an acute sense of embarrassment" on the part of the would-be critic of pop music.[1] But proceeding to use the case study of Radiohead to answer such questions, and proposing that Radiohead's work "incarnate[s] a particular historical situation"[2] marked by anxiety, paranoia, and dread, Greif strikes a tone that is determinedly unembarrassed, even confident or aggressive. Nor does embarrassment remain a sustained object of critical scrutiny in the essay, which echoes quietly Russell Nye's assertion, so foundational to American versions of cultural studies, that popular arts, including popular musics, take their inspirational cue from The Unembarrassed Muse:[3] as Greif notes provocatively—but only in passing—pop music is "a singularly unembarrassed art" that allows its enthusiasts "to hold on to and reactivate hints of personal feeling that should have been extinguished . . . and [embarrassing] things that should not be articulated because they are selfish, thoughtless, destructive."[4] Indeed, Greif could be understood as reflecting mimetically the very aesthetic and political operations that he seeks to demystify: he is "a singularly unembarrassed" critic whose lack of embarrassment allows him "to hold on to and reactivate" the ideological and affective propulsions that animate Radiohead's music, ranging from a critique, in the paradoxical form of chilling incorporation, of "distant soft tyranny" in contemporaneity, to the likely toothless "defiance" asserted in the face of such soft tyranny.[5] Perhaps it is none too surprising that Greif should be ultimately unmarked by the embarrassment with which he nevertheless marks his foray into philosophizing pop, for n+1 is not only a forum for the avowed reinvigoration of public intellectuality, but also a manifestation of the millennial hipster postures that it purports merely to interpret—and what better calling card for the cool (in the senses of both poised and fashionable) critic of pop music than his affiliation with Radiohead, whose bona fides and credentials in the realm of hipster reception are long established and remarkably, durably unassailable?

Yet what if Greif had chosen a truly embarrassing pop band or artist's body of work through which to route his ruminations on mass culture at the millennium?

What if, for instance, he had written about Tori Amos?

Over the past decade or so, I have often thought that, because of the co-constitution of my deep knowledge of her corpus and my extensive attachment to large parts of it, Tori Amos would make a terrific object for my own critical inquiry—and I have just as often thought, and for precisely the same reasons, that Amos would make a terrible object for the kind of critical inquiry in which I typically engage. In describing my attachment to Amos's music as "embarrassing" and thus "terrible" for a project such as the very one on which I have now embarked, I should hasten to add that no obsolescently (if not obsoletely) disdainful reluctance to engage mass culture critically— and no equally disdainful move, in critically engaging it, to dismiss it as mere kitsch—has driven my reticence about Amos; quite to the contrary, my scholarly work heretofore has been characterized by a robust reckoning with mass cultural products across a range of decades, media, and genres, from Britney Spears's album Blackout (2007) to the film Showgirls (1995) to the television serial Big Love (2006–11). Nor do I invoke this constellation of formerly taken-up commodities to plead specially, and by way of comparison, about some exceptional quality or qualities that I see inhering formally or materially in Amos's recordings and live performances: I do not think, for instance, that Amos's Scarlet's Walk (2002) is "more" awkwardly aspirant to American mythologizing than Big Love, or her Boys for Pele (1996) more vulgarly histrionic than Showgirls, or her To Venus and Back (1999) more conspicuously manufactured than Blackout, such that writing about Amos's albums and related phenomena should yield a greater dividend of embarrassment than may be generated by reckoning with similarly constructed and conditioned artifacts (like Blackout) and should thus give me critical pause. Rather, the hesitancy stems in part from the aspects and angles of my affective relation to Amos's output—and from the potential necessity to announce, or the potential inevitability of otherwise exposing, the aspects and angles of that relation.

To be sure, any number of influential critics of mass culture, building on Nye's charge to "erase . . . boundaries created by snobbery and cultism,"[6] announce—without embarrassment—affective attachments to their objects of inquiry; think, among a great number of possible examples, of Henry Jenkins's exuberant account of fandom in *Textual Poachers* or of Jane Tompkins's unabashed opening salvo in *West of Everything* ("I make no secret of the fact: I love Westerns").[7] Yet such late twentieth-century scholarly enterprises, adhering to what Joseph Litvak has called "hipper, more 'populist' postmodern protocols" than those governing earlier (for instance, Frankfurt School) and later (chiefly, Frankfurt School–indebted) critical accounts of mass culture,[8] pose no clear response to Litvak's compelling and provocative call that "we might in fact set a better example, and be better critics," by mobilizing an Adornian sophistication that would likely give rise to embarrassment in the face of, say, Tori Amos's music. Ironically, this sophistication may itself "cause . . . embarrassment" in an intellectual landscape in which "retaining our expensive tastes [rather] than . . . repudiating them" has been routinely indicted for its potential (though by no means guaranteed) collusion with classist hauteur.[9] If we simultaneously take up Litvak's charge to credit such sophistication and take up the study of mass culture, embarrassment about the awkward collisions among sophisticated intellection, ostensibly unsophisticated objects of inquiry, and perhaps equally unsophisticated attachments or relations to those objects, seems inevitable. In other words, what kind of inquiry except an embarrassed one is possible for the critic who admits honestly, if uncomfortably, that "a specifically institutionalized literariness" persists (however superficially disavowed) even in cultural studies projects that have otherwise moved away from the literary—and who is caught in the double bind of "invest[ing] one's cultural capital . . . in objects one has [probably] had to renounce," if only imperfectly or fragmentarily, "in order to acquire that capital in the first place"?[10]

By way of routing an answer to this question through the local and the specific and thus giving some color and dimension to my more metacritical reflections, I offer here a partial catalogue of my own embarrassments, enunciated in a version of what Eve Sedgwick has called the "impossible first person" or (by way of pointing proleptically toward a later, crucial part of this analysis) perhaps articulated under the sign, if not the weight, of what Rei Terada nominates as "an infinite abysm of transpersonal perspectives," "a string of Humean 'who's' who are all the I's I have."[11] I am embarrassed by my intimate, adolescent investment in Amos's early work, including the albums *Little Earthquakes* (1992) and *Under the Pink* (1994). I am embarrassed by the ways in which that investment has survived adolescence and persisted into adulthood. I am embarrassed by my related investment in every article of work that Amos has produced since recording *Little Earthquakes*, including her 2009 "solstice album," *Midwinter Graces*. I am embarrassed that Amos has made what many consumers would call a Christmas album—and that, refusing to acknowledge it as a Christmas album or, more benignly, as a holiday album, she has attached the modifier "solstice" to the effort.[12] I am embarrassed by Amos's frequent invocations, in interviews and elsewhere, of the value to her work of Jungian perspectives and their popular offshoots and equivalents. I am embarrassed that these Jungian perspectives form the central lineament of the 2005 book *Tori Amos: Piece by Piece*, coauthored by Amos with rock journalist and critic Ann Powers. I am embarrassed by the book's repeated attempts, in the words of an unnamed "avant-garde jazz saxophone player" quoted therein, to position Amos's work as "high art pop music."[13] I am embarrassed that the 2010 DVD *Tori Amos: Live from the Artists Den*, which is patently not a book, is packaged to resemble one. I am embarrassed by the small body of musicological books and articles about Amos, which focus almost exclusively, and with impoverishing narrowness, on tracks from *Little Earthquakes*; which put insufficient critical pressure on such insidiously naturalized terms as *confessional*,[14] *interior, self-expression*,[15] *authentic*, and *truthful*;[16] and/or which yoke otherwise fine close readings of Amos's songs to dreary revisions of Schenkerian analysis or to warmed-over articulations of feminist discourses that have been rendered outmoded by theoretical developments in feminisms coeval with—or often made prior to—the appearances of these close readings.[17] I am embarrassed by the accrual of these embarrassments and the ease with which they have accrued.

To furnish this catalogue with its items is not, I hope (and will warrant), a mere exercise in bathetic wallowing but a precondition for asking three related questions that will steer the remainder of this chapter: What is embarrassment, exactly? What distinguishes critical embarrassment from other versions and varieties, chiefly everyday or "garden" ones, of the emotion? And how might risking critical embarrassment—courting, enduring, and pushing through it, rather than sidestepping or otherwise bypassing it—situate one to speculate profitably about an object of inquiry, especially a "bad" object (like the music of Tori Amos), in ways that would have remained unaccessed and, indeed, inaccessible had the critical embarrassment not been entertained? I ask these questions in the service of valuating—but also, and more fundamentally, of valuing—critical embarrassment as an intellectual disposition and, when sufficiently disposed, as a methodological tool for cringe-worthy tasks, which (to redeploy the words of one recent, judicious commentator on Tori Amos fandom) are "not cool," which are indices of our "forbidden and dorky love," and which are undertaken "shyly, or with a self-deprecating smirk and shrug."[18]

An Embarrassment of Richness

As a way of beginning to establish the contours of embarrassment as such, I want to detour through two striking caveats concerning what embarrassment is not. Embarrassment is not one of the *Ugly Feelings*, at least insofar as such a minor emotion or affect (or, precisely, such a feeling that troubles the distinction between emotion and affect) is comprehended in Sianne Ngai's groundbreaking and influential book of that name.[19] For one thing, embarrassment is not an intrinsically "weak" affect but, as Luke Purshouse observes in a philosophical analysis of the feeling, "admit[s] of a range of strengths. It is possible to be . . . extremely embarrassed."[20] For another, embarrassment is not a necessarily or even preponderantly "negative" feeling but one that, in social psychologist Rowland S. Miller's estimation, has the salutary effects of "reassur[ing] observers of our good nature after some . . . transgression," of "reduc[ing] one's distress," and of encouraging *audiences usually [to] respond in reassuring, supportive, or cooperative ways that help embarrassed actors regain their poise.*"[21] And, for yet another, it is possible and even likely that embarrassment's relationship to the aesthetic is not (always) nearly so vexed or vexing as is that of ugly feelings like disgust; to borrow literary critic Christopher Ricks's compelling formulation, "one of the things for which we value art"—an art understood as "freed from the possibility . . . of an embarrassment that clogs, paralyses, or coarsens"—may be "that it helps us to deal with embarrassment, not by abolishing or ignoring it, but by recognizing, refining, and putting it to good human purposes."[22]

To the extent that it may be "put to good human purposes," Ricks suggests compellingly,[23] embarrassment's cultivation may resemble the transformational shame of which Eve Sedgwick and other queer theorists have written so thoughtfully—but embarrassment is not a version or subspecies of shame.[24] Where shame "makes identity"—that is, figures as "integral to and residual in the processes by which identity itself is formed"—and "remain[s] in very dynamic relation to identity, at once deconstituting and foundational,"[25] embarrassment, as a "failure in self-presentation, . . . does not undermine the individual's *general identity*; rather, it discredits a much more restricted *situational identity* [that] he is projecting into [a given] interaction."[26] In short, the "antecedents [of embarrassment] tend to involve violations of social conventions"—and thus they "differ from the antecedents of shame, which concern the failure to live up to expectations that define the 'core self.'"[27] So thoroughly does shame involve the factitious production of the "core self" and thus sharpen the distinction between self and other—as opposed to embarrassment, which depends on the environmentally situated dance between other and self—that it is possible and plausible for Douglas Crimp to write even of the shame inspired by identificatorily witnessing or otherwise partaking of another's abjection that "in the act of taking on the shame that is properly someone else's, I simultaneously feel my utter separateness from even that person. . . . I feel alone with my shame, singular in my susceptibility to being shamed for this stigma that has now become mine and mine alone. . . . In taking on . . . shame, I do not share in the other's identity."[28] In contrast with the singularizing shame that puts the self "in the place of the other only insofar as I recognize that I too am [as] prone to shame" as the other is,[29] embarrassment has a collectivizing tendency or communitarian force that is constituted by its embeddedness in relationality and predicated on the possibility that the place of the other could also be or become the place of the self—an important issue to which to return.

But first, and by way of further clarifying and specifying this distinction between shame and embarrassment, let me offer a serendipitous piece of anecdotal evidence from the repertoire of phenomena that have hovered or clustered around my experience developing what we may think of as the "cringe criticism" simultaneously enacted and reflected upon here, as well as in some earlier incarnations. After the first public presentation of this work in cringe criticism was announced on one of Cornell University's websites—and after a search trawler alighted on the mention of "Tori Amos" in the presentation's title and brought the presentation to the attention of the maintainers of the website "Undented: News & Information for the TORI AMOS Fan Community," where the presentation was reannounced—a colleague warned me that the as yet unpresented (indeed, unwritten) work was "already . . . receiving some buzz around the Tori internet communities (misunderstood buzz, but buzz nonetheless)."[30] The misunderstanding concerned the erroneous assumption, predicated only on the title of the presentation (and in the absence of any further information about its content), that my work was somehow designed to disparage or malign the "Fan Community" interpellated by "Undented." And, sure enough, my colleague's warning, sensitive to this misunderstanding, was almost immediately followed by my receipt of an unsigned email from a user with the handle "Just Me," in which I was not directly addressed but which rather began thus:

> While I don't want to make assumptions or preconceived notions about what this colloquium event will entail with regard to . . . "Cringe Criticism: On Embarrassment and Tori Amos[,]" . . . I can only imagine what your alleged so called research entails based on some feedback and chatter I hear out there already.
>
> But, I don't want to jump the gun. I'd like to encourage you to do a well-rounded analysis on your chosen topic. Dialogue is so paramount in these ever so changing times. . . .
>
> I have done research (USC Norris and UCSF Medical Center) and know a thing or two about data collection and analysis.
>
> Here are some facts that may have eluded you.
>
> - The fans that often times get a bad name are those of us who travel to numerous shows a tour. Most are fairly well educated in that we have studied some form of higher education. . . .
> - Many are quite artistic. Books, movies and music have all been published as a result of inspiration from Tori.
> - Most all of those crazed fans have some sort of spiritual component in which we serve other human beings selflessly.
> - Rarely will you find a racist or narrow minded fan. We are loving and accepting of ALL humans. . . .
> - We are well traveled and . . . have embraced other cultures worldwide BECAUSE of Tori.
>
> I implore and challenge you to do some background work that you may not have considered.[31]

Based on the presupposition that my chief intention is to ridicule or belittle fans like and including the writer of this missive, her or his own rhetoric was, in turn, wielded with the chief intention of shaming me: that is, of impugning me, in the texture of my person ("Just Me"?), as selfish, biased, "narrow[-] minded," hateful, intolerant, and culturally insensitive in whatever proportion and to whatever degree I do not recognize the writer and similar fans of Amos as, conversely (as well as distinct and distinguished from me), "selfless," anti-"racist," open-minded, "loving," "accepting of all humans," and "embrac[ing] other cultures." Yet far from shaming me and inciting me to question, ontologically, the ostensible ground of my being or shape of my subjectivity, the email—prompted by and, in its own way, participating in a public circulation of discourse ("feedback and chatter I hear out there")—provoked in me a sharp and truly empathic sense of embarrassment on the writer's behalf, for everything from the stylistic infelicities that reflect, perhaps, the volatile affective conditions of the email's composition, to her or his and others' woeful misperception of the nature of my work and, more generally, of scholarly inquiry like mine.

The understudied issue of embarrassment on another's behalf (and its implications, more broadly, for an understanding of intersubjectivity and empathy) remains to be addressed more fully—and addressed, to my mind, most fruitfully from within a positive articulation of embarrassment's coordinates and stakes. The elaboration of its negative counterpart has already and inevitably produced some definition to this positive effect, and its further unfolding is one that I would like to position, following critics like Max Black and Ben Singer, within a "cluster concept" approach to embarrassment.[32] As Singer suggests in thus approaching the unstable, if not turbulent, concept of melodrama, this methodology defers any search for the likely elusive, if not phantasmatic, "essence or foundation" of a concept and admits, instead, the way in which a concept's "meaning varies from case to case in relation to different configurations of a range of basic features or constitutive factors."[33] Where embarrassment, in particular, is concerned—and having surveyed a wide range of philosophical, sociological, psychological, literary critical, and other meditations on the concept—I would identify five "features" or "factors" as most salient to embarrassment's ongoing constitution. From such a perspective, we could provisionally say that embarrassment "is" (1) a quintessentially adolescent feeling, which arises when (2) there is an exposure of the performative self, (3) in a social or relational situation (whether real or imagined, actual or hypothesized), (4) as undesirably or nonideally multiple and divided—and which is often (5) manifested in such paradigmatic physical or gestural signs as the blush and the cringe.

To tackle each of these dimensions of embarrassment in its turn, I find it fitting to start with the feeling's adolescence, a term indexing the site where varied commentators have sought to identify the putative origins or most intense manifestations of the feeling in the (developmentally understood—and probably damagingly so) human life span. Echoing Ricks's attestations that adolescents are "especially liable to contemptuous self-rejection" and "particularly good at blushing" and that "what they [thus] know about, and can help us to know about, is embarrassability,"[34] Miller proposes that embarrassment's predication on "public self-consciousness, the ability to think about and be concerned with what other people are thinking about us" makes children much less susceptible, if susceptible at all, to the so-called "mature form of embarrassment familiar to adults"—that is, "until they gain both the socialization and the cognitive abilities of young adolescence."[35] Whether or not a bounded time of life recognized as adolescent is indeed the verifiable crucible of embarrassed feeling, embarrassment's pulsations are certainly perceived, constructed, inflected, and impacted as adolescent "in nature"; a crucial element of embarrassment's force stems from its imbrication with the "extraordinary *novelty*," "unfamiliar *impulses*," "issues of privacy and propriety," and "chronic awareness of others' evaluations" associated, in ways that now seem indelible, with adolescence.[36]

That nigh-indelible association, however historically or geographically determined and determinative (for instance), is at the same time wholly understandable to anyone who has ever felt the stinging, not-quite-naked exposure—ironically more pressurized than actual, public nakedness—of a junior high school gym class. For Purshouse (working against the grain of a cluster conceptualization of embarrassment and rather in the service, common to analytical philosophy, of bracketing the perceived contingencies of embarrassing scenarios and thereby distilling embarrassment to its essence), such exposure provides the key to understanding embarrassment's operations. As he writes, "Embarrassment involves a construal of oneself as involved in an interpersonal exposure to which one is averse," whether that aversion stems from one's positioning as the "exposee" or as the "recipient" of the exposee's vulnerably revealed "physical body, mental states, dispositions of character, [or] actions."[37] In thus describing embarrassment (and plausibly so), Purshouse takes pains to put to one side what he perceives as the unnecessary and extrinsic elements of Erving Goffman's account of embarrassment—probably the most celebrated account or, at least, worthy still of such celebration—and its emphasis on (sometimes perilously conflictive) social roles or personae. But without some such account of social roles and their fragility—that is, an account of what, exactly, makes some kinds of interpersonal exposure aversive (and others not)—I do not see how Purshouse's leaning on the aversiveness that motors embarrassment can acquire thickly descriptive, rather than only formally argumentative, force.

Goffman's explanation of role deviation's place in the unfurling of embarrassment, worth quoting at length, holds:

> Often important everyday occasions of embarrassment arise when the self projected is somehow confronted with another self which, though

valid in other contexts, cannot be here sustained in harmony with the first. Embarrassment, then, leads us to the matter of "role segregation." Each individual has more than one role, but he is saved from role dilemma by "audience segregation," for, . . . ordinarily, those before whom he plays out one of his roles will not be the individuals before whom he plays out another, allowing him to be a different person in each role . . . without discrediting either.

In every social system, however, there are times and places where audience segregation regularly breaks down and where . . . individuals confront one another with selves incompatible with the ones they extend to each other on other occasions. At such times, embarrassment, especially the mild kind, . . . clearly shows itself to be located not in the individual but in the social system wherein he has his several selves.[38]

Even an account of subjectivity less flatly sociological than this one (an account, say, like this chapter's eventual own, to which I am looking ahead) must find much to admire, and to mine, in Goffman's sleek rendering of the part played by what we might variously call the dissonance, disjunction, collision, or rupture in the social fabric that obtrudes when embarrassment obtains. As a further gloss on this state of upheaval, I might add that the social conditions imagined by Goffman may in fact be imaginary. Merely contemplating the public occasion on which "role segregation" breaks down—merely conjuring the audience in whose presence I don't wish for some aspect of my calculated performance or unstudied performativity of self to be disclosed—may be sufficient to produce the disquiet of embarrassment (though perhaps not quite as emphatically or loudly as in the hurly burly social field toward which Goffman gestures).

How Goffman knows that some mode of embarrassment has been activated—though perhaps not yet precisely "by whom . . . the embarrassing incident [is] caused[,] to whom [it is] embarrassing," or "for whom . . . embarrassment [is] felt"—owes a good deal of its detectability to embarrassment's visceral symptomatology: the array of "objective signs of emotional disturbance" that he lists with loving attentiveness and that includes "blushing, fumbling, stuttering, an unusually low- or high-pitched voice, quavering speech or breaking of the voice, sweating, blanching, blinking, tremor of the hand, hesitating or vacillating movement, absent-mindedness, and malapropisms."[39] It is no accident that the blush enjoys pride of place at the head of this list, for, though blushing is not necessarily an indicator of embarrassment, it occurs to just about every commentator on the subject to mention it and recurs in manifold, embarrassing situations; as Miller has it, "Blushing and embarrassment are not synonymous [,]. . . but they overlap considerably. In particular, blushing rarely occurs in situations that do not trigger simultaneous embarrassment. On the whole, blushing is a reliable signal of embarrassment."[40] What strikes me as missing, though, from Miller's account, as from Goffman's list of somatic (and other) profusions and, indeed, from any authorized account of embarrassment—and what I had wanted, as a consequence, to signal uniquely with the title of the public presentation, "Cringe Criticism," invoked earlier—is just how powerfully the cringe, as well as or even in place of the blush, may connote the production of embarrassment. There are a number of likely reasons why the cringe, that distinctive flavor or range of shrinking and flinching and shivering, has been overlooked in studies of embarrassment. Perhaps most important, those studies, even as they acknowledge subjects' relative aptitudes to be embarrassed by or for another, tend to focus on one's embarrassment for the self—and the blush that suffuses the face, given all of the face's deeply embedded associations with subjectivity, emerges as a privileged marker for such self-embarrassment. Conversely, the cringe, a mode of contracting and thus withdrawing, is likelier to be associated with withdrawal from another and thus with embarrassment on that other's behalf. Indeed, it is harder, though by no means impossible, to imagine the circumstances under which one would blush for another empathically rather than for oneself; and easier to imagine the conditions within which one would cringe in a complex disidentification—predicated, in the first place, on identification—from another rather than from one's self (probably, in that case of auto-disidentification, a self that is former and recollected).

Historical considerations may likewise account for cringe's conspicuous absence from the literature on embarrassment, whose reckonings have yet to catch up to the full—and fully recognizable as such—mass cultural force of cringe. That force seems to be of quite recent vintage, covering a period of about the last twenty years (also, and not incidentally, the period of Amos's successes in the commercial music industry) and defined by the emergence of a new brand of "cringe comedy," from Seinfeld to The Comeback and beyond; a new genre of reality television, inaugurated by MTV's The Real World; and a host of related phenomena that allow Ira Glass of This American Life to declare boldly of our contemporaneity that "cringe is the new horror."[41] Whether or not we cringe more now than before is far from certain, but the available lexicons and sites for attending to the cringe, as adequated with the blush, are readier to hand in a discursive field populated more fully by the craven workers of The Office than by the haunted house dwellers of Wes Craven. This vivid field is one in which it becomes increasingly possible to grasp embarrassment's power in generating bonds among its feelers; it is no accident, for instance, that live studio audience laughter and shots of comedy club habitués, modeling responses for other, later audiences, are so crucial to the respective sonic and visual landscapes of Lucky Louie and Louie, television experiments by cringe comedian par excellence Louis C.K. that aim at the rippling creation of ever-wider rings of cringers. Indeed, a cringe of mutual embarrassment—so different from the more probably isolating blush of shyness or shame[42]—has the potential to forge communities, however fragile (extreme, sustained embarrassments are likelier to produce durable communities than are their more passing and less intense equivalents) or toxic: for every cringing withdrawal from another followed by that other's embrace in ultimately empathic inclusion, there is a cringe whose making of collectivity depends more simply on exclusion (you and I cringe together at another, who remains outside our magic circle of embarrassment) or is competitively, perhaps even maliciously, motivated (by cringing at another, I test my capacity to get you to cringe, too).

What is further productive about thinking of cringe diffused across a cultural landscape—or, more modestly, of a cringe that is provoked by another or others and that may, thus, blur certain distinctions among them—is the consequent capacity to decenter, in the study of embarrassment, the feeling as definitively locatable in or owned by a particular, bounded subject. Sensitive to and enlivened by work, like Rei Terada's in Feeling in Theory: Emotion After the "Death of the Subject," that refuses to offer accounts of "ourselves without representations that mediate us, and . . . through [which] emotions get felt" and that "demonstrates how experience survives [the death of] subjectivity," I see embarrassment, poised potentially to "contraindicate the idea of the subject," as contributive to an ongoing project of the self's interrogation, inspired by and indebted to poststructuralisms.[43] For Terada, advancing a Derridean reading of the "classical picture of emotion" as always-already infused with announcements and indications of the death of the subject supposed to be the feeler of such emotion, pathos emerges as the feeling most exemplary of feeling as such.[44] In her account, "pathos is indeed the Cartesian emotion, because in sustaining thought"—understood as the self-difference that constitutes (non-)subjectivity and experience—"I feel for myself as I announce myself to me."[45] In thinking about embarrassment alongside a pathos thus defined, we might recall Goffman's perhaps related emphasis on the divided self and its unstably segregated roles. If, in Terada's account, pathos is the paradigmatic emotion qua emotion because it is an "other"-oriented feeling about the self (a self that is understood to be, in the moment of cognition, divided), then embarrassment might disclose, equally paradigmatically, how emotion works—but would appear as a more fully social, public equivalent of the pathos that otherwise allegorizes emotion's operations. In the case of embarrassment, the thinking, divided self would recognize and feel its own self-difference in relational (or the hypothesis of relational) circumstances and would thus be embarrassed by, rather than inspired to pathos for, that self-difference. Embarrassment, then, would be the paradigmatic emotion in and of the world, a counterpart in its exteriorizations to the inwardness of pathos as Terada comprehends and presents it. To pathos's refrain, "I feel for myself as I announce myself to me," embarrassment echoes, "I feel my self's otherness as it announces itself to others," or, more radically, "I feel my self's otherness as others announce my selves to me."[46]

The Richness of Embarrassment

But how is this feeling, constituted by the play of self and other, more specifically inflected when it is experienced in the field of criticism? By what mechanisms or relays does critical embarrassment communicate its local difference from an embarrassment more globally understood? In one possible iteration of addressing these questions, we would need look no further than Goffman's strong theory of embarrassment to proffer some answers. The critic (in this case, me) has opened himself to embarrassment by collapsing the separation of one or more selves (again, in this case, my onetime adolescent self, a Tori Amos fan, and my ongoing, adolescently marked self, likewise—though differentially—a recreational Tori Amos listener) from a sphere or spheres (professional ones, constituted by colloquium attendees, conference copanelists and audiences, peer reviewers, journal readerships, and so forth) where those selves (nonprofessional, or even unprofessional) do not properly or easily belong. On some intuitive, and perhaps more than intuitive, level, this Goffmanian version of events seems "right." I have felt no embarrassment talking about Tori Amos—even as she figures in my work, this work—with at least three different colleagues, also friends, on at least three different bar-going occasions, but the moment I imagine those same friends assembled in an auditorium, flanked by other colleagues (friendly and possibly otherwise),[47] and hearing a version of the very words you are now reading, I am seized by embarrassment. Role segregation's failure—in this case, more precisely understood as role segregation's refusal—creates the conditions for embarrassment's irruptions.

But is that really where the ride ends? In attempting to push further, to see around the next bend, I would submit that what distinguishes critical embarrassment from garden-variety forms of the feeling is not that it happens when one is or imagines one is interacting with professional, intellectual interlocutors (one could, after all, be just as embarrassed by tripping in front of the department chair as by giving a bad paper in her hearing—and that trip wouldn't invite critical embarrassment) but that it almost always bursts forth from, fastens to, cathects around, or centers on an intransigent sense of one's intractable (if localized) stupidity. Indeed, what undergirds or subtends all of the statements in my catalogue of embarrassment is just this common sense, variably inchoate or refined, of my own and others' associated stupidities. Thus each statement could be understood as implicitly enacting or deictically announcing the following metastatement of regret, also a problem: "This allegiance or belief or practice was or is stupid; yet if only I were smart, dexterous, and critically facile enough, I would find a way to make talking or writing about it somehow brilliantly un-embarrassing."

Limning the regret in this way has hinged, in part, on my thinking about Henry James's short story "The Figure in the Carpet," in which James has addressed the very same sort of problem with his characteristically maddening, charming, and paradoxical combination of obviousness and obliquity. So thoroughly the lodestone of Jamesian embarrassment, the story not only appears as the first item in the 1896 collection titled, simply, Embarrassments, but is also the only of those Embarrassments to leap, as if magnetically, from that book to the fifteenth volume of James's New York edition, a volume whose stories' common denominator is, according to the preface, "that they deal all with the literary life, gathering their motive, in each case, from some noted adventure, some felt embarrassment, some extreme predicament, of the artist enamoured of perfection, ridden by his idea or paying for his sincerity."[48] To turn to Jamesian modernity for answers about a critical issue of contemporary significance—and, worse, to allow myself to be taken, perhaps, as suggesting some contiguity between the intellective and affective topographies of James's prose and those of, or at least inspired by, Amos's music—may seem like a curious move. I make it not because I see an uncomplicated identity between one era's embarrassments, critical or otherwise, and another's, but rather because of how staggeringly much recent critical inquiry, especially among James scholars, reenacts the problem faced by the narrator (also a critic) of "The Figure in the Carpet" and thus positions that narrator, insistently, to tell us something about "ourselves." Indeed, it is hard to find a contemporary critic writing about "The Figure in the Carpet," even the one purporting to address the topos of embarrassment,[49] who is not, in disclosing one or another version of James's unshared "secret," replicating the narrator's own stymied quest to discover the unnamed, enigmatic, and uniting element among—the secret thread running through—all of the works by a cagey novelist, Hugh Vereker (that is, to discover, metaphorically, the eponymous figure in the carpet).

Thus searching for "deeper" meaning—or even in efforts to read the story as a sly, ironic, and allegorical critique of (the search for) deep meaning—critics tend to pass quickly over what is glaringly on the surface of James's story: its anatomization of a specifically critical form of embarrassment. And a painstaking, if not painful, anatomization it is, as James makes his narrator "blush to the roots of [his] hair," when the novelist Vereker induces him to feel, publicly, like "a rare donkey"; or "colour" when he is caught short in the face of the question, "What . . . is criticism supposed to be?"; or feel "humiliated at seeing other persons derive a daily joy from an experiment which had brought [him] only chagrin"; or feel "rather ashamed—[hating] to remind [a friend] that . . . [he] had irremediably missed [the friend's] point" about Vereker's works.[50] If only he were smarter, the narrator thinks, he would discover what the figure in the carpet is. If only he were smarter, we ought to think, the narrator would not discover what the figure in the carpet is, per se, but would rather find just as dazzling a way to write or converse about not finding the figure in the carpet—and perhaps even refuting the existence of the figure in the carpet—as he would if he had the (impossible) key to reveal that figure. In other words, he would find a way to push through the embarrassment that hounds him in almost every interaction, that impedes him at almost every turn, and with which his yoked stupidity obstructs or damages his social and professional relations. (As an aside, it's worth noting here that one key connotation of the French *embarras*, so richly linked to *embarrass*, is "obstacle" or "obstruction.")[51]

Stupidity, as the nagging instigator of a critical embarrassment like the Jamesian narrator's, poses a curious epistemological problem, since it seems to blur the line between thinking and feeling. Why is it that we tend to say, "I feel stupid," not, "I think I'm stupid"? Living with and even courting, rather than avoiding, our critical embarrassment and the undoing of poise that it engenders could be a way of (riskily avowing that we are) forcing ourselves to confront the obstructions created by our stupidity, one of which is the obstructive state in which thinking and feeling may be thoroughly entangled and, indeed, incapable of disentanglement. Whether we reject the obstruction as such and choose to categorize stupidity as belonging either to the province of thought or to that of feeling—or whether we refuse, following Avital Ronell, to categorize stupidity at all[52]—this sense of doggedly living with it is what the narrator of "The Figure in the Carpet" must finally impress on us. Thus he leaves us with a question to my mind more urgent than, "What is stupidity?" (or, more exactly, "How do I know what stupidity is?")—and that lingering question, also a hope, could be expressed this way: "If I choose likewise to live doggedly with my embarrassing stupidity, will it paradoxically yield some kind of wisdom, of the sort that James finally (sadistically?) denies his narrator?" Another way to put this question, and to invoke E. S. Burt's thoughtful reading of Rousseau's *Dialogues*, would be to ask after what happens (as in those *Dialogues*) when embarrassment isn't merely tongue tying or gap-stopping, but when the writer decides to "put pressure on the obstacle and write in an embarrassed vein"? Then embarrassment is "not a defense, but a signal of the writer's coming to face with the impossible but necessary task imposed by a regard for the other," whether that other, thus carefully and caringly regarded, is the one in the invoking of whose name the act of writing proceeds (say, a pop musician, about whom more in a moment) or the other one—you—to whom the writing is addressed.[53] Understood and performed in this way, critical embarrassment could have a tender and generative quality quite different from the preservative utility, in guaranteeing a social status quo that Goffman attributes to everyday flashes of the feeling:

> When situations are saved [by displays of embarrassment], . . . something important may be lost. By showing embarrassment when he can be neither of two people, the individual leaves open the possibility that in the future he may effectively be either. His role in the current interaction may be sacrificed, and even the encounter itself, but he demonstrates that, while he cannot present a sustainable and coherent self on this occasion, he is at least disturbed by the fact and may prove worthy at another time. To this extent, embarrassment is not an irrational impulse breaking through socially prescribed behavior but part of this orderly behavior itself.[54]

Here, Goffman sees the salutary social quality of embarrassment as conservative in nature, but could his line of thinking indicate, inadvertently, a more radical set of possibilities for the interactions that embarrassment may reshape, especially if actively risked or undertaken—and critically so? In other words, what if embarrassment, rather than safeguarding the possibility that an individual may be "either" of two selves in a future social or institutional (or intellectual) relation, were rather yoked to the agenda or demand that an individual be *both* of two selves, or more—simultaneously—in such relations?

Among other things, he might then begin to write about Tori Amos.

Embarrassment of the Catalogue

I have deferred my promised reckoning with and close reading of Tori Amos's work, not in an attempt (as should by now be clear) to stave off the embarrassment of the task but as a way to reflect mimetically, in writing's dilation, the period of living with and pushing through critical embarrassment (and its interlining stupidity) that it has taken for me to arrive at the version of observations about Amos that I am now, as a consequence, prepared to deliver. Having submitted to this emotional and intellectual gestation—as if to be embarrassed really were, in some sense (and as some Romance languages would have it), to be pregnant—I find that, far from merely figuring as a source of embarrassment, Amos provides an abundant source of instruction about embarrassment, along with and even along the same lines as Goffman, James, Rousseau, and others. Consider, to begin with, her 2005 concert performance of the song (made famous by Cyndi Lauper) "All Through the Night," in which, after spoonerizing the lyric, "We have no past / we won't reach back" as, "We have no past / we ron't weach back," she pauses, clears her throat, and says to her audience, "Well, fucking hell. That's a tricky one. Those lyrics? Let's try it again."[55] Prior to this moment of mild, embarrassed fluster, Amos has performed an uncharacteristically restrained, even decorous, rendition of the number, which she sings in a shimmery head voice and accompanies with spare, straightforward, and rhythmically regular piano playing. Then, after the embarrassed pause, something clicks, not unlike the taxi's meter in the song's lyrics: reaching down into her chest to vocalize *reach back*, prolonging the vowels of the word *through* with staccato emphases, and bending notes toward dissonantly sharp ends, Amos transitions to a style of singing more like wailing, sustained for a full half-minute of the song, accented with snarls and growls, and amplified by abandoned thrashing of the piano's keys. Tellingly, the song's lyrics insist on not reaching back, on looking forward, but every theatrical choice that Amos makes after the embarrassing stumble is precisely in the mode of reaching back—and referring—to the moment of embarrassment. Rather than acknowledging and moving swiftly past this embarrassment (which her brief, self-deprecating "interruption" of the song, applauded by a generous audience, would have more than accomplished), she decides to elongate it, musically: to risk living with it and to see how living with it will reshape what follows. And it does reshape what follows, making the remaining time of the song (as its own lyrics would have it) "new time" and as the very grain of Amos's now raspier, literally grainier voice captures the brazenness of a reveling in embarrassment, perhaps akin to the reveling in abjection that Michael Moon and Eve Sedgwick identify as the basis for "divinely" transmogrified and transmogrifying shame.[56]

"All Through the Night" could be construed, then, as a positive, if miniature, model for critical embarrassment not unlike the negative, almost cautionary counterpart provided by "The Figure in the Carpet." More fundamentally, Amos's musical project seems, on an inspection that would have remained unavailable to me prior to this assay of approach to her career and catalogue, to have been for quite some time concerned with the embarrassment as such, more encompassing than critical embarrassment, that I have otherwise been tracking in this chapter. Indeed, embarrassment—of a particularly public, exposing, and painful sort—plays a prominent role in a story about her early career that Amos has told on a number of occasions and that figures, in fact, as a kind of origin story for her breakout success in the early 1990s. Prior to that breakout—and after an adolescence and young adulthood spent performing in countless piano bars—Amos, grasping for commercial success in late '80s Los Angeles and fronting a band called Y Kant Tori Read, allowed that band's eponymous 1988 album to be pulled in every cheesy, clichéd direction imaginable within the framework of a synth- and power ballad–driven pop idiom, the writing of whose death was already splattered across any number of walls by the time of the album's release. Given the waning interest in such pop styling—and given, too, the excruciation with which that styling was rendered on Y Kant Tori Read—the album unsurprisingly tanked, a moment registered not only by Billboard's withering association of it with "bimbo music" but also by the following social encounter,[57] recalled by Amos:

> They called me a bimbo in Billboard. . . . [Then] I walked into this restaurant and saw an acquaintance, and I went over to the table, and he was, like, pretending he didn't know me. And I felt these snickers 'cause my hair was totally pumped up six feet high, and I had my plastic boots that went up to my thigh and my little miniskirt. And I understood for the first time that I was a joke. And I walked out of that room going, "They can laugh at me, but I'm walking out of this place with dignity. Hair spray and all."[58]

Assessing this moment as one of revelatory "embarrassment"—and learning from it, in words reminiscent of Goffman, "I was playing a role then, and . . . I decided, no, that doesn't fit me very well"[59]—Amos proceeded to compose and record the songs of Little Earthquakes, a much-discussed platinum effort for which the debacle of Y Kant Tori Read provides a complex context (or, better, intertext), one riven with tensions. On the one hand, considerations of marketing and publicity have sometimes prompted a desire to disappear the Y Kant Tori Read episode from Amos's career (and, quite literally, to disappear the album, which is out of print and difficult to acquire),[60] as if it were a cringe-worthy "adolescence" best left unremembered, and to replace it with another origin story: that of the shamed, as opposed to embarrassed, child prodigy admitted at five to the Peabody Conservatory, only to misfit there—and to be made, palpably, to feel that misfit—because of her unorthodox style of playing piano, devotion to rock music, and difficulty with conventional musical notation; eventually, Amos's scholarship was revoked, a failure experienced emotionally and materially as getting "kicked out" of the conservatory.[61] (Ironically, this shame-filled childhood past is embedded in the name of the band Y Kant Tori Read itself, as though the ultimate need to return to the less tainted, more saleable, and more "original" origin story were already comprehended before the band's dissolution and within its very signatory—pun intended.) On the other hand, the mythologization of "inspired" artistic production and of concomitant aesthetic cultivation has sometimes led fans, critics, and Amos herself not to ignore or erase the embarrassment of Y Kant Tori Read but to figure her as cathartically overcoming it, in a pivotal catalysis for the work of Little Earthquakes—positioned, in retrospection after the album's breakout success, as also a breakthrough endeavor.

Patently skeptical of the latter narrative's causations and teleology, I am nevertheless interested in its investment in embarrassment's capacities and in dislodging the emphasis on shame produced by the former narrative and its occlusions. For while a number of the so-called "breakthrough" songs on Little Earthquakes ("Crucify," "Leather") are, as often heralded, records of shame—sometimes transformational, sometimes not—at least one pivotal (and, to my ear now, embarrassing) song, "Precious Things," is alternatively a texturally detailed chronicle of embarrassment: "I remember, yes / in my peach party dress / no one dared / no one cared to tell me / where the pretty girls are," its speaker warbles, the word cared sticking in Amos's constricted throat as she incarnates that speaker's recollected adolescent embarrassment.[62] What's more, this sort of thematization of embarrassment persists, as much as or more than the foregrounding of shame, in a number of Amos's

1.1 and 1.2 In the video for "The Big Picture," the opening track and lead single from Y *Kant Tori Read*, Tori Amos teases her hair and dances with motorcycles.

later songs: a direct lyrical echo of the "peach party dress" is imaged in the "lilac mess in your prom dress" of the song "Liquid Diamonds,"[63] which could be thought on a spectrum of embarrassment with "Glory of the 80s," the sonic equivalent of a cringe as Amos's speaker conjures a repudiated former self, one from the period of the hair "totally pumped up six feet high," "plastic boots," and "little miniskirt" that Amos herself has exchanged for a radically different set of looks and public personae (arguably "witchy"—and thus no less embarrassing, perhaps, to some consumers of her circulating image).[64] Most vivid on this song spectrum is the hit single "Cornflake Girl," whose elliptical lyrics sketch, impressionistically, a scenario of obstructive rivalry and betrayal among women that mortifies the feminist-identified speaker describing the intimate scenario; her mortification is anthemized in the refrain, "This is not really happening / you bet your life it is" (what more compact motto for the slings and arrows of embarrassment?), on the first line of which Amos plays vocally with the idea of the embarrassed fluster as she produces a calculated, rhythmic stammer of the four words *this is not really*.[65] That Amos, who also sings herein, "Never was a cornflake girl," did actually appear in an embarrassingly trite television commercial for Cornflakes-like Just Right cereal before the rise of her star, amplifies deliciously and ironically, for the informed listener (and Amos is appealing to her), the song's meditation on embarrassed feeling. Taken together, these songs suggest a productive continuity or even slippage in Amos's work between confrontational depictions of literal adolescence or personal liminality and metaindustrial depictions of professional "adolescence" or liminality—a powerful slippage to exploit when one's output, the industrial involutions of which are nigh impossible for consumers to ignore, is largely pitched to a youth market who want, whatever cognitive dissonance it requires (the less dissonance and the more lubrication from the artist, the better), to map life narratives, constructed as private and intimate, onto the exigencies of commercial performers' highly public career displays.

Yet, as I have already indicated in a number of ways, embarrassment in this work is not just Amos's to embrace and thematize compositionally, but mine (and that of many other listeners) to experience in response to her compositional choices, as well as her performative idiosyncrasies. Consider, again, the song "Precious Things," whose catalogue of arguably embarrassing features includes Amos's mid-song shriek, italicized with an echo effect; her nasal lingering on and stretching out of the word *girl*; and the "adolescent" quality of her frenetically repeated, arpeggiated stroking of the piano keys, reminiscent of practicing a lesson (obsessively). Think, too, if you have

1.3 A witchy Tori Amos straddles the piano bench, in this instance to play two keyboards at once as she reimagines a song from Y Kant Tori Read.

heard Amos's live or studio music, of her extravagant breathiness ("China," "Horses"), her outrageous pronunciations of vowels ("Siren," "Bliss"), the overripe arrangements of orchestral-inflected tracks ("Yes, Anastasia," "Girl Disappearing"), the melodramatic excesses of songs with leaping notes and soaring whoops or cries ("Pretty Good Year," "Hey Jupiter"). To return to one of this chapter's key, framing terms, none of these effects are cool—unlike Amos's famously shivering, "icy" voice—as if such aspects of production and performance constitute Amos's organized, ongoing effort to inject some heat, however embarrassing, where and how she can, despite voice's frostiness. But in describing the production of these effects as likely "organized," I mean to emphasize that none of them, however uncool, registers as unconsidered, unstudied, or unpoised. Rather, as a practiced and disciplined performer, Amos yokes poise to an actively risked—indeed, aggressively staged—loss of control; and, in a similar mining of contraries, she stylizes her "self"-exposure and lavishly artifices such a self's vulnerability to others and to relational otherness. For instance, her lyrical and performative addresses confound, even more than usual in pop music, the line between such music's endlessly elaborated "you's" and "me's." That confounding works not only to interrogate the easy differentiation of a narrating speaker from her direct addressee, figured again and again—and predictably enough—

as a lover (as one lyric paradigmatically has it, "If the rain has to separate from itself / does it say / pick out your cloud"),[66] but also to graft that slippage between speaker and addressee onto the relationship between Amos and her live auditors. Staring with more than predictable intensity at what feels, through a performative sleight-of-gaze, like individual conferees of recognition in a given roomful or even arena full of audience members, Amos makes her lyrical "you's," also blurrily the "me's" of those lyrics, register simultaneously as the special, singled-out "you's" (potentially any of us) in the darkened crowd—and thus (and at the same time), she makes those special, audient "you's" register as one with her lyrics' enunciated "me's"; if, as she declares in a favored song on her concert set lists, "All the world is all I am,"[67] all the world stands, in a kind of reverse synecdoche, for all the smaller fan world eager to absorb these words as referring most intensely to its own habitants.

Yet in one telling performance, Amos breaks (somewhat) from this routine mode of address in order to hail (ostensibly) a more explicit and singular—and explicitly and singularly embarrassed—addressee: none other than Britney Spears, with a very different invocation of whom this chapter began. At the height of Spears's public embarrassments in 2007 (ranging from the exposure of an under-undergarmented crotch to the exposure of a bald head whose ill-considered shaving was read as a sign of "breakdown"), Amos dashed off an occasional song, "When a Star Falls Down," which she performed before a Melbourne audience on a leg of her concurrent international tour, which she framed with the explanation, "I have a comment to make," and which began with the lyric, greeted with laughter by the audience, "Britney, they set you up."[68] The laughter is understandable (any number of other public figures were simultaneously using the occasion of Spears's rapidly accreting embarrassments as grist for their comic mills), but it quickly died down as the audience came to comprehend the empathic intent of Amos's address. Listening to the sounds of Spears's tribulating mishaps and to various pundits' attendant, derisive chatter with charity—and, more important, with identification—Amos lent Spears a generous (if curious) ear, in the form of her voice. We might, following Derrida's punning account of "otobiographical" countersignature, call this lent ear the ear of the other, the "uncanny" ear that "can become" "double":[69] in this case, that becoming ear positioned the addressed "you"—Spears—as a double of (one sliver of) the speaking I, namely the Amos who had likewise experienced such painful, potentially career-ruining embarrassment on the occasion of the Y Kant Tori Read debacle and who could thus plausibly sing, with implicit acknowledgment of one of her own performing selves as well as with explicit reference to Spears, "This is what it looks like / when a star falls down." As if wishing that her address could spark Spears's (or her management's) recognition of and capitalization on her perceived "breakdown" as another *Little Earthquakes*–style "breakthrough"—and as if intuiting Derrida's mostly subterranean implication that when the uncanny ear is "large," it connotes a maternal largesse[70]—Amos sang, in an identificatory maneuver to haul Spears's star into her own, putatively more courageous wagon, "You may be a mother / baby, you still need a mother / yes, I may be a mother / but I still need a mother / to pick me up / yes, to pick me up / when it all falls down."

But did anyone else at the concert really think that Amos was picking up Britney Spears? From their perspective, wasn't she rather attempting, as on so many other occasions (though with more topical idiosyncrasy, here), to lift up an audience that might more readily identify with her avowed embarrassment—and with her mediating identification and avowal of Spears's embarrassment—than with Spears herself, at whom they were all too ready to laugh? That collective laughter can be interpreted as the live audience's camp effort to forge a "badge of identity" (with Amos, with each other),[71] one that Amos refuses in the interest of letting sing, as it were, a less sophisticated and more unalloyed feeling of embarrassment that she shares with Spears and, by musical invitation, with her audience.[72] Camp, here rejected by (or simply unavailable to) Amos, may be profitably understood as a strategy for the negotiation of enduring relationships to "bad" objects that *preempts* the instigation of embarrassment by marrying, ambivalently, two other feelings: affection and disdain, often congealing into simultaneous (and paradoxical) identification with and disavowal of the objects in question.[73] But when abiding affection for such an object persists at intransigent odds with the potential disdain to which camp would otherwise yoke that affection—that is, when affection refuses, awkwardly, to be prosthetically modified by disdain—then the resultant, secondary embarrassment that accrues and attaches to the more primary affection must be managed other than winkingly or cuttingly, as camp would do. Comprehended in the light of this consideration, the term *critical embarrassment* could nominate not just the brand of embarrassment that arises in intellective circumstances, but also the reflexive management of this brand of embarrassment: the brand that dogs the subject whose thought, coalescing into a system of taste (the object should be construed as bad), and whose feeling, evading such systematicity (the object's impact won't be reduced to such a construal), can't be rendered compatible or, more forcefully, can't even be so neatly disentangled as "thought" and "feeling" that their incompatibility can be reliably measured. Into this putatively obstructive breach, critical embarrassment steps to keep productively in tension and at play the knotted thoughts and feelings, as well as gestures and activities, whose braiding would otherwise provoke disenabling cognitive dissonance.

According with this account, I would venture that Amos, on the occasion of singing to and about Spears, performed her own version of critical embarrassment by putting her embarrassed feeling to work in two divergent registers, appealing at once to a phantasmatic Spears and to a real audience (one that is, as Amos well knows, potentially, exponentially expansive; thanks, YouTube). À la Goffman, we could understand this work as predicated on a refusal of role segregation—that is, on a delicate tightrope walk that allows Amos, marrying agendas in confrontation with one another, to hail an embarrassed celebrity (in her capacity as a fellow, sometime embarrassed celebrity) and to acknowledge the literally juvenile needs of her audience (in her positioning as their putatively, likewise needy, but also abundantly maternal, proxy and surrogate). Yet, as otherwise explored in this chapter, we could also push beyond Goffman's emphasis on role segregation and see in Amos's framing of her song as a "comment" a pointed refusal to distinguish its emotive work (for Spears, for the audience) from its intellective capacity to furnish "explanatory or critical notes" on the cruelties of the commercial music industry.[74] In this way (and in a variety of others that I have sketched), Amos makes a fitting, if also discomfiting, companion for her embarrassed critic, who likewise must—to make his embarrassment work, and to affirm the work that it does—perform a related set of antipodal marriages: in his case, of stuckness and movement, of grasping and loosing, of making peace and making trouble. Or perhaps the work of cringe criticism, as enlivened and enjoined by parrying with the productively embarrassed artist, is rather a matter of making peace *with* making trouble. Surprised as I remain by this outcome, I find genuinely instructive Tori Amos's routinely (if not consistently) publicized endurance, her chronic (if not unalleviated) making available, of her embarrassingly competing personae: her willingness, that is, to be perceived simultaneously, rather than consecutively or otherwise segregably, as both the maker of "bimbo music" and its overcomer; as both the cornflake girl and the raisin girl;[75] as both unhappily embarrassing and happily unembarrassed. In this exercise, I have likewise embraced the exposure of conflicting positions: I have tried to be both one of the "ears with feet," as Amos nominates her fans,[76] and a (dissenting) mouth with (animated) hands; both stupid and smart; both cringing critic and critic of cringe. If the experiment yields any fruit at all, then the fruit is, I think, a pineapple: what better offering to interlocutors whom I'm asking to consider, in their turns, the value of ineluctably conjoined prickliness and sweetness, foreignness and familiarity, suspicion and savor?

Of course, pineapples are not the only fruit. To underline yet further what is specially, critically instructive about Tori Amos's embarrassments, let us consider them alongside the pedagogies made available by conspicuous moments in two other pop stars' recent careers, also shot through with embarrassment: Janet Jackson's infamous "wardrobe malfunction" at the 2004 Super Bowl, and Sinéad O'Connor's much less noticed (though still buzzed about) 2013 open letter to Miley Cyrus, in which the chiding former urged the twerking latter to "care about [herself]" rather than "be . . . pimped" by the commercial music industry[77]—and to which Cyrus responded with a pithy tweet impugning O'Connor's sanity; in turn, O'Connor's own embarrassed and embarrassing responses were wrought, even riven, with signs of emotional distress, and the responses to those responses were often baldly cruel. What, exactly, is to be learned from these public mortifications in tandem with my meditation here on Amos? Regarding the first, we ought to take note that despite the careful, politically astute responses of Jackson to the so-called controversy of her exposed breast (recall the dignity with which Goffman imagines that the salutary player of her social role will greet and smooth over embarrassments and assure us of her respectability)[78]—and despite Jackson's status as a megastar—her words were drowned in a sea of blather, christening the halftime show and its aftermath Nipplegate. To many onlookers, the real shock came not from the show but from the circus whose motions it incited, testifying to the sad, worn way in which a trivial misfire in performance could still in the twenty-first century acquire the status of a scandal when attached to the performing body of a woman of color. Yet more than what I am calling blather, and what I am also calling racism, obtained on this occasion. As Lynne Joyrich observes in a sharp essay that positions the Super Bowl show in a larger meditation on television, its liveness, and its queerness, a changed and changing industrial landscape constitutes the most pressing horizon within which to ponder the "live" mishap and its surprisingly sobering and consequential aftershocks:

> The Nipplegate case . . . didn't only impact the incorporation or exclusion of the black female body on television; it had an enormous impact on television as a whole. . . . On the one hand, the ensuing FCC crackdown put a damper on broadcast television, particularly on daytime program-

ming: broadcast soap operas had been trying to maintain their position in the media marketplace amidst growing competition by becoming more "risqué," but with the fear of those skyrocketing FCC fines, they had to curtail that strategy. Yet, just as this case weakened broadcast TV, it, on the other hand, strengthened other televisual forms, such as cable and satellite TV—platforms that are not bound by FCC rules since their delivery systems do not rely on the publically owned over-the-air broadcast spectrum. Perhaps not coincidentally, their dramas soon began taking on many of the strategies once only associated with broadcast soaps. . . . More so, even beyond boosting cable and satellite platforms (which are still delivered by the TV industry as commercial products sold to viewers to play on TV sets), "nipplegate" jumpstarted online video, for which it was truly a boon. . . . It gave rise, that is, to the more "sophisticated," "mature" programming ushered in by cable and pay TV (as these venues' immunity to FCC rules provided a production environment and sure selling point for new sex- and violence-filled programs that could never air on broadcast TV), and it equally led to the development of even other venues like YouTube, which stretch—without breaking—the very bounds of the "televisual" itself.[79]

That YouTube cocreator Jawed Karim could plausibly (if questionably) cite Nipplegate as instigating the desire to create the platform—and that, as Joyrich suggests compellingly, *Game of Thrones* and its kin wouldn't pursue their lines of "racy" development in quite the same way if not for the more plainly raced alterations of broadcast network television that Nipplegate also occasioned—constitute big stakes. Indeed, they are stakes in the face of which the topos of embarrassment, well beyond its nonlocalized diffusion, is obscured to the point of disappearance—just as Jackson herself has opted largely to disappear from the toxic industrial, political, and aesthetic scene that would "'brand' her body" and into a life now much more seldom on public view.[80]

As for O'Connor—at the other end of the spectrum of stardom as a performer, viewed as "declining" and also as mentally ill, whose opportunities for remunerative musicianship in the twenty-first century are much more slender than Jackson's (or Amos's)—she draws nonetheless, weirdly near to Jackson as a participant in a public discourse that exceeds dramatically and embarrassingly (indeed, excruciatingly) her effort to play a shaping role in it. Making a bid for relevance with her open letter and related blogging activity, O'Connor is charged with irrelevance—or, worse, the compromised relevance only to inspire a fleeting flurry of headlines in an infotainment cycle whose capital flows are predicated precisely on such tactics as briefly resuscitating attention to "wash-ups" and "has-beens," with the express intent of then generating mass schadenfreude by reconsigning them to the social abjection of the dustbin. To observe as much is not to suggest that, by contrast, Amos has some transparently, easily volitional or voluntaristic relationship to her embarrassments and their contouring; no subject, least of all Amos, does. It is rather to indicate that, on the economic and entertainment spectrum imagined at the top of this paragraph, Amos—having negotiated her way out of a constraining contract with Atlantic Records at a pivotal moment in her career, long and since consistently marked by producing or coproducing credits on her albums; having salted away enough money from near chronic touring in mostly modest venues for two-plus decades to (for instance) lay her hands on such means of production as a state-of-the-art studio installed in her Cornwall home;[81] and having the consequent cushion and latitude to risk giving an album like 2014's *Unrepentant Geraldines* one of the most embarrassing, recondite, and pretentious titles in the annals of pop music's history (and counting on its eager reception by a relatively small, yet fervently devoted, fan base who, she knows, will push to hear past its title to its actually lyrical and listenable songs)—lands squarely in the middle, receiving neither blinding attention nor blistering dismissal. Concomitantly, that middling position lands her embarrassments in a terrain where they can work for her and for the modeling of a critical practice poised in tandem, situated on a fault line between opportunity and its possible miscarriage.

Coda: Cooling

To translate back into a more literal statement part of the meaning metaphorized by the pineapple near the end of this chapter's previous section, let me assert, comparatively plainly, one crucial upshot and purchase of work in the mode of cringe criticism: such criticism may move us beyond the choice, as famously nominated by Eve Sedgwick, between paranoid inquiry and reparative inquiry (a choice, were we to follow Sedgwick's lead, that would privilege reparative inquiry and highlight paranoid inquiry's comparative limitations).[82] Cringe criticism may allow us instead to oscillate between a hermeneutic of suspicion and its compensatory obverse—even, in the process, to repair and renew suspicion itself by emphasizing its dialectical interplay with a strategy of amendment.

Yet there is another, perhaps more embarrassing reason at this juncture to (re)consider the pineapple, which enjoys an imagistic pride of place in the song "Cooling," originally released by Tori Amos as a B-side for the single "Spark" and available for understanding, in the moment of the single's release, as an epilogue to the album *Boys for Pele*. Where that album foregrounds, often through images of lava and fire, the fury of women in the aftermath of relationships' dissolutions (one appreciator calls it "one of the best breakup albums ever made"),[83] the jilted speaker of "Cooling" substitutes resignation for hostility, the trickling graduality of peacemaking for the burning immediacy of indictment—with a corresponding, reflexively announced shift in imagery: "So then I thought I'd make some plans / But fire thought she'd really rather be water instead."[84] To read this fire and water imagery, as the song would seem to invite, as passionately elemental—as, say, forces of (woman's) nature rather than of culture—becomes happily less available in Amos's live performances of the song, regularly trotted out during the portions of her shows in which her accompanists leave the stage and she performs solo at the piano for typically hushed, reverent crowds. This reverence is leavened by Amos's mercifully jocular framings of the more "intimate" insets of the shows, which have, on different tours, been variously identified as belonging to the space-times of "The Roadside Café," "The Lizard Lounge," and so forth. With names (and sometimes lighting schemes) thus evoking the textures of the myriad piano bars in which Amos toiled during her adolescence and young adulthood—bars aiming at twilit or starry romance but more often achieving seedy dimness—the insets invite a recalibrated interpretation of the songs performed therein, especially the ones, like "Cooling," that have become the signature pieces of these insets. Resituated in the lounge, the fire and water imaged at the beginning of "Cooling" become the flame of the just-struck match and the club soda flowing over tinkling ice cubes. Later, when the "storm" of the speaker's feeling manifests as "this ocean" wrapped around "that pineapple tree," the roiling waves read more as those of *South Pacific* than of the South Pacific, the pineapple tree an artificially wrought ornament of the tiki room.

A host of theatrical choices facet Amos's evanescent flash, during her short insets, as a reinterpreter of the lounge idiom. Costumed (during her 2009 tour) like the kittenish Julie London of the mid-1950s or (during her 2011 tour) like the matronly robed Rosemary Clooney of the early 1980s, Amos takes the insets as occasions to relax from the coiled intensity with which she usually perches, in a famously unorthodox pose, at piano bench's edge, a corner of the bench jutting from between her rigid legs. Instead and by contrast, the Amos who sings "Cooling" in The Lizard Lounge, cheating out toward her audiences, crosses her legs casually and then waves calmly in invitation as she intones the line, "Let's go for a ride."[85] White-hot piano playing and aggressive soprano head-singing give way for Amos to more limpid keystrokes, more languid rhythmic choices, and less determination to signal poignancy in the highest registers of her vocal range. In short, the cooling of "Cooling" is not just that of a love affair or of the feelings conjured at its end, but also and, to my eye and ear, more powerfully that of a performance style, one whose routine un-coolness has, as I have noted, been often remarked. In this cooler mode—and thus as a parodist, broadly understood as a renegotiator (but not necessarily a satirist),[86] of lounge style—Amos may then wave not only in invitation to her audiences but also in anticipation to us as we turn fully, in the next chapter on "Laziness," to the issues of lounging, relaxation, and liquidity highlighted more fleetingly in The Lizard Lounge.

2. Laziness

"Around Lounging"; Lounging Around

Otium is an essential part of a mental economy.
—James Simpson, "The Economy of Involucrum," in *Reason and Sensuality*

Every writer I know (and no doubt countless others besides) has a story to share about an unproduced piece of writing, whose sharing would amount to a curious bereavement for a thing that was only ever no thing; likely accompanying the story, which is why so many of them must go untold, is a sense that its telling would disclose the necessary and, worse, narrow limits of the story's interest to anyone else but the (in this case, non-) writer. At the risk of thus compromising your interest in this chapter and embarrassing myself in the process—a risk of whose undertaking I hope to have intimated the promising and suggestive possibilities in the previous chapter on "Embarrassment"—I aim here, to begin, to demonstrate the value of launching (or better: slinking, with insinuation) into a meditation on laziness with a eulogy for one such "nothing," an essay-length piece of writing contemplated for a long time before I realized definitively that its existence could be no more, or less, than notional. Part of that value inheres in the extent to which the writing's failure to materialize does not merely haunt but actively, even virally, shapes the pages that you are now reading.

The impetus for this writing that never was came from my recognition that a significant, cohesive, and contemporary strand of experimental American theater took its inspiration from—and subjected to varying degrees of parody—a history of lounge music or, more broadly, of lounge performance. I found and wanted to parse an affinity among recent work by Karen Finley, whose 2003 *Make Love* is, in the words of its creator, "a cabaret-driven, lounge-style act that channels Liza Minnelli in song, dance, glamour, and glitter[,] . . . a complex amalgam of pee-in-the-pants humor, pain, and compassionate outpourings of sorrow" that Finley enlisted to anatomize the post–9/11 American political scene;[1] Peggy Shaw and Lois Weaver's *The Lost Lounge* (2010), "a behind-the-scenes peek into the labor and romance of two lounge act performers" and thus an oblique assessment of the (d)evolution of Shaw and Weaver's romantic relationship as it intertwines both with their ongoing friendship and professional collaboration as Split Britches and with threats posed "by the wrecking ball of . . . greed-driven culture";[2] and an array of performances by Justin Vivian Bond and Kenny Mellman, the infamous partners better known as Kiki and Herb who, in those respective personae as a demented, intoxicated chanteuse and her shyly long-suffering, gay accompanist, turn "would-be standards . . . inside out, eviscerating them . . . and emphasizing the lyrics' haunting and/or perverse content" alongside "psychosocial and sociopolitical commentaries . . . as funny as they are rawly emotional . . . in ways that violate all rules of political correctness or private space."[3] At all of these sites of performance, the lounge idiom, at first blush retrograde and reactionary, is unexpectedly galvanized in the service of a progressive (more specifically, feminist and queer) politics and aesthetics, whose interpretations would situate me, or so I supposed, to ruminate on the conspicuous place of beyond-ironic—that is, encyclopedically comprehensive and affectively comprehended—forms of recycling in a contemporary landscape.

So I had an archive. I had a nascent argument. I even had a dim idea for a possible coda on the louche impostures of Steven Mellor (Spin) and Deirdre O'Connell (Marlene) as The Dream Express, an end-of-the-line lounge duo appearing in various versions of a performance piece by the same name, written by playwright Len Jenkin in collaboration with Mellor and O'Connell and evolved over the 1990s and 2000s. Best of all, I had a working title: "Around Lounging," whose clever (I flattered myself) inversion of the elements in the familiar phrase *lounging around* would gesture toward the defamiliarizing inversions (of systems of sex, gender, and sexuality; of near-yet-not-quite broken and still recognizable hierarchies of taste; of neoliberal schemas of economic and emotional value) at stake in the performers' play with lounge effects and would, as well, signal a move from ease or idling to the hard work, discipline, and skill brought to bear in the making of the various pieces. Yet I was not so done with idling—or immune from being undone by ease— as I might have supposed in this early stage of prewriting. Whatever rigor or commitment Finley et al. had marshaled as artists, I found myself, in my scholarly response, turning lazy every time I confronted this project. I read a book about the history of American hotels (in which buildings a complex and interlocking elaboration of lobby, lounge, and bar spaces unfolded over time) at such a glacial pace that it seemed to mirror the hotel's own lumbering mutations. I looked slackly at the taut shrink-wrap enveloping the DVD *Karen Finley Live*—and yet more slackly brought myself, eventually, to consider the package's contents. I could listen to *Kiki & Herb Will Die for You* regularly, but only as selections from that concert recording shuffled through my iPod and piped through substandard car speakers, half-drowned out by overlapping chatter, on meandering road trips. Homing in yielded to hanging back and hanging out, "Around Lounging" to lounging around.

To be sure, any number of writers' false or half-starts are identified as such at just the moment of stalling that I describe here; and from an otherwise than perverse perspective, nothing could be more routine than jettisoning these projects or more mundane (for any writer possessed of less genius than Borges, anyway) than cataloguing the flotsam generated along the way to the projects' abandonment. If I reserve an entry for "Around Lounging" elsewhere than in the annals of triviality, it is because of the paradoxical intensity of my investment in this project with which I could seemingly do nothing, my intractable refusal to relinquish, at the very least, some etiolated version of its currency in my intellectual life—and because, in consequence, I flapped my gums overmuch about the essay "in progress" and thus invited a serious number of interlocutors to ask, too often for comfort, some version of the question, "How's 'the lounge article'?" Having made myself a bed in a comedy of errors, I could only lie in it with a lame joke for a bunkmate: I explained the inevitability, given the subject matter, of "loafing," "lingering," "loitering," or "languishing" with lounge. If there was a truth embedded in or at least indicated by this jest, I tellingly realized as much not in the form of a "Eureka!" moment, but liquidly, in a set of lapping reflections; and better to call this liquid insight the discovery not of a truth but of a trickling toward a different project simultaneously inspired and impeded by "Around Lounging." Namely, I could use the obstruction posed by my lingering or languishing as an occasion to meditate on what (insights, if not essay) that obstruction *had* yielded: insights precisely about what we tend to identify as laziness and what might better be called lazing, a phenomenon to which I will turn my attention more directly in the remainder of this chapter.

Whatever euphoria would erupt at the parallel "Eureka!" moment was attended, over the course of this gradual "discovery" of laziness, by a more modest and sober reversal of feeling from despair to cautious hope—a reversal that I would describe with a concomitant rhetorical one (not unlike "Around Lounging") of a phrase made famous by Stevie Smith: I was *not drowning, but waving.* (Here and throughout, I deploy the chiasmus as an ostensively easy-to-use figure that therefore and thereby becomes, too, a useful figure for—only ostensible—ease or easing.) For I was still at sea and just barely treading—but treading—water, for at least two reasons. Having amassed a great deal of historical and theoretical material on lounge, I would now have to reconsider that material, and amass much else, to hone my sense of laziness. Likewise, having thought of only a "possible coda" on *The Dream Express*, I realized, as Spin and Marlene eddied around me, that the rippling course of that piece over time and through space would tell me a greater deal about "laziness" than would my other objects of study and that I would thus have to dive into its analysis much more fully. And if nautical, oceanic, and otherwise watery language seems to have soaked, to the point of oversaturation, the sentences of this paragraph and the prior one, then I plead my justifiable desire to build toward—indeed, to enact at the level of style—a third insight to accompany the two just enunciated: having stepped foot into a number of lounges or loungy spaces, I would also have to swim or float in the baths, boats, and pools that recur abundantly in the scenes animating the genealogy of laziness.

The fear of drowning has passed; the wave is firmer. Giving in (afloat) and up (aloft) to lazing—a project of several years' duration since "Around Lounging" was first hazily conceived—allows me now to appreciate the value of what often passes for laziness and to explain that value in three tidal movements. To begin, I argue that, far from "doing nothing," as they profess regularly, a long line of laziness's literary-philosophical theorists are in fact practicing a particular, relaxed kind of thinking, the proof of which inheres in how routinely those thinkers produce currents of and give volume to an equally particular, liquid kind of writing. Further, because of a special relationship, in the form of a declension, between lazing and lounging, a meditation on lounge style is poised to disclose and, indeed, to engender the manner in which lazing producers of work outside a literary-philosophical tradition may nonetheless be tellingly in dialogue with it. This declension is reflexively, if obliquely, anatomized in the otherwise and more capaciously reflexive performances of the duo The Dream Express, one eminently sensible—even sensibly ethical—approach to whose (post) work is thus a lovingly lounging or lazing one. Because the laze-inducing lounge is the site of performances of The Dream Express (and *The Dream Express*), that site is also one of instruction for the lazing critic, who may profitably learn from them (and it) ways to go with the flow of her or his intellection: ways, that is, to understand that lucubration may require acts of surrender to lubrication.

Doing Nothing? Nothing Doing

It is awfully hard work doing nothing. However, I don't mind hard work when there is no definite object.
—Oscar Wilde, *The Importance of Being Earnest*

Doing nothing, a phrase whose manipulations and echoes I worked variously in this chapter's introduction, likewise furnishes Tom Lutz with the title for his "history of loafers, loungers, slackers, and bums in America"[4]—a history that happens also to take stock of those American subjects' lazy kindred in England and elsewhere throughout Europe and whose peregrinations span a course of roughly 250 years (suggesting, misleadingly, that laziness and closely related states, like idleness, are strictly phenomena of modernity).[5] Among the many loafers and slackers nominated as such (and otherwise) and engaged closely by Lutz, I find most interesting—and wish, here, to expand the list of—one special subset of them: those who philosophize "doing nothing" and who, in the process, are not only doing *something* but also *making* something: thinking in a transmittable form, almost always a form of writing. (Indeed, nearly all of the so-called lazy are doing something. Absolute stillness or total absence of activity is extremely rare, and that rarity helps to explain what is fascinating, for instance, about the paradoxical ostentation with which Bartleby the scrivener asymptotically approaches the "accomplishment" of doing nothing.[6] This accomplishment also places Melville's story to the side of the tradition, traced here, in which lazing enterprise is theorized.) Lutz does not identify as such the writers and thinkers, cited in his book, who philosophize doing nothing; neither does he segregate them from the other lazing subjects who fill his pages nor otherwise specially highlight their contributions to what we could provisionally call an ongoing field of "laziness studies." I revisit figures hailed by Lutz and add others to their number not only in the interest of delineating such a field more clearly, nor even of producing a less incomplete genealogy of laziness's theorists, but also and, more important, to determine what exactly these theorists tell or show us, at different angles and to various degrees yet nonetheless commonly, about the tension consistently animating the slippery notion of *doing nothing*: about what is done under that banner and related ones ("nothing" as something), about why it is done (as a refusal of dominant, historically mutable modes of intellectual, educational, and/or economic organization), and about how it is done (stylistically, by which one could mean, in assessing so many of these authors, *stylishly*).

Indeed, because style, as we shall see, is so crucial to the various projects of this suite of writers, it should come as no surprise that the great stylist Samuel Johnson takes a place among them as a prominent, early theorist of laziness, chiefly (though not exclusively)[7] in the writing of and in his guise as *The Idler*. If the Idler, as Lutz argues compellingly, "rejects Franklinian striving toward accumulation and achievement, rejects precisely that ethos at the center of the new industrial capitalism that is transforming social life" in the mid-eighteenth century and afterward,[8] that rejection does not entail a wholesale abandonment of work, but rather of the still-emergent modes of commerce with which almost every imaginable form of work is becoming aligned. In contradistinction to those alignments, the Idler's work, his relationship to which positions him so that, according to Johnson in the first number of *The Idler* (1758), "the man of business forgets him; the man of enterprize despises him," cannot be seamlessly coordinated with dominant forms of production and distribution.[9] He does indeed work, and that work takes the particular form of intellection and its recording and dissemination—"for to form schemes is the Idler's privilege," and "there is perhaps no appellation by which a *writer* can better denote his kindred to the human species" than that of Idler—but the work is enabled neither by striving nor by enthrallment to the ruses of exchange value but by their obverse: a delight in ease and, more specifically, a celebration of the use value of what is easily at hand.[10] "The Idler," as Johnson has it, "who habituates himself to be satisfied with what he can most easily obtain, not only escapes labours which are often fruitless, but sometimes succeeds better than those who despise all that is within their reach, and think every thing more valuable as it is harder to be acquired."[11] Through this framing of the Idler's work, Johnson removes it rhetorically (the Idler "escapes") from the sphere of capital transaction, connoted by the distinction between "obtain" and "acquire"; he thereby situates it to participate in an alternative scheme of valuation of "every thing," including implicitly what would appear to "the man of business" or "enterprize" as, in Johnson's words elsewhere in the same essay, the "*doing nothing*" for which the Idler is "most"—but inaccurately—"famed"; and, as a consequence of this shift in valuation, he figures as successful and fruitful that work whose "execution" may be subject to "tardiness," perhaps because the "always inquisitive" mind of the Idler must reserve for itself the right to be "stimulated" precisely through *idling* contemplation of its many objects.[12]

Praise for such contemplative pursuits—without definite direction or end, and thus with no sure relationship to the punctual rhythms and mercenary obligations of the market or predetermined susceptibility to commodification[13]—similarly animates almost-contemporaneous writings of the late nineteenth century, Paul Lafargue's "The Right to Be Lazy" (1883) and Oscar Wilde's "The True Function and Value of Criticism, with Some Remarks on the Importance of Doing Nothing: A Dialogue" (1890). Laziness, as apostrophized by Lafargue near the end of his manifesto, is no condition of mere indolence but "mother of the arts and noble virtues"; if, as Lafargue advocates polemically, a three-hour workday should be implemented throughout Europe, "the rest of the day and night [reserved] for leisure and feasting," then the *leisure* thereby provisioned and perhaps misleadingly nominated must,[14] as his later apostrophe indicates, provide time and space for ethical and aesthetic activities, as well as for "hygienic and callisthenic exercises" that will "re-establish [the] health" required to feed (so much better than the "spicy indigestibles and syphilitic debauches" of the capitalist class) those activities.[15] Lafargue conjures nostalgically as the backdrop for such activities a series of bucolic scenes in which the emancipated proletarian workingmen and women will distinguish themselves from the labor-enslaved shopkeepers of the petit bourgeoisie, "crouched in their little shops, burrow[ing] like the mole in his subterranean passage and never stand[ing] up to look at nature leisurely";[16] here he draws imagistically near to Wilde, who likewise posits an easy yet deliberate contemplation of nature as a key ingredient of "doing nothing" when he rhapsodizes about those who do not attend to their "daily labour" but instead "wander, it may be, through the city gates to that nymph-haunted meadow where young Phaedrus bathed his feet; and, lying there on the soft grass, beneath the tall wind-whispering planes and flowering *agnus castus*, beg[i]n to think of the wonder of beauty, and gr[o]w silent with unaccustomed awe."[17]

These contemplators of nature, to whom Lafargue points constatively and whose contemplation Wilde enacts performatively, are not so much lazy as *lazing*, a phenomenal cultivation of attention and rumination that we might profitably distinguish from the sense of stasis or ossification (as well as pejorative judgment, so often classed and racialized) connoted by the nominal form of *laziness*. And, like Lafargue, Wilde promotes the notion that lazing in this way is conducive not only to a feeling of sublimity in the apprehension of nature but also to ethico-aesthetic work. Playing, as do so many others that we have encountered or will—yet with his singular penchant for arch inversion—on the idea of doing nothing, Wilde presents those committed to "earnest industry and honest toil" as the "people who [actually] have nothing whatsoever to do," in contrast with whom a class of lazing dreamers, artists and critics alike, take up "the contemplative life, the life that has for its aim not *doing* but *being*, and not *being* merely but *becoming*."[18] If this life, dedicated to "the development of temperament, the cultivation of taste, and the creation of the critical spirit," is perceived negatively by the toilers who in fact, according to Wilde, "have nothing whatsoever to do," as doing nothing, then that misperception is predicated on their failure to appreciate "*that to do nothing at all*"—in its contemplative rather than commercially industrious incarnation—"*is the most difficult thing in the world, the most difficult and the most intellectual*."[19] And, in the end, that difficult intellection is, even for the seemingly work-averse Wilde, an idealized form of work—indeed, the aspiration toward which "the methods [of] education should *work*"—that positions the pursuer of the contemplative life to produce, among other things, essays like "The True Function and Value of Criticism."[20]

Like Wilde, Robert Louis Stevenson is, in his "Apology for Idlers," concerned with the educative possibilities that will—or won't—dispose subjects to embrace a lazing mode of intellection. (And he is also bluntest, among the thinkers assembled here, in challenging the routine indictment, leveled at the putatively lazy, that they are doing nothing: "Idleness so called," he asserts, "which does not consist in doing nothing, but in doing a great deal not recognised in the dogmatic formularies of the ruling class, has as good a right to state its position as industry itself.")[21] Lamenting the "lack-lustre periods between sleep and waking in the class" that mark, and mar, so many scenes of ostensible pedagogy, Stevenson contrasts the semiconscious torpor of the classroom with the "full, vivid, instructive hours of truantry" that pupils of life's idling possibilities may find, much as Lafargue and Wilde suggest, in "meadows by the wayside, lying with a handkerchief over their ears and a glass at their elbow."[22] Yet in Stevenson's bolder—and lazier—account of such affordances for meditative cogitation, one need not meander as far as the meadow to achieve relaxed or reposeful thinking; the site for such an experience may be found "in the streets"—and not even very rare ones, but those of the sort that could be appellated "Commonplace Lane," where the idler "shall command an agreeable, if not very noble prospect; and while others behold the East and West, the Devil and the Sunrise, he will be contentedly aware of a sort of morning hour upon all sublunary things."[23] Extending yet more radically Stevenson's notion that knowledge of "the warm and palpitating facts of life" is "all around about you,"[24] Roland Barthes, in his lecture course on *The Neutral*, raises the delicious possibility that one might not even have to leave the house—and the country or summer house, no less—to participate in such a full-blooded epistemological-cum-ontological project. As he, in the first lecture, admits unabashedly of the course's construction, specifically of the choices of texts to engage, "Then, what library? That of my vacation home, which is to say, a place-time where the loss in methodological rigor is compensated for by the intensity and the pleasure of free reading."[25] Theorizing further how a most conducive kind of "place-time" enables the "whimsical *sourcery*" that is, for him, at the heart of lazing, Barthes argues for a relationship to time and place that would not only "transform [the] self"[26] but also transform the place in which such a self is (non-)located: "The present-day world is full of [the demand for a position] (statements, manifestos, petitions, etc.), and it's why it is so wearisome: hard to float, to shift places. (However, to float, i.e., to live in a space without tying oneself to a space = the most relaxing position of the body: bath, boat.)"[27] Moving us from the vacation home's library to its bathtub—yet refusing to calcify our position there (the bath transforms metonymically into the boat), just as he refuses the terminological calcification of his philosophico-political "position"—Barthes aspirates into his language a figure of floating that may stand here, in miniature or synecdochically, for the myriad representations of floating (in baths, on boats, in pools) that recur powerfully, yet lightly, in so many discursive constructions of laziness.[28] Barthes also refuses, in this instance, the weariness to which he opposes floating or what I am calling lazing; and though later in *The Neutral* he contemplates what creativity weariness may prompt, the condition for that creativity is that weariness does not remain such, nor is it even a transformed weariness, but that it is superseded in the creative act (an issue to which I will return in this book's conclusion, in a meditation on exhaustion). A similar, implicit distinction between fatigue and lazing—and another key image of floating—emerges in Wendy Wasserstein's *Sloth*, where we find a circumscription of the lazing producer's space even yet more radical than that of Stevenson's local street or of Barthes's vacation house. In a biting satire of self-help languages and cultures, Wasserstein adopts the narratorial persona of "a regular guy whose life was totally changed by sloth," announces triumphantly that he "wrote this book entirely lying down" in bed and can only, from that bed, imagine lazily rather than enact even the recumbent posture of "floating on a raft" or the motions of "the book tour [that] consists of writing one chapter in the bedroom and the other in my backyard."[29]

Taken together, the writers whom I have put here on strolling parade are more or less commonly liquidifying certain regimes of truth, order, education, economy, and labor as they celebrate lazing and the kind of work that it conduces. Yet these writers are also more or less consistently embracing a liquid style for the expression of what liquefactions are at stake in their work and why those liquefactions matter. To be sure, superficial, obvious differences distinguish the style of Wilde from that of Barthes, or Wasserstein's from Stevenson's, but on a more fundamental level, all of these lazing producers write with liquidity as they generate prose that is sleek, supple, propulsive, porous: as they embrace, in other words, what Pierre Saint-Amand has lovingly identified as the art of the "levitationist," not "the lazy man . . . bogged down, trammeled by lethargy" but "on the contrary" the one "buoyed up by the air," whose "genius unfolds in the fluid element."[30] To circle back to the historian of laziness with whom this section of the chapter began, Tom Lutz could likewise be understood not just as a chronicler of such figures as Johnson and Lafargue, but (rare in academia, though perhaps less rare among scholars who come aslant at critical enterprise and who attempt, like Lutz, to ignite the ever-elusive alchemy of the "crossover" book) as a liquid writer in his own right, whose pellucid, smooth prose in *Doing Nothing* poises him to be placed in the genealogy that I have been tracking. Just as important, Lutz himself thematizes his potential nomination as a member of the lazing tribe in his most personal excursions, which are also the passages in which the hardest (unanswered) inquiries and biggest (unclarified) stakes of his work emerge; invoking the persistent myth of the lazy professor—and complicating it with a turn of the screw—he writes both of his "life of sloth," as he worries that "maybe the academic life has become a haven for the lazy," and at the same time of the paradoxical way in which his life of sloth "blends imperceptibly into my pathological flip side, my workaholism, and this is the odd thing: I can just as easily argue and believe that I work, not too little, but entirely too much."[31] Extending the reach and purchase of this confessional meditation, he poses some tough questions for others in "the academic life": "Everyone I know is in the same boat. We are all lazy imposters, and we are all workaholic slaves. We work way too hard and not nearly enough. What can this possibly mean? Is slackerism somehow as much a part of our lives at this point in history as our vaunted work ethic? Are the two simply two sides of the very same coin?"[32] To some extent, Lutz intends these questions as rhetorical ones and means, in a manner that I find unsatisfying (lazy?), that goal-oriented industry and aimlessness are indeed mutually constitutive in academia (and elsewhere)—a notion that does little, directly, to dispel the intractable stereotype of the layabout professor. A better response to Lutz's line of questioning, which is admirably inspired by an open acknowledgment of the contradiction or tension animating the feelings of professors who perceive themselves ambivalently and simultaneously as overworked and lazy, might reside in another question: Can the overworked help but feel lazy when the expectations placed on them are high and unrelenting? Some of Lutz's colleagues would answer with a resounding yes: as Ellen Schrecker notes, for instance, in her judicious (and thus misleadingly, because melodramatically, titled) history of university corporatization, *The Lost Soul of Higher Education*, "It's not as if the nation's academics [have] been loafing. By the early 1970s faculty members were putting in some fifty hours a week, with professors at the University of California working sixty. In 1988–89, according to another survey, the average college professor was spending fifty-five hours a week on the job";[33] she proceeds to (re)quote approvingly a particularly incisive plaint from a professor who asserts, "Whoever thinks faculty life is the leisurely pursuit of knowledge should follow me around for a while."[34] The valuing of what this colleague calls the "leisurely pursuit[s] of knowledge" (if not leisure as such, with its routine mobilizations of vexed and vexing class dynamics), as I have done thus far in these pages, must be recognized as embedded in materially specific contexts (as such pursuits themselves always are) and must appear alongside acknowledgment of the constraints on such lazing—including, for professors, publication imperatives and bureaucratic duties—even among those who enjoy, for instance, job security in the form of tenure. Those are of course a dwindling number in an academic world whose traditional perquisites are ever more steadily eroded and have all but disappeared for casual employees of colleges and universities.

At the same time, I find myself, as one of a handful of incredibly privileged members of my profession, identifying with Stanley Aronowitz's position in "The Last Good Job in America" that, at its best, academia affords a buoying blurring of lines between work and ludic activity—a recurrent notion, even ideal, in the theorizations of lazing that I have invoked—that allows those like Aronowitz (and me) to "enjoy . . . the ability to procrastinate and control [his] own worktime, especially its pace: taking a walk in the middle of the day, reading between the writing; listening to a CD or tape anytime . . . calling up a friend for a chat," even as he contends with "administrative garbage, too many students . . . and taking on too many assignments."[35] That there is space at all for the pleasure and agency that attends the lazing form of work that Aronowitz praises is a—too—rare opportunity,[36] and thus it is no coincidence that his personal paean to his own good fortune appears in the same volume as the much more polemical "The Post-Work Manifesto," written by Aronowitz in collaboration with others, in which the logic of the workday in late capitalism, too routinely "seen as a reflection of who we are and what we want rather than [as] an enforced structuring of human energy to the impulses and tendencies of an economic system bent on breaking the human spirit," is subject to trenchant and eloquent critique.[37] I point to this work not simply in sympathetic endorsement of its principles (such as advocacy of shortened workdays for most paid laborers and for the institution of guaranteed income in the United States and elsewhere), but also to suggest an opening up, a lazing *relaxation*, of the fairly taut genealogy of thinkers and writers spun thus far. Laziness's theorists, as well as its historians (like Lutz), need to be thought on a spectrum with key theorists of postwork like Aronowitz and Kathi Weeks[38]—as well as on a spectrum with key theorists of work as such, like Hannah Arendt (about whom, more below)—because they are likewise coming, albeit through their paradoxically otiose negotiation of the challenge of "doing nothing," at the questions of what work is and of what value should be placed on its various forms, including especially its "post" forms.

In our contemporary moment, many of these forms of work or "postwork" are also versions of knowledge's manufacture, of which the scholarship made in a university setting, theorized by Aronowitz, is just one incarnation. Across the terrains laying claim to knowledge production that we, following Tiziana Terranova, could call constitutive sites of "network culture" for the "information age," lazing may have a special, curious value because its *unpredictability* makes it potentially less capturable by capital, tentacular and capacious enough in its neoliberal guises to capture just about everything else: affect, as Michael Hardt and Antonio Negri document in their analysis of "immaterial labor";[39] so-called "free labor," whose cooptation Terranova describes with particular attention to the building and maintenance of the Web;[40] flexibility, on whose pervasive, even hegemonic insistence the contemporary collapse of distinctions among historical forms of fluid, latent, and stagnant un(der) employment and employment as such depends, according to Paolo Virno;[41] and, in Franco Berardi's polemical account, "our very souls," through which rhetoric he means to indicate such aspects of subjectivity's constitution as "intelligence, sensibility, creativity and language" itself.[42] Like all of these attributes of consciousness or social embodiment, lazing, as is this chapter's effort to demonstrate, *can* be made to work, but how much of such lazing will work, on what occasions, and with what force are highly uncertain and thus less susceptible than, say, putative free labor to territorialization; yet more volatile in its uncertainty are the ends to which lazing may—or may not—be put, making lazing an especially loopy and intractable business, still capable of the "wandering and unpredictable" motions whose likely, contemporary eclipse Berardi asserts and decries.[43]

With the issue of ends in mind and at stake, we may valuably turn to Arendt, who, despite the different historical circumstances of her writing, makes insights relevant to the post-Fordist economic context assessed by Berardi, Virno, and others. Famously distinguishing among labor, work, and action in The Human Condition,[44] Arendt also underlines a difficult dilemma through whose consideration to put pressure on what may otherwise be too facilely celebrated as the "achievements" of the lazing, what Johnson nominated as their fruits and successes. As if in implicit dialogue with Arendt, the writers whose imbricated ideas about laziness I catalogued above are all offering eccentric examples, indeed weird exemplars, of how Homo faber—the subject who, by Arendt's reckoning, works rather than labors or acts—may make things: in these cases, an unorthodox series of makings of equally unorthodox pieces of writing that form the material proof that "doing nothing" may consistently yield something (an essay, a pamphlet, a book). For her part, Arendt worries over just such makings, insofar as they are likely predicated upon the instrumentalization of thinking and almost certainly entail thinking's reification: these makings, according to her, are "always paid for, and . . . the price is life itself"; the thing, such as the book, "is always the 'dead letter' in which the 'living spirit' must survive, a deadness from which it can be rescued only when the dead letter comes again into contact with a life willing to resurrect it, although this resurrection of the dead shares with all living things that it, too, will die again."[45] Yet even as Arendt mourns the deadening of thinking-in-action necessitated by fabrication—as well as the deadening repetitions of that deadening—she concedes (to my ear, with subtle ambivalence) the value of such fabrication:

> Acting and speaking men need the help of homo faber in his highest capacity, that is, the help of the artist, of poets and historiographers, of monument-builders or writers, because without them the only product of their activity, the story they enact and tell, would not survive at all. In order to be what the world is always meant to be, a home for men during their life on earth, the human artifice must be a place fit for action and speech, for activities not only entirely useless for the necessities of life but of an entirely different nature from the manifold activities of fabrication by which the world itself and all things in it are produced.[46]

When Arendt identifies the carving of a space, the rendering of a container, for the strictly "useless" as the paradoxically special use to which Homo faber "in his highest capacity" orients his work, I cannot help but hear an invitation to evaluate *Homo otiosus* as a yet more special version of *Homo faber*—precisely because his heightened attunement to uselessness (so called) characterizes his disposition toward work and the kind of work produced in that disposition. In other words, if Arendt endeavors, despite her reservations about dead letters, to find a way to value, ethically, the congealing of thought into a shareable thing—a valuation that is not merely reducible to one's subjugation to or subjectivation through the operations of reification—then the lazing writer, whose product is more liquid than lapidary, more recline than rigid, may offer up work uniquely lubricated to satisfy such a valuation. Miguel Balsa notes astutely of Arendt that she "derives [an] essential characteristic of action, its unpredictability, from the opposition between *praxis* and *poiesis*. While in fabrication the end product is measured against the model or plan that guided the entire process, action does not happen as a result of any previous design."[47] Yet products (for instance, essays or books) made through a process of lazing may be, one might say, "usefully" situated to deconstruct this binary opposition between work and action, poiesis and praxis, by registering—in the things themselves, on their very surfaces— their fabrication according to a plan or model so loose as hardly to constitute a plan or model, or their fabrication in liquid departure from a solid plan or model, or, more extreme, a condensation of these two kinds of fabrication (loosely following a loose model). And this proposition requires thinking through a further question: in addition to the writings already constellated in my genealogy of lazing, what forms or kinds of making most especially deserve this nomination? More particularly, might they be the kinds of making that happen in or around the lounge?

Uneasy Listening: Unlistened Ease

Crooning is a hotel mode.
—Wayne Koestenbaum, *Hotel Theory*

To approach a robust answer to the previous section's lingering question about the lounge requires, preliminarily, a more concrete assay to lounges, loungers, and lounging—yet an assay, in line with the relaxed thinking trickling across and through this chapter, that is nonetheless capacious in its concretions. Alongside and following Amy Villarejo, who, in her parsing of *lesbian*, shares that she "like[s] that dimension of rote involved in the grammatical breakdown of a noun, the commonplace and commonsensical repetition of people, place, and thing modified with a lesbian inflection or provenance,"[48] I want similarly to appeal through the triad of person, place, and thing to a fairly stable spirit or flavor of *lounge* as it nonetheless pulses across different registers, shifts dimensions, and acquires new resonances: from the lounger, a subject with a long and variegated history, through his more particularized appearances in a series of spaces identified as lounges or loungy, to the kinds of performed lounging—including, eventually and especially, the making of a set of musics collectively identifiable as "lounge"—that typify those spaces and related ones. Consulting a range of sources—including Lutz's history (which names *loungers* in its subtitle), the *Oxford English Dictionary*, and a volume, *Lounge: Webster's Timeline History, 1466–2007*, whose existence defies believability—we may grasp fairly easily that the lounger or the loungy sort has been hanging around for a long time; as early as the late eighteenth century, "some young men" with literary or aristocratically inflected anticapitalist pretensions (or both) "proudly called themselves . . . loungers," insouciantly adopting a label with negative valences; producing publications like the Edinburgh-based *The Lounger* (1785–87), a direct descendant of Johnson's *The Idler*; and "claim[ing] that they . . . were devotees of contemplation rather than crude mammon."[49] Associations of the word *lounge* with the kinds of haunts, ranging from taverns to coffee-houses, in which such loungers were likely to idle—and thus the association of the lounge as a space with languorously convivial contemplation—are at least as old as these self-nominations of loungers and perhaps older.[50] Given this history of associations, it is ironic that, after the modern hotel (as distinct from the inn) emerged in the United States in the late eighteenth century and developed in complexity in the nineteenth, the spaces within that hotel that should first have been designated as lounges were the ones "less open to nonguests than the hotel's other public spaces" and where women, accompanied by male escorts, could enjoy "respectable," semi-private colloquy:[51] spaces, that is, unlike hotel bars, lobbies, and public parlors—and thus spaces where loungers, rapidly on their way to morphing into lounge lizards,[52] could not as easily take advantage of their would-be conquests by likewise taking advantage of the "hotel's distinctive combination of privacy, anonymity, and transience," which "made it a highly sexualized space, its lobbies, bars, and bedchambers charged with both possibility and peril."[53] Eventually, of course, the use of *lounge* to identify a hotel space—or, latterly, a motel space—was subject to relaxation, and the word became attached in hotels and motels, as it long had (and continued to do) outside them, to bars, which, by the 1950s and early 1960s, were in the middle of the mixological revolution marked by the popularized reimagination of the cocktail.

This moment in lounge's history—when the word could, identifying a certain kind of venue, be modified by both cocktail and tiki and could, in its turn, modify a spectrum of musical performances (ranging from crooners' swing to space-age pop to exotica)[54] marketed chiefly to middle-class audiences in just such venues—is perhaps its most vital and, pardon the pun, intoxicating moment; for it is in this charged moment that a person, the lounger's, habitus coincides with a space, the lounge's, energies, as amplified by a set of tonic entertainments, collectively understood as lounge music, to make a powerful conjuncture. That conjuncture marks lounge as a signifier for a unique expressive mode of sociality and sexuality—one manifesting in "the 'swinger' image as a kind of desperate, if confused, response to the enforcement of heterosexual family lifestyles"[55] and modeling "expansive sophistication, in which the 'disgusting' or vulgar body is not repudiated but stylized"[56]—whose iconic coolness had a remarkably quick expiration date and whose ongoing, twilit presence in (un)popular culture has consequently been haunted by an especially desperate kind of charm.[57] Indeed, as we consider lounge's specific (mis)adventures, in the mid-twentieth century and afterward, within the longer historical trajectory sketched above, we could profitably think of the lounge—and, more expansively, of lounge—as often a site of failed aspiration, for at least three reasons: (1) Many spaces called (cocktail, tiki) lounges in the fifties, sixties, and later have meant, through this appellation, to evoke the languid grandeur of spaces where the rich or fashionable (or both) consort and thus to secure their patronage (including, newly in the postwar period, in the lounges of luxe, if outré, Las Vegas casinos);[58] but the misfit of nomination and destination is palpably striking in the myriad cases of down-at-heel, fringe, or otherwise depressed and depressing lounges whose seedy, roadside proliferations are likely, today, to be primary in the average imaginary of lounge. (2) At the same time, grand spaces, such as those in premier hotels, have themselves long had an anxiety about their precarious grandeur or status, since one quintessential figure, as intimated above, hanging out in such spaces has, for at least a century, been the lounge lizard, the poseur whose aspiration might not, in fact, fail to secure him a woman's affection and largesse; (3) and this anxiety is inscribed in the word lounge itself, which connotes both luxuriant reclining and the wasting or spoiling of time—and perhaps with it reputation. Again, some times, as well as spaces, spoil faster than others: how short the span between the Rat Pack's glory days and the retrospective (and retributive) classification of their "cool" sound as the epitome of lameness.

Having established these (by no means exhaustive) contours of lounge—and having already hinted at its lazy features—I want to reckon, in a consequently more informed way and as promised in both the introduction and previous section of this chapter, with what I have described as the declension uniting lazing and lounging. To describe the relation through the route of a *declension* may appear to suggest a decline from lazing to lounging, but I rather wish, more charitably and generatively, to emphasize the space of the declension as one of variation or inflection. For one thing, the appearance of decline could be viewed from two directions when we consider the movement from lazing to lounging, or vice versa: a putative decline, for instance, from the aesthetic-philosophical tradition that embraces Samuel Johnson, Paul Lafargue, and Roland Barthes to its mass cultural counterpart in the music of Frank Sinatra, Martin Denny, and Julie London; or, to turn the gaze reflexively back on myself and the failed project "Around Lounging," a putative decline from lounging with material for a scholarly enterprise to languishing with it to lazing with it in a way that threatened to sediment into a passive state of laziness—but in this case didn't, precisely because of a recuperation of lazing in part via its dialectical interplay with lounge and lounging. For another thing, I reject the line—if ever there were one, a line in the (Nevada) sand—that would separate from each other figures that have as much in common, if weirdly so, as Oscar Wilde ("The gods live thus: . . . watching with the calm eyes of the spectator the tragic-comedy of the world that they have made. We, too, . . . might make ourselves spiritual by detaching ourselves from action, and become perfect by the rejection of energy") and Dean Martin ("Milton Berle is an inspiration to every young person that wants to get into show business. Hard work, perseverance, and discipline: all the things you need . . . when you have no talent").[59] And, for yet another, one of the key principles on which to alight through lazing intellection is that valuable possibilities may course through, rather than inhere in, the liquid movements of lazing—or lounging, or idling, or what you will: that is, movements producing flashes of insight that fly, lightly, in the face of any insistence on rigidly taxonomic demarcations among, say, the very terms *lazing, lounging, idling,* and so forth.

So, in the sanguine spirit of thinking of lounging as a local variation on or special inflection of lazing, how to understand this relation in a more fine-grained way? To begin, we might take a detour with Sigfried Kracauer, whose 1963 essay on "The Hotel Lobby" still provides a seminal point of departure for any thinker seeking to understand the dynamics of lounges and lounge-

like spaces—and thus the dynamics of the lounging that obtains therein. Kracauer paints a sharp—and ultimately unflattering—picture of the "aimless
lounging" of subjects in hotel lobbies, who, "sitting around idly" in "tasteful
lounge chairs," are disposed to enjoy a "nirvana of relaxation"; to consider
disinterestedly "a world creating itself, whose purposiveness is felt without
being associated with any representation of a purpose"; and to indulge in "the
mere play that elevates the unserious everyday to the level of the serious."[60]
Word choices like *mere* (and, in more frankly devastating passages, nomi-
nations of those "coming and going" through lobbies as "people who have
become empty forms because they have lost their password, and who now
file by as ungraspable flat ghosts") indicate Kracauer's sense that pleasurably
lounging, nondirected contemplation of the sort that he describes typifies for
him a decline, specific to modernity, from the purposeful, "revelatory" contemplation that obtains, by contrast, for devoted subjects sitting upright in
hard "church pews" rather than sinking into plush cushions.[61] Yet there may
be a way to celebrate the vividness of Kracauer's portrait of lounging—and
the spatial specificity of the unfolding of that lounging—without acceding
to the damning assessment that he attaches to it: a way, that is, to disarticu-
late the observation from the judgment and thus to value rather than indict
the relaxed and playful contemplation, a form of lazing, that he theorizes.
Villém Flusser, writing a couple of decades later and forecasting the imminent emergence of a telematic world (arguably a prescient, if of course not
wholly accurate, imagining of the networked, digitized one in which we now
live), provides a good model for the way to make this shift when he reserves
a space to praise, rather than condemn, the possible coming of a time "in
which everyone lives at leisure, . . . the very situation that Plato called life in
the love of wisdom."[62] Far from distinguishing such a social model from one
rooted in worship, as Kracauer does, Flusser suggests that rest and repose
will, on the contrary, restore for human subjects (and here he betrays the close
correspondence between utopian and nostalgic vision) a religiously inflected
form of celebration, the ability to navigate which we have lost. As he writes:

> Our incapacity to celebrate can be observed in the way we use the word *idle*.
> We use it in passing, with a dismissive gesture, for example, when we say
> it's idle to speculate about something. *Idle* clearly means "pointless." But
> the ancient Greeks knew that *pointless* is a synonym for *pure*. They knew
> that philosophy depends on idle speculation about something. And the
> ancient Jews kept the Sabbath holy expressly to keep it distinct from the
> working day, to be able to speculate idly about holy texts for that length of

time. For both these prebourgeois traditions, idle is an expression for the human capacity to rise above the purposeful. It is a celebratory expression. And unless we can remember the meaning of the word, we will remain incapable of recognizing unemployment as a blessing.[63]

Less boldly and speculatively than Flusser, though nonetheless in dialogue with and inspired by him, I wish to suggest not that we "recogniz[e] unemployment as a blessing," but that we recognize alternative—lounging or lazing—modes of employment as valuable, because celebratory or even ecstatic, phenomena. (If we do, then we can, for instance, attempt to make our sabbatics, the version of Flusser's "Sabbath" most relevant to some readers of this book, occasions to follow flights of fancy rather than to-do lists.)

These phenomena are, moreover, ones that we can locate, like Kracauer (if much less crankily), in the present and near past and not only in equally hazy postulations of the distant past and potential future. Indeed, they constitute part of the historical record of lounge expression as it was enacted by its most lazing—and thus, arguably, its "loungiest"—practitioners; consider, for instance, singer and variety show host Perry Como, who inspired the *New York Times* article, "How to Relax: The Como Way," in which he invokes a golfing metaphor to advise to other would-be lazing successes, "Walk slow, swing slow—and win."[64] Even more fully epitomizing the lazing ethos of lounge is Dean Martin, invoked specially above, a singer, actor, and television personality routinely charged with being "flippant and lazy," with "truly ha[ving] no work ethic."[65] More generously and generatively, and as I argue in a review of Mark Rotella's *Amore: The Story of Italian American Song*, we could understand Martin as bodying forth a distinctive form of sprezzatura, a quality "central to the performance idiom of Italian American crooners," as he "brought the easy energy of the 'layabout,' . . ."[66] of the one 'slouching around the house,' 'lounging in his own living room,' not only to the practice of listening to music 'on the radio or on the family Victrola'" when he was a teenager "but also to its live and recorded performance" in his adult, professional life.[67] Biographers trying to conjure the textures of that life cannot help but imagine Martin occupying something like what Vivian Sobchack calls "lounge time," a time "spatialized from nightclubs, cocktail lounges, bars, anonymous hotel or motel rooms, boardinghouses, cheap roadhouses and diners" and predicated on the substitution of "impersonal, incoherent, discontinuous, and rented space for [the] personal, intelligible, unified, and generated space" associated with "family contiguity and generational continuity";[68] in such an evocative frame of mind does Michael Freedland, for example, assert that

Dean's real home seemed to be Las Vegas, where the smoke-filled, low-lit gambling rooms offered a womb-like comfort to him. It was all dreadfully artificial in a land where no building has a clock for fear of bringing people back to reality. To Dean, who seemed ready to escape from the responsibilities of other mortals, it was the ideal life. He kept a suite reserved for himself at the Sands, full of pine panelling and the kind of carpeting in which unsuspecting feet all too easily lose themselves.[69]

Popular writers like Freedland are drawn to imagine Martin (and guests) "los[ing] themselves" in this way precisely because the resonant traces of the lounging that these writers, like Sobchack, associate with the loss—that is, the rejection—of intimate domesticity are evident in the actual work that Martin produced, whatever the largely irrecoverable details of his offstage hours. Paradigmatically, his 1959 album, *Sleep Warm*, produced at the height of the lounge ascendance and epitomizing the laze of lounge, is a gauzy, somnolent paean to the pleasures of sleeping, dreaming, and their narcotized or narcotizing equivalents in wakeful—but languorous—pursuits of love, sex, and song (and every bit as material a proof of generative lazing as, if formally different from, an essay by Wilde or a book by Wasserstein); as Shawn Levy notes in an extremely astute close analysis of the record, "the effeminate little spin [Martin] gives his sibilants on numbers like 'All I Do Is Dream of You' and 'Sleepytime Gal'" registers, among other potential meanings, Martin's winking amusement over "the fact that he was actually getting paid so much to do something so easy."[70] Equally loungy and potentially instructive for those who would build achievement through some version of lazing is the work that Martin did as host on his wildly successful television variety show in the 1960s, for which he refused to "rehearse in the conventional way. It would have to fit in with his golf schedule—and that's when he learned his lines and his songs"; of his relaxed preparation for and performance in the series, Lucille Ball reportedly claimed, "You make cooked spaghetti look tense," a quality that pleased both viewers and critics for whom Martin's easy-appearing sensibility and light touch "worked" to convey spontaneity and to avoid the feeling of "embalming" that would come from an overly clinical or sterile approach to entertainment.[71] In addition to comprehending lightness and ease, though, we might think of the ways in which Ball's invocation of spaghetti, connoting softness, rings in time with the other conjurations of softness, both material and representational, that this detour with and through lounge has brought into view: plush cushions of lobby chairs, tufty grass of golf courses, thick carpeting of hotel rooms,

2.1 Dean Martin epitomizes seeming ease, languor, and relaxation in his television series.

fluffy pillows of bed and song alike; taken together, these soft sites suggest that what may in part distinguish lounging, as a declension of lazing, from other varieties of the phenomenon is the set of textural modifiers and cues, arrayed across loungy spaces and scenes, that prompt the kind of lazing in which Martin, striking among others, engages.

I call Martin's model of lazing only "*potentially* instructive" not because the lesson runs a great risk of ineffectiveness but because many progressively oriented subjects, whose interpellation I am imagining with these remarks, would likely not wish to tarry with a teacher like Martin, given the misogyny and racism with which his legacy, as well as much of that of the Rat Pack, is associated. (It is for this reason that I position lounge music like Martin's as "uneasy listening" and suppose that his hypothetically educative ease has gone "unlistened," at least by a certain audience: hardly any scholarly work on Martin's corpus has yet been published.) Instead, they might move with me to a consideration of The Dream Express, who turn whatever is antiprogressive about lounge on its ear and who offer just as robust and pedagogical—and, in their case, class-aware—example of what can be accomplished through the kind of lazing incubated or marinated in the lounge.

Unlocal Stops, Unstopped Locals

God sees . . . all locality in an unlocal manner.
—Ludwig Feuerbach, *The Essence of Christianity*

This unlocal, uncentral world where the pubs are bad and the people are sly.
—Daniel Jones, *My Friend Dylan Thomas*

Spin Milton and his ex-wife Marlene, the lounge act whose name also furnishes the title of *The Dream Express*, were first imagined as two minor characters in Len Jenkin's *Careless Love* (1993), where their banter and song help to frame the play's kaleidoscopic action and in whose inaugural production they were portrayed by Steven Mellor and Deirdre O'Connell, two prominent actors in New York's downtown theater scene who had collaborated with each other and with Jenkin, as well as with playwrights like Sam Shepard, in a number of earlier projects.[72] As O'Connell explained to me in an interview, she and Mellor, whom she describes as having a "weird chemistry" that enables them not to "get in each other's way at all" even as they're "completely connected," "had so much fun being Spin and Marlene that [they] just prevailed on Len" to "write a whole piece for [them]" as *The Dream Express*.[73] In slowly responding to the actors' "haranguing" and answering for himself the question about the compositional process, "Huh, how would I do that,"[74] Jenkin took inspiration from, in his words,

> every late night lounge act in every cheap hotel lounge or bar I've ever hung out in, a lot in Albuquerque, Los Angeles, Seattle, and New York. The clientele is everyone who can't sleep, everyone looking for love, everyone with no place to go, everyone who's in between jobs, in between loves, in between lives. The bands were often couples, a man and a woman, sometimes partners in life, sometimes just in the show—some in their early 20s, others in their 60s . . . playing covers, talking a bit about this and that, occasionally playing an original song. . . . I'm always looking for the forgotten side of America, the places the "media interstate" has passed by, the places with echoes, and by chance I had to stay in one hotel in Florida, actually a Howard Johnson, that had a succession of lounge acts in their lounge/bar—2 local rockers picking up $50 a night, or a husband and wife (him on piano) doing a lot of 40s numbers—and I would always go down and see the show, sometimes the only customer for the late set. Then I wrote the original piece, and started actively looking wherever I went—

retro-hip places like the Dresden in L.A., but more the kind of nameless lounges in Ramada Inns or faded hotels on Main Street in small towns.[75]

In the years since this "original [version of the] piece" was drafted and then revised with input from Mellor, O'Connell, and sound designer John Kilgore, "the show"—which, like its models, integrates songs with narratives from and talk between Spin and Marlene, sometimes directed pointedly to the audience—"keeps changing"[76] (Jenkin has made available a Dream Express subtitled Set I on his website, whereas I saw a production called Set III at Long Island City's The Chocolate Factory in December 2009). What has remained constant over these ever-evolving incarnations of the project is, ironically, the inconstancy—or, rather, indeterminacy—of the show's setting, conjuring so many of the different yet united "cheap hotel lounge[s] or bar[s]" in which Jenkin has "hung out." At the top of the show, Spin hails audiences as visitors to the Briarpatch Lounge in the Uncle Remus Motel, where, he reports, he and Marlene have been playing for three months; yet just as those audiences are assembled, in a version of lounge time, on "a nite where the outlines blur, [where] things slide into one another," so, too, does space blur and slide as the Briarpatch Lounge morphs, in Marlene's later nomination of the show's location, into "the Shalimar Lounge. Our music works best when we communicate on the edge of town—between the check cashing place and the Blood Donor Center. Between the Jack in the Box and the interstate off-ramp."[77] Later still, we're informed that we're "coming around a curve here at the Jack O' Hearts Lounge, the fully mentholated nitespot of the Royal Flush Travel-lodge," and thus the site of The Dream Express's performance becomes what I have identified in this section's heading as unlocal: paradoxically retaining a relationship to (in part through verbal invocation of) local specificity even as, in a form of the liquidity that we have otherwise encountered in this chapter, that local specificity is subject to a "meltdown"[78] in the service of Jenkin's more global meditation on or "continued obsession with the American vernacular."[79]

This unlocality works, too, in the service of The Dream Express's multivalent metatheatricality (we are invited to reflect consciously on the relationship, for instance, between the real, material dimensions of playing spaces like The Chocolate Factory and the largely derealized or dematerialized textures, given minimal stage design, of the Briarpatch-cum-Shalimar-cum-Jack O' Hearts Lounge), another crucial strand of which emerges in the piece's citational, parodic relationship to lounge music and culture. Measuring, through pointed humor, a critical distance from the Orientalism of 1950s- and

'-6os-era tiki lounges and the faux cosmopolitanism of suburbanites consuming, in the same era, representations of newly available forms of jet-setting, Jenkin furnishes "The Milton Version" of "Let's Get Physical," a 1980s hit for Olivia Newton-John, with the alternative lyrics, "You took me to a Polynesian restaurant / (Tell me Samoa) / Then to a Lithuanian movie / (Viva Vilnius, baby)."[80] Indeed, the very fact of making an '80s cover a prominent set piece in The Dream Express signals an oppositional relationship to traditional lounge expressivity's unexamined, retrograde politics, since "the 1980s was the decade of destruction—the abolishment of Tiki and his culture" after a long decline initiated as early as the late 1960s, when "exotica and the Tiki style were denounced as contrived rituals of the imperialist establishment at the same time that the Vietnam War developed into an ugly mistake, with native huts and palm trees burning on TV."[81] That decline was marked, in the 1970s, by "a certain 'Jimmy Buffetization' [of lounge's Orientalism]—the introduction of a generic tropical island theme with no definite identity. Be it the Caribbean, Mexico, or Polynesia, everywhere was Margharita-ville [sic],"[82] a disturbing, racist erasure of local specificity quite different from the self-aware form of unlocality articulated in The Dream Express—and no less immune than tiki style to Jenkin's critique when he has Marlene offer this withering coda to the demented "Milton Version" of "The Pina Colada Song," in which a violent shootout disrupts the lunch hour at Denny's: "I don't like pina coladas. I like sad carnivals, drawings of the devil, extravagant operas, childhood storybooks, religious wars, living rooms at the bottom of lakes, fog, black silk sheets, churches, snow." The ethos conjured in Marlene's litany, reminiscent perhaps of a Henry Darger illustration or a Goth ball, works to yoke The Dream Express's politically progressive distancing from lounge's regressive features to its aesthetic assault on lounge's sometimes Technicolor brightness, in contradistinction to which the (descended from John?) Miltons' lounge, for spells a chthonic one, is marked by darkness.

That aesthetic darkness, albeit leavened by humor, suits the piece's exploration of subjects, as described above by Jenkin, as "looking for love, . . . with no place to go, . . . in between jobs, . . . in between lives." Though the lovelorn and loveless are imagined, addressed, or ventriloquized most emphatically over the course of The Dream Express, reflections on work are just as importantly, if more sinuously, braided through the show; and those key reflections situate The Dream Express to speak powerfully with and to the discourses on lazing and postwork central to this chapter. For instance, in a pivotal, spoken-word number, "Town Well" (one of only three Dream Express songs recorded, over many years of work, for posterity and available on a lazily [non-]maintained MySpace page for the project),[83] Spin and Marlene enact the daily depredations of an array of marginalized figures marked by their nonnormative relationships to work: an unemployed mother (the kind regularly hailed in rightist cant of the late twentieth century and later as a "welfare queen") buying a mass-produced snack for her crying child at the Price Chopper; an old blind man who "lost [his] sight in a work-related accident" for which he received no compensation, who concedes that he drank prior to the accident but insists that "hav[ing] a drink in the parking lot don't mean [he] can't run the damn roller," and who asserts that he "worked like a fucking cart horse and broke [his] health" in ways irreducible to his supposed "negligence" at the roller; and a would-be student at the Technical Institute of America, who waits for a loan to pay for his enrollment and whiles away time at the Launderama, "watch[ing] college girls fold their underwear with [his] dick hid inna box of Tide" and dreaming to learn "what makes [computers] light up. How they actually work, you know."[84] Denizens of an unnamed and thereby unlocal town (which could be anywhere because it is everywhere in the United States of the 1990s and 2000s), this underclass of putatively lazy or shiftless subjects is revealed rather, through Spin and Marlene's sympathetic investment in them, to have complex relationships both to work and to laziness—and a comparatively simple relationship to the title figure of the song, "Fuck You, I'm a Millionaire," who owns "hotels in Martinique" implicitly contrasted with the shabby motels hosting Spin and Marlene's act; who says *fuck you* to the "hobo on the corner" asking for a nickel; and whose "tax breaks" are likewise designed to fuck the un- and under-employed characters brought to life in both songs.[85]

In the *Set I* version of *The Dream Express*, the critique of neoliberal capitalism's inequities manifested in the latter song appears, tellingly, in near-juxtaposition with an episode that features Spin and Marlene's death and resurrection and that positions their ghostly apotheosis as a statement on their own complex relationships, like those highlighted in "Town Well," to both work and laziness. The duo recall for their audience a marathon car ride through the desert with their manager, Uncle Wolfie, whose lupine obsession with relentlessly booking and thus overworking the act is contrasted, throughout the piece, with Spin and Marlene's appropriately indifferent responses to their underwhelming sites of employment—a contrast made most vivid in the account of the car ride, during which they recline, narcotized by drugs, in the backseat of the car while Wolfie, determined to speed them to their next gig, hunches rigidly over the steering wheel all night.[86] His insomniac effort is mocked when he discovers, upon arrival at the Hi-Hat Lounge, that his conversely somnolent clients have in fact succumbed fatally to the contents of a "bad bag"; this death, literally a "double overdose," operates metaphorically to enact Spin and Marlene's resistance to work as enjoined by Wolfie, who can only think, upon discovering their corpses, "Five nights five hundred a night out the fucking window. Money in the grave," and who thus refuses them that grave as he calculates the comparatively small expense of driving "out to a picnic spot he knew by the banks of the Ohio, . . . stripp[ing] the bodies, [tying] on enough concrete to keep them down in the mud with the catfish, and roll[ing] them into the river."[87] Yet like the bathtubs and pools in which so many relaxed subjects float in the representational history of laziness, this river, far from a space for sinking Spin and Marlene, levitates them miraculously into the post-life "shadows" we see in performance.[88] Both as and in the haunts of those patrons who "may very well have ruined [their] whole fucking [lives] already," their postlife is, rather, a transcendence of the ruination or spoiling that otherwise sticks to lounge and situates their performing as a kind of postwork, undertaken for the love of playing (badly) and as a loose, meandering salute to those driven to desperation by the Wolfies of the world; guided by the generous barroom philosophy, "No cover, no minimum," Spin and Marlene produce minimalist covers as gifts to capitalism's losers, otherwise and oppositely hailed by "the preacher and the politician . . . on TV, in the newspaper and on the street" with the message, "Them that hath shall be given some more, and them that ain't got never shall get, world without end, thus and forever, amen children."[89] As living-dead loungers who don't, like the millionaire of "Fuck You," have the ear of the president and a "couple dozen senators," Spin and Marlene can't advocate for labor reform or guaranteed income on behalf of "them that ain't got," but they can, in their languid way, give voice to the stories of those, like seventeen-year-old Marlene when she first meets Spin, who work "at the Taco Bell . . . full time so I can get enough money to buy a car, drive outta town so fast they'll think I dematerialized"—as, indeed, she does eventually dematerialize into a revenant.[90]

In ways related to the postwork of their creations Spin and Marlene, Jenkin and his collaborators could also be understood as having engaged in a process of lazing as they have, with relaxed ambition, transformed The Dream Express over time. Indeed, O'Connell captures well their embrace of a slackened pace and an easy-seeming energy in their evolutive revisions to the piece over the course of the 1990s and 2000s:

Sometimes we're writing the songs from scratch, sometimes we're covering something that one of us found. . . . Once in a while, we think, "We should learn how to play some actual instruments," but we don't do it [*laughs*]. We've become very dependent on [sound designer] John Kilgore [who prerecords the instrumental sound that is supposed to be emanating from their "electronic keyboard and rhythm machine"].[91] . . . We'll usually go in and have a meeting; we'll sit around and drink coffee in John's studio for a couple of hours, then we'll play each other a whole bunch of—we'll just go like, "Alright, let's just all, like, find everything that we like right now and play it for each other." So we'll just play for each other everything either we think Spin and Marlene should cover or something we've just heard that we really love. . . . And then John will go, "OK, I'll make you a track," and then he won't make one for two months, and then finally he'll make a track and it'll be—. . . in the middle of the night he'll have had an idea. . . . And then he'll come in with the track and we'll just work-and-work-and-work and, half the time (maybe not half the time, maybe a quarter of the time), we end up discarding it. You know, it's like very hard to find something that fits . . . that Spin and Marlene thing. . . . We'll make a lot of stuff that we throw away. . . . And there's some underscoring that was, like it'll be a track for a song that we threw away ten years ago, and we'll be like, "You know? Let's play that old track. Does anybody have it?" And we all have these piles of CDs, and we're like, I mean, a big old mess, so we'll be like, "Wait, I found it, here's that track that went under that song," and it was just so bad, . . . and it will be uncanny sometimes, it times out exactly to the end of [a new] monologue, and then it makes this really cool sound right when we were supposed to be opening the door, and you can't believe it, so we'll have the underneath track for the piece. . . . That's one good thing about doing this for, whatever, seventeen years, is that we have a lot of piles and piles of stuff—our clothes, and our music, and pieces that Len wrote that we never did—and we'll be like, "Let's resurrect that, and maybe that is a song."[92]

From the performers' jocular unconcern about not playing instruments, to the creation of dilatory time and fluid space in which to let inspiration strike and to develop, tweak, and redeploy material, to the casual handling of the Dream Express archive, O'Connell and her collaborators epitomize a lazing approach to work—one that, indeed, *works* for them as they achieve "uncanny," "cool," and (to add to O'Connell's list of modifiers) effervescent, shimmering, or even at times hallucinatory effects in sets of *The Dream Ex-*

press. I would also say about their approach that it constitutes a potent version of what Stefano Harney and Fred Moten call, in *The Undercommons* and elsewhere, the genuine, collective *study* that obtains, in their reckoning, either altogether to the side of the university or in the less institutionalized, more under-the-radar zones and relations that the university may still produce despite its corporatization.[93] Indebted to each other in ways that, consonant with Harney and Moten's advocacy of such debt, exceeds the terms of calculation and resists the logic of credit, Jenkin, Mellor, O'Connell, and with them Kilgore treat *The Dream Express* like a palpating, unruly gift. And, given the piece's coordination of a class analysis through the sympathetic imagining of a litany of precarious lives, as described above, studying in tandem with the project the process of its making invites imaginative speculation about collectivity of the sort that Harney and Moten affirm: how might various members of the undercommons come together to laze in the manner of Jenkin et al., "play[ing] for"—and with—"each other"? This question, unlike others raised or implied here, does not and cannot have an unlocal answer, though it is one toward which every subject hailed by *The Dream Express* ought to remain disposed—as it were, expressly to dream.

Where the disposition of the Dream Express archive is concerned, one consequence of its makers' lazing that could be construed as a downside is the lightness, not to say carelessness, with which "piles and piles" of material are let to languish "mess[ily]" in corners of rooms and under beds, indexing an idle regard for the piece's posterity that extends to the collaborators' never having made a video of any of the myriad live performances of *The Dream Express*. Indeed, for me, the nonexistence of such a recording eventually became a matter of consequence. Having only hazily or half-thought about writing on *The Dream Express* in a coda to "Around Lounging" when I saw *Set III* of the project in 2009—and having, as a consequence, taken very few notes about the performance at that time—I felt the telltale signs of worry (the lump in the throat, the perspiration on the brow) when I later realized both that the piece's analysis would be crucial to this chapter and that I would have no video footage of it to study. Faced with likely failures of memory, I indulged the paranoia that Spin's words about inattention to history in *The Dream Express*—"Amnesia is your birthright in the USA"[94]—had some special, stinging meaning for me. How, after a gulf of years, could I do honor and justice to the rich details of the piece and communicate properly to readers the thrills produced by experiencing Marlene's beyond-gravelly "purr"[95] (if "the crooner is the vocal materialization of a drink, . . . alcoholic and subtly intoxicating,"[96] then Marlene offers the vocal materialization of a hangover);

2.2 The Dream Express (Steven Mellor, l, and Deirdre O'Connell, r) gets lit and rocks out on a carpeted stage at the Chocolate Factory. (Photograph by Brian Rogers.)

or the magical tonal alternations from goofy to sinister to plaintive wrought by "Spin" at the Musicmax 5000 keyboard; or the chic shabbiness of Spin's porkpie hat, Marlene's spangled halter; or the palpable precarity with which a drink perches on a keyboard or one of the tripping Miltons grips a mike stand?

The possibility of generating this question and its contours corroborates Pierre Saint-Amand's assertion that "laziness allows 'the rising to the surface of memories and sensations' in 'free-flowing remembrance,'"[97] as well as the value and wisdom in taking to heart Eve Sedgwick's insight (following Melanie Klein) "that it can be a relief and relaxation, rather than a big tragedy the way it is in Freud, when one manages to get disabused of the fantasy of omnipotence, together with the reflex fantasy of utter impotence."[98] And this lesson—to relieve oneself of worry, to surrender to relaxation even or especially in a scholarly pursuit that threatens to be poisoned by toxic aims at mastery—is one likewise furnished by *The Dream Express* itself: "Relax," Marlene instructs the audience after Spin has followed a creepy, monologic tangent that might "make [us] nervous," and Spin himself tells us to "equilibrate . . . ourselves" after our minds have been blown by the number "Town Well."[99] To follow these twinned pieces of advice meant, for many viewers assembled at the Chocolate Factory in December 2009, myself included, to hail discreetly one of the servers more than happy to (re)fill a glass of wine or beer. *The Dream Express* has been expressly dreamed by its creators as a piece to be enjoyed in a mode of relaxation, so much the better if eased by intoxication; if I felt the importance of re-creating for readers some sense, say, of the 2009 production's soundscapes or other design elements, then shouldn't I also endeavor to re-create the imperative to recreate, unto a state of liquefaction, equally central to the show? And not only might a scholarly response to *The Dream Express* generatively convey the importance of that liquefaction to the experience of the piece in production; it might also, in its turn, embody a related form of liquefaction or lubrication: what I have been tracking throughout these pages, yet not with so embodied a specificity until this engagement of and with *The Dream Express*, as meaningfully intellective lazing. Indeed, it might entail a surrender, not literal but nonetheless material, to Spin's call at the end of *The Dream Express*—"We're back at the Briarpatch tomorrow night. Join us. Meanwhile, enjoy the garden"[100]—that would find in conversation, rather than at odds, the fleeting pleasure and the eternal return.

Coda: To Slack or to Swing?

In the spirit and interest of relaxation described at the end of this chapter's previous section, I have had, as also intimated in the chapter's introduction, to let go of what I once imagined would have been a tight grip on *Make Love*, to lose, which in this case is to say *loose*, *The Lost Lounge* so that lessons for lazing, not to be found in those pieces as they are in *The Dream Express*, could obtain instead. Yet without rigidly attempting to close the rather purposively open circle that "Laziness" traces, I do find worth in briefly resituating *The Dream Express* alongside these other lounge parodies by way of looking ahead to the next chapter's archive and concerns. Performance practitioners like Jenkin, Mellor, and O'Connell—as well as Bond, Finley, Mellman, Shaw, and Weaver, invoked alongside them earlier—ought to be understood as producing responses to lounge's idioms and expressive styles that are not just historically but generationally specific; if not the actual parents of these particular performers, then certainly the avatars for *mom* and *dad* in the mass culture of their youths were imaged again and again with martini glass in hand, "Hawaiian" shirt on back. The generational specificity of such artists' approach to lounge parody—constituted by their simultaneous attachment to and detachment from lounge material, a movement of coupling and decoupling that measures their formerly embodied experience, their palpating memory, and the ongoing repercussions for them of Cold War ideology, repressive domesticity, and youthful rebellion—marks their distinction from other artists and consumers, belonging to a later generation, who likewise embraced lounge in the mid- to late 1990s and early 2000s. That later generation is, of course, chiefly responsible for the runaway success of *Swingers* (1996), of the *Ultra-Lounge* compilation albums released by Capitol Records between 1996 and 2009, and of a host of related phenomena and products ranging from swing lessons to vintage cocktail dresses. These two generational, historically coincident uptakes of lounge share a participation in ironic display, but the inflections of their respectively ironic modes of engagement are quite different in tone. Where the older generation's lounge ebullience is tempered by melancholic, caustic, or demented colorations (or all of these colorations—and more), the younger one's enthusiasm for lounge is much more singularly cheerful and sanguine, to an extent that no amount of scare-quoting or self-consciousness can quite temper.

Equally important, (mostly) twentysomething neo-swingers have not tended, like Jenkin and his collaborators, toward lazing, and the makers among them have certainly not been lazy in their rush to capitalize on nostalgia, of however reflexive a sort. Rather, the laziness mantle for the generational peers of Jon Favreau and Vince Vaughan goes to the slackers among them, and the very legibility of *slacker culture* as a categorical term indicates the extent to which slacking, just as much as swinging, defines the version of contemporaneity in question. Among the many enunciations or representations of this defining slacker culture on which we might alight, director Kelly Reichardt's *River of Grass* (1994)—which debuted at Sundance in the same year as the ultimately much more famous *Clerks*—is a singular, unusual, and therefore not very "representative" representation (and all the more interesting for it), largely because of the ways in which it imagines slackers, rather than lizards or swingers or even their parodists, in the loungy spaces like cocktail bars and seedy roadside motels that are otherwise almost never imagined as the haunts of skateboarders, video gamers, and their kindred.[101] In this case, the slacking protagonists, Cozy (Lisa Bowman), a bored wife and mother, and her shiftless, would-be lover Lee (Larry Fessenden), meet in a bar and later imagine—mistakenly—that they are responsible for the shooting death of a stranger; their response, to go "on the lam," takes the lam-less, literally lame, form of holing up in a motel, where they fail to achieve the level of arousal to engage in their promised affair, fail to hatch a plan for their next move, indeed fail to do much of anything except peer, occasionally and listlessly, through mostly drawn shades. The physical and existential stasis of these slackers is mirrored visually in Reichardt's use of actual still photographs (of Cozy as a child, from album covers) to fill the screen, in dialogue with which hyperstatic shots of various figures and locations become evocatively reminiscent of specimen views under microscope lenses (as when Cozy, caught by the camera's exactingly unmoving, overhead gaze, scissors languidly and repetitively in a pool like a bacterium under a slide); of crime scene photography (in, for instance, the case of the camera's lingering dully over rummaged drawers that appear deceptively to have been ransacked); and of "picture postcards" (as filmmaker Todd Haynes has dubbed the exteriors of buildings captured in the "long, flat, frontal frames" of establishing shots).[102]

As Cozy and Lee's absurd failure simply to produce change for a highway toll makes plain, sometimes the fruit of laziness is just stuckness; and sometimes movement—any amount of it, and however halting its form—is better than none, a notion suggested by the final scene of *River of Grass* when Cozy's (homeward bound?) car moves slowly along a trafficked road and Reichardt's camera, following it with a barely perceptible increase in speed, threatens for a moment to draw too near to its bumper. What's more, even if laziness isn't just stuckness but takes the shape of the more generative lazing anatomized here, sometimes the duration that such lazing requires (recall my years' worth of time spent lounging with lounge) isn't, in fact, available, in which case a different—but nonetheless aslant—orientation to temporality may have to supervene for the subject who can't afford the toll of the pace of Cozy's car. In suggesting a transition, at the end of *River of Grass*, from torpor to crawling, from stopping to proceeding with caution, Reichardt, whose later, less static, and more arresting (because not so wholly arrested) work will figure at the center of the next chapter, also provides a conceptual model for thinking about the transition from laziness to slowness, one in which spending time must give way to the fraught effort of saving it.

3. Slowness

Arresting

I can think of no better way to begin this meditation on "Slowness" than with a very long quotation that I ask you to read slowly. The source of the quotation is an interview that Jacques Derrida gave to Bernard Stiegler and that was "shot by Jean-Christophe Rosé under the auspices of the INA (Institut National de l'Audiovisuel), on Wednesday, December 22, 1993":[1]

> I would like to evoke what is happening here when, instead of pursuing the necessary course or relatively interior consequence of a meditation or discussion, as we would if we weren't surrounded by this technical apparatus, all of a sudden, as if we had been interrupted, we had to start speaking in front of the camera and recording devices. A modification is produced—in any case, in me, and I don't want to pass over it in silence—which is at once psychological and affective. Another process is set into motion, if you like. I don't speak, I don't think, I don't respond in the same way anymore, at the same rhythm as when I'm alone, daydreaming or reflecting at the wheel of my car or in front of my computer or a blank page, or as when I'm with one of you, as was the case a little while ago, as will be the case again in a moment, talking about the same questions but at another rhythm, with another relation to time and to urgency. This does not mean that, at that moment, one has enough time—one never has enough time—but the relation to urgency and rhythm would be different and now it has suddenly been transformed by this system of scenographic and technical devices. As soon as someone says "Roll tape!" a race begins, one starts not to speak, not to think in the same way anymore, almost not to think at all anymore. . . . One's relation to words, to their way of

coming or not coming, is different, you know this well. The first thing to do, if what we are doing here has any specificity, would therefore be not to forget, not to subtract, not to neutralize this effect, and to record on tape, to archive the re-marking of this fact that we are recording, that I, in any case, am recording with a certain amount of difficulty. This is in general part of the experience, shall we say, of "intellectuals," of people who write or who teach, etc.: when they are in front of the camera or microphone, the more they ask themselves questions about this situation, as I am doing here, the more they exhibit reticence, scruples, a shrinking or retreat—not a gratuitous or negative retreat, but a retreat in which they try not to do just anything, to be more "responsible"—the more they are removed from this experience, the less they are accustomed to it, the less they are able to forget the artifice of the scenario. . . . I say this under the heading of process and of stasis, of the arrest, the halt.[2]

In framing this quotation, I introduced two related but crucially different concepts that are also addressed implicitly by Derrida within the quotation: length and slowness. The length of the quotation—448 words—is calculably quantifiable and thus basically (or at least relatively) indisputable, but to write of the slowness with which I invited you to apprehend the passage involves, conversely, the introduction of an ambiguity in meaning. *Slowness* could refer to an activity, in this case reading and comprehending, that *takes time*—indeed, a time whose length may correspond more or less plainly to the length of the quotation itself. But *slowness* could also indicate something about the quality of the time—in your phenomenal experience of it, and however long (or not) that time is—for whose duration you read and comprehend the passage; in this case, slowness would consist not necessarily in taking time but in *making time*, or in time making itself felt as, expansive, extensive, even stretched: in a word, slowed. One could, to heighten the difference between these two kinds of slow time as well as to begin to parse their relationship to one another, call the first kind simply *long time*, the experience of which involves (unusual) duration, endurance, and the imbrication of the two; whereas the second kind of slow time, stretched time, concerns dilation, a notion that doesn't have (commonsense, anyway) purchase until one has accepted measurable, as opposed to "pure" or Bergsonian, duration as a temporal principle—even if only one imposed in its spatializing and homogenizing tendencies on the phenomenal, heterogeneous (for instance, sometimes "slow," sometimes not) experience of time.[3] I might plausibly assert that some hours move more slowly than others, but thinking of such subjective "warping" of the duration of an hour is, for most, especially nonphilosophically oriented subjects, difficult until and unless the quantifiable duration of, say, an hour is a meaningful category (given the powerful and historically long imposition of measurement on time that I have just identified, itself available to be understood as an intractable warping).[4] Thus temporal dilation is likelier than not to be graspable as a quality or an aspect of duration—one of the things that can happen to duration in our perception or experience of it.[5]

Everyday users of language mobilize routinely—and perhaps sometimes confuse—both meanings of slowness charted here, but I will want to insist on their distinction, at least in part to focus attention on the second, less often and carefully attended meaning of slowness as stretching, dilating, expanding. Derrida himself points toward this distinction in expressing his frustration with the constraints of the recorded interview and the phenomenal experience that those constraints incite for him. When he contrasts the kind of time that he spends thinking behind the steering wheel with the kind of time that he spends speaking before the camera, we must not assume that the former time is necessarily longer than the latter (or that Derrida drives slowly); indeed, the interview of which this speech comprises a part is quite long, whereas many car rides are much shorter. Rather, it is the manner in which Derrida may dispose himself, his time, his self in time, in the car that conduces favorably to the thinking whose value lies in its fullness or intensity and whose intensity owes to what Derrida calls its "rhythm": a complex of attributes that I would identify as the thinking's slowness, in contradistinction to the speed exacted by and enacted before the camera (again, for however long or not one is shot there) whose embeddedness in an industrial system with economic and affective imperatives, if not its technical specificity, prompts an inevitable-seeming "race" that disturbs Derrida and that has the ironic effect of paralyzing him (implicitly directed to speed up, he freezes up instead). In his turn, Derrida wants to contest the ostensible inevitability of the race and to disturb the recording process that disturbs him by marking it as such, by ruminating on it, by philosophizing it. And in so doing, he attempts (successfully, in my estimation) to make the obstruction that he experiences as an "arrest" something more than a mere obstacle or impasse: indeed, to make what could otherwise be only an arrest an occasion that is rather *arresting* for him, for Stiegler, and for the eventual audience for these remarks; that is, to endow the remarks, however compromised or fragile the effort (one less so because the threat of fragility and compromise is reflexively identified), with some portion of the slowness that more readily obtains for Derrida in moments of "daydreaming," that very word conjuring the expansiveness or extensiveness, simultaneously an intensiveness, of which he feels robbed by the camera.

It is telling that Derrida does not feel thus robbed in front of the computer that he would otherwise align with the camera as two important manifestations of what he calls "teletechnology."[6] In this, as in so many other, boons, Derrida proves to be a singular thinker and writer, for how much more used are we to hearing of the blockage that the blank screen prompts for myriad subjects who, like Derrida, have committed themselves to the enterprise of scholarship? That blockage may relate crucially to the play, not always felicitous, of the arrested and the arresting that I have begun to trace here through the rubric of slowness. On the one hand, scholars are routinely told and tell themselves that their work's specialness inheres, at least in part, in the care, the deliberation, the rigor of its execution, which would seem to necessitate some version of or at least something like slowness. On the other hand, professional imperatives (the mantra "publish or perish" is intoned to the point of cliché for a reason) just as routinely put many scholars in a position in which an expectation of output, measured against often-intransigent deadlines for review and reward (or its withholding), would seem to dictate speed. Slowness, in the sense of taking time, is a problem (more bluntly, not a typically viable option; as Derrida says, "one never has enough time") for those who nonetheless want to make time—the time that they spend thinking and writing, as well as the time that interlocutors spend with the fruits of their intellection—valuably dense, intense, slowed, and not dull, dulled, or, worse, paralyzing in its slowing. (It should be no surprise that subjects faced with such a double bind experience a panic before the blank screen not unlike Derrida's tensing before the camera.) Thus the making of slowness is an obstruction of a sort somewhat different from, say, the embarrassment anatomized in this book's first chapter or even the laziness of its second. Where a salient, tricky proposition entailed by those obstructions is how to put them to good use, the perhaps even trickier proposition for the would-be embracer of slowness is how to arrive, in the first place, at the means of its manifestation as spiriting rather than seizing. An eccentric version of this otherwise mundane challenge to render and share a positive slowness, as I have been suggesting, is one that we can locate in Derrida's approach to "exappropriating"[7] his recorded performance for the INA.

Far from alone in preferring slowness to speed and in wishing to disrupt the operations whereby the camera tends to collude with the latter, Derrida mounts an effort in his interview with Stiegler at affecting time, at endowing it with a slowness, that has been likewise and yet more powerfully accomplished by artistic makers of recorded media (or artists working in related arenas) themselves. To be clear, the kind of slowness that I am attributing to Derrida in juxtaposed invocation with such artists is *not* the long one—based directly on endurance—that has found a prominent place in contemporary culture and that has been a hallmark, for instance, of performance art like Marina Abramović's and theatrical experimentation like Elevator Repair Service's for some time; rather, it is the more unusual feeling or sense that time has slowed in a piece of whatever duration—and perhaps all the more special and striking in a piece of short duration—through which I am chasing (slowly) a pedagogical model for critical enterprise. For this reason, I turn to director Kelly Reichardt, an examination of whose work will be central to this chapter and whose films of the early 2000s engender for the viewer the fascinating, underthought phenomenon whose contours I have begun to sketch here: again, the experience of time moving slowly in a good, generative, and pleasurable, rather than boring or frustrating, way. Reichardt's films configure a sort of duration that is marked by *concentration* in two senses: the presentation of a density of information in a given series of frames, and thus the concomitant intensity of focus that it takes to grasp, appreciate, and take pleasure from that dense spool of information. Paradoxically, this "concentration" of material and of attention takes, in fact, the form (in production) of minimalism, understatement, and seeming absence, and (in reception) of a sense of dilation—but not of dilution: Reichardt's films position what material there is, however little of it there may be, in such a way that it all seems arresting because almost arrested, as becomes the viewer's sense of duration itself. Learning from this cinematic slowness, with its invitation to be arrested, the scholar may share the task, in working, to try to make a parallel sense of dilation obtain more regularly and in a more "concentrated" way—so that the putative obstruction of slowness is galvanized to charge the experience of (thinking, writing) time as densely and intensely as possible. En route to the terminus that this lesson, as disclosed by Reichardt, comprises, I take a necessary detour through the most prominent critical literatures on speed and slowness, which foreground what I have called taking (slow) time rather than making time (slow)—and which thus raise the question, if only implicitly, of what relationship obtains between taking time and making time. Supposing that the relationship is a transductive and mutually beneficial one—but requiring the slow (s)pace of a temporal delay and rhetorical gap to make a warrant of this supposition—I turn to and through two braided areas of inquiry where the underinvestigated phenomenon of making time slow *has* been considered, if briefly or tangentially: cognitive psychological studies of optimal experience and flow, and Buddhist explorations of temporal dimensionality. Putting pressure on the attraction in both of these discourses to what may be described as "cinematic consciousness," I advocate the pedagogy offered neither quite by psychology nor precisely by Buddhism but by slow cinema like Reichardt's itself—and offered therein through both that cinema's formal gambits and its production histories: a pedagogy of slow tempos, the contemplative activity that those tempos promote, and the preparedness required for contemplation at those tempos.

Speeding

Where some modern or contemporary thinkers of various stripes have been slow to take up slowness as a problematic or analytic, they have been comparatively quick in their uptake of speed; and these relative rates of velocity—with their corresponding rates of abundant, or scarce, writerly output—should come as no surprise, given the widespread ways, stretching far beyond the more or less rarefied realm of critical discourse, with which speed has made itself felt as one of the most pressing, if not alarming, attributes of global modernities and their afterlives (in this case, perhaps more aptly their aftershocks). As Sam See notes astutely of the abundant literature of speed, two of its most influential avatars have been Stephen Kern's *The Culture of Time and Space* and Paul Virilio's *Speed and Politics*, "methodologically divergent texts" that nonetheless "concur that, especially between the world wars, technological innovations in the automotive, film, radio, and martial industries created a 'cult of speed' for a generation" with appetites whetted for ever faster "products . . . that could not only contract but imperil the time and space of modernism."[8] Of the two, Virilio's text—with its bleak account of "dromocratic-type progress" and of the hegemonic ways in which the instigators of this so-called progress make designs on "the future" and "the infinite" under the sloganeering banner, "*speed is the hope of the West*"[9]—continues more impactfully to exert force on current theoretical and political conversations, if in sometimes un- or underacknowledged ways;[10] it finds its most striking contemporary counterpart in Bernard Stiegler's magisterial, multivolume *Technics and Time*, which moves from a "quasi-transcendental" account of "technical speed" qua *tekhnē* to a more materially grounded, "historical narrative concerning a quasi-apocalyptic acceleration of the speed of technics."[11] In the latter mode, Stiegler understands subjects of "the technics of virtual reality and telepresence together with the biotechnologies" as assaulted combatants in a "war of speed" that threatens,[12] via such technics, to move those subjects and their worlds "tendentially"—and with volatility—"towards the absolute speed of light,"[13] an account of speed vibrating resonantly with Virilio's worrying of and over the dromocratic "annihilat[ion of] time and space."[14]

For the present purposes, one salient thread to draw out of the knotty and knotted field of speed studies, as dominantly shaped by such writers as Virilio and Stiegler, is the vital extent to which this field produces implications about—and sometimes explications of—slowness. When Virilio points to the motto "*Stasis is death*" as the West's blinkered yet "*general law of the World*," corollary to the notion that speed is hope, and when he advances the related proposition that "the more speed increases, the faster freedom decreases,"[15] he suggests, without asserting or affirming outright, that subjects resistant to dromologics might rather find hope in slowness and perhaps develop an oppositional politics, a measured embrace of something like freedom, through slowness. Similarly, when Stiegler argues that "contemporary disorientation," the prevailing condition, in his contestable account, of the neoliberal subject "is linked to speed, to the industrialization of memory resulting from the struggle for speed, and to the specifics of the technologies employed in that struggle,"[16] he raises the specter of the possibility that slowness might provide not only the pace but also the ground, contra the "extermination of space" that he and Virilio attribute to speed,[17] for the re-orientation of that subject, a reordering of her or his consciousness and phenomenal experience that could obstruct the manufacture of dislocatedness, amnesia, and malaise.[18] Where such potentially salutary effects of slowness are concerned, other critics working in the domain of speed studies make central and plain what remains marginally insinuated in these foundational accounts. For instance, Thomas Hylland Eriksen, who devotes most of his *Tyranny of the Moment* to a reckoning with speed, turns in that book's final chapter to a careful celebration of "the pleasures of slowness,"[19] which he presents as a mode of taking time and space away from fast flows of information and which, he insists with an eye to the scalar dimensions of such slowness, must be cultivated at both personal and sociocultural levels, requiring pragmatic recommendations for policy makers.[20] In a similar vein, William E. Connolly asserts in *Neuropolitics: Thinking, Culture, Speed* that the structuring of "a world marked by asymmetrical zones of speed" makes critical the task of providing "citizens in a variety of walks of life . . . with structural opportunities for periodic escape and retreat from a fast-paced life," even as he remains skeptical about the homogenizing and hierarchizing conditions of traditionally slow lifeworlds and cautiously affirmative of the ways in which speed can be mobilized in the service of a cosmopolitan, ethical, and democratic pluralism.[21]

A still-emergent discourse of slowness—chiefly concerned in its popular manifestations with such neoliberally tractable (that is, globally monetizable) agendas as slow design, slow food, and slow travel—can and should be understood as responsive, if sometimes obliquely or unwittingly, to the literature of speed canvassed here and, in its best critical manifestations, as thoughtfully extending that literature's concerns and as modeling a challenge to or refusal of post-Fordist models of productivity. John Urry's *Sociology beyond Societies* remains a touchstone in this slowly burgeoning field of slowness, particularly for its multireferential account of ways to inhabit the "glacial time" that is not only incredibly "slow-moving" and thus "beyond assessment or monitoring within the present generation," but also, and precisely because of its "mimicking [of] the enormously long 'timescapes' of the physical world," less available for capture by "the clock-time of the national state and the instantaneous time of much corporeal, imaginative and virtual travel" and more amenable to forms of "reflexive awareness" and protest.[22] Though less politically far-reaching and more beholden to the class privileges and tacitly nationalist presumptions of the so-called slow food "movement" (yet thoughtfully responsive, at times, to just such critiques of slow food), Wendy Parkins and Geoffrey Craig offer a nonetheless stirring account, detachable finally from the art of cooking, of the wonder, generosity, care, reflection, attentiveness, and sense of collectivity that can emerge in formations whose participants reject the "temporality of speed" and demand "the need to protect slowness" at both "private" and "institutional" levels.[23]

Worth underscoring at this point is that, whether (in my evaluation) at their "best" or otherwise, all these writings on speed and slowness—and the related doings of slowness toward which they gesture or that they entail—have in common their responsiveness to and enlivening of what, in the introduction to this chapter, I identified as the kind of "slow" time that could equally well be nominated *long time*, the kind whose activity and relationality take time. (As Parkins and Craig write, paradigmatically, "At its heart, slow living is a conscious attempt to change the current temporal order to one which offers *more* time, time to attend to everyday life.")[24] Part of what makes long, slow time long—what makes it take time—is the tempo at which activity or relationality happens in such time. Yet a slow tempo might also characterize—in fact, tends almost unilaterally to characterize—the other kind of slow time to which we will turn fuller attention, the stretched or dilated time, of whatever short or long duration, that has attracted so much less commentary than long time. Indeed, following anthropologist Robert

Levine's compelling claim that tempo is "salien[t]" to all manner of temporal experience, "no matter what area of temporal experience" is under consideration—and that this salience owes to the "overlaying and interconnectedness of tempo with the many dimensions of . . . time"[25]—we could leverage this salience and pivot from the easily graspable commonality of slow tempo to versions of both long time and stretched time, in order to ask a series of overlapping questions: What other commonalities do these two forms of time share? How might we extrapolate from these commonalities—as well as from related differences—the precise nature of the relationship between taking slow time and making time slow? May they be in some way mutually constitutive? Does taking time, so much less curious and more explored a phenomenon, have lessons or resources to offer making time? And how would discerning the nature of these potential resources depend on and emerge from more carefully parsing the relationship, perhaps coconstitutive or transductive, between makings and takings of time?

To pose these questions as genuinely open questions and not, in the opening, to move directly to their answers is also to create a punctuation, by which I mean not only a temporal and temporary intermittence, but also a dimensional space in which the questions may be kept in a state of attention and contemplation even as, and paradoxically because, other questions or concerns are getting activated and more actively addressed. This move is not the one that Giorgio Agamben, following Heidegger and Bataille, makes when he inhabits the open as the site of inoperativity and the potentiality that inoperativity begets,[26] but rather a move to incarnate an alternative operativity, an operativity by other means, for whose concretion I find an arresting—but only approximate—image in Karen Wendy Gilbert's essay "Slowness," where she "writ[es] of time as rivers of different rates of flow" and asks, open-endedly, "What happens (in terms of open systems) if one steps from a river moving at one mile per hour into one moving at ten miles per hour? And back again?"[27] To tweak this question: what happens when one keeps a foot in each river at the same time, in such a way that the very words *same* and *time* begin to lo(o)se their meanings? Let the questions posed above move at their relatively slow rate and nonetheless catch up to us—or us to them—after the fashion of the tortoise in Zeno's paradox and after, which is in a manner to say as, we explore a parallel field of inquiry that also demands attention if our attunement to slowness is to be properly orchestrated: psychological and Buddhist writings, indexical to each other, in which the otherwise undertheorized phenomenon of slowed time, as opposed to long time, makes its way.

Flowing

While it would be an overstatement to describe certain texts in cognitive psychological and Buddhist discourses as shaping or deeply informing each other, some of those texts do point referentially to one another in ways that reveal common concerns. To furnish a couple of examples, Mihaly Csikszentmihalyi, the foremost researcher and theorist of what he calls optimal experience and flow, sees as related to those phenomena and writes approvingly of the "mental discipline" and "cultivat[ion of] constant spontaneity" that animate practices in "Zen varieties of Buddhism";[28] and, in turn, the popularizing writer and teacher Lama Surya Das invokes Csikszentmihalyi and his conceptualization of flow—which Das understands as "the state of being when we seem to accomplish everything without effort and we know instinctively what needs to be done to reach our goals"—in order to assert that one's "Buddha self lives in a constant state of [this] flow. The Buddha within is always awake."[29] The subtitle of the text in which Das writes thus of flow and its implicit relationship to Buddhism—*Awakening to the Infinite Possibilities of Now*—indicates that as his writing contributes to an ideology of self-enhancement by way of self-discipline, it participates simultaneously in a meditation on time and, for him, its paradoxically timeless dimensions. So, too, does Csikszentmihalyi's work yoke an investigation of temporality to an agenda of self-refashioning; as he writes in a deftly terse articulation of the effortful achievement of happiness to the dwelling in time's passage—that is, an articulation of psychological flow, "The state in which people are so involved in an activity that nothing else seems to matter; the experience . . . so enjoyable that people will do it even at great cost, for the sheer sake of doing it," to temporal flow: "Optimal experience depends on the ability to control what happens in consciousness moment by moment."[30]

More specifically, the "moments" and "nows" of which Csikszentmihalyi and Das write, respectively, are ones that they understand—though they only address the issue in passing—as instances of slowed time, time whose extensivity (and corresponding intensivity) cannot be reckoned by the measurement of duration. Csikszentmihalyi claims of achieving "flow experience," with its "deep but effortless involvement that removes from awareness the worries and frustrations of everyday life," that such flow may cause "the sense of the duration of time [to be] altered; . . . minutes can stretch out to seem like hours";[31] similarly, Das avers that living a "dedicated spiritual life," informed materially by "meditation practice," can "lend time an infinitely expansive quality,"³² an expansiveness that may take the more concrete form of stretched or dilated time:

> When we understand and connect with our true, timeless natures, we will automatically slow down. And when we slow down, time slows down as well, so that we perceive that we have more of it. The more aware we are and the more quickly our minds process things, the slower they seem to occur—just as time seems to slow down on that first glorious autumn morning, when the colors and the breeze come alive under our intensely focused attention.³³

Reading Csikszentmihalyi and Das together underscores their shared privileging of heightened awareness and of the cultivation of focus that summoning heightened awareness requires; and while this horizontal reading practice helps to clarify what is vitally at stake—what is valued—in contemporary and contemporaneous discourses of self-improvement, one could also benefit, following Eve Sedgwick's cue, from reading the popularizing Das on a dense, if fraught, vertical continuum with other Buddhist thinkers and writers. Questioning the dominant model of identifying figures like Das as adapters—who, in the process of adapting Buddhist concepts and ideas for mass, largely American audiences, distort or otherwise misrepresent those concepts and ideas—Sedgwick wonders (even as she registers that "to a certain degree the aptness of this topos [of adaptation] is undeniable") whether a more nuanced and generous understanding of Das and others like him would emerge from an approach grounded in Buddhist pedagogy itself: that is, by "try[ing] out more, different resources from the great treasury of Buddhist phenomenologies of learning and teaching. What if, for example, an equally canonical topos such as *recognition/realization* describes some dynamics of Western Buddhist popularization better than does the one-directional topos of adaptation?"³⁴ Recognizing or realizing that Das is participating in a genealogy of Buddhist thinking—and, more important for the present purposes, a genealogy of Buddhist thinking about time in its slowed manifestations—would mean, for example, reading him with medieval writers and teachers and their more recent academic interpreters who, like Das more than unlike him, theorize slowed time as emergent from the dimensionality of time, specifically the presence (and comprehension of the presence) of time's fourth or "timeless" dimension in any and every present moment. Along these lines, Das makes his work available to be positioned alongside Dōgen's thirteenth-century *Shōbōgenzō*, in which the teaching on uji, or being in time, asserts the difference between temporal duration and the phenomenal experience of that duration ("we may not yet have measured the length of these twenty-four hours as to whether they are ever so long or as short as a sigh, still we speak of them as 'the twenty-four hours of our day'"),[35] as well as alongside the scholarship of Kenneth K. Inada: following "such Buddhists as Nāgārjuna and Buddhaghosa (5 A.D.)," Inada proposes that the full and aware apprehension of "a becoming of an event . . . 'takes time' for its fruition but not in the usual sense of the phrase" because time has been made "a kind of 'arresting to see' phenomenon of the experiential process," a felt, phenomenal arresting or slowing of the time taken to see, to experience.[36]

What unites all of these Buddhist teachers and commentators is the seeming or likely incompatibility of their models for the enlightened arrangement of consciousness and phenomenality with the kind of intellective work in whose investment this meditation on "Slowness" began. Hubert Nearman, a onetime scholar of theater studies, Buddhist monk, and recent translator of Shōbōgenzō, makes plain that, even though "modern scholars have" read Dōgen's teachings as "a form of philosophical speculation akin to that of . . . Western existentialists" like Heidegger (a reading that aligns those scholars' work with contemporary readings of the fourteenth-century Tibetan teacher Longchenpa),[37] the "type of mentation" that animates humanistic and post-humanistic Western discourses is precisely the sort "that trainees" learning from Dōgen "are working to disengage themselves from so that they may progress towards realizing spiritual Truth, which lies beyond the reaches of speculation."[38] Inada makes a similar, implicit distinction between the Buddhist temporal slowness achieved through "concentration," aligned in his account with "the development of [a] state of rest (samatha) or tranquility (passaddhi)," and the kind of intellectual slowness associated with the making of work like his own, a very different kind of "meditative discipline" from that which "offers a dimension of rest, a coolness of being, to our experiential process."[39] Weighed against the claims of these authors, Das's promises to his reader both to provide instruction for "tapping into the timeless [in order to be] a happier, more present, more patient, more aware, more engaged human being" and to offer wisdom "for strengthening memory, enhancing intelligence, giving lectures, engaging in debates . . . or writing" appears to put him at cross-purposes with himself (and to render what Sedgwick calls "the topos of adaptation" relevant, once more, for evaluating popularizing Buddhist work of this sort);[40] "meditation and mindful practices [may] work to slow down time," and Das may be able to demonstrate a correlation between the slowed time in and of meditation and "the imaginative energy . . . productively channeled into [the] work" of his students when they are not meditating, but correlation is not synonymous with causation, and Das's work does not evidence that his students' work-time is valuably or intensively slowed, just that it is "productive."[41]

On somewhat different but related grounds, Csikszentmihalyi's program for the maximal optimization of optimal experience seems inadequate to the cultivation or engendering of slowness with which he flirts in his writing. And it is indeed a flirtation, taking up little space in his prodigious *Flow* and, when taken up, emerging as a matter on which he is reluctant to hypothesize because of the absence of empirical data in which to ground such hypothe-sizing; as he writes, fastening on "the safest generalization to make about" slowed time:

> One of the most common descriptions of optimal experience is that time no longer seems to pass the way it ordinarily does. . . . Ballet dancers describe how a difficult turn that takes less than a second in real time stretches out for what seems like minutes. . . . The safest generalization to make about this phenomenon is to say that during the flow experience the sense of time bears little relation to the passage of time as measured by the absolute convention of the clock. . . .
>
> Most flow activities do not depend on clock time. . . . It is not clear whether this dimension of flow is just an epiphenomenon—a by-product of the intense concentration required for the activity at hand—or whether it is something that contributes in its own right to the positive quality of the experience. Although it seems likely that losing track of the clock is not one of the major elements of enjoyment, freedom from the tyranny of time does add to the exhilaration we feel during a state of complete involvement.[42]

Far more disappointing than Csikszentmihalyi's reluctance to speculate fur-ther about slowed time, arguably one of the most curious and scintillating aspects of flow experience—a reluctance wholly and understandably in line with his disciplinary training and investments—is the wedded vagueness with which he conceives a praxis for achieving "exhilaration . . . during a state of complete involvement," specifically when the involvement is mental or intellectual. Of making "the simplest *physical* act enjoyable when it is trans-formed so as to produce flow," he advises a five-part process—"(a) to set an overall goal . . . and [feasible] subgoals . . . ; (b) to find ways of measuring progress . . . ; (c) to keep concentrating on what one is doing, and to keep making finer and finer distinctions in the challenges involved in the activity; (d) to develop [necessary] skills . . . ; and (e) to keep raising the stakes"[43]—but when the translation of this "simplest" advice into a more complex register and for the transformation of more complex processes (like thinking and writing) comes into play, he demurs and, like Das, devotes his recommendations to championing activities finally extrinsic to such complex processes but putatively fueling their eventual enrichment: for example, and in Flow's moment of most shocking banality, the applauding of "working crossword puzzles," an "illuminating example" of "produc[ing] a sense of pleasing order that gives one a satisfying feeling of accomplishment."[44]

If neither Buddhism nor the cognitive psychology of flow, two rare sites of slowed time's invocation, offers a textured, nuanced teaching of slowness, where to alight on one? Csikszentmihalyi's and Das's shared, magnetic pull toward cinematic experience—or at least toward implied metaphors of cinematicity—suggests, as I have also done, that the refinement of something like one's cinematic consciousness may fill the pedagogical lacuna regarding time and slowness toward which their endeavors point.[45] Indeed, Das likens the operations of cinematic movement explicitly to perceptive awareness and its temporalization when he writes of his "love [of] the diaphanous nature and flickering phantasmagoria of the silver screen, so akin to consciousness itself and its workings."[46] A more rigorous account (if rightly challenged in its sweep)[47] of such a kinship between consciousness and cinema gets developed in the third volume of Stiegler's *Technics and Time* and suggests the ways in which a turn to cinema may not only yield lessons for the seeker of slowness but also, and in the process, generate pleasure: an experience to which Stiegler devotes brief, uncharacteristically tender regard and,[48] suspectly, one sidelined or even impugned in the works of Csikszentmihalyi and Das[49]—suggesting yet another reason to move not on their trail but to, with, and through slow cinema, and the slow pleasures that it affords, for clarity and guidance about the sanguine slowing of scholarly time.

Slowing

Having used the end of this chapter's previous section to call particular attention to the pleasure of slowness, likewise signaled in the chapter's introduction as a crucial critical concern, I should avow that my motivation has stemmed in part from a need to turn to a frank acknowledgment that not all viewers of slow cinema take pleasure from it and that some have charted rather their much less surprising—and much less interesting—feelings of boredom when confronted, for instance, with work like Kelly Reichardt's feature films. Regarding the annals of such boredom chronicles, we might fasten, briefly, on the journalistic firestorm initiated in 2011 when Dan Kois published an essay in The New York Times that used his viewing of Reichardt's most recent film, Meek's Cutoff, to launch a complaint about the film critic's responsibility to "Eat . . . [His] Cultural Vegetables," as the piece was titled, with incendiary intent, in the online edition of the newspaper.[50] For Kois, "slow-moving, meditative drama" like Meek's Cutoff produces a "grueling experience" as he has "trouble staying planted in [his] seat with [his] attention focused on the screen," and as "the long dissolves from one wind-blasted plateau to another sen[d] [his] thoughts blowing in a dozen directions."[51] In turn, Kois's account of this phenomenal experience prompted a series of challenges to his perspective that registered tonally just as much irritation as did his own piece—yet an irritation harnessed ironically, in those cases, to the cause of defending the salutary reception, opposed to frustration or anger or sheer boredom, available to the viewer properly oriented to slow, putatively tedious films. Indeed, in one of the most thoughtful, measured, and unhurried (I am tempted to write slow) pieces written amid the flurry of responses to Kois, Manohla Dargis deconstructed the ostensible singularity and transparency of boredom itself when she asserted of cynically made films like The Hangover Part II that their "grindingly repetitive . . . scene[s] after similar scene[s] of characters staring at one another stupidly, flailing about wildly and asking what happened" constitute the kind of "boring that Andy Warhol, who liked boring, found, well, boring," in contradistinction to which Reichardt's films may be understood as a deliberate effort to jerk the viewer out of the numbness with which such films are apt to be greeted.[52]

All too easy to glide over in visiting "the great boredom debate of 2011" is the fundamental agreement between Kois and his otherwise departing interlocutors that Reichardt's films are, in fact, slow films—and their reciprocal disinclination to say anything very detailed or substantive about how and why those films merit the attribution of slowness.[53] Dargis, for instance, makes no meaningful distinction between short, slow films like Reichardt's Old Joy and Wendy and Lucy, both of which clock under ninety minutes, and slow, long films, among which she cites "minimalist epics like 'Empire,' eight hours of the Empire State Building that subverts the definition of what a film is" and "Béla Tarr's seven-hour 'Sátántangó,'" which "take[s] time away even as [it] restore[s] a sense of duration, of time and life passing, that most movies try to obscure through continuity editing."[54] My emphasis here on the difference between long and short forms of slowness—predicated on a further difference between what Dargis calls "tak[ing] time away" and such an act's emphasis on "a sense of duration," on the one hand, and making time approach arrest through that time's endowment with dilation, on the other—may provide the basis, already and otherwise the ground of this chapter, for understanding more precisely Reichardt's slowness and its capacity to stretch the viewer's being, with that slowness, in time. In embracing that capacity, she may also be understood as an exemplary maker of the first of two kinds of direct time-images, the "peaks of present" (as distinguished from "sheets of past") that Deleuze, reassessing Bergson, conceptualizes in his treatise on cinema. According to Deleuze, these peaks of present are the cinematic time-images in which "there is *a present of the future, a present of the present and a present of the past*, all implicated in the event, rolled up in the event, and thus simultaneous and inexplicable. From affect to time: a time is revealed inside the event, which is made from the simultaneity of these three implicated presents, from these de-actualized *peaks of present*."[55] Deleuze then offers a number of examples of how these peaks of present might obtain (narratively, for instance)—and one of these examples could be taken to provide a perfect description avant la lettre, as we shall see, of what and how time happens in *Old Joy*: "Two people know each other, but already knew each other and do not yet know each other." More specifically, Reichardt cultivates ways to slow the time-image precisely so that we can grasp the complexity that is "rolled up in the"—seemingly simple—"event," the "simultaneity" of knowings and not-knowings that mark the work.

The ground of Reichardt's slowness is the consistency of her camera's *stillness*, the central artistic gesture through which she routes all of her related strategies for generating slowness—of which I will identify five as most salient (and others, briefly, along the way). In the case of making a film like *Old Joy*, the camera's stillness is, to a certain extent, predicated on the material constraints of dealing with a shoestring budget, limiting the production crew to five collaborators,[56] depending for illumination strictly on the manipulation of natural light,[57] and working without the advantage, also an expense of time and money, of laying dolly tracks.[58] As Reichardt has said of shooting both *Old Joy* and *Wendy and Lucy*, "I can never really move the camera,"[59] yet she has chosen to see this constriction not as an impoverishing limit but as an enabling condition of her artistry and its innovations; faced at times with provocations from interviewers who "don't buy that [she's] uninterested in exploring" what compositional effects might emerge, for instance, from "the joy of dolly shots,"[60] she asserts that a "good thing is if you can keep the whole machine small enough [so] you get a certain physical freedom where you can shoot without everyone being so aware of the camera"[61]—and, further, that her "ideas are so small . . . that it kind of works, aesthetically, for the stories we're telling and the amount of money we've had" to create in spaces, often outdoors, quite unlike the "sets [where] you tell someone, 'I'd like to move the camera an inch' and it's like, 'We're moving the camera!' and it's this whole moment-killing thing with everyone running with this shit all over them, the walkie-talkies and the Blackberries and all this stuff."[62] In tandem with the quiet and resultant intensity of focus with which Reichardt has sought to suffuse production, her still camera invites a mimetic stillness and concentration from the viewer in the reception of her work; that habitus may not be engendered (recall Kois's fidgety distraction, his "trouble staying planted in [his] seat with [his] attention focused on the screen"), but when it does, the effect is calmly profound: I have, for instance, observed imperceptibly incremental—yet ultimately significant—shifts in my straightened posture, my craned neck and head, as I have responded to Reichardt's camera and its interpellating cues to slowness.

Tending, then, not to move the camera "an inch" but to mine its stillness for her audiences—a stillness flirtatiously approaching but never settling into stasis; arresting in its evocation of, but without sedimentation as, arrest—Reichardt proceeds to calcine her slowness in the crucible of this stillness, chiefly through five cinematic operations: (1) *Longish takes*. It would be misleading to nominate many of Reichardt's takes as long in a standard sense (given, for example, her use in *Old Joy* of a "small Eton camera that holds 200-foot rolls," with which one "can only shoot five minutes at a time," and Reichardt's consequent decision to advise her actors, "Feel the space . . . take the time to get to what [is] in the script, . . . but you only have five minutes to do it in. Slow down, but hurry up"),[63] yet her takes are nonetheless longer than the ones found, say, in frenetically cut, mainstream Hollywood films and contribute to the simultaneous expansiveness and intensiveness of her scenes. (2) *Depth of field*. An astonishingly sharp and penetrating level of detail is achieved in Reichardt's compositions, many of which are executed as medium or long shots. In the case of *Old Joy*, Reichardt attributes this visual plenitude in part to the input of director of photography Pete Sillen, who urged her away from her thought "about maybe shooting [the film] in Super 8mm," because Sillen "has this A-Minima camera and he was like, 'I'm in, but there is so much motion and you want the depth for the forest'—a lot of things that Super 8 is just too low-gauge to pick up on. So we went to this idea of Super 16mm and using Pete's camera."[64] (3) *Figure behavior*. Sillen identified "so much motion" in Reichardt's storyboarding and their conversations about shooting *Old Joy* because of her routine inclination to work, pointedly, the movements of actors and animated objects (like cars)—movements within frames but also and especially across their edges—against the camera's corresponding stillness. As she says of this carefully choreographed dance between camera and figure behavior, the camera may be construed as "static, but it's not always static. It's not Jarmusch. In addition, there are many things crossing through the frame. The camera is deliberate."[65] (4) *Camera movement*. Despite all my necessary emphasis on stillness, and as my last quotation of Reichardt begins to indicate, her camera does indeed move—all the more impactfully, if subtly, because stillness is the norm against which these deviating movements (a gentle tilt here, a languid pan there) are precisely calibrated. (5) *Recurrent motifs*. A number of images acquire the power to arrest attention because of their vibrational conjuring of earlier, striking images with which, taken together, they constitute some of the signature visual elements of a Reichardt film.

To see how a version of this multipronged approach to slowness's cultivation works in practice, we could turn to any number of moments in *Old Joy*, among which I begin with the central scenic lineament of the "fireside chat" between principal characters Kurt (Will Oldham) and Mark (Daniel London) for the elegance and clarity of the example.[66] Old, largely estranged friends who reunite for a weekend trip through Oregon's Cascade Mountains en route to the mountains' Bagby Hot Spring, Kurt and Mark lose their way; in the black of night, and after disorienting backs and forths along paved as well as dirt roads, they settle on makeshift camping in a forest clearing where previous visitors have left behind considerable detritus. In a longish take of about two minutes' duration, the still camera is trained in a medium shot on two abandoned, background objects, vivid for their sharply captured surfaces: a plush, cushioned couch with a floridly floral pattern of warm reds and browns, and a contrastingly hard cooler with a cold, green exterior and a slate-grey lid. Read against the equally vivid, smoldering wood and flickering flames of a campfire in the shot's foreground, the couch and cooler recall a series of manufactured items in the film's opening sequence in Mark's yard, where the positioning of those items against environmental elements likewise highlights the porous, if not hopelessly blurred, line between "natural" and "cultural" objects (an imagistic recurrence that underscores and amplifies Kurt's laconically intoned observation, "It's not like there's any big difference between the forest and the city, though. You know what I mean? It's all one huge thing now. There's trees in the city, garbage in the forest"): in the earlier sequence, we see a swallow perched, fluttering, on a gutter

3.1 Kurt (Will Oldham, l) and Mark (Daniel London, r) have a fireside chat in *Old Joy*.

against a backdrop of roof shingles; brick steps and meditation bowls in re-lief against grass and flowering bushes; ants crawling across a sere leaf that partially covers a garden hose, its green and white lines arcing in parallel with the twisting stem of a leafy piece of groundcover. In the correspond-ing fireside scene, the precisely juxtaposed couch and cooler not only jibe with these other, earlier objects but also divide the shot into a neat grid of two near-halves—and likewise divide relaxed Kurt, who sinks into a cush-ion, from uptight Mark, hunched on the cooler. Kurt's comparative mobility, ease, and freedom is further registered by his movement into the foreground to stoke the fire and out of the shot as he wriggles from that task back to the couch—where the barely perceptible movement of Lucy, Mark's dog, on the edge of the couch (and frame) into which she has comfortably nestled, in a new allegiance, next to Kurt, suggests the evolving, intricate sense of com-petition between the two friends. It may take about two minutes for a typical reader, working at an average pace, to read my thick description here of an exemplary, longish take in *Old Joy*; what may or may not obtain for that reader is the experience of those minutes' slowing as they would likely do in their corresponding unfolding for a viewer of the scene in question. Mark says in that scene of his impending fatherhood and the anxieties associated with it for him and his wife, Tania (Tanya Smith), "We're both stretched so thin with work that it's almost impossible to imagine, but it'll have to work itself out. We'll just . . . find another rhythm"; unlike Mark's nod to the future, what has been "imagine[d]" and "work[ed] . . . out" in the present of the scene is a "stretch[ing]" not obstructive but conducive to "find[ing] another rhythm," one that mobilizes clarity, repetition, contrast, and delicate movement, as well as—pardon the pun—pregnant pauses (such as the one within Mark's dialogue marked above by an ellipsis), to achieve the feeling that two minutes have slowed stirringly to something like two or even three times the length of that duration.

Effects of this sort only accrue more intensely—and make themselves available for likewise more intensive, critical appreciation—when we look not merely to the central shot in a scene but to a scene as a whole or, more capaciously, to a sequence of scenes. In one indelibly memorable, spatiotemporal sequence of about four minutes in *Old Joy*, as Mark and Kurt (back on track) traverse a winding trail to the hot spring, a series of constellated shots produced at myriad ranges and angles offers the viewer the pleasure of slowing into a set of scenic variations on a theme—one into which they are inaugurated by a brief sample from the "dreamy score" of Yo La Tengo, used "to create a delicately intimate soundscape enveloping the spectator in a mood of reflection."[67] The imagery that follows rewards this beckoning to reflection, as we focus on—and yield in focusing to the "enveloping" sights of—Lucy running gamely from the foreground to the background of a medium shot, or Kurt striding expansively (and Mark following him with ginger care) into and then out of a long shot; the latticework of trembling fern leaves, the ridges of thick tree trunks, and the insinuations of moss across logs all "popping" in deep visual fields illuminated by glistening sunlight; an arrestingly hard cut from a very still shot of water, trickling crisply and with dynamically contrasting movement over a bed of rocks, to one in which rhythmic tilts up and down simulate, but also play subtly against, the eager jumping up and down of Lucy in response to the yet giddier wiggling of a stick by Kurt. Giving one's attention to this array of visuals is also to give oneself over, in a delicious slowing of perception, to their complexly striking sensuousness.

Crucially, what I have dubbed here a paradox of yielding into focus is not a yielding of related mental activity but rather provides the occasion and basis for that activity's heightening. Indeed, one of the critical results of slowing time is the (s)pace that such slowing produces for intellection; and we may begin to get a sense of how intellection in slowed time works by weighing it against fast cinema's contrasting seduction away from thinking, of which Dargis writes wryly:

> Thinking is boring, of course (all that silence), which is why so many industrially made movies work so hard to entertain you. If you're entertained, or so the logic seems to be, you won't have the time and head space

3.2 Kurt, Mark, and Lucy walk through the woods in *Old Joy*.

to think about how crummy, inane and familiar the movie looks, and how badly written, shoddily directed and indifferently acted it is. And so the images keep zipping, the sounds keep clanging and the actors keep shouting as if to reassure you that, yes, the money you spent for your ticket was well worth all this clamor, a din that started months, years, earlier when the entertainment companies first fired up the public-relations machine and the entertainment media chimed in to sell the buzz until it rang in your ears.[68]

Opposed in every stylistic gambit to the kind of "zipping" that Dargis describes, a film like *Old Joy* asks rather for audiences to dwell in its stillnesses—and, in dwelling there, to think about what is seen, what is heard, and what is not. But of what are we likely, thus disposed in time, to think? To begin, we must surely think about the personal relationship between Kurt and Mark being explored in great detail—or, more accurately, being explored in depth through a paradoxical economy of detail. Within the openness produced by Reichardt's slowed time—within the expansive space created by her pace—Oldham and London enact with subtle ambivalences the equally subtle ambiguities of Reichardt and collaborator Jon Raymond's script, such as those that inhere in spare dialogue, in order to develop a sense of the open-endedness of these characters and their relationship—and, by implication, the open-endedness of character, of relationality itself.

At the same time, we also have space to think about time—and about the peculiar relationship that obtains between space and time when one gets lost, as Kurt and Mark do in a way that invites us to situate *Old Joy* in the (surprisingly small) lineage of films, identified by Vivian Sobchack, that deal with such losings of way and the disorientations that they provoke. Sobchack categorizes these disorientations as tending to belong to three respective phenomenal orders with three corresponding, spatiotemporal, and affectively marked coordinates: going round and round, which (dis)orients the goer-round uncannily toward the past and to a circular sense of space; not knowing where one is, which (un)grounds one, panicky, in the present and in a vertical—and vertiginous—spatiality; and not knowing how to get where one is going, a frustrating state that (mis)leads one toward the future, along a linear spatial trajectory.[69] *Old Joy* is a remarkable, in part because remarkably rare, example of a film that aims to represent not one of these kinds of disorientation but all three—and all three at once, as they are imbricated with and co-constitute one another on Kurt and Mark's drive through the mountains, an imbrication that Reichardt captures through a dense concatenation of shots that emphasize repetitive circularity (as the camera swings in time with multiple turnings around of the car), dizzying verticality (as the camera points up into the sky, where the tops of trees appear to bend), and dogged linearity (as the camera tracks the movement of the car along a white-lined road). What's yet more remarkable about this condensation of disorientations is the effect that they produce: not a multipronged disorientation of the viewer to match that of Kurt and Mark, but a slow(ed) *re*-orientation of the viewer to and through phenomenality and intellection. The surety, evenness, and deliberation—in short, the slowness—of Reichardt's camera focus us on a situation in which the characters' focus gets dispersed and gives us a steadily attentive way to respond to a way that is lost. And, because of the setting of these scenes in a landscape of mountain and forest that is sharply rendered, Reichardt also invites us, in the space of her pace, to think about glacial time and its relationship—lacking? indifferent? bemused?—to the time of weekending road-trippers.

Finally, Reichardt's slowness generates a space-time in which to think about progressive politics, or to think progressively about mainstream politics, not least because of the near bookending of the film with scenes in which Mark listens, and we listen with him, to Air America segments in which callers give voice to frustration with the ineffectiveness of the Democratic Party and with the increasingly dire socioeconomic prospects of working-class Americans. And, though I have, for convenience and clarity, identified one by one the likely kinds of thinking prompted by *Old Joy*, I should hasten—

slowly—to add that the film's logic underscores at every turn the coimplica-
tion of the personal, the temporal, and the political, particularly through the
variously faceted trope of loss. The loss of closeness between Kurt and Mark
as the latter embraces bourgeois normativity and the former drifts from one
fleeting interest to another; the loss of time to domestic commitments or,
alternatively, the loss of time in which to evade those commitments without
facing the indictment, or perhaps condescending sympathy, of one's peers
(as Reichardt has said of Kurt, "He walks a fine line: at what point are you a
wanderer and what point are you homeless");[70] the loss of a thirtysomething
generation's formerly vibrant political and aesthetic enthusiasms, mapped
onto the micro-losses of indie bands (and the vendors of their records) and
the macro-losses of electoral contests and legislative agendas: all of these
losses inform each other complexly and are arrayed delicately by Reichardt
and her collaborators as inseparable from one another. Old Joy's most emphatic insistence on this inseparability of the personal, political, and temporal emerges in a scene in which Mark veers toward self-satisfaction in his
account of his volunteer teaching and cooperative gardening efforts—and
adds of Kurt's implicitly compared investments, "Not that you don't give to
the community. It's just a different community . . ." It's a scene that asks us,
in its slowness, to think carefully about how we value—or judge—how one
gives one's time, how one disposes oneself—or not—to giving in time; and,
in line with the openness and open-endedness that I have otherwise been
charting in and through Old Joy, the film offers no easy, direct, or clear answer
to the question as posed but prefers precisely (and paradoxically) to animate
the ellipsis of its answer.

What is comparatively clear is that such a question, however important
and challenging, is one borne of the relative privilege that Kurt and Mark
share and that they share with their creator; as Reichardt has revealingly disclosed of herself and of her investment in Kurt's representation:

> After I made River of Grass, I lived in New York City for five years without an
> apartment, just out of a duffle bag, and that put me in a position to relate
> to Kurt's situation, to understand how it changes your friendships with
> the people who you are depending on. If you are building your own free-
> dom, you sort of become reliant on a lot of other people. You can roman-
> ticize this behavior if you're doing it in your 20s, but if you start living like
> this in your 30s, it actually becomes somewhat questionable. Even your
> punker friends start to wonder. So many things that become our identity
> have to do with where we live and things of that nature.[71]

To choose a long-term, itinerant way of living, in an effort to "build . . . [one's] own freedom," is quite different from a qualified embrace of temporary itinerancy in an effort to find desperately needed work—and then facing the alarming prospect that temporary itinerancy will shade into semipermanent homelessness because of the evaporation of material resources and, with them, access to the very prospects for their replenishment: exactly the situation confronted by Wendy (Michelle Williams) in *Wendy and Lucy*, made by Reichardt two years after *Old Joy*, two years further into the second Bush administration, and on the other side of the fallout of Hurricane Katrina, among other events of the 2000s that have highlighted, like the film, the precarity of life in poverty.[72] In its diligently unsentimental examination of such precarity and its tolls, *Wendy and Lucy* would seem to have moved far from the terrain of *Old Joy* (not literally: both films are set and shot in and near Portland, Oregon), yet an abiding commitment to cinematic slowness unites the projects, the more recent of which hews to the formal strategies of slowness enacted in the predecessor film and likewise deploys them to force an intellective reckoning with the complex braiding of the personal, political, and temporal.

What makes the slowness of *Wendy and Lucy* even more striking, arguably, than that of *Old Joy* is the way in which its pleasurable experience for the viewer (and it's a complicated pleasure, not least because of its partial determination by the loving, aching beauty with which depressed locations and their depressed inhabitants are captured onscreen) is yoked to the excruciation with which Wendy experiences time: as money, affirming capital's woeful adage; as way too fast, given the escalation with which her money-as-time dwindles (and her ledger calculations grow ever more urgent) in the face of food running out, a ticket for shoplifting, and devastating car breakdown; and, simultaneously, as way too—brutally—slow, when she must endure the grinding pace of contemporary bureaucratic and technical organization in the form of booking and fingerprinting at a police station, standing in line or filling out a form at a dog pound, and waiting for creeping, underscheduled buses. That the viewer's slowed time situates her or him to comprehend the pointedly other deceleration of time for Wendy, at once its paradoxical acceleration, means that *Wendy and Lucy* asks its audiences to learn, in real time and through its phenomenal recalibration, expertise in differential velocities, a pedagogy whose visual crystallization comes in three differently paced movements that are imaged, likewise differently, in the film: an opening, medium-long shot of Wendy and her dog, Lucy, walking unhurriedly along a wooded trail, the camera's equally unhurried, punctually occasional

3.3 and 3.4 In shots of different lengths, Wendy (Michelle Williams) walks at different speeds through the woods and past a wall in *Wendy and Lucy*.

movement with them evoking the rhythmic satisfaction of time spent in companionate fellowship; numerous, crisply still long shots of Wendy walking solitarily down depopulated roads, the shots' length emphasizing the distance Wendy has traveled, in losing her dog and their material supports, from opportunities for intermittent respite to continuous hardship—and their stillness conveying the fatigued, depressed pace, the seeming inching forward, of the traveler who has to walk almost everywhere; and a final, meditative tracking shot of trees as seen in medium view from a lumbering train, which Wendy has hopped, alone, to a life of whose betterment we can be no more certain than what comes after the next tree. Much faster than walking, train travel from Oregon to Alaska is nonetheless slower than the driving Wendy plans or the flying that never (could have?) occurred to her; the train was once also the paradigmatic emblem of modernity's "new spatiality [as] linked to speed, a temporal diminution that is registered as a shrinkage or overcoming of space"[73]—a bygone status whose very bygoneness suggests the altogether different kind of "diminution" with which Wendy may aim agentially for an "overcoming of space."

In the ways that I suggest here, *Wendy and Lucy* offers us an object lesson in relative rates of speed and slowness that aligns with recent, compelling work by Sarah Sharma, whose *In the Meantime* addresses "the multiple temporalized flows and time-spaces of globalization": multiple flows that, as in Reichardt's film, do not stay tidily apart but come together and, because of the unevenly distributed ways that they come together, teach us "how time is worked on and differentially experienced at the intersections of inequity."[74] The issue of inequity, marked in *Wendy and Lucy* more specifically as a class issue, is an important one to which I will return at the end of this chapter; but I want first to mark a space, to the side of what distinguishes this latter film of Reichardt's so pointedly from *Old Joy*, in which to tease out how both films may offer lessons—a key target of my effort to think with and through this cinematic work—for the scholar who wishes, like Reichardt, to slow time generatively. That scholar is not, in thinking and writing as I do, using a camera or working with actors. But he may nonetheless learn valuably from Reichardt and with the cinematic consciousness that she has slowed—which is, after all, just one local manifestation of the ever rescalable and otherwise adaptable *textual* consciousness that Susan Stewart theorizes when, writing of miniaturization and gigantism, she claims that

> convention holds time to be linear, narrative, and undifferentiated by hierarchy; it is a convention that defines "being" in everyday life as "one thing after another." But from another stance—that offered by the model of fiction—the time of everyday life is itself organized according to differing modes of temporality, modes articulated through measurements of context and intensification. Time in the everyday lifeworld is not undifferentiated and unhierarchical—it is textual, lending itself to the formation of boundaries and to a process of interpretation delimited by our experience with those boundaries.[75]

If slowness is one of the crucially "differing modes of temporality" that "organize" or even help to "define . . . 'being' in everyday life," Reichardt's films may not only give her audiences access to that slowness but also, and not unlike "the model of fiction" of which Stewart writes, model for those audiences ways to achieve slowness in noncinematic experiential modes, such as the ones that characterize academic thinking and writing. A scholar aiming to slow time may cultivate a multivalent praxis parallel in its particulars to the filmmaking praxis developed by Reichardt. To spend a longish number of minutes measuring the shape of a clause or the weight of its argumentative substance; to penetrate the very joints of the words that constitute his intellection; to consider reflexively and then to highlight the movement from one sentence, or paragraph, or section of prose to another (and to consider and highlight what appears and what disappears across those movements); to recalibrate with delicacy and nuance a perspective on a topos or idea; to repeat a key word with a modulation, a stylistic maneuver with a variation, a governing premise with *différance*; and to deploy all of these tactics in a spell or on a page marked, paradoxically, by an absence of turbulence or noise: such a layered effort would constitute an approximation or, better, translation of the strategy whereby Reichardt uses stillness, as well as the takes, fields, figures, movements, and motifs arrayed within that stillness, to slow cinematic time—and, if the effort is a successful one, the scholar will have managed the slowing of time not just for himself in the act of thinking, of writing, but also for the reader of work generated in this way.

Nor does the ride end there. As Reichardt has avowed in a number of contexts, she has been able, in shooting films like *Old Joy* and *Wendy and Lucy*, to "be much more comfortable and creative" as a filmmaker not only by "embracing limits" and working without the support of the usual "outside entities" and their "apparatus" (and thereby to achieve her stunning effects),[76] but also because of the strategic ways in which she has used her time before the shoots to prepare for them—and in those uses of time, too, there may be an instructive model for the critic responsive to Reichardt's films and their slowness. Consider Reichardt's work with Neil Kopp, the producer of *Old Joy* who, according to Reichardt, knows "every back road in Portland" and with whom she grew close as they spent "six, eight weeks before [they] started shooting . . . scouting and going to the locations so [she] could figure out how [they] were going to shoot stuff."[77] Or her extended road trip, constituting something at once more rigorous and more idiosyncratically digressive than mere scouting, which preceded the making of *Wendy and Lucy* and during which Reichardt "drove around the country for six months going to Walgreen's parking lots."[78] Or her ongoing collaboration with Jon Raymond, with whom she co-wrote the screenplays for both films and who, through the development of close intimacy with Reichardt ("Jon and I speak every day, so we're really involved in each other's lives"),[79] has been "able to comprehend" her "rhythms" and "write in . . . silences knowing that she'll dilate them as she wants to."[80] In all of these cases (and they are just a few, key examples among many possible features of the films' production histories that could be discussed), the preshooting time that Reichardt takes—to drive, look, devise, talk, befriend, and more—yields palpable effects during the subsequent shootings, which she routinely describes as magical in their unfolding. To wit, Kopp, no mere producer, acted as an ad hoc grip and assistant director on *Old Joy* in what felt, for him and for Reichardt, like the only logical extension of the relationship they developed during scouting.[81] Likewise, only after driving for six months could Reichardt comprehend, during a snowstorm in Butte, how special it would be to shoot *Wendy and Lucy*'s parking lot scenes next to the very Walgreen's that "Jon wrote about that's two blocks from his house."[82] And only because Reichardt and Raymond "racked [their] heads forever" thinking about how to rework a pivotal but unusable monologue from the short-story version of "Old Joy" could she, making the film, hear in an anecdote shared by Will Oldham the serendipitous substitution for that monologue.[83] Time taken in various efforts before shooting is, in each instance described here, not just preludic but seminal to the ways in which the much more limited time of shooting itself is made so generative, so full—and so slowed.

Or, to put it another way (and to channel Dusty Springfield, circa 1968), *taking time to make time* may be the necessary prerequisite for time made slow. And if Reichardt proves exemplary in manifesting ways to take (slow) time before and in order to make time (slow), then she does so not only as the singular sort of filmmaker who (reminiscent, here, of Derrida) "driv[es] around with [her] dog" for a long time because "it just helps [her] to figure things out,"[84] but also because she took twelve years (working largely as an instructor of film production) between her first feature, *River of Grass*, and *Old Joy*—a much more radical form of preparation—in order to arrive at the readiness to make her recent, mature work. As Reichardt says of her own learning curve:

> The thing about technical chops, figuring out how to make films all came in the 10 years between my two features and you figure it out through teaching. . . . I aim my classes to what I'm most interested in and where my questions lie and you deconstruct the narrative in a room full of people and every time it reveals more and more and more. I never went to film school, I never studied any of that stuff. I'm a high-school dropout.[85]

Who better than the motivated "high-school dropout"-cum-accomplished professor to show scholars working in the same academy the value of taking time—to teach, to converse, to develop collegial relationships, to research—as a founding and grounding condition for the turn to another, familiar time (a spring break, a summer, a sabbatical) whose renovation in, through, and as slowness may comprise a less familiar, differently felt fulfillment: a kind of new old joy. Another such joy: if it takes twelve years to make twelve shooting days work well, because slowed—or three months of research to make three minutes of writing dense and intense, and so on—then the pleasure of making time's slowness may consequently inform the return to taking time and one's willingness to invest in it. Something like the opposite of a hangover (not to speak of *The Hangover Part II*), the residual good feeling that may persist after having felt slow(ed) time can, in that persistence, encourage or buoy the scholar who then has to return to what for many feels comparatively like drudgery in the otherwise slow time spent at the archive or in the stacks, conducting field work, transcribing interviews, chasing footnotes—in short, the long.

Coda: Capitulating?

In the culminating gestures of "Slowing," we have at last a speculative answer to the question arrested at the close of "Speeding" regarding the relationship between long time and stretched time, taking time and making time. Lest that movement seem too tidy, I add this coda to trouble such tidiness in a couple of key ways. First, that troubling requires a return to what I called a "complicated pleasure" that, if it is a pleasurable experience at all, must for ethical and political reasons produce at the same time an *uneasiness*: specifically, an uneasiness in the face of *Wendy and Lucy*'s anatomization of Wendy's slide into a homelessness marked by seismic loss, drawing Wendy's slowness far from whatever we may take to be comparatively, if not wholly, voluntaristic about the slow movements of Kurt and Mark in *Old Joy*. As I imply in my reading of the ambivalent and ambiguous open-endedness of the film's final scene, which reserves some space, however likely etiolated, for hope, we cannot be sure whether or not Wendy is living a version of the "slow death" that Berlant theorizes in *Cruel Optimism*, the "condition of being worn out by the activity of reproducing life" that, because of such factors as "unequal access to health care, the cramped conditions of everyday life, and the endemically unhealthy workplace" (as well, we could add, as unemployment and its consequences), marks "most notably the bodies of U.S. working-class and sub-proletarian populations that fray slowly from the pressure of obesity on their organs and skeletons."[86] Working in implicit dialogue with yet all the same to the side of something like Berlant's conceptualization of slow death, *Wendy and Lucy* tracks not the relationship between diet and obesity but rather the precarious oscillation between eating junk food and "fray[ing]" from starvation; and of course, in focalizing the experience of a white "subproletarian" character, the film does not work like the many representations, cited by Berlant, in which the bodies of people of color "stand in . . . for the entire culture of U.S. nonelites" and thereby both "shape particular aversions to [putative] people of excess (already negated as both too much and too little for ordinary social membership)" and foreground "the topic of excess as a general issue of public health."[87]

One question inspired by this engagement with Berlant concerns what difference the representation of race may make to the kind of cinematic slowness that will or will not obtain in contemporary culture. Attending to the system of U.S. slavery that in so many ways demands to be understood in its articulation to today's forms of "morbidity, the embodiment toward death as a way of life,"[88] the 2013 film *12 Years a Slave*—exemplary for its slowing of time—is, at a formal level, in some ways quite like Reichardt's films (when the camera is still or reframed with minor calibrations, when similarly minor modulations in figure behavior demand attention, when motifs like the imaging of trees against the sky are established and reused) and in others working a different set of tools to let slowness obtain (through an unusually meditative deployment of flashback and flash-forward, in the literal repetition of shots, and in almost exactly repeated scenes).[89] In this case, the slowing of time works at a general level to conjugate for audiences a sense of the crushing impasse, the arrest arcing beckoningly toward despair, in which Solomon Northup (Chiwetel Ejiofor) finds himself for the eponymous twelve years of his enslavement—and at other particular instances to imagine versions, from an earlier moment in capitalism's development, of what Sharma calls the condensation of "multiple temporalized flows and time-spaces." Arguably most striking in the latter regard is the sequence in which, almost lynched, Solomon hangs from the branch of a tree for an unbearably long time, flexing his feet so that their tips will make contact with the muddy ground below and will thus prevent the noose from tightening around his neck. Just as two slowed hours aim to convey a feeling for twelve years' passage, so here do a few minutes slowed largely by the work of unflinching close-ups and longish takes suture us to the horror of Solomon's predicament—except that, at the same time, a different angle on and amplification of that horror comes from its juxtaposition with the other imaged characters who move in different "temporalized flows" and inhabit "time-spaces" distinguished from Solomon's (namely, the slaves ambling through the background of one shot, to whom a deep field gives us unnerving access as Solomon hangs in the foreground; and Master Ford (Benedict Cumberbatch), whose horse eventually speeds him to the tree and who makes, with devastating irony, "swift" work of cutting the noose). In the end, what we learn from this slowness, so far in its limning of pain from what I called the uneasiness with which audiences may greet the aesthetic pleasures of *Wendy and Lucy*, cannot be quite in identity with the lessons for scholarship that I have tracked here. Rather, I would venture that it asks us in tandem, if we engage in scholarship of the sort that I am advocating, not just to take time to make time (as I described above) but to take time to make space for the consideration of dimensions of experience, such as injustice and trauma—real and imagined, historical and contemporary—in the face of which work, life, the gaze may just have to halt and dwell rather than, more modestly, slow or stretch.

I mentioned above that this coda's work of troubling the chapter would emerge in a couple of ways, and the second, related one comes now from the explicit posing of what has been an implicit, potentially disquieting question haunting "Slowness"—especially in the denouement of the section "Slowing": Is the scholar who slows time happily and who, in so doing, makes the duration of hard work more endurable, merely rendering himself pliable to an academic system whose norms and mandates—particularly concerning "productivity," a disturbing if inevitable rubric through which that system (like almost any extant system) will assess the work of its participants—need rather to be questioned, vexed, even thwarted? A related question certainly emerges for me when I take up *Flow* and find Csikszentmihalyi advocating the cultivation of optimal experience in order to make otherwise "dissatisfying" labor feel more enjoyable and thereby rewarding: in whose or what interest?[90] When ought workers of various stripes embrace goals that are coordinated with and through capital, however complicatedly, and when are they just capital's suckers? In addressing this question's specific pertinence to academia—and in routing their meditations on academic work through a rhetoric of *speed* and *slowness*—Harney and Moten ask their colleagues to remain vigilantly cognizant of the uneven distribution of work opportunities and compensations in academia as they worry over the "new and jarring ways," specific to the contemporary scene, in which

we can feel [the] motion [of academic labor]. . . . For some, the motion feels like someone has cranked up the belts of the line, like a traditional factory speed-up. For others, the line has been slowed, painfully, not in the traditional form of a protest by labor, a work to rule for instance, but through new techniques of extracting surplus and controlling labor, like sourcing-out, just-in-time production, and flexibility.[91]

Are scholars responsive to the hails and rewards of productivity—and, in their productivity, contributive to "The Academic Speed-Up"—only ever mystified capitulants to a fantasmatic "pleasure of purity . . . [a] dream of craftsmanship" that offers them equally fantasmatic access to "a special and limited brotherhood" and that runs the risk of foreclosing their solidarity with another "brotherhood" (and sisterhood), "those who must slow down" and who "are prevented from work almost entirely"?[92] Worse, if they are not mystified in their capitulation, are such scholars (and here I am looking ahead to the next chapter of this book) plain old cynical?

These questions have no easy answers, and I would not wish to offer any that are more than tentative—and slow. Indeed, if one assumes too quickly that I, and others like me, are just cynically replicating versions of efficiency that contribute to the impasse (quite different from a valuable obstruction) in which we may find ourselves in the academy, then that assumption requires that work like mine, this work in fact, be interpretively defined in saturating identity with—rather than understood partially in the context of—the institutional field and professional imperatives that help to coordinate it. I wouldn't wish to be so quick for a number of different reasons, including the positive benefits (for oneself, for the world) of doing committed work without sentimentalizing or misunderstanding it and while affirming other ways of doing work that could and should also be explored, such as the admirably collaborative, cross-disciplinary, and explicitly political work done by Moten with Harney. Indeed, many important advocates for institutional change, like Moten, persist in "individualized" work that makes them mappable in "the vulgar system of stardom" even as they call for other forms of work to emerge alongside it (and perhaps, eventually, to displace it)—making it hard not to be at least a little bit "cynical" about, say, their more sweeping pronouncements on vulgarity and stardom.[93] Yet if such cynicism is to be entertained or inhabited at all, its experience must, for now, be scare-quoted as a signal that its further entertaining requires scruple and its provisional inhabitation care.

4. Cynicism

Head-Butt

Because the last chapter of this book ended with a citation of scholars writing, from positions of relative privilege within the academy, about the work of its potential transformation, I am attracted to the complementarity of beginning this one with an invocation of an obverse, more precarious voice: that of a scholar who aims likewise to contemplate the academy's betterment, yet who has left her adjunct position within it; who confesses to having found a more sanguine way of being in the world as a yoga instructor; and who renders this confession in an essay about, among other things, the MTV animated series *Beavis and Butt-head*. In that piece, "Talking Out of School: Academia Meets Generation X," Traci Carroll concludes with a provocation incited by her concern about what she sees as a worrisome cynicism pervading cultural products like *Beavis and Butt-head*, as well as about the intellectual attention lavished by interpreters on such products:

> Despite the courageous acts of creativity performed in these Gen X texts, the residual sense of cynical resentment [in them] is troubling to me, as is the sense that a great deal of energy is being wasted on . . . textual games, energy that could and should be directed toward helping someone (even yourself) live better or feel better. This does not necessarily have anything to do with raising material "standards of living." It may start with just learning to experience your experience for what it is. I know how many unhappy, disaffected academics there are out there, whether they are Gen Xers or not. My hope is that we can all learn to feel a little happier, or even a lot happier, by being more honest in and about our work, by taking risks that might make learning institutions more responsive to the entire range

of human needs, and by staying open to the possibilities of renewal held out by alternative institutions and independent inquiry.[1]

Initially, I came to Carroll's essay through due diligence as a critic planning to write about *Daria*, a spinoff of *Beavis and Butt-head*, and thus as part of a comprehensive survey of the extant scholarly literature on both series. In the process, I was not prepared to encounter Carroll's poignant meditation on cynicism, the conceptual object of the inquiry of which my thinking about *Daria* comprises one smaller part, nor could I have predicted the keenly felt pressingness with which I would want to answer Carroll's call to risk "being more honest in and about [my] work"—an honesty that, in this context, necessitates clarity about cynicism, which sometimes either atmospheres or impels or, in a more middling way, tinges my work and which, as the quoted passage from Carroll's essay implies, imbues the work of many academics who may plausibly, if not always quite accurately, be hailed as "disaffected."

To the end of achieving that clarity and furnishing such honesty, let me offer three related anecdotes about cynicisms of mine that will not otherwise continue to animate this chapter but could be nevertheless comprehended as "of" it, to the extent that they identify signposts on the path that I ambulated toward the chapter's writing. (1) As part of a larger concern about what could be perceived, in my chapter on "Slowness," as an imbalance between (rather than a calculated risk regarding) the relative number of pages devoted to *Old Joy* and those addressing *Wendy and Lucy*, I feared that eventual peer reviewers of my manuscript would critique that I have, at least on this occasion, next to nothing to say about the crucial role of the dog in the latter film (or about the vital contributions to studies of animals, ranging from work by Jacques Derrida to Cora Diamond to Donna Haraway, that could help one understand that role)[2]—and then imagined cynically, because without much substance but merely as a possible, neatly engineered sop to readers, that the introduction to this chapter could pivot from further analysis of *Wendy and Lucy* to a rumination on cynicism via dogginess, etymologically as well as conceptually crucial to classical constructions of the "dog-philosophers" of Cynicism (following scholarly convention, designated with a capital C to distinguish the philosophical contributions of antiquity from later cynicisms, whose relationships to anterior formations in ancient Greece and Rome are, as we shall see, often quite complicated). (2) Before alighting definitively on *Daria* as an exemplary object of analysis in an examination of cynicism, I half-entertained the idea that another contender televisual text, the USA Network police procedural *Silk Stalkings*, could make for a rich and stunning case study in a chapter like this one—yet cynically dismissed that possibility because of the gapingly differential levels of respectability and perceived quality between a series like *Daria* and one like *Silk Stalkings* (and thus the likelier potential for dismissablity of a chapter focused to some extent on the latter series). (3) In my first encounter with Carroll's aforementioned essay, I read it in a cynically hurried way because of an impression, based on impatience with its first pages, that deeper engagement with its argumentative contours would have ultimately limited utility for me—only to discover, by its headbutting end, that rereading it more carefully and less cynically would yield so much more intellective satisfaction than when I approached it more or less as an item on a checklist.

If you have never thought cynically along any of the several lines or at the various scales identified here, then you may well, with impunity, and from a position of relatively unalloyed purity judge me for these imbricated cynicisms; but a cynical voice is whispering, more than a little impishly in my ear, that the number of yous positioned for interpellation by this sentence's first two clauses is much smaller than the corresponding audience of identifiers with my copping to cynicism. In turn, how might the "we" thus constituted cope with this copping? Should we abandon our cynicism and follow courageous colleagues like Traci Carroll into better practices of self-cultivation, including the yoga to which she attributes her insights about care and relationality? What if we're not, literally and otherwise, that flexible? Should we take, in however modified and translated a way, the satirical advice to stay mired and wallow in our cynicism that Carl Elliott offers in his extremely mordant essay, "How to Be an Academic Failure"? Elliott begins to answer the question this way:

> How to be an academic failure? Let me count the ways. You can become a disgruntled graduate student. You can become a burned-out administrator, perhaps an associate dean. You can become an aging, solitary hermit, isolated in your own department, or you can become a media pundit, sought out by reporters but laughed at by your peers. You can exploit your graduate students and make them hate you; you can alienate your colleagues and have them whisper about you behind your back; you can pick fights with university officials and blow your chances at promotion. You can become an idealistic failure at age 25, a cynical failure at 45, or an eccentric failure at 65. If failure is what you're looking for, then you can hardly do better than the academic life. The opportunities are practically limitless.[3]

Having himself opted for a version of the forty-something's trajectory, Elliott proceeds to attribute no small portion of the "cynical" feeling named in his opening gambit to the experience of "publish[ing] dozens of articles nobody has read and giv[ing] public lectures so dull that audience members were actually snoring."[4] I take seriously the pain that interlines Elliott's rhetorical recourse to hyperbole, as I do the extent to which his exaggerated account of "the academic life" rings nonetheless in time with myriad, less Jeremianic flag-raisings (like Carroll's) about the purpose and value of scholarly work that threatens to be undone by cynicism—or, perhaps worse, described with brutal realism in cynical terms.

In response, my ambition here is to uncover what unexpected forms of value may be mobilized for scholars through cynicism—and how a perhaps equally unexpected recalibration of cynicism's very meaning(s) may be necessary to that project of detection. In so aiming, I look, as already intimated, to television, not least because of the abundant, various ways, threatening to congeal into a set of truisms, in which television's makers have been charged—in a manner not unlike the indictments of academia's self-critics—with what would seem to be irredeemable forms of cynicism. (Most influential in this camp of television critics may be Pierre Bourdieu, who indicts television journalists for their "cynical view of politics," as well as the so-called "'ironic and metatextual' messages cynically manipulated by television producers and ad people";[5] but almost any account of cynicism—and numerous accounts of television—will inevitably alight on television as one of cynicism's chief purveyors. For the writers of such accounts, television is, for example, "a sure source from which vast quantities of naked cynicism ooze abundantly day and night,"[6] or essentially "cynical" "more than it is false, censored, biased, or annoying.")[7] Given the tellingly consonant ways in which writers of various stripes find television saturated with cynicism, on the one hand, and associate academic enterprise with cynicism, on the other, an investigator of cynicism's possible recuperation for scholarship would seem to have much to learn from television—in such a way that she or he would simultaneously learn about television that it is not only or ever manifesting cynicism in the monstrous ways that it has been characterized as doing (even though many of those characterizations are fair). To learn as much, in the present context, will entail rejecting some prominent rejections of cynicism—but will also, and perhaps less expectedly, require moving beyond some rather weak embraces of it.

In the differently inflected embrace of cynicism to which I give flesh in the pages that follow, I comprehend cynicism as a multifaceted experiential phenomenon, one that complexly interleaves Cynical and cynical elements, and I affirm its manifestation not by sidestepping what has been pervasively—and plausibly—named obstructive in cynicism but by drawing out potentially generative elements in it that tend to get dismissed precisely as obstructive. More specifically, three central elements interpenetrate, sometimes in unusual and counterintuitive ways, in the version of cynicism anatomized and advocated here: hardest to swallow but necessary to the endeavor, a tactically accommodational cynicism that does not sediment into an accommodationist strategy but that does risk serviceability to structures whose overriding tendency is to shore up unethical interests, chiefly those of capital (routinely shorthanded hereafter, and for clarity, as accommodational cynicism); a countervailing, ethically critical cynicism that exposes precisely such accommodations (hereafter, critical cynicism); and a renovated Cynicism for our age whose paradoxically ascetic theatricality, entailing strategies of protest and display, obtains in the service not just of negative critique but of positive philosophico-political commitment (ditto, renovated Cynicism). Often common to critical cynicism and renovated Cynicism are versions of truth telling nominated by both classical writers and their more recent commentators as acts of parrēsia, acts whose risks are not simply at odds with but are rather enabled—and not, in being so enabled, automatically undermined or disqualified from ethical affirmation—by the complicatedly related risks of accommodational cynicism.

As suggested above, one key model for the multifaceted—and historically specific—cynicism outlined here comes from the MTV series *Daria*, which was originally broadcast from 1997 through 2002. At the level of characterization (Daria's sarcastically-cum-cynically affective flatness) and of style (Daria's formal flatness), the series does not quite produce antianimated or antiexpressive effects, as has routinely been suggested; rather, and rather paradoxically, its flatness has a critical sharpness, pointedness, or punch that is better understood as aiming (to some extent in the service of an accommodational cynicism) at an ascetic animation aesthetic: one that aligns with—and manifests a local, medium-specific version of—the ascetic theatricality that I have begun to associate with renovated Cynicism. Indeed, the series' accommodatingly spare, critically flat—in short, ascetic—theatricality performs the work of a philosophical asceticism that has crucial qualities in common with the likewise (though more vulgarly) theatricalized asceticism of ancient Cynics and, at the same time, rests on a different, contemporary set of ethical principles. Where Diogenes of Sinope is credited with finding the justification for Cynical asceticism in fidelity to (human) nature, in itinerant citizenship in the cosmos, and in the extreme pedagogy required to promote that fidelity and such cosmopolitanism, *Daria*'s makers locate the imperative for a more and less similarly theatrical asceticism in anticorporatism, in global cosmopolitanism, and in the explanatory power with which flatness and related techniques limn these values. Yet, in a further turn of the screw, this latter-day, renovated Cynicism could be understood as compromised by the series' very dance with corporate consumerism and its clear pliability to the schemes and schemas of neoliberal, global capitalism. The challenge, then, of interpreting the series, as of this chapter on the whole, is to explain how the interplay of renovated Cynicism and of cynicism, in both its critical and seemingly compromised (because compromising or accommodational) forms, renders work that is defensible and valuable rather than self-contradictory, falsely conscious, and "merely" cynical.

"What Evs"

If the sound bite, tagline, and slogan interrelate as some of the most dominant rhetorical forms of cynical cultures, then it should be no surprise that accommodational cynicism itself comes frequently to recognizability through a handful of such ready-made statements: "Everybody else is doing it, so why can't we," "What are you gonna do about it," "It is what it is," and, most bluntly and wearily, "Whatever" (or, as the *Urban Dictionary* catalogues the "lazy way of saying *whatever* when you care so little that you don't even feel like saying *whatever*,"[8] "What evs"). More than a little ironically, given the status of *whatever* or its variant as a key mantra of accommodational cynicism, certain commentators on such cynicism have, it would seem unwittingly, approximated an enactment of this very mantra as they have allowed the word *cynicism* itself to stand for just about *whatever* in uncareful accounts of what constitutes a cynical behavior, disposition, or worldview. Where some of the would-be definers of cynicism are too vague ("concisely, cynicism is the condition of lost belief"),[9] others are overprecise in accounting for the affective dimensions and historico-political conditions of cynicism ("cynicism, by which I mean a melancholic, self-pitying reaction to the apparent disintegration of political reality (in the form of 'grand narratives' and 'totalizing ideologies'), is the result of a process [of] the 'reification' of postmodernity"),[10] while yet others take *cynicism* to be substitutable for terms, like *nihilism* and *pessimism*, with which it is not exactly synonymous or coincident and on discursive occasions when, say, *nihilism* or *pessimism* itself would serve perfectly well—indeed, better—to advance an argumentative claim.[11] Perhaps yet more damaging (precisely because more thoughtful and sophisticated) to the clarity with which *cynicism* might be deployed is the advocacy of a tripartite understanding of the term that would disclose the overlapping and co-constituting relationships among cynical publics, the "master-cynics" who benefit from those publics' inertial "what evs," and the equally inertial "insider-cynics" who, as middlemen and not infrequent scapegoats, cravenly serve the interests of those master cynics.[12] To my ear, little is illuminated by describing the so-called "master" manipulator through the rubric of *cynicism*: at best, he is calculatingly dishonest, at worst evil; and in neither of these two cases is his dishonesty or evil better comprehended by calling it *cynical* and, in tandem, cramming in the margins all the different, otherwise interesting currents that the term may electrify.

To the side of these tendencies, and equally ironic, some of the better understandings of accommodational cynicism emerge in contexts in which the term *cynicism* is not a crucial—or even explicit—referent. Paradigmatic in this regard is Alan Liu's magisterial *The Laws of Cool: Knowledge Work and the Culture of Information*, a text that does not name cynicism as such but that strikes me as providing one of the most lucid comprehensions of its accommodational form and of one of that form's pervasive manifestations. In so doing (on my reading), Liu is also, in his own terms, offering an idiosyncratic definition of coolness and of how it operates attitudinally—typically, as a diffusely and hazily bad attitude—among subjects who have climatized themselves to depressed and depressing conditions of contemporaneity but can't or won't face recognizing that climatization as total resignation:

> Cool is an attitude or pose from within the belly of the beast, an effort to make one's very mode of inhabiting a cubicle express what in the 1960s would have been an "alternative lifestyle" but now in the postindustrial 2000s is an alternative *workstyle*. . . .
>
> At once wise to it all and profoundly ignorant, simultaneously arrogant and vulnerable, and . . . both strangely resistant to and enthralled by the dominating information of postindustrial life, cool is the shadow ethos of knowledge work. It is the "unknowing," or unproductive knowledge, within knowledge work by which those in the pipeline from the academy to the corporation "gesture" toward an identity recompensing them for work in the age of identity management. Whether watching cool graphics on the Web or cool dinosaurs in that Spielberg film allegorizing the fate of knowledge workers in the age of global competition . . . knowledge

workers are never far from the cubicle, where only the style of their work lets them dream they are more than they "know."[13]

Liu locates coolness—a version of it that I would instead nominate as cynicism—in the paradoxical manner in which accommodators to neoliberal capitalism make their accommodation bearable: regarded by them as no mere accommodation, its "wise to it all" patina is nonetheless never glossy or incrusted enough to layer over the "ignoran[ce]" at its core or to mitigate just how damaging that core accommodation and its entailment of ignorance are; the accommodators' "arrogant" sense of besting a system that "they 'know'" is designed to use them belies the "vulnerab[ility]," indeed a profound precariousness, with which they submit to that use. This coolness or accommodational cynicism is a contemporary, renovated version, for "the age of identity management," of what Peter Sloterdijk famously nominated some twenty years earlier as the cynically "enlightened false consciousness" of postmodernity.[14]

Indeed, though cleaved by their different historical situations, Liu and Sloterdijk cleave, in the other sense, as they both register a tensional interaction, routinely shading for them into a worrisome slipperiness, between accommodational cynicism and what I have dubbed the *critical* cynicism that would take to task the very accommodations that coolness, or in another guise enlightened false consciousness, obliges. With whatever "ambivalent, recusant oppositionality" contemporary subjects, especially the knowledge workers on whose conditions Liu is focused, greet "the new rationalization," that oppositionality can, in his bleak account, almost "only protest equivocally with the very voice of the new rationalization"[15]—a whimper that hardly deserves the nomination *critical*. Similarly, Sloterdijk asserts of his own, earlier moment that "the critical impulse has never been more strongly inclined to let itself be overpowered by a sour temperament. The tension between what wants to 'criticize' and what should be 'criticized' is so taut that our thinking is becoming more morose than precise. . . . Hence the . . . abdication of critique."[16] If a "sour temperament," elsewhere and with a slightly different tonal shading characterized by Sloterdijk as a "certain chic bitterness"[17]— very near to Liu's coolness—passes glibly for critique only to constitute its "abdication," then a call emerges for an alternative mode of critique to dislodge the "cynical reason" that manifests so sourly, bitterly, and as Sloterdijk elaborates over the course of his thick tome, in a variety of other flavors. His own solution is to reject cynicism for and to replace it with a Cynicism (or, in his more eccentric rendering, kynicism) rejuvenated for postmodernity, one that would defiantly respond to the bitterly chic subject's grimace with a gut-driven roar, the essential gesture of an ethically valuable "scandal":

> When Diogenes urinates and masturbates in the marketplace, he [accomplishes] . . . the unified act of showing and generalizing (the semantic system of art is based on this). The philosopher thus gives the small man in the market the same right to an unashamed experience of the corporeal that does well to defy all discrimination. Ethical living may be good, but naturalness is good too. That is all kynical scandal says. Because the teaching explicates life, the kynic had to take oppressed sensuality out into the market. Look, how this wise man, before whom Alexander the Great stood in admiration, enjoys himself with his own organ! And he shits in front of everybody. . . . Here begins a laughter containing philosophical truth, which we must call to mind again if only because today everything is bent on making us forget how to laugh.[18]

With this invocation of Diogenes of Sinope (by some accounts the "first" Cynical philosopher) and the most notorious public acts that history and legend alike have attributed to him—and, indeed, throughout the *Critique of Cynical Reason*—Sloterdijk romantically misrepresents Diogenes as a pleasure-seeking sensualist, an avatar of plenitude and *jouissance*, rather than portray him as a happiness-oriented naturist, a hardcore ascetic, who would much more plausibly align with accounts of the figure as he emerges in the slender, extant literature from antiquity and in the careful work of classicists documenting and responding interpretively to that literature. Yet far more disquieting (after all, "Diogenes" has only ever been a literally fabulous reconstruction; no serious historical harm is done when an obviously fancifying writer takes an imaginative flight in the dog-philosopher's name) and perhaps grievous, given Sloterdijk's avowed commitment to the renovation of thought itself, is the unthoughtful ease, the undercomplication, with which he advocates Cynicism as a panacea for cynicism; that ease, as Leslie Adelson, one of Sloterdijk's most trenchant respondents, has noted, fuels a volume that, for all its heft, "never identifies or even circumscribes the locus of radical change, either on the personal level or in the social sphere; neither does [it] address the real relations of power in which cynics and *Kyniker* stand opposed."[19] As we shall see, those relations and the spheres of which they are constitutive do not now furnish, and arguably never have, a field in which the simple opposition of Cynicism and cynicism(s) is either credible or creditable.

Bark, Bite

Almost all commentators on either classical Cynicism or later cynicisms turn eventually to the vexed question of the relationship of the one to the other(s); and, with the exception of a few outliers who insist on the radical discontinuity of Cynicism from manifestations of cynicism,[20] the overwhelming majority of these commentators posit some kind of dialogic, dialectical, genealogical, or otherwise transductive truck between the two—if only, at the most extreme, to critique cynicism as a devolution from or insincere imposture of Cynicism. Indeed, as early as the beginning of the second century C.E., Epictetus was advising his interlocutors not to take up Cynicism if they were to do so in a manner that we would call cynical: anyone who supposes that following the ascetic life of a Cynic is merely a matter of outfitting himself with the right clothing, accoutrements, and attitude—the "cloak," "little bag," "staff," and corresponding preparedness to "abuse those whom [he] meet[s]"—but who is not capable of more substantive transformation, in the form of exerting "the power of the will" and of evacuating "anger," "resentment," "envy," "pity," and, above all, "desire," should "keep far away from [Cynicism]: . . . it is not at all for [him]."[21] For some much more recent critics, remarkably little has changed in assessing the relationship of a cynical bark to a Cynical bite; in tracing a link from ancient Cynicism to modern cynicism through satire, William Desmond, for instance, asserts that even though both Cynic and cynic may "satirize their own contemporaries mercilessly," a pessimistic undergirding to latter-day incarnations of such satire—a cynical disbelief that the satire will effect change—is, for him, at profound odds with the ancient Cynics' "astonishing . . . optimis[m] regarding human nature. . . . [Human beings] may have been corrupted by the bad customs and needless artificialities of 'civilization', but all this can be cured" with "satire," "humbling," "frugality," "simplification of one's life," "renunciation of all unnecessary possessions and desires," and "renewed living in the present moment."[22]

Whether Desmond's uncharitable—indeed, arguably cynical—appraisal of the modern cynic's motives and beliefs constitutes a fair assessment is a matter of debate; tracing a pivotal, emergent moment in the development of this modern cynicism, "our" cynicism, to the thinking of eighteenth-century *philosophes* (who, as Louisa Shea demonstrates vividly, had a complexly ambivalent relationship to classical Cynicism),[23] Sharon A. Stanley argues instead that what I have called critical cynicism, in contradistinction to its accommodational form, may be one tactic (rather than a monolithic strategy or singular disposition) in the arsenal of an otherwise eminently optimistic, would-be reformer of human endeavor, including especially political endeavor.[24] In making this argument—and making it compellingly—Stanley is also breaking pointedly with claims, like Sloterdijk's, that critical cynicism (or, in his language, cynical reason) can only ever constitute an attenuation of, or a phantasm in place of, genuine, proper critique. At the same time, she is admirably answering Adelson's implicit call to think with greater historical care about Cynicism, cynicisms, and the sites of their interpenetration; even as she proposes that "the constitutive cynicism of sociability necessarily yields a cynical moment within democracy itself,"[25] she takes care to distinguish the nascent democracies of the eighteenth century from the very different versions of it through which political theorists like herself—and political subjects, period—move and are moved in the twenty-first.

Despite my esteem for Stanley's nimble thinking and the eloquent prose in which she expresses that thinking, I would, for a couple of key reasons, want to question the proportional relevance to the contemporary classroom, conference, or protest, as opposed to the eighteenth-century salon, of her central claim that one can imagine—and, indeed, particular historical actors have imagined—a "counterintuitive but revealing marriage between familiar currents of progressive optimism and less familiar tendencies toward a thoroughly modern form of cynicism," with the crucial upshot that cynicism, conceived "as a tactic[,] . . . is no longer an intrinsic, unalterable possession of particular subjects but rather a weapon that can be taken up to navigate particular epistemological and social dilemmas and laid aside when it no longer appears useful."[26] To assert as much, however vitally, is nonetheless to leave unquestioned the value of the putatively "progressive optimism" to which the occasionally cynical subject may make recourse as part of a multipronged, "continued engagement with [a] world" in which both the critical, "clear-eyed willingness to confront and engage with the baser impulses in human beings" and the hope that "propitious moments for sincere, collective action could well arise" get carefully weighed against and powerfully inform each other.[27] What if our moment is one in which the optimism alongside which tactical cynicism is arrayed is, far from progressive, much likelier to be, in Lauren Berlant's seductive formulation, a "cruel optimism" because "something [one] desire[s]," such as "a fantasy of the good life, or a political project," "is actually an obstacle to [one's] flourishing"?[28] If a "counterintuitive but revealing marriage" between critical cynicism and optimism reveals, in fact, that the optimism in question makes "a person or a world . . . bound to a situation of profound threat,"[29] to what else, rather than this threatening optimism, should the critical cynic bind herself and her cynicism? Whatever allegiances she chooses, her cynicism, though it need not be, as Stanley plausibly argues, an "exhaustive identity," does seem poised to fill more of the field with its "critique of worldly corruption and hypocrisy"[30] than in the scenario where, one small tactic among others, that critique cedes major ground to optimism—an optimism with which Berlant contrasts "collective detachment" as a potentially fruitful "protest" of the world's "normative" demands and their tendency to lead to "the wearing out of the subject."[31] Seeking to find a third way and thus to navigate between an exhaustive cynicism, against whose volatility Stanley finds ballast in progressive optimism, and an exhausting optimism that Berlant finds equally dangerous, I imagine an alliance of cynicism(s) to Cynicism, trickier to theorize or enact than the simpler substitution of Cynicism for cynicism that Sloterdijk proposes, yet soberer in a contemporary landscape in which, even more than in the postmodernity that Sloterdijk assayed, an intensification of "impassivity and other politically depressed relations of alienation," including cynical relations, may conspire to yield "the attrition of the subject of capital."[32]

In attempting this tricky imagining, I find generative some key ideas animating Foucault's final lecture course at the Collège de France (the scripts for which are now published in English as *The Government of Self and Other*), in which an athletic and not at all predictable reckoning with Cynical philosophy marks Foucault's ethical investigation of the care of self and others, an abiding preoccupation of his late career. Turning to and through the Greek concept, explored by Cynics and others, of parrēsia—in Foucault's account, the simultaneous "virtue, duty, and technique" of "free-spokenness" or "free speech," defined not discursively or performatively but by the speech act's relation to, and its necessary entailment of, risk—Foucault locates parrēsia's value in its capacity "for directing others, and particularly for directing them in their effort . . . to constitute an appropriate relationship to themselves," as well as in its establishment of the recourse, the "only one" of its kind, through which "someone weak, abandoned, and powerless proclaims an injustice to the powerful person who committed it" (hence the risk or "unspecified price" of parrēsia: the extent or scale of the consequences for such a speech act cannot be known in advance to the relatively powerless subject who courageously undertakes it).[33] As Foucault develops a theory of parrēsiastic truth-telling through a close reading of classical texts, including Diogenes Laertius's *Lives and Opinions of Eminent Philosophers*, the vivid scene (as chronicled therein and elsewhere) of Diogenes of Sinope's famous encounter—and parrēsiastic interlocution with—Alexander the Great emerges as a crucial source for thinking in a fine-grained way about the contours and predicates of parrēsia. Foucault, worth quoting at some substantial length in order to follow the careful steps of his intellection, contextualizes, describes, and interprets the encounter (and a related one) as follows:

> In Cynicism there is . . . a very marked, very emphatic connection between philosophical truth-telling and political practice. . . . This mode of connection is one of confrontation, and derision, of mockery and the assertion of a necessary exteriority. We should remember that opposite Plato, who advises the tyrant Dionysius, there was Diogenes. Diogenes, taken as prisoner by Philip after the battle of Chaeronea, was confronted by the monarch, the [Macedonian] sovereign. The [Macedonian] sovereign asks him: Who are you? And Diogenes replies: "I am the spy on your greed." Or again, there is the famous dialogue between Diogenes and Philip's son, Alexander. There is the same question again: "Who are you?" But this time it is Diogenes who puts the question to Alexander, who replies: I am the great king Alexander. And at this point Diogenes replies: I will tell you who I am, I am Diogenes the dog. In this way the absolute exteriority of the philosophical and the royal personages is asserted, which is exactly the opposite of what Plato proposes. What could be further removed from the philosopher king, the philosopher who is king, than this typically, exactly, word for word anti-Platonic reply? I am the great king Alexander. I am Diogenes the dog. Diogenes Laertius . . . reports . . . that Diogenes the Cynic explained his aphorism "I am a dog" by saying: I am a dog "because I fawn on those who give me something, I bark at those who don't, and I bite those who are wicked." So you can see the interesting interplay between philosophical assertion (philosophical parrēsia) and political power. The philosophical parrēsia of Diogenes basically consists in showing himself in his natural nakedness, outside all the conventions and laws artificially imposed by the city. His parrēsia is therefore in his very way of life, it is also apparent in this discourse of insult and denunciation with regard to power (Philip's greed, etcetera). Faced with political power, this parrēsia appears in a complex relationship since, on the one hand, in saying that he is a dog he says that he "fawns on those who give me something." Consequently, in fawning on those who give him presents he accepts a certain form of political power, integrates himself within it, and recognizes it. But at the same time he barks against those who give him nothing and bites those who are wicked. That is to say, with regard to the power that on one side he

accepts, he feels free to say frankly and violently what he is, what he wants, what he needs, what is true and false, what is just and unjust.[34]

As a dog-philosopher who is prepared respectively to fawn, bark, and bite, according to circumstance, Diogenes of Sinope could be uncontroversially construed as enacting a movement from something like what I have identified as accommodational cynicism ("in fawning on those who give him presents he accepts a certain form of political power, integrates himself within it, and recognizes it") to a legibly critical cynicism ("he barks against those who give him nothing") to a two-pronged demonstration of values most essential to his Cynicism (he "bites those who are wicked" verbally and evidences theatrically through "his very way of life," "outside all the conventions and laws artificially imposed by the city," the starkly oppositional relationship between his pure poverty and the compromising "greed" of those wicked). Potentially far more controversial is the way in which Foucault maintains, tendering what could be fairly counted as an underacknowledged paradox, both that "a necessary exteriority" to power characterizes Diogenes' parrēsia and that, at the same time, the power in question is of a sort "that on one side he accepts." How can Diogenes simultaneously accommodate power and preserve an exteriority—one whose necessity Foucault highlights—to its operations? Is his Cynicism not compromised by his cynicism?

Clearly, Diogenes, held up as a model parrēsiast in this passage and others, is not radically compromised in Foucault's estimation; and though Foucault doesn't quite spell out why, I would hazard that, for him—and for any thinker who will, as I do here, want to contemplate an affirmable interplay of cynicisms and Cynicism—the beginning of an explanation inheres in exteriority's nonidentity with the kind of totalizing extrinsicalness, apartness, or disengagement that Berlant imagines, for instance, when she advocates "collective detachment" from toxic norms. Diogenes' exteriority to power is, by contrast, an inner outerness, an outward- or otherwise-oriented disposition articulated nonetheless within a discursive field that can never fully capture or contain it. More completely abjected from this field, Diogenes would not be able to speak his risky truth; accommodating to the field provides not only the occasion but also the enabling condition for the dance of critical cynicism and Cynicism and for the kind of truth telling that, together, they incite. In other words, how else to become the fly in the ointment (as critical cynics and Cynics alike are often hailed), the one whose truth-telling constitutes a risk, without access to the ointment, without an interlocutor to hear one's risky parrēsia? And yet accounting for exteriority in this way does not quite put to the side the question of what may be troubling about accommodation. If parrēsia constitutes a risk, then the risk is not only, say, that the king might throw the parrēsiast in prison or order his execution; as I have begun to intimate, a corollary risk is that the dog's bite will be a toothless one, that his fawning will have accomplished, alongside his feeding, his defanging.

Whatever Diogenes, or those conjuring in his name, would say about this nagging problem, I take guidance, in thinking about our own historical and political moment, from the thoughtful work of Sanford F. Schram, who, in a stirring revisiting and rereading of *Poor People's Movements* (and elsewhere),[35] advocates a dissensus politics rooted in what he calls "radical incrementalism"; as he explains it, and unlike the more routine incrementalism that has a deserved reputation as a dirty word in progressive conversation, its radical counterpart is "strategy—not theory—using a politics of disruption as a critical but contingent tool for creating political change" in contexts where "the all-pervasive reality of political contingency" cannot be denied: an "orientation . . . where activism pushes for fundamental changes by forcing concessions from those in power, taking what incremental gains can be had[,] . . . using them to build a better future," and "effectively combining a 'politics of survival' with a 'politics of social change.'"[36] Circling back to Foucault with Schram in mind, we could embroider his reading of Diogenes and understand the dog-philosopher as approximating the position of the radical incrementalist avant la lettre. Living contingently, and avowing as much as he fawns for survival, he makes the aptest, most disruptive critique he can in the most opportune instances that avail themselves to him—and that critique hinges on the grounding principle that radical social change, in Diogenes' case dependent on corresponding ethical changes that would likewise radicalize subjects' ways of caring for themselves and others, may be incrementally prompted by his bark and bite: "Recogniz[ing] his potential kinship with others, and . . . therefore a certain obligation to help them,"[37] the Cynic urges followers and detractors alike—whatever "potential kin" will listen—toward "cleansing . . . the mind of all unnecessary and disturbing thoughts, . . . the removal of inconsequential and poorly conceived ideas, . . . the abandoning of impediments and hindrances that clutter the human consciousness, and attainment of a lasting state of intellectual . . . lucidity" as the basis for then organizing, equally lucidly, the happy life of oneself and one's community.[38] That Cynical urging, as I'll explore in greater detail as part of the project of imagining a renovated Cynicism for our own moment, is accomplished chiefly through forms of castigation, of making a theatrical example of one's own everyday life practices, and of the imbrication of the two.

Neither the instantiation of a renovated Cynicism nor the critical cynicism with which it trucks is discernibly accomplished, in just about any contemporary scene on which we might alight (and especially any televisual scene), absent their semireliance on an accommodational cynicism from which we may be inclined to shrink but that has its necessary place—just as necessary as the assertion of exteriority—in a program of radical incrementalism or one approaching it. The making of *Daria* discloses as much, and the representations therein gesture as far, with a concreteness that helps to limn these ideas further, as well as with a historical specificity to which we attune profitably if we want to know what a latter-day Diogenes says—no longer *I am a dog*, if a declaration discernibly parallel to that self-nomination—when asked by authority, *Who are you?*

Deadpan

Daria—and *Daria*—were first, if not foremost, glimmers in the eyes of MTV network executives. In an arguably cynical concern that *Beavis and Butt-head*, sometimes dripping with misogyny, was not sufficiently inoculated from feminist critique and perhaps also stemming from a likewise cynical desire to attract more female viewers to the series, then-president of MTV Judy McGrath registered "a criticism," in 1993, "that there were no smart people and no girl characters in the show"—in response to which the cynically "time saving solution was to take care of two birds with one stone":[39] voilà Daria Morgendorfer, a brainy classmate of the series' eponymous duo whose earliest design and development fell to vice president of animation John Andrews and whose ongoing appearances in *Beavis and Butt-head* were mostly crafted by staff writer and story editor Glenn Eichler,[40] bucking the otherwise hands-on approach to the series' evolution taken by its creator, creative supervisor, and executive producer, Mike Judge. Indeed, as "*Beavis and Butt-head* were killed" by Judge as he planned ventures into other projects,[41] it was once again MTV executives who had the initial notion to spin off Daria into the world of *Daria*, construable as a cynical move simultaneously to capitalize on creative content from *Beavis and Butt-head* that was not Judge's intellectual property and yet to continue to attract that series' target audiences, or ones nearly akin to them, despite its imminent discontinuation. Approached in this context to create *Daria*, an assignment that he undertook with fellow *Beavis* staffer Susie Lewis,[42] Eichler, who would proceed to write myriad episodes of *Daria* and closely to oversee most aspects of its development, was faced with a task reminiscent of Diogenes' navigation of the potentially conflictive imperatives to fawn, bark, and bite: how to accommodate a platform provided by the net-work and yet to endow the resultant series—as, we shall see, Eichler and his collaborators were keen to do—with a critical oomph? As parrēsiasts with critically cynical and renovated Cynical designs, the *Daria* team undertook a form of truth-telling whose risk was at least twofold: facing network disap-proval and censure of the series' ethos and thus the threat of cancellation, on the one hand, and, on the other, losing credibility in cultivating that ethos be-cause of accommodations to a cynical system of production and distribution.

In Eichler's and others' estimation,[43] fear of compromising network over-sight was mitigated by lack of scrutiny of projects in MTV's Animation Di-vision in the late 1990s and early 2000s: a time when television's "second golden age" (as industry insiders appraised it) of traditional,[44] limited cel animation was on the wane, largely in the face of exploding competition from CGI—and, indeed, right before MTV shuttered that very division.[45] Yet even in a context of relative industrial latitude, accommodation to the liter-ally defining limits of limited cel animation—one constraint among others acknowledged by Eichler in an account of *Daria*'s budgetary leanness and the tightness of the series' production schedule[46]—constituted a challenge to leverage those very accommodations to good, critical, even Cynical, purpose. In formal terms, *Daria* intimates its ambition to take up such a challenge by reflexively acknowledging its likewise ambitious situatedness in a televisual genealogy of limited cel animation and of its marriage to sitcom conventions. "Utilizing a heavier line, more streamlined look and richer palette than *Bea-vis*,"[47] the series draws allusively nearer in style to *The Flintstones*, whose look was defined by "earthy" colors and "thick-textured" lines,[48] yet it also marks its critical difference from such forebear series by eschewing the "playful disobedience, misbehaviors, and even malfunctions"[49] that characterize an-imated worlds like Bedrock and by flirting with the sitcom's three-act struc-ture only to thwart consistently the rhythmic beats, pacing, trajectories, and closures usually commanded within that structure.[50] What's more, limited animation itself may provide a set of rubrics through which to frame, as it were, a further understanding of how Eichler et al. embrace the challenge of accommodation and achieve something like radical incrementalism in the process. A harsh critic of such cel animation and the Fordism in which it has historically participated, experimental animator George Griffin nonetheless offers a helpful conceptual model for understanding its processual move-ments and their potential implications for broader thinking about movement as such. "Central to the technique," he writes, "is . . . compartmentalization of labor, beginning with the separation of two basic functions—'design' (the look of a single frame) and 'animation' (the spatial displacement that occurs *between* the frames), and percolating down through other stages: backgrounds, inking, opaqueing, camera, editing."[51] Let's linger for a moment over the "*between*"-ness that Griffin emphasizes as essential to the very ontology of cel animation. Could this between-ness, and the movement of which it is constitutive, provide a metaphor with which to conceive more fully the between-ness inhabited by *Daria*'s makers, themselves moving across modes of cynicism and Cynicism (and back again) as they animate—that is, breathe life into—a series of critical images and messages not finally reducible to, and indeed aiming at cross-purposes with, the "assembly-line" logics against which Griffin chafes?[52]

However best to conceive the metaphorical movements of *Daria*'s creative personnel and the literal movements of, say, the animation rostrum affected and sometimes determined by their choices, one thing the latter manipulations do not achieve is a "movement into depth," that "sense of movement into the world of the image" that "many consider the hallmark of the cinema," that can be aped in animation by innovative technologies like Disney's multiplane camera system, but the pretension to which limited cel animation forgoes almost entirely.[53] Such animation relies on often open compositing techniques, which loosely synthesize layers of celluloid images designating fore-, back-, and middle grounds; which "force . . . a confrontation with effects . . . at odds with Cartesian perspectivalism"; and whose routinely "sliding or gliding movement[s]," deemphasizing and indeed dehierarchizing the distinctions among cel layers and "encourag[ing] *lateral movement of* eyes," "may look cheap" or flat to the viewer habituated to—and thus habituated to privilege or prioritize—cinematic effects (and even defenders, like Thomas Lamarre, of "animetism" as a distinct and distinctive practice with its own histories, imperatives, and values acknowledge that the sustaining of "cinematism demands a great deal of technical attention, time, and money" unrequired of limited animators).[54] *Daria* itself provides a wry gloss on these issues of flatness, depth, and perspectivalism—as well as the motions of capital that always shape the projects of art and commerce in attending to which such issues are most germane—when, in the second episode of the series, "The Invitation," Daria offers a lesson in perspective to typically clueless cheerleader and classmate Brittany; alongside a transcript of its dialogue, a sense of the scene's visual humor is well captured in the meticulously descriptive language of the fans who maintained the (sadly, now-defunct) website *Outpost Daria*:

(*Daria and Brittany are sharing a table in Ms. Defoe's class; Daria is effortlessly drawing, while Brittany is having a tough time*)

BRITTANY—Perspective is hard.

(*Ms. Defoe comes to their table and examines Daria's drawing*)

MS. DEFOE—Good work, Daria. Your cube is bursting out of the picture plane. You've really created the illusion of depth.

DARIA—I'm thinking of going into politics.

BRITTANY—Ms. Defoe? I need a new pencil. I used up the eraser.

MS. DEFOE—Here, Brittany, take another pencil and a fresh piece of paper, and try again. (*walks away, exasperated*)

BRITTANY—If I don't figure this perspective thing out, I'll have to take remedial art. I heard they make all the lefties become righties.

DARIA—But . . . you are a righty.

(*Brittany examines her hands, confused*)

BRITTANY—Daria, you're smart. Show me how to do this.

DARIA—Well . . . okay. You know when things seem very far away?

BRITTANY—Like the weekend?

DARIA—Distant things, like mountains and buildings.

BRITTANY—But, Daria . . . we're in a building.

DARIA—Yes, but . . .

(*Daria turns over her paper and starts drawing a stick-figure Brittany, complete with skirt and large bust*)

DARIA—Make believe you're at the mall. You're standing in front of J. J. Jeeters.

BRITTANY—Oh, like I would shop there.

DARIA—(*very slowly*) You don't have to go in. You're looking at Cashman's Department Store . . . (*draws small rectangle representing the store*)

BRITTANY—Now you're talking.

DARIA—. . . way down at the other end. (*draws arrows pointing to store*) Everything seems to be pointing to the entrance and saying, "Come shop, come shop." (*beat*) "One-day sale."

BRITTANY—I get it! That's really realistic, Daria.

DARIA—That's one-point perspective. All the lines are pointing to one spot on the horizon. (*draws more arrows to further illustrate the point*)

BRITTANY—I get it! Except . . .

4.1 Daria explains perspective to Brittany in *Daria*.

DARIA—Yes?

BRITTANY—Is Cashman's really having a one-day sale?[55]

A stunningly complex piece of meta-television, the scene abounds in a series of overlapping doublings, each of which also accomplishes a conceptual sliding or figural gliding that, among other effects, allegorizes the literal sliding and gliding of openly composited cel animation: (1) Daria's drawing doubles *Daria*'s drawing, yet the relatively dynamic latter exceeds and glides away from the crude, static former; (2) linguistic puns ("illusion of depth," "lefties become righties") mobilize words to slide across aesthetic, affective, ethical, and political registers; (3) visual puns (the white "cube" in Daria's picture mirrors layered white rectangles of paper arrayed before Brittany, which mirror the whiteboard before which they sit) invite the eye to glide and compare multiplied compositional elements in the cels; and (4) Daria's putative explanation of perspectivalism retains formalist terms but doubles their meanings to engender a sly slide from art historical pedadogy to a critique of capital's relentless seizures. Taken together, these doublings and their slidings or glidings have the cumulative effect of pointing, not unlike the lines in Daria's drawing, toward a provocative idea: just as the "definition" of perspective produced within the animated world through which Daria and Brittany move concerns techniques conducive to a cinematism at a remove from that world's animetism, so, too, does *Daria*'s articulation to and through the commercial imperatives of television, its accommodating movement with capital, nonetheless provision a critical perspective on that movement, a redoubling of that movement aslant to or at a shrewd remove from what is maintained in the less complex "thesis," the "one-point perspective," about Cashman's. Daria's and *Daria*'s critical cynicism suggests that sliding and gliding through capital—with a flatness that turns out to be remarkably textured—may achieve sharper and punchier effects than would be galvanized by a pretension to escape into a depth at once material and metaphysical; and part of what gives this flatness its texturality is the sonic portion of it working in concert with its visual dimensions: chiefly, the famously deadpan intonations with which Tracy Grandstaff voices Daria's withering assessments (contrasted vividly here with the exaggerated chirps, squeaks, and squeals of Janie Mertz as Brittany).

Pursuing a more detailed analysis of *Daria*, a scholarly critic would do better to keep in mind (and in view and hearing) the multivalent flatness whose features are charted above—one marked by a conceptual refusal of the metaphysics of depth, open compositing techniques, and deadpan tone of voice—than to follow most journalistic commentators on the series, as Kathy M. Newman does, in reductively identifying its flatness with a "static," "visually unchanging" animation aesthetic.[56] Far from static, the series' aesthetic, though ascetic, nonetheless produces a set of formal effects that are more plausibly described as theatrical—stylized, citational, heightened—and enlists those effects in the service of its cynical and renovated Cynical agendas, for which Daria, herself routinely accused of cynicism (particularly by her mother),[57] becomes the avatar within the representational world of suburban Lawndale as she bodies forth the tripartite cynicisms-cum-Cynicism of her creators.[58] That animated bodying, necessitating that Daria become a kind of Cynical theatricalist, also marks her difference from precursors like the composite "Diogenes" of history and legend, especially as he emerges in accounts, such as Sloterdijk's, that emphasize the tactics of his theatrical self-display-as-pedagogy most available for reading as lurid and shocking (e.g., masturbating and urinating in public venues). If, as Andreas Huyssen asks in his trenchant foreword to the English translation of *Critique of Cynical Reason*, "What *are* women to do while Diogenes 'pisses against the idealist wind,'" and how do they participate in or counteract the cynicism of domination?"—and if, as Huyssen proceeds to argue, "Sloterdijk's male kynicism remains ultimately unsatisfactory" "for a new politics of subjectivity"[59]—then Daria emerges at a later but intimately related historical moment to disclose what a differently gendered yet nonetheless theatrical Cynicism might entail. Her "pointedly" flat chest (so unlike the Barbiesque bustline of Brittany) contrasting, too, with the phallic tricks of Diogenes—and working as another tool in Daria's flatness arsenal—she shares instead with the Cynic of yore a penchant for moving from "clever uses of language (puns, extended wordplay, etc.)" to defenses of "plain speech,"[60] as well as a delight in devising scenarios in which object lessons emerge for the more benighted denizens of her corrupt world. If she figures as an actor in as well as a director of those scenarios, her gestural repertoire does not include "farting, belching, . . . rolling about in the sand, . . . sleeping in a *pithos*, . . . and innumerable other contortions, twists and shapes [that] loudly trumpet the brazen freedom and antinomianism of Cynics,"[61] but rather smaller, more subtle gestures that acquire their power precisely from their contrast with the more literally cartoonish behaviors of her classmates, family members, and neighbors *and* from their relief against the backdrop of her otherwise Bartleby-like preference not to gesture at all; perhaps the most famous of these tiny, biting gestures (in part because repeated weekly in the series' opening credit sequence)[62] is the purposefully belated and ineffectually minimal raise of her hand as a volleyball whizzes past her in a loathsome, mandated gym class. The fact that the ascetic gesture does not require much work to draw, is repeated multiple times in the credit sequence, yet on each of its repetitions *does* involve additional animation, undertaken with cheeky deliberation, works both to show us the *Daria* team's accommodation to the constraints of limited cel animation and to signal their winking acknowledgment of that accommodation and the ways in which marking it can spark a critical movement.

Alongside this sequence, Daria's work as a theatricalist—and the thoroughgoing interlocking of her representation as theatricalist with her creators' accommodations to the exigencies of limited cel animation—inform in a likewise and especially powerful way the pilot episode of the series, "Esteemsters."[63] Here we encounter, for the first of many times, the upper-upper-middle-class Morgendorfer family partaking in one of an absurdly endless series of unpalatable lasagna dinners, the repetition of which, in reused cels, will much later be explained in narrative terms as mother and workaholic Helen's go-to, quick-fix answer to harried meal-making[64]—yet which also clearly reduces the amount of ongoing time, energy, and money needed to render the kitchen table over which the Morgendorfers hover. At the same time, the makers of *Daria* use this gambit to more critical ends as

4.2 In *Daria*'s opening credit sequence, Daria "prefers not to" try too hard in gym class.

they offer an ongoing vision of a family wealthy enough to eat more variously but whose richness is banal, as is the richness of their lasagna-centric diet. Moreover, sitcoms, the series suggests, are likewise banal and trade on such canned repetitions without, as is endeavored here, capitalizing on an obstacle like budgetary constraint to achieve a familial characterization, also a meditation on habitus, that is complex and multidimensional. In the local case of "Esteemsters," that complexity and multidimensionality also fuels a form of ascetic, yet theatrical, Cynicism when Daria, given the opportunity to choose a meal out (and a relief from lasagna) and thus poised to do the work of Cynical *régisseur*, hijacks the invitation and directs the family to the direly kitschy and unhealthy Pizza Forest, as if to say, ascetically, "Nothing but jarred tomato sauce and processed cheese for us!"—and, as the family is serenaded by animal-suited singers in a routine that Daria was made repeatedly to endure as a child, likewise as if to say (in Chekhov's oft-quoted words), "Have a look at yourselves and see how bad and dreary your lives are!"[65]

If Daria's ethical effort, like Chekhov's, is to make "people . . . realize that [badness and dreariness], for when they do, they will most certainly create another and better life for themselves," then she has, as a Foucauldian parrēsiast, not only the cultivation of theatrical *as ifs* but also more direct forms of risky truth-telling at her disposal as she aims at the transformed care of self and other that such truth-telling might provoke (though she might also, and again like Chekhov, suppose cynically—and Cynically—that she "will not live to see" such transformation "but . . . know that it will be quite different, quite unlike our present life"). The many adult viewers of *Daria*, characterized by Kathy M. Newman as "cerebral, writerly types," have delighted in just this status of Daria as parrēsiast or "outcast she-hero who dared to say things they were too scared to say in their own teenage years. As Walter Belcher remarked, 'this ultimate outsider says things I wish I had said in school.'"[66] Yet such delight is not simply backward-looking, since the situatedness of Daria at a suburban high school only provides a local set of occasions for more globally oriented acts of parrēsia, the most delicious of which is perhaps the definition of the word *edgy* that Daria offers to skewer Lawndale visitor and one-name-wonder Val (founder and editor of *Val!* magazine, likely a parody of *Sassy* guru Jane Pratt): "As far as I can make out, *edgy* occurs when middlebrow, middle-aged profiteers are looking to suck the energy—not to mention the spending money—out of the 'youth culture.' So they come up with this fake concept of seeming to be dangerous when every move they make is the result of market research and a corporate master plan."[67] (If one were in the cynical habit of making tee shirts, *I am not edgy*, Daria's implicit version of *I am a dog*, would do well to be pressed on one.) As we have seen in an investigation of the complex commingling of fawning, barking, and biting, such risky speech runs the bummer-risk that its impact will be so small or ephemeral that nothing much is moved by it: indeed, within the diegetic world of this episode of *Daria* (whatever extradiegetic effects Daria's much-loved *edgy* monologue may have or have had),[68] Daria only has Val's ear because she is being courted for writing an essay, "My So-Called Angst," deemed *Val!*-worthy; and, after one beat's worth of awkwardness, a humiliation-resistant Val attempts the cooptation of Daria's parrēsia with the blithe rejoinder, "I love this girl! Is she smart, or what? Where'd you sharpen that mind of yours, Daria? That's edgy!"

Though the interval opened by this instance of Daria's parrēsia may be too incremental, at last, to fuel a sustained project of radical incrementalism—a concern clearly registered (as on other, like occasions)[69] by the episode's underlining of Val's unstoppability—other episodes, in which Daria's anticorporatism, parallel to Diogenes' antistatist naturism, is likewise foregrounded, are more sanguine about the possibilities of taking up a radically incrementalist project. Whether resisting the access that a modeling agency is granted to Lawndale High School,[70] thwarting the installation of soda machines in the school's halls in exchange for corporate sponsorship of school initiatives,[71] critiquing the consumer logic of a "Teen Fashion Extravaganza" hosted (where else?) at the local mall,[72] or affirming that an agenda of "voluntary simplicity" is not only an ambition of her parents' aging hippie friends but is also compatible, in a complex, fragile, yet meaningful way with her "bitter, nineties cynicism,"[73] Daria routinely impacts a policy, a practice, a family member's perspective, or a friend's ethical self-care, respectively; the gradual, punctual (and thus quintessentially televisual) accretion of these victories, some more minor than others, resembles in form something very near Schram's radical incrementalism. Furthermore, Daria's anticorporatism is just as routinely if punctually represented in contexts in which she recognizes the global reaches of capital's tentacles and is concomitantly figured (again, parallel to Diogenes, who "frees himself. . . to become a 'citizen' of himself, the cosmos, and other Cynics[,] . . . wander[s] from city to city," and is "at home here and everywhere because . . . radically at home with [his] present sel[f]")[74] as a kind of global cosmopolitan who "take[s] seriously the value not just of human life but of particular human lives, which means taking an interest in the practices and beliefs that lend them significance.[75] People are different, the cosmopolitan knows, and there is much to learn from our differences."[76] This sense of global cosmopolitanism is not just a property of Daria but of *Daria*, manifested curiously but compellingly in ever-changing closing credit sequences in which we see the ascetic slate of characters who populate the show theatrically attired like a plenitude of subjects, real and fictional, contemporary and historical, from a variety of global contexts. On the one hand, and given limited cel animation's "favor[ing] of . . . schematized and iconic styles for rendering locations and characters,"[77] this repeated gesture could be understood as a colonizing arrogation of difference, an accommodation of that difference to the series' iconicity-generating machinery, such that anyone could be yoked in identity with Daria (or a related, iconic character) or any look, point of view, or subjectivity translated, with effacement or disfiguration, into *Daria*'s iconic style.[78] On the other hand, and thinking in a more critically cynical and renovated Cynical mode, I would submit that the closing credit sequences may be read in precisely the obverse way: as indicating the openness of the series' makers to otherness, or the capacity with which otherness, in myriad manifestations, may be appreciated by a *Daria* viewer—with the consequence not that everyone can, via animation's relatively easy transformations, be made a version of Daria or every signifier subsumed to *Daria*, but rather that thinking like Daria or with

4.3 In *Daria*'s closing credit sequence, Daria's look is reimagined on the left side of the screen while information about labor scrolls quickly by on the right.

Daria can keep one kaleidoscopically attuned to and eager for encounters with difference whose contours are not predicted or determined in advance, thus deferring the very kinds of (fore)closure with which a final credit sequence could otherwise align.

And yet, as the eye is invited to contemplate, fairly slowly, Daria as Gulliver, Brittany as Inquisitor, or history teacher Mr. DeMartino as *Pink Flamingos'* Divine (among many other permutations) on the left side of the closing-credit screen, words scrolling superfast on the right include the attribution of animation work to "overseas studio" Plus One Animation and its supervising director: acknowledgment that *Daria*, like most network and cable primetime series of its moment that used limited cel animation, inexpensively outsourced much of the technical work of that animation's completion to Asian enterprises (in this case, one based in South Korea). With the various versions or dimensions of cynicism ever in mind, how ought we to square the anticorporate, globally cosmopolitan sensibility of *Daria* with its participation in a system of globally decentered, neoliberal capitalism—a participation that includes not just cels made on the cheap by a South Korean subcontractor, but also the ads that appeared between segments of *Daria* episodes when it aired on MTV, the licensing of commercially produced pop music to provide the show with its distinctively millennial, alt-rock-sympathetic soundtrack, and the various product tie-ins that proliferated during the series' run and even well afterward (surely most wonderful and horrible, at once, is the recent prospect that deadpan Daria, courtesy of MTV's joint venture with NavTones™, may "voice . . . your Garmin or TomTom GPS. And after you do[wnload my voice]," "she" adds in an advertisement for the product, "maybe we can go for a double tall, extra hot, no foam, lobotomy")?[79]

With ideas of between-ness and movement in mind, I find that this question remains for me an abiding question, one I would hesitate to follow with an answer that is (the accommodational cynic in me would say) too facilely ungenerous, (the critical cynic in me would say) too relenting, or (the renovated Cynic in me would say) too undisciplined; after all, having definitive answers to such questions may be dilutive rather than refining for sustained critical inquiry of the sort required to write a book—or for producing a television series, inhabiting a pedagogical or administrative role in the academy, or doing pretty much any of the forms of work that *Obstruction* asks us to think together. Instead, what examining intertwined cynicisms recommends is a willingness, without dismissing but vigilantly maintaining rigor, to make up provisions as one goes along, all the while remaining committed to and on the lookout for the openings in which radical incrementalism can make its gains: to learn that being the fly in the ointment requires a simultaneous gingerliness in doing it on the fly. Such delicate, improvisatory choreography is highlighted and championed in two episodes of *Daria* in which Daria plays the role, broadly understood—and initially unmooring to her—of teacher: "Pinch Sitter," where she unexpectedly finds herself with a babysitting assignment and flummoxed by it, then models impromptu for her overobedient charges the pleasures of critical thinking (and of watching bad television);[80] and "Boxing Daria," where just-graduated Daria and best friend Jane Lane, the sunnier Crates to her prickly Diogenes,[81] are at first nonplussed when approached to give a tour to incoming Lawndale High students, then offer one last, series-ending parrēsia as they descriptively catalogue for the "middle school veterans" (shocked despite their veteran status) the "food poisoning of every variety" of the lunchroom, the showers that have "all been peed in," and the "fine industrial grade lockers, which make the perfect noise when you bang your head against them."[82] Banging our heads against the lockers: an apt metaphor, to those of us with ongoing scholastic investments, for the challenges that attend teaching in corporatized universities, writing with an eye to publishing via those universities' presses, and performing the related activities that can seem hopelessly obstructed by the cynicism that they generate but that may, as I have been arguing, be better embraced by not getting mired in and instead moving with—and, through dexterous recalibrations, moving—that cynicism. The "noise" made in the process will not be "perfect," but it may sound—accommodatingly (yet riskily), incrementally (yet radically)—like, and as, a telling of truth. It would certainly be plainer, cleaner—and make a more rousing manifesto—to use this chapter just to advocate renovated Cynicism, in general, and its positioning as a feminist riposte to Sloterdijk, in particular. Yet as Daria herself would likely say, "I am . . . and I am not." That is, I believe that advocating renovated Cynicism is salutary—and at the same time narrower and easier than the task of navigating renovated Cynicism's (and critical cynicism's) relationship to accommodationism, which I have otherwise tackled in this chapter. For (multiply) cynical reasons, an endorsement of this latter navigation can never, in motto-like or sound bite-esque form, be fostered only or simply under the rubric *cynicism*, chiefly because of how intractably damning that word will, I expect, remain. This bind is the one in which the "gingerliness," "improvisat[ion]," "dexter[ity]" and "recalibrations" that I affirm in this paragraph become all the more urgent, if also slippery and perhaps wobbly.

Coda: Track Sound

With the notion of imperfect sounds, conjured in the last section of this chapter, still in mind, I would be remiss in departing "Cynicism" before saying a word about the 2010 DVD box-set release of *Daria: The Complete Animated Series*, long awaited by an intense fan base and delayed, as Glenn Eichler explains in a liner note accompanying the discs, "because the cost of licensing the many music bites we used would have made it impossible to release the collection (and for many years did)."[83] In response to the obstacle created by licensing fees, and thus choosing to change "99 percent of the music," Eichler and his collaborators chose also to embrace—or rather, to continue to embrace—the obstruction of cynicism. Defending the decision, he adds, "To put it bluntly, replacing the music had to be done. Does that mean this box set is compromised? Season I Daria would have said, 'Yes.' Season V Daria would have said, 'Shut up and pass the remote.' Let the raging begin." As I hope my engagement with *Daria* has helped to demonstrate, the series reveals, contrary to Eichler's retrospective perception of a narrative of progress, rather that all the Darias of Seasons I through V would have said, "Yes. *And* shut up and pass the remote." Moreover, cynicism—of some sorts, plural—is not the exclusive property of a "compromised" DVD box set but always-already animated the decision to use contemporary music, both popular and unpopular, mainstream and alt, radio-friendly and underground, in the series, which leveraged the selections to give *Daria* a powerful sonic interface, at once accommodational, critical, and theatrical, with the massier as well as fringier musical cultures of its period. Whether it's unbearable to some audiences that a scene involving a direct parody of R.E.M.'s "Everybody Hurts" and its iconic video may be marred beat to beat (or simply cease to make perfect sense) once the scene is stripped of that song[84]—or that the historical specificity of a lame party's lameness is evacuated from a sequence when "FastLove" is likewise evacuated from a scene therein,[85] or that a montage of excessive amorousness between Helen and husband Jake is not skewered as hilariously when it's not set to the bombastic "Vision of Love,"[86] and on and on—is finally less worth "the raging" that Eichler anticipates than is the question posed by the band Cake in a song that is in fact retained in the box-set version of *Daria*: "How do you afford your rock-and-roll lifestyle?"[87] It's a question whose best, implicit beginning of an answer may come from musical material original to *Daria* and voiced by Jane's brother (and Daria's longtime crush) Trent and his punk band, Mystik Spiral: "Every dog has his day."[88] (And every dog-philosopher his moment in the sun, if only for Alexander to block it?) One way and another, every "rock-and-roll" statement, however ascetic (or luxe), is paid for, however inexpensively (or exorbitantly), and the costs—literal and metaphorical, direct and ancillary, material and psychic—associated with the price tag need to be weighed against the related costs that would be incurred if the "lifestyle," or song, or box set, remained notional instead of getting actualized. In the case of *Daria*, a transportable, navigable archive of the series is better for the public record and good, for the democratization of investigations of the series, than a number of imaginable alternatives.

Of course, there are also real alternatives—and highly democratized, if not legal, ones, at that—to consulting the box set; they take either the form of VHS recordings of *Daria* broadcasts that have been digitized and uploaded online or, via a massive project of restoration (and piracy), the form of remastered versions of the DVD's episodes in which the official, licensed soundtrack is replaced with the original "music bites" (also snatched from VHS recordings of old broadcasts). One can go down a rabbit hole—or several, as I have—reading these different *Darias*, their contents, and their contexts of production and distribution against each other, especially when the paths into and through those holes are so helpfully made possible by hyperlinks. Probing the value of such Web forays will be one of the chief concerns of the ensuing chapter on "Digressiveness." In a more tangential way, that chapter will speak obliquely with and to this one's exploration of flatness by considering the digresser's relationship to what Manuel DeLanda has called, in a reading of Deleuze, a confrontation with the world as a reckoning with its radically "flat ontology."[89] Something near that flat ontology gets modeled in the closing credit sequence of *Daria* discussed in detail above; more dramatically and vividly, the digresser, especially in her paradoxically simultaneous guise as a sort of encyclopedist, does "flat" work, insofar as that work discloses, via digression as well as encyclopedism, the potential non-hierarchization of the assemblages that, together, make up flat ontologies. In a more metaphorical vein (and looking ahead to the next chapter's mash-up of contemporary Web-based projects and the eighteenth-century Enlightenment efforts that beg weirdly to be identified as their predecessors), I might venture that the aptest spatial metaphor for the journey of digressiveness is neither scrambling up and down the topographies of an "untamed," romantic wilderness nor rounding the labyrinthine corners of a neoclassically pruned landscape but taking a long, flat, city walk—where the flatness in question describes both a quality of digressive ambulation itself and the relations among the phenomenal perceptions and critical appraisals that the digressive movement makes possible.

5. Digressiveness

Step Aside

Thinking about how to open this chapter, I became briefly distracted by the question: Is it strictly possible to *begin* with a digression? To answer this question means at least to presuppose and—better—to proffer a definition of digression, en route to a more expansive meditation on digressiveness as style (of self re-presentation), strategy (of orientation toward lifeworld or worlds), practice (of work, play, and their imbrication), and method (of artistic expression or scholarly investigation). Considering the figure of speech *digressio* "as a figure *for* speech and mental, interior, movement," Anne Cotterill discloses that the movement most centrally characterizing digression—and thus meriting centrality in a definition of digression—is the "step aside":

> The Latin root of digression, *digressio*, translates a Greek rhetorical term, *parecbasis*, that means "to step or go aside or depart"; and digressions have stepped "alongside the subject" in poetry and oratory, in fiction and in historical and critical writing since antiquity. The movement of stepping aside has proved richly allusive yet by definition elusive: digressions have been read as lightly pleasurable and darkly sinuous, as the harmless vehicles of gossip and romance and the heroic wandering of epic liberty.[1]

Whether or not any given digression is trivial or consequential, benign or shattering, to be given as a digression means, in its substance, to have given the step aside from an explicit or implicit course already underway. From this perspective, to (claim to) begin with a digression betrays the premises, however factitious, on which the idea of digressing depends. Even if, as Cotterill proceeds to suggest, notions of beginning and ending, on which the fabrication of closed narrative (for instance) relies, are at odds with the tendency "of all discourse to digress" in a manner that, when examined, highlights the illusoriness of beginnings and endings,[2] these illusions are, all the same, ones in which subjects invest, if only provisionally, to give coherent shape to language, sociality, historicity, and more: an ostensively originary shape or line, only in relation to which the asideness of a digression can appear as such. As Thomas M. Kavanaugh argues in a similar vein yet with an emphasis on *level* rather than, in my account, *shape* or *line*—and in a very fine reading of Diderot to which we will return after some further swerves—"Digression: *dis-gradi*, to step aside, to depart from, but with the key notion of the level, the grade (*gradus*) designating that from which the deviation is made."[3]

So—if not, "First, a digression," then: Now, a digression. And the digression with which I invite you to step aside with me from definitional work on digressing concerns, in fact, a step aside or detour that I made from the very focus on this chapter, taken shape in the form in which you now encounter it. In that detour, during what I conceive as the long middle of my tackling "Digressiveness" (in the "end," I also gravitate away from notions of beginning and ending, however tactically necessary I demonstrate them to be in the preceding paragraph), I wrote a pocket monograph on the television series *Knots Landing* for Wayne State University Press's TV Milestones series; and, while the accomplishment of that work may seem superficially to have constituted a huge step, if not a leap, away from the investments and concerns of "Digressiveness," stepping back to them in the way made possible only because of the digression put me in a position to treat key elements of this chapter with much fuller consideration and rounder perspective than I would otherwise have brought to bear on them. To research *Knots Landing* was lubricated by time spent exploring a fan website devoted, with meticulous care and attention, to the series' production and reception histories. To write about the series in both synoptic and detailed ways posed the challenge to think, often at once, at very different scales about the televisual text and about televisuality as such, which itself poses scalar challenges to any grasp of its ontology. And to furnish the monograph with its images required the tedious but necessary tasks of generating many screen captures, of selecting the most compelling among them, and of editing and framing the stills thus made so that they would work to best effect alongside the words that they accompany. Beyond their immediate, salutary consequences for the book on *Knots Landing*, these forays furnished me with new or renewed capacities to attend to the work of the present chapter. The first gave me a richer understanding of what it means—and what level of labor it takes—to produce a website or blog with comprehensive attention to a sprawling television series, as do not only the webmasters responsible for the maintenance of the *Knots Landing* website but also the journalist Rich Juzwiak, whose blog *fourfour* figures here as my case study of a digressively styled yet simultaneously encyclopedic project. The second prompted my more textured reflections on the scalar slipperiness not just of the televisual archive but also of the related and in many ways overlapping archive—one for whose apprehension the very notion of the archive may be "wildly inaccurate"[4]—inhering in and evolving as the Web. And the third gave me practical instruction in the time, patience, and manipulation—with an emphasis on the *manual*, which is to say digital (in both senses), aspects of manipulation—required to generate effective images for a blog or for a book, however simple the final results may sometimes seem to the consumers of those images and however much, consequently, the embodied work of that image production threatens to be occluded from view unless marked in some further way (a marking to which the final section of this chapter, like the blog that is the object of its close analysis, will turn).

What I aim to indicate with the digression constituting the prior paragraph is that the related, yet more prior digression constituted by my work on *Knots Landing* was not a mere distraction from this book chapter but a boon whose very aside or aslant relationship to this chapter enabled the more contoured, more comprehensive—and, paradoxically, more attentive—thinking and writing with which I establish the chapter's value by also and in the same movement establishing the value of digressiveness as a phenomenon, a maneuver, and a provision. "Not a *distraction*": to write in this terminological way is to follow, at least conditionally and for the moment, the cues of Damon Young, whose book of that title, *Distraction*, proceeds from the convictions that "the cultivation of concentration can be a struggle" and that "attention is a scarce and precious resource," in part for perceptual and psychological— that is, phenomenal—reasons.[5] These presumed constraints form the basis for Young's ensuing argument about ethics and value (a target, as indicated above, of my own venture here):

> The good life warrants an ongoing struggle to be clear about what's important, and to see it with lucidity and passion; not to be distracted by false ambitions, or waylaid by dissipated consciousness. This conundrum is captured in the Latin root of the word *distraction*, meaning literally to tear apart or pull asunder. When we are distracted, we're dragged away from what's worthwhile.
>
> Hence distraction is ultimately a question of value. To say that we're "distracted" is to admit that we're squandering our mental and physical assets; something we value less is diverting our efforts from something

we value more (or should). Values represent our choices of what's most significant, desirable or necessary.[6]

One enlivening challenge of digressiveness—a mode of stepping aside that I distinguish from the conceptualization of distraction as variously "dragg[ing] away," "tear[ing] apart," and "pull[ing] asunder"—is to treat it not as an obstacle or impediment to focusing our attention on what we should value, per Young's rallying call, but as an obstruction that calls generatively into question our schemas of (e)valuation and forces us to recalibrate them, such that the relatively valuable and relatively (putatively) valueless are brought into a closer proximity, an altered choreography, perhaps even a dialectical interplay, with one another.

In other, more doggedly mundane words, when is Web surfing—the routine, paradigmatic example of contemporary distraction in Young's account and in many allied texts—a baleful distraction, when a valuable digression? It would be facetious at best and disingenuous at worst to value surfing as such (an inapt metaphor, as it happens, for the bulk of Web engagement—and one for which I will propose alternative metaphorizing) without distinguishing more carefully among its varieties and their putative ambitions and effects; and, of course, the anecdotal example invoked above of visiting a fan website for a side research project is at one extreme, and extremely purposive, end of a spectrum of Web traffic and negotiations. The taxonomic, and more than taxonomic, work of identifying and assessing various distractions will steer the next section of this chapter—toward its terminus in the assertion that a recent, staggering emphasis on distraction in both scholarly and popular writing is itself a distraction from digressiveness, away from which we may propitiously veer. In so veering, I take a step not only aside but also historically backward to consider Diderot's digressiveness, as yoked to an encyclopedism with which it would seem to be at odds but to which it has a more complexly obverse relationship. I do so in order to argue for a renovated understanding of encyclopedism that would rescue a perverse, indeed perversely digressive, version of it from its association with the worst cornerstones of Enlightenment ideology—and in order also to demonstrate how this Diderotian digressiveness, as yoked to encyclopedism, paves the way and provides a model for a mode of sanguine encounter with so-called "new" media. To determine what isn't new about emergent media, what is, and to vex the ease of that very project, in a manner likewise indebted to Diderot and with one crucial upshot in (re)theorizing the hyperlink, is also to move one step closer to the already promised navigation of Rich Juzwiak's *fourfour*, whose haptically oriented approach to remixing—the central gesture of the blog—brings touch, as it were, into view and, in the process, remixes with instructional value the ways and reasons to digress encyclopedically.

To recap and remix, then, as Juzwiak does, and thereby to signal ways in which my scholarly performance here owes some of its rhythms to the pedagogy modeled in Juzwiak's online writing, this chapter on "Digressiveness"—inevitably and constitutively—heads in a number of directions. In order to distinguish digressiveness, a finally, if weirdly, valuable obstruction, from distraction as a mere impediment—and, in the process, in order also to suggest what is missing from or problematic about some contemporary discussions of (in)attention—I take up recent writing, both scholarly and journalistic, that constitutes a field of "distraction studies." In order to define digressiveness not only negatively (that is, as not distractive) but to limn further and positively the coordinates of this obstruction, I look (recalling Melas, invoked in this book's introduction) to Diderot's uncanny, noncontemporaneous contemporaneity, inhering in the artful strolls that allow him not to prioritize digressiveness there and then and encyclopedism here and now but to make the magic that comes from their confrontation and interleaving. In order to give further heft to the idea that a noncontemporaneous contemporaneity merits Diderot's emplacement in this chapter—and to propose how it does (and doesn't) have a special relevance to thinking about mediality—I engage some "older" and some "newer" new media theorists whose work also helps to orient and pivot us more knowledgeably toward blogging as a practice. And in order, with key blogger Juzwiak at the center of the effort, to show how he, too, invites a way to think about the theorization of contemporary media and at the same time to think about putting digressiveness valuably into play, I provide a close analysis of his blog *fourfour*, with particular attention to the prominent place of television recaps in that work. Of course, along the way, digressions from these four central aims punctuate the effort (and bring into view such issues as the phenomenology of reading, flat ontology, racial disidentification, and hapticality); and, if they work, they form no mere asides but necessary—albeit more minor—steps in the theorization and demonstration of digressiveness's movement.

Step Away

In a neat irony, the attraction to distraction as an object of inquiry has become so magnetic and has yielded such a copious literature in "distraction studies" that the field threatens to fuel the very information overload, ostensibly particular to a digital, networked age, over which many of its representatives wring their hands. Indeed, the bulk of writers contributing to this bulky discourse interweave versions (with local, idiosyncratic inflections) of two basic claims: that distraction, understood as an attrition of concentration or dissipation of attention, is a problem, and that the problem is more urgent and grievous now than in earlier historical moments because of the various, emergent technics that incite distraction as such a prevalent technique of (non- or weakened) engagement with the world. Within this discursive field, a slightly smaller subset of its participants introduces a third, related claim as they worry over or make predictions about the status of reading (slenderly understood as literarily oriented, close, deep, and lengthily sustained reading of words on pages in books), which is treated either as an already lost species of another time or as endangered, at least, to become one. Arguably most prominent in advancing such arguments, Nicholas Carr distinguishes "the world of the screen . . . from the world of the page" as the basis for his assertions that "the Net seizes our attention only to scatter it" and thus "prevent[s] our minds from thinking either deeply or creatively";[7] likewise prominent, and in language that closely resembles Carr's, Sven Birkerts identifies "technologies" associated with the "digital paradigm" as largely responsible for the "rapid erosion of certain ways of thinking—their demotion, as it were. I mean reflection, a contextual understanding of information, imaginative projection."[8] Though Carr tempers his diagnosis with an acknowledgment that distraction isn't necessarily "bad" if by *distraction* we mean, narrowly, the "temporary, purposeful diversion of our mind that refreshes our thinking when we're weighing a decision" (and not instead the "constant distractedness that the Net encourages"),[9] others are inspired to more alarmist and inflammatory language and lean more heavily than he does on the idea of living in stuckness with a static, even ossified form of distraction, "constant distractedness." Johann Hari goes so far as naming ours an "age of distraction" as part of a proposal for "how to survive it,"[10] while Robert Hassan, ratcheting up the rhetorical stakes (and endowing a whole book and not just an article with the name *The Age of Distraction*), calls "pathological"—because "chronic"—the distraction with which he sees contemporary subjects "becoming disconnected from the rhythms of time . . . that have made the worlds that we still take for granted."[11] A little more cautiously calling ours an "Age of Interruption," Thomas L. Friedman nonetheless resorts to a similarly medicalizing language of "malady" to assess the dangers of "continuous"— that is, also interpreted as chronic—"partial attention."[12]

Those interested in dissenting from these lines of reasoning could follow a variety of alternative paths, of which three have been most prominent and laudable. To begin, a number of thinkers disclose how distraction—even defined in terms more or less coincident with the ones cited above—may not be as toxic as supposed by its detractors. Most cautious in this camp is Michael Wood, who, elaborating on Walter Benjamin in the development of his "Distraction Theory," makes plain that he has no intention to recuperate distraction (for him, distraction "contains . . . elements" to appreciate, "but not enough to make it respectable"), yet he locates the value, alongside "concentrating," in also "try[ing] to tune into our distraction, to hear some of its beguilingly plausible, mostly disorderly messages."[13] So attuned—indeed, far from nonattuned in our inattention—we would have less partial (in both senses of the word) understandings of the texts, among other objects, arrayed before us. Pursuing a related line of argumentation—yet more buoyantly celebratory as he identifies the good uses to which distraction may be put, and thinking more of creative production than aesthetic reception—Hanif Kureishi finds an "Art of Distraction" in subjects' willingness to let their minds wander down the distractive paths that "might be more like realizations and can be as informative and multilayered as dreams. They might be where the excitement is." As Kureishi lets his own mind (and mimetic prose) wander toward such "multilayered . . . dreams," he also makes a rhetorical move precisely converse to the one made by a number of distraction's naysayers: where they, as we have seen, mystify the operations of distraction in medicalizing language, Kureishi demystifies a hegemonic relationship that many subjects have to actual medication and faults Ritalin, in particular, for leading them to "prefer . . . obedience to creativity," a preference serving a broader regulatory regime of "psychological policing" that is "the contemporary equivalent of the old practice of tying up children's hands in bed."[14] Similarly taking up—and literally taking—the sister drug Adderall as part of a thought experiment on the perils not of distraction but of (over) attention, Joshua Foer reports that with Adderall-fueled concentration comes rigidity of thinking and loss of access to the distractingly "day-dreamy": the "rogue thoughts" that he associates not only with "creativity" but also with a sense of self from which he becomes uncannily and unnervingly estranged.[15]

A reader could get distracted by yet further versions of these (to borrow Wood's language) "beguilingly plausible" arguments in favor of distraction.[16] To do so would, however, be to focus too much and too rigid a form of attention on the strategy of taking for granted a more or less transparent definition of distraction as inattention, which serves its opponents just as much as its champions. Still more ambitious are the writers who redefine distraction itself—or, more precisely, direct us to dimensions of distraction that we have not properly attended—by way of alighting on its uses. Undertaking one such project of distraction's renovation, and hailing distraction's "value" as "an intellectual resource" and in its "link[age] to rebellious creativity," Joseph R. Urgo deconstructs the very opposition between attention and inattention on which more routine accounts of distraction hinge:

> Commonly considered, distraction is the absence of attention. But inattentiveness is not the whole of what distraction is. Distraction is also itself a form of attention, a mode of attentiveness more privately conjured or submitted to. When one is distracted, one is still attentive, but one may also be made aware of being attentive to something aside from, or apart from, something else. . . . Distraction thus depends on something *not thought about* for its existence; it fills the gap left in consciousness when attention to something else is let go. Distraction depends on absence for its existence, as when we refer to a distracted person as absentminded.[17]

To "let go" of one mode of attention is not, in Urgo's account, to let go of attention altogether but to let in other sensations and perceptions, perhaps in their "more privately" colored "conjur[ation]" also "resistan[t] to external controls over what one thinks about and what one does."[18] Following distraction down another of its roads, Cathy N. Davidson underscores its potential relationship not to oppositional interiority but to the outward-oriented efforts of a harmonizing collectivity who get distracted together (if in different ways and by different stimuli) as part of a project of "shar[ing] our perspectives" and "figuring a way out of our own minds."[19] All the same, the imperative to transcend "our own minds," necessary in Davidson's view because of "the way in which *attention* limits our perspectives," presupposes a redefinition of distraction that comes nearer to Urgo's than we might expect on the basis of their otherwise divergent accents and emphases. Davidson proceeds to clarify what precisely she means by *distraction* in a move that resembles Urgo's in its sensitivity to distraction's dance with, rather than severance from, attention:

> One guide to keep in mind—almost a mnemonic or memory device—is that when we *feel* distracted, something's up. Distraction is really another word for saying that something is new, strange, or different. We should pay attention to that feeling. Distraction can help us pinpoint areas where we need to pay more attention, where there is a mismatch between our knee-jerk reactions and what is called for in the situation at hand. If we can think of distraction as an early warning signal, we can become aware

of processes that are normally invisible to us. Becoming aware allows us to either attempt to change the situation or to change our behavior. In the end, distraction is one of the best tools for innovation we have at our disposal—for changing out of one pattern of attention and beginning the process of learning new patterns.[20]

In the abstract, one may wish to affirm the first part of this account that itself affirms openness to the "new, strange, or different," but we must also pay attention to the fact that there is, finally, very little abstraction for Davidson in then identifying distraction as a practical, material "tool . . . for innovation": an innovation, she does not conceal, working blatantly for (in the language of her book's subtitle) corporatized "schools and business for the 21ST century." (Digressive aside: Davidson, a sometime university administrator, was by her own account the object of some criticism and, in her view, misunderstanding when in 2003 she spearheaded an initiative to "g[i]ve a free iPod to every member of the entering first-year class [of Duke University]" with "no conditions.")[21] More politically sympathetic to Urgo's speculation that distraction may fuel resistance to regimes of productivity playing out "in corporate settings" than to Davidson's fantasy of distraction's capture for the vested interests of neoliberal capitalism,[22] I wish nonetheless to refuse any overhasty generalization about how the openness she salutes may be torqued, given the unpredictability and diversity of the hands in which (and the devices with which) that torquing is and will be rendered.

I also wish, building on these two accounts of distraction's redirection of attention, to torque this discussion in its own different direction and highlight a third strategy for approaching, with skepticism, the discreditation of distraction: namely, to discredit in turn elements of that effort by deemphasizing the importance of distraction to our recent historical circumstances and conditions, ones likely misassessed when distraction becomes the privileged marker of the contemporary. (One could also, in step with Jonathan Crary and at a tangent to work on the present and recent past, historicize the fetishization of attention as dominant in "Western modernity since the nineteenth century" and thereby call into question some of the values associated with that—ongoing—fetishization, bound to ideological currents of the 1800s long and deservedly subject to critique.)[23] N. Katherine Hayles, the writer most perspicaciously pursuing this third way in her recent book, How We Think, tackles the literature on distraction, with particular attention to Carr's work, in order to demonstrate the inadequacy of distraction as a central term—let alone the master term—through which to understand our peregrinations as readers, thinkers, and sentient, sensuous beings. In dislodging an emphasis on distraction, she gravitates instead to the words *hyper* and *close/deep*, instructive modifiers both of forms of attention that contemporary subjects experience routinely and of manners of reading associated respectively (though not in perfect identity with) those forms of attention:

> Deep attention is essential for coping with complex phenomena such as mathematical theorems, challenging literary works, and complex musical compositions; hyper attention is useful for its flexibility in switching between different information streams, its quick grasp of the gist of material, and its ability to move rapidly among and between different kinds of texts. As contemporary environments become more information-intensive, it is no surprise that hyper attention (and its associated reading strategy, hyper reading) is growing and that deep attention (and its correlated reading strategy, close reading) is diminishing, particularly among young adults and teens. The problem, as I see it, lies not in hyper attention and hyper reading as such but rather in the challenges the situation presents for parents and educators to ensure that deep attention and close reading continue to be vibrant components of our reading cultures and interact synergistically with the kind of web and hyper reading in which our young people are increasingly immersed.[24]

This measured account of attention and technogenesis ought to seduce readers not only because of its sane tone but also because of the correspondingly sanguine agenda—taking the form of an admirably *focused* pedagogical recommendation—that it entails. Beyond admiring its evenhandedness, Hayles's less distracted (though potentially more digressive) readers may also reflect on a footnote, attending this passage, in which she anatomizes three distinct kinds of attention studied by cognitive psychologists—none of which is nominated by those researchers as *distraction*.[25] One crucial upshot of distraction's depriviledging is to understand how, in Hayles's compelling formulation, "the flood of surveys, books, and articles on the topic of distraction is now so pervasive as to be, well, distracting"[26]—and distracting in particular from other, better ways to conceptualize such phenomena as, indeed, modes of conceptualization.

Pivoting my own conceptualization away from the dichotomy *close/deep* and *hyper* and toward digressiveness stems in part from my reluctance to deploy terms, like these three, that can too easily obscure the fine-grained acts and attitudes that obtain in different reading environments or situations. Though Hayles notes briefly that "skimming, scanning, and pattern identification are likely to occur in all . . . reading strategies" and that "their prevalence in one or another is a matter of scale and emphasis rather than clear-cut boundary," her repeated conjuncture of hyper reading with Web-based hypertexts and of close reading with "typical print" texts runs the risk, despite the care with which she writes, of leaving the misimpression that close reading is synonymous with print reading and hyper reading with screen reading (a misimpression even though and as these synonymities may be statistically likely)—especially when *How We Think* ends up in the page-turning hands or on the Kindles of skimmers and scanners.[27] In short, some subjects skim and scan printed material relentlessly; some readers of digitally mediated material pore over it with care; and the overwhelming conclusion to draw from the abundant literature I have been surveying—even when its authors point us to it unwittingly, and especially when they write most confessionally about their own reading experiences and those of their intimates—is that astonishingly banal criteria that precede the rise of screen reading still (over) determine the occasions on which subjects read in focused versus less focused ways: participation in taste formations (do I "like" this kind of material?), submission to rhetorical tactics and strategies (is the material "grabbing" me?), and acculturation to logics of expectation and sustainability (will it *keep* grabbing me?).

Thus grabbed or not, one kind of reader worthy of further attention, compensating for the paucity of critical literature to this effect, is the one whose mode of engagement can be most profitably understood as digressiveness. In making the move from the digression as step aside discussed in this chapter's introduction (not so different from, and certainly no more complex than, Urgo's redefinition of distraction involving "something aside from . . . something else") to a more multilayered assay on digressiveness as a repeated and repeatable suite of performances, I take a cue from the two critics (again, among a very small number), Anne Cotterill and Jack Undank, who have attended to digressive performance with the most finesse and insight. En route to the close reading of early modern English poets who write with "digressive voices," Coterill identifies four common reasons why "wandering"—following "unexpected turns and byways"—is enabling for the subjects of her study: (1) "step[ping] aside" gives them access to "a deeper, more personal subject"; (2) it likewise provides them with the camouflage, alibi, or plain old métier in which "to defend, to complicate and resist, and to attack" received notions, hegemonic forms of power, and more; (3) they "digress to recollect," that is, "to collect and connect together . . . disparate fragments of experience"; and (4) they enjoy the "life-giving power" of "movement and breath," a syncopated "pause, . . . rest, or delay" in which to experience "the expansive pleasures of variety."[28] Along near lines, though meditating on eighteenth-century incarnations of digressiveness, Undank locates their chief boon (what Cotterill similarly calls "the expansive pleasures of variety") in the "delight" that comes from "profusion, waywardness and circumstantial particularity."[29] More ambitious, as well as more phenomenological (and recalling both Cotterill's lingering on "collect[ing] and connect[ing]" and her invocation of "movement and breath"), he theorizes of digressiveness's "unpredictable linkage[s]," "insist[ing]" (and depending) again and again on "the intake of a new breath," that they constitute "nothing less than the erratic, not entirely irrational movement of perception, pleasure and curiosity—all three continuously bound together in the organic adventure of knowing and telling."[30]

Drawing on, putting together, and moving beyond elements from these rich accounts (as well as looking ahead from early modernity to contemporaneity), I amble toward digressiveness through the trope—and name it as the art—of *strolling*, a keyword through whose consonances I invite you to hear the echoes and think at once of the meanings of (at least) two other terms, *scrolling* ("to move [text displayed on a screen] up or down as if it were on a scroll stretched vertically across the screen," but also "to engross") and *trolling*: the latter a word I nudge here from one recent, unfortunate connotation ("to post a deliberately erroneous or antagonistic message on a newsgroup or similar forum with the intention of eliciting a hostile or corrective response") back to a more robust set of meanings with which it has been associated ("to ramble, saunter, stroll, 'roll'; *spec.* [. . .] to walk the streets, or 'cruise', in search of a sexual encounter"; "to turn over and over, or round and round"; that is, "to turn over in one's mind; to revolve, ponder, contemplate").[31] A cruiser and a (re)turner, propelled by curiosity and pleasure but also contemplation and its convolutions, the digresser comes best to attention as a stroller whose signature movement is—movement, yet not just movement but flexible movement perpetuated, even curated, as praxis. Moreover, that praxis engenders rotations that may also be its (re)collections, an issue to explore further in approaching Diderot's digressive encyclopedism.

Step Back

Some readers may be surprised by my magnetic attraction here to Diderot, given my remarks in the previous chapter on "Cynicism" and the reluctance with which I approached, in my nonetheless sympathetic reading of Stanley, her advocacy of an Enlightenment-inspired, progressive optimism that could be compatible with and translated for contemporary life. Admiring Stanley rather for her insistence on what differentiates contemporary versions of democracy from that of the *philosophes*, I put my reading of her work briefly in dialogue with Adelson's critique of Sloterdjik. That critique is worth revisiting now because of the appropriateness with which she takes him to task for his "striking underestimation of the dark side of Enlightenment, even in the eighteenth and nineteenth centuries," most conspicuously manifesting, on her view, in his total nonmention of Horkheimer and Adorno's *Dialectic of Enlightenment*.[32] Not wishing to be guilty of any similar "omission," in Adelson's phrasing, I turn now to that work with a slightly digressive confession that I was surprised, in my recent rereading of it, to find (an element of the book's 1944/47 preface that I had forgotten) Horkheimer and Adorno briefly saluting "the uncompromising *encyclopédistes*," whose "oppos[ition]" to rightism was sadly compromised when "the apologetic school of Comte usurped the succession" to those *encyclopédistes* and their version of and claim to enlightenment.[33] To note this salutary nod to Diderot and his compatriots is worthwhile in a context in which a further and fuller embrace of Diderot will figure, yet to read that nod as constituting a dichotomous distinction between eighteenth- and nineteenth-century incarnations of Enlightenment would constitute a grievous error: one key thrust of Horkheimer and Adorno's argument (their "petitio principii") is to demonstrate the major ways and extent to which "the self-destruction of enlightenment" was always already a constitutive dimension of the multistranded Enlightenment project.[34]

At the same time, and less digressively relevant to the task at hand, I want to mark a dialectic of Enlightenment—not the one of Horkheimer and Adorno's title—that slithers away from their consideration because of their trenchant focus on enlightenment's dialectical interplay with and cannibalization of the myth that it is supposed to supersede, rendering enlightenment proto-"totalitarian" in its "enslavement of creation," elsewhere called its "sovereignty over existence."[35] To attend single-mindedly to this crucial feature of Enlightenment is to miss another of its features, arguably just as crucial, to which I have already gestured: its digressiveness moving not just alongside but with and through its encyclopedism. For the "ordering mind" of Enlightenment, disposed through order to mastery, "number became [its] canon"—as well, we could add, the knowledge-tree of the encyclopedic hierarchizer—but certain nodes in Enlightenment thinking and textual production could be construed as anticipating this Frankfurt School critique and as containing within them the tools for order and mastery's confounding: not the confounding into myth and irrationality of which Horkheimer and Adorno write—and with that confounding, the opening onto fear and fascism that rightly dismays them—but a confounding through digression and dispersion, and thus potentially (if waywardly and erratically) toward the "freedom in society," the "liberat[ion] from . . . entanglement in blind domination" that provides Horkheimer and Adorno with their guiding principle.[36]

To speculate thus is to align with any number of critics who find, for instance, in Diderot's *contes*, his *Jacques le fataliste*, and similar fictions the unfolding of a "digressive manner," which works as "a frequent refusal" of the ordered "integration, identity, and repose" otherwise animating, indeed "orchestrat[ing]," Enlightenment discourse.[37] My more exceptional claim, extending this line of argumentation in a direction that some of these critics would likely find perverse, is that not just to the side of projects like the *Encyclopédie*, supposed to be sites of "the more rationalizing tendencies of the Enlightenment," but directly within them, as Andrew H. Clark also suggests (though not looking explicitly to the *Encyclopédie*), may we find stunning, shimmering examples of the digressiveness whose "*jouissance*" gives the lie to "technique and science";[38] and, moreover, that this digressiveness, not ornamentally incidental but constitutive to the kind of encyclopedism engendered by their dialectical interplay, saves that encyclopedism—at least in the hands of certain practitioners, most especially Diderot—from the tyrannical aspiration to "denote . . . the total of all knowledge" that we could associate with related historical endeavors like the fashioning of the *Encyclopaedia Britannica*.[39] In so asserting, my effort at "extending [a] line of argumentation," as I call it above, is also and more explicitly an extension of an approach to Diderot's corpus modeled by Thomas M. Kavanaugh, whose close reading of *Jacques le fataliste* gives way to a more or less passing—but revelatory—glance at the *Encyclopédie* that works to deconstruct the opposition between digressive Jacques and the ostensibly "rational," "fixed," and fixing *Encyclopédie*:

> The "lesson" of *Jacques* . . . is that of a limit to our understanding of the world as a rational, preordained universe governed by definable laws of causality. . . . *Jacques* represents, by reason of its meditation on the very form of the "romanesque," what is perhaps Diderot's most eloquent statement as to why he should have undertaken a project so ambitious as that of the *Encyclopédie*. What the reader finally takes away from this novel is an unfettered vision of chaos and indetermination, of a world which is fundamentally recalcitrant to man's attempts to impose upon it his various systems of reason, law and predictability. Only, I would argue, a consciousness so acutely aware of that resistance could formulate the project

of challenging it with so unparalleled a gesture of defiance and affirmation as that of Diderot's attempt, as the very title of his enterprise indicates, to encircle the whole of human knowledge. . . . The entire enterprise of the *Encyclopédie* is meant to initiate a series of innovative confluences within the turbulent flux of human knowledge not as a fixed, predetermined *histoire de ce qu'on savait* but, in the words of Francis Bacon, as the purely future-oriented, always potential *histoire de ce qu'il fallait apprendre*.[40]

What has mitigated most against readings like this one of the *Encyclopédie*'s tenor is the *encyclopédistes*' prominently displayed illustration of a treelike system through which to schematize the branches of human knowledge, as well as a number of d'Alembert's remarks thereupon in the *Encyclopédie*'s "Preliminary Discourse," which challenge any flatness—in the DeLandian sense[41]—that would otherwise be more available to ascribe to the alphabetically and thus arbitrarily arranged, perhaps even rhizomatically deranged, entries that constitute its volumes' assemblages (ones perhaps especially deranged by the work's *renvois*, about which more below). To be sure, d'Alembert's embrace of the tree as a metaphor for the organization of human knowledge is complicated, vexed—and arguably undone—by his introduction in the "Preliminary Discourse" of two other competing metaphors, the labyrinth and the map, through which to understand not the putative, intellective premise for the *Encyclopédie* but rather the material and phenomenal experience of engaging the work. This experience, as David S. Ferris notes, betrays a presumably central principle of the Enlightenment project, its affirmation of a priori reason, if the "disorder produced by [the] discontinuity" of navigating a labyrinth indicates a "movement from direct sense experience to reflection. . . . In short, the experience of the encyclopedia ends up annihilating the image in which its principle of organization is presented. The Enlightenment already appears more problematic the more it reflects on its own promise."[42] Turning with Robert Darnton from d'Alembert's problematizing labyrinth metaphor to his equally problematizing map metaphor—which on Darnton's view discloses not how to diagram the design of the *Encyclopédie* or the assay of its terrain but rather how "no map [can] fix the indeterminate typography of knowledge"— we could likewise conclude that, far from aiming at mastery, the *encyclopédistes* "thought they could limit the domain of the knowable and pin down a *modest* variety of truth. True philosophy taught modesty. It demonstrated that we can know nothing beyond what comes to us from sensation and reflection."[43]

Likewise emphasizing sensation as a condition for reflection in his famous, reflexive *Encyclopédie* entry on the "Encyclopedia"—as we shall see, the forum for the quintessential manifestation of digressiveness's interinanimation with encyclopedism—Diderot takes a step further than displacing the tree metaphor with the labyrinth metaphor. In turn, he displaces that very labyrinth metaphor with another, more attractive one for the encyclopedia as he imagines the sensible (in both senses) subject who strolls its "broad, vast avenue which extends into the distance, along which others are encountered at intervals, leading to remote and isolated objects via the easiest and shortest path."[44] Of the various metaphors that Diderot and his collaborators generated to describe and indeed to conceive the Encyclopédie (and there were many), the "broad, vast avenue" emerges, arguably, as the strongest because of the sheer volume of tropological work that it accomplishes: (1) "Extend[ing] into the distance" and thus conjuring a horizon that has not been reached and, it is intimated, can never be reached, the avenue stands in this extensivity for the "future-oriented, always potential histoire de ce qu'il fallait apprendre" of which Kavanaugh writes—and which Daniel Brewer has more recently named as "the temporality and historicity of knowledge."[45] (2) Evoking strongly the traveler of this avenue, who will encounter a variety of "objects" along the way and who must (to cite immediately prior language from the entry) make "simple," "clear and accessible" connections among those objects—that is, find the best "path" from one to another, however "remote" or "isolated" they may seem—Diderot positions the implied figure of the traveler to stand for the encyclopédiste, collecting and arranging items as well as determining the cross-references or renvois among them; (3) yet that figure of the traveler also stands for the reader of the Encyclopédie, who must similarly take measure of the "intervals" of the work by walking its "avenue" and "encounter[ing]" the side streets along which he will divagate from and return to that avenue.[46] (4) Most metadiscursive, the avenue and its branches stand not just for the Encyclopédie as a massive work with interconnecting parts but also for the one, magisterial part in which the metaphor appears:[47] the "Encyclopedia" entry, which is itself a "broad, vast" essay at over thirty thousand words and in its ambitious ranging over many related topics (the encyclopedia's "possibility, its purpose, its materials, the general and particular ordering of those materials, the style, method, references, nomenclature, the manuscript, the authors, the censors, the editors, and the typographer")—and which, in its highly digressive structure and style, mimes the ostensible spontaneity of the wayward sensational experience, leading to reflection, whereby an investigation of these related topics "came to [Diderot's] mind," and thus redoubles that experience for the reader. (Tellingly, the list of topics that I cite here is one with which Diderot concludes rather than begins the entry, so that we stroll its avenue and streets without a map—a gambit through which he implicitly rejects d'Alembert's map metaphor, however self-undermining that metaphor may already have been, alongside his explicit insistence that the encyclopedia "must not be a tortuous labyrinth").

To investigate further the "Encyclopedia" entry's conjuncture of digressiveness and encyclopedism is work for which this close inspection of the avenue metaphor has, as it were, laid the ground . . . but first, a digression. To reinvoke Darnton's account, Diderot can only advocate the "modest" course and view connoted by the avenue stroll after rejecting a more would-be omniscient and, it is implied, omnipotent version of encyclopedism. In perhaps the most famous and discussed passage of the "Encyclopedia" entry, he says of that rejected way that its effort at completism would pointlessly, if not dangerously, blur the "difference . . . between the reading of an opus in which all the mechanics of the universe were expounded, and study of the universe itself." On this understanding, the universe, figured as a "complicated . . . machine . . . in every sense infinite" and with likewise infinite "connections . . . between its parts," cannot possibly be comprehended in its entirety by the human mind; to attempt as much could only lead to *distraction*, approaching its sense as madness (the attempt would, in Diderot's words, "interrupt the course of our observations, introduce disorder into our readings," and "fragment" "our knowledge"). Better to avoid such distraction by also avoiding the ambition to reproduce mimetically the universe-as-infinite-machine in the design and execution of an encyclopedia; indeed, better to digress in and through an encyclopedia whose form does not aim to approximate the world but only one part of it, satisfying our "curiosity" without overtesting our "impatience": the part construed and constructed as a series of connected roads—akin not to a whole wide world but to a worldlike web (a phrase to unpack further, but not yet, as to do so here would constitute a distraction rather than a valuable digression on a digression).

Within his part of the encyclopedia, Diderot writes with the charm of a digresser who is confident that he can digress from the "broad, vast avenue" onto a side street (and digress from that side-street digression down an alley, where he angles his perspective digressively toward a door) precisely because he is likewise confident that he will always find his way back to the avenue, even if, and better because, the phenomenal experience of the avenue— indeed, the avenue itself—will have changed as a consequence of his straying from and then reengaging its flows. The strategy is one that suffuses the exemplary "Encyclopedia" entry, very near whose opening Diderot introduces a first digression on dictionaries—and within that digression, a digression on childhood (and within that digression on childhood, a digression on luxury items)—through which he begins, slowly, to come back to a general point about the necessity to produce dictionaries collaboratively, which feeds a basic argument about the "mutual beneficence" of "dispersed" but none-theless united encyclopedists. Enacting a similar move later in the essay, Diderot introduces a digression on language (and within it a digression on style: "let it be said in passing" of style . . .), which could be construed as a digression from a digression on an imagined dystopic future in which an encyclopedia like this one would be discovered and would help to enlighten the lost subjects of that other, imagined time. As in the previous example, Diderot endeavors to render the general points about language, style, and what makes them compelling (or not) serviceable to a basic argument about compelling principles for ordering the Encyclopédie ("But after treating . . . language, or the means of communicating knowledge, let us seek the best way of tying it together")—and this endeavor to bring the digression back into dialogue with a theory of encyclopedism leads into the famous passage on the universe-as-machine discussed above. Of that passage, and in the larger context of discussing the "Encyclopedia" entry's sociable, distinctly Diderotian digressiveness as central to the entry's maddening, perhaps not-always-charming charm yet genuine intellective and affective searching ("It is a document of luminous humanity, as well as exasperating vanity"), Philipp Blom asserts that "analysis and contemplation of each given detail" of the machine "can lead to the particular understanding of the whole" machine of which "the human mind" is capable—and "that makes the world what it is" for us.[48] In other words, digressiveness is not just a matter of style but struc-turally enables the fine-grained attention to "each given detail" that fuels "whole"—or at least holistic, modestly encircling—"understanding": that is, encyclopedism. Digressiveness and encyclopedism cocreate what Richard Yeo, in his attention to this entry, calls Diderot's "adventurous browsing."[49]

Yeo's pun on "browsing" is as deliberate as my echo of World Wide Web in the phrase, "worldlike web," as he, like me, seeks to think of Diderotian encyclopedism—and, more broadly, "the idea" of the encyclopedia—in re-lation to such Web phenomena as, for instance, "the increasing power of search engines."[50] In the current case, such thinking becomes crucial, most specifically in this chapter's next section, to theorizing what the Diderotian movement of digressiveness with encyclopedism may clarify about contem-porary modes of networked activity. Yet even more basically, and practically, a reader like me of the Encyclopédie in its online, English translation does well to reflect on the impact of reading this Encyclopédie rather than some other and to mark that close analyses like mine of the "Encyclopedia" entry are calcined in a Web crucible. Following Philippe Roger and Robert Morrissey when they assert that (in her paraphrase) "the virtual *Encyclopédie* would limit the circulatory freedom and subversive readings that Diderot and d'Alembert sought to facilitate," Joanna Stalnaker wonders whether "virtual readings of the *Encyclopédie* do not force us to grapple with the gargantuan proportions of the work, or with its evolution over time. By appearing to cut through the mass and reveal the underlying systems of human knowledge that structure the *Encyclopédie*, virtual readings thus mask the difficulties Diderot experienced both as an editor and as a describer."[51] While I do not wish in any way to discount the sensuous materiality of the *Encyclopédie* as a multivolume print work or the effect that this materiality has on phenomenal apprehensions of its words, I question the ease whereby Roger, Morrissey, and Stalnaker contrast that materiality with what they deem the "virtual[ity]" of Web-based versions of those words; for reading the *Encyclopédie* on a screen constitutes every bit as much, if differently coordinated and registered, an embodied experience of the material world as does book reading. And far from "cut[ting] through the mass," online readers are confronted quite powerfully with a mass of Web pages, hyperlinks that reproduce the *Encyclopédie*'s *renvois*, and yet further links specific to incarnating the work for the Web,[52] which do not in some unilateral way "reveal the underlying systems of human knowledge that"—supposedly—"structure the *Encyclopédie*" but may rather amplify the sense of the philosophical "difficulties" with which Diderot grappled and that I illustrate in my accounts of the avenue and machine metaphors.

While I also don't wish to endorse any strictly instrumental value in reading the *Encyclopédie*, I find it worth questioning the ends to which these critics imagine that print-based and so-called virtual encounters with its text(s) will be routed, for they are implicitly indicating such ends when they worry that readers of the University of Chicago's "ARTFL" version of the *Encyclopédie* (with which the University of Michigan's Collaborative Translation Project is closely allied) will somehow be badly led astray—rather than led astray well, which would seem to mean on a model of "circulatory freedom and subversive reading" of whose bona fide subversion and freedom these scholars have, with heavy and unintended irony, appointed themselves the guardians. Whatever perceptive-cum-interpretive scenarios they imagine—and worry that they cannot pedagogically guide—the fact that they cannot guide them is itself worth underlining, by way of complicating. A reader sitting in an archive to look at volume 5 of the *Encyclopédie* as published in Paris in 1755 may for instance catch—or miss, just as a screen reader of the Collaborative Translation Project may for instance notice or pass by, Diderot's complex claim about the ontological status of "beings" (as "subversive" as it gets in its treatment of the "circulatory" relations among such beings, including ipso facto readers and their encyclopedias):

> The universe offers us only individual beings, infinite in number, and virtually lacking any fixed and definitive division; there is none which one can call either the first or the last; everything is connected and progresses by imperceptible shadings; and if throughout this uniform immensity of objects, some appear, which like the tips of rocks seem to break through the surface and rise above it, they owe this prerogative only to particular systems, vague conventions, certain unrelated events, and not to the physical arrangement of beings and to nature's intention. *See* the Prospectus.[53]

If ever there were an elegant and vivid explanation of DeLandian flat ontology avant la lettre (like the "tips of rocks" whose "break[ing] through the surface" of the "immensity" is not "certain" or predictable, an earlier footnote about this philosophical concept is one that may or may not have "rise[n]" for you), the first sentence quoted here is it. Readers may or may not subscribe to this flat ontology; indeed, my own attitude toward its (non?) reckoning with what Lauren Berlant calls "ordinary hard hierarchy" is agnostic.[54] Yet contemporary subjects, whatever their obligation to understand how "eighteenth-century readers [did and] did not consult the *Encyclopédie*" (and that obligation may be deemed significant),[55] will very likely and very well ought to think of the Web itself when onscreen they read the words, "Everything is connected and progresses by imperceptible shadings," then wonder to what extent this flat ontology describes their media environments and the worlds that those environments help to constitute. If so disposed, some of those metareaders will hopefully exert intellectual pressure on what the putative connectivity of "everything" could mean (and conceal from rising to meaning) in a networked ecology, as well as on how "imperceptible" or not the movements enabled by connectivity turn out to be. Certainly, some of those readers will wish to "progress . . . by" clicking a hyperlink to the Prospectus—only in its absence to discover, if they click rather on links to editorial notes, that the 1750 Prospectus to the *Encyclopédie* is not part of the Collaborative Translation Project . . . and will aim then to find it elsewhere online via searches and links beyond this site. However erratic or orderly the navigation of these links may be from case to case, such links are a key element in assessing the explanatory force with which Diderotian digressiveness may speak to Web forays.

Stepchild

Just as I write above of Diderot's theory of being as flat ontology avant la lettre, so, too, have the *Encyclopédie*'s *renvois* been recently invoked as a prototype for hyperlinks—but only after at least two earlier generations of scholars have looked to the past for other practices through which to metaphorize this particularly attention-drawing feature of hypertext. Indeed, to consider what is old about and to put pressure on the newness of so-called new media are intellective moves as old as *new media* itself. These moves, as well as the larger critical conversation of which they form a part, are insightfully summarized and interpreted in Wendy Hui Kyong Chun's introduction to *New Media, Old Media*, an anthology that adds powerfully to that critical conversation.[56] Among other insights, Chun writes of the caution that scholars of emergent media must take when making transhistorical claims about media, not because "no overarching argument can ever be made about mediums or media" but rather because "any such argument" would do well to contend "with the ways that mediums have changed, rather than concentrating" more singularly "on the remarkable yet overdetermined similarities between entities now considered media."[57] I read this advice in implicit dialogue with Wolfgang Ernst's parsing of the differences between two dominant approaches to media studies—media history, which privileges "continuity against the experience of ruptures," and media archaeology, which "insists on differences"[58]—and wonder whether a method rooted in cultural studies could, along the lines that Chun indicates, find a third way that acknowledges the ruptures in continuity or insists on the similarities that inhere in differences. More specifically, I mean to signal my attunement to the possibility of finding this third way when I call this chapter section, "Stepchild," a deliberately attenuated genealogical metaphor with which to think the relationship between the Diderotian and the Webby. In pursuing what lines of descent may link one medium and attendant knowledge formation to another, care may be registered by the modification of the *step-*, announcing the manner in which the discerned lines of descent result from epi- and techno-genetic workings more like the inputs and outputs of a marriage act than of a parental bearing. Moreover, we cultural critics ourselves have a role in performing such "marriages" by discerning, and declaring our discernment of, the lines of descent in question. The hyperlink, for instance, is more fully the *renvois*'s descendant when a critic intervenes—steps in, as it were—to identify the relationship than when that relationship remains (im)potential.

But first, there is the footnote. As Peter Krapp observes, early theorists (some of them enthusiasts for what they took to be the radical possibilities) of hypertext, including Jacob Nielsen, Norbert Bolz, and Friedrich Kittler, follow Theodor Nelson, "who coined the term [hypertext] in 1963," in conceptualizing the hyperlink through the master metaphor of the footnote.[59] Taking this move to have been a less than thoroughly reflective absorbing of Nelson's proposition—and proposing in turn that "if one were to maintain a truly innovative character of hyptertext, a more promising model might be the database"—Krapp names the card of the card index, in place of the footnote, as the more appropriate precursor (one whose anachronism he avows) and metaphor for the hyperlink.[60] In yet another turn of the screw, Michael Zimmer's account of the "hyperlinked text" and its "long history" proposes not the card index but the encyclopedic *renvois* or cross-reference, often used by the *encyclopédistes* (and by Diderot in particular) to subversive ends, as the best "antecedent" for the hyperlink, which to a limited extent has already been activated—and could, in Zimmer's utopic vision, be yet further activated—to perform as *renvois* do when they "defer . . . absolute meaning or knowledge to another article, often leading to unsettling juxtapositions and unexpected meanings that force . . . the reader to think anew."[61] Responding to this work, I admire Zimmer's genealogy in particular for the way in which it may be used to situate the faulty encyclopedic *renvois* as the precursor for the broken Web link.[62] Likewise, I admire Krapp's account in general for the reflexivity with which, in Chun's reading, he understands the move to "turn much of what new media has supposedly superseded into new media *avant la lettre*" as "*the symptom of new media*" (but one through which he can nonetheless generate insight and value).[63] At the same time, Krapp and Zimmer both repeat the essential—and questionable—strategy of prior critics like Nielsen and Kittler in their insistence on one master metaphor through which to understand better the phenomenon of hyperlinking. The attraction to the strategy is understandable even as it is questionable: the hyperlink simultaneously invites (because of its resemblance to and adaptations of older modalities for a newer set of contexts) and resists (in part because of the evolving ecologies in which it is situated) reducibility to such master-metaphorization.

What if instead one were to look for a deliberately, paradoxically *weak* "master" metaphor not only for the hyperlink but also for the hyperlink's combination of courting and rejecting metaphorization? With an eye to the earlier discussion of Diderotian strolling and ahead to a further stroll back to strolling, I propose that the metaphor might come in the form of the *footstep*. Each critic cited above is taking a footstep, venturing elsewhere ("Thinking means venturing beyond," as Ernst Bloch has it);[64] and each hyperlink could likewise be understood as a modest footstep, a metaphor that recalls Darnton's leaning on the *encyclopédistes'* own modest reckoning with plural, nonuniversal truths. The footstep metaphor also answers Collin Gifford Brooke's call to think simultaneously about the matter and the manner of hyperlinking:[65] though the weight in the earlier metaphors for hyperlinks rests in the nominal part of each semantic formation (foot*note*, *card* index, cross-*reference*), we may in turn, and in an obverse way, look to what those metaphors commonly disclose about movement (*foot*note, card *index*, *cross*-reference). In so doing, we may see how the idea of the footstep was already present to these writers' thinking and was waiting, like a hyperlink that had yet to be clicked, to be pursued in the trajectory of further inquiry—an inquiry responsive to Dave Ciccoricco's urging that scholars work against the misleading emphasis on spatiality in many accounts of hypertextuality and turn instead to the mobility and temporality central to navigating hypertextual ecologies.[66] And, to take one more step in thinking about the footstep: one can't know precisely in advance the size, direction, or speed that any footstep will take, as with hyperlinks and as with the theorization of hyperlinks (some theorists look—step—backward, some forward, some sideways to cite precedents, tweak existing accounts, imagine utopias; in the process, some make more imaginative "leaps"—on occasion stretching credulity—than others).

If I foreground modesty, movement, and uncertainty—all key elements of Diderot's digressive stroll into encyclopedism—as I liken or link the hyperlink to the footstep, I do so in part because it would be irresponsible to make grander claims (recalling Stalnaker's language) about how subversive or freeing any circulatory, even digressively circulatory, navigation of the Web may be(come); and to say as much is not new or news but simply to recall a chorus of important voices, Alexander R. Galloway's perhaps most prominent among them, about how, in very material terms, the Web has ever been thus in colliding possibility with constraint. (And indeed the *Encyclopédie* before it, and in certain ways [un]like it, opened onto some exciting readerly and intellective experiences precisely by foreclosing others.) In step with Ernst's reminder that "world-wide order and hierarchies in current hypertext programming languages . . . oppose . . . fluidity,"[67] as well as with Tara McPherson's meditation on the extent to which most experience is still linear and unidirectional online and restrictively directed to serve the interests of corporate capital,[68] Galloway historicizes these issues: "*Control has existed from the beginning*," he literally emphasizes as he traces the manner in which network protocols that adistribute organization depend in the first place on protocols that "focus [it] into rigidly defined hierarchies." The resulting, "generative contradiction that lies at the very heart of protocol is that *in order to be politically progressive, protocol must be partially reactionary.*"[69] As a consequence, and as Alan Liu intimates through his close inspection of the "the inter-network of the Internet" that "only developers" or "programmers" engage, the statistical lion's share of subjects may be able (to return to a key term for the present inquiry) only to digress so much, so far, or so deep given the inherent limitations placed on those subjects' experiences of the Internet on which the Web is built, as well as more mundanely of the Web itself.[70]

Questions about practice, policy, and futurity are raised by these imbricated scholarly insights. For her part, McPherson asserts that her "hope [is] not entirely foreclosed by corporate rhetoric";[71] and perhaps that hope is not foreclosed because, like Zimmer, she (and we) may look away from corporate rhetoric or structures and toward still-emerging developments in "the semantic web and the growing use of folksonomies online," which may "allow . . . readers to relinquish their position as passive receivers of pre-organized information, to subvert traditional knowledge structures and hierarchies and to become active and integral participants in the production of knowledge."[72] Alongside these important speculations about what comes next, I still feel the freight of history, the drag of memory, and wonder further about what has come (online) before. Training her view on just these networked pasts—and the bizarre forms of persistence with which they inhabit the present—Chun, describing the bizarreness through the paradox of the "enduring ephemeral" (as well as undoing a persistent, semantic, and damaging conflation of *memory* and *storage*), raises some "pressing questions": "Why and how is it that the ephemeral endures? And what does the constant repetition and regeneration of information effect? What loops and what instabilities does it introduce into the logic of programmability?"[73] These questions come on the heels of her account of the rapidity with which blogs tend to be produced and consumed—yet the questions also attend her attempt to topple the "dictatorship of speed" in new media studies because of how suspectly this dictatorship "can blind us to the ways in which images do not simply assault us at the speed of light."[74] Thus to address Chun's genuinely open-ended questions may benefit from slowing down to revisit the "old" "new" blogs that would seem to have grown stale but that have the capacity to instruct us precisely because of the complex ways in which they have outlasted their ostensible shelf lives. As a blog that in its own, distinctive way revisits "new" "old" material, Rich Juzwiak's *fourfour* offers one key site through an exploration of which to produce this address, as well as to revisit—and remix—our sense of the digressive / encyclopedic dialectic.

Step Up; or "Touched for the Very Second Time"

On the one hand, Juzwiak's *fourfour* (2005–12) is a typical Web 2.0 blog, resembling what Aimée Morrison calls the vast "middle ground" of blogs that have appeared since the watershed year 2004 (when Merriam-Webster named *blog* its word of the year and when the blogosphere's readership spiked almost 60 percent): at a formal level, these middle-ground, composite blogs hybridize aspects of notebook or filter blogs (efforts increasingly professionalized and corporately sponsored in the 2.0 era) and of personally inflected, diaristically oriented blogs; and at a structural level, they incorporate hyperlinks to external sites, permalinks, trackbacks, blogrolls, posting functionality for readers' comments, and browsable categories with which entries are tagged and by which they are organized, often in a column on the right side of the screen that mirrors the blogroll on the left.[75] On the other hand, Juzwiak, a professionally trained journalist freelancing prominently and staff-writing for VH1.com at the time that he launched *fourfour*, has enjoyed atypical success and attention and become, in the words of one recent assessor, "that rare thing: a respected Internet presence";[76] and the blog itself, even as it uses a generic Typepad template into which to incorporate its texts, images, and soundtracks, became audiovisually distinctive for its featuring of "supercuts," a Web genre that Juzwiak helped to pioneer and popularize when his 2008 video, "I'm Not Here to Make Friends," among the very first supercuts to be produced, "stitched together a full 3 minutes and 20 seconds of reality show contestants exclaiming, 'I'm not here to make friends' or variations thereof" and, in its deft skewering of banality, cynicism, and cliché, was "the first supercut to go super-viral."[77] Hovering somewhere between typicality (in its indebtedness to *Television without Pity* and other forums that preceded *fourfour* in the generation of television episode recapping as a genre) and atypicality (because of Juzwiak's pointed and eccentric approach to the genre's development),[78] *fourfour* is arguably most famous and certainly attracted its biggest following for Juzwiak's hilarious, poignant, and highly idiosyncratic recaps of over ten full cycles of the competitive reality series *America's Next Top Model*. These recaps constitute a relentless effort to stay in lockstep with the speedily, contemporaneously produced television series, an ambition for the blog that Juzwiak couldn't have anticipated fulfilling when, in its opening

5.1 Journalist Rich Juzwiak and his blog *fourfour* became famous for his pioneering efforts in "supercutting" reality television segments.

salvo, he declared that it would provide a forum for returning to "old" savors rather than for generating coverage of the "new" material that would, in fact, vie increasingly for space in the blog:

> I intend fourfour to be a collection of my interests, particularly of the pop-culture sort, specifically those of the musical variety and especially that which has the 4/4 stomp. My baby girl's name is house music (the post-acid period of '89-'94 is my fav), but I love disco almost as much. My taste doesn't stop there (I'm an avid fan of electronic music, including contemporary R&B, in particular). But my main intention with fourfour is to write about and share things the ever-snappy world of musical journalism deems too old to cover (i.e. EVERYTHING), since I frequently get my timeliness on in print (via MAGNET, BUST and The Miami New Times, among places). In addition to my words, I'll be posting MP3s and, whenever I can get my shit together, my own vinyl mixes.[79]

In a lovely condensation of figures and ideas, this introductory gambit positions the blog's name not only as an allusion to a musical rhythm but also as a synecdoche for an set of expressive styles, the ethos that they conjure, and their putative superannuation: that is, a trope for a predigital, pre(-post)-postmodern feel—but one that can be reactivated in new ways via technologies like the MP3 format, a container for a practice of remixing that nonetheless inheres in vinyl's (literal and other) grooves.[80]

More capacious in its reach than its stricter usage in the realms of DJing may suggest, *remixing* offers a compelling analytic through which to understand the "mixed" cultural work that Juzwiak performs—not just in producing the tracks that he labels explicitly as mixes or remixes, but also in the creation of supercuts that position audiovisual material anew in the service of critique; of recaps that comment wryly on their source episodes (and beyond wryly, bordering on the fantastical); of screen captures and their moving GIF counterparts, which accompany recaps and which, in their unusual arrests or slowed, repetitive animations, make the images more "hypnotizing" than in their original television contexts;[81] of reframings of other sites that Juzwiak lists in cheeky categories and not merely alphabetically in the blogroll on the left side of his site's pages; of allusive language that is almost but not quite quoted in titles for entries (as in, "Touched for the Very Second Time," which I borrow from an entry title to give this chapter section part of its own title, which rings a promiscuous change on lyrics from Madonna's "Like a Virgin"[82]—and which furnishes a nice gloss on the art of remixing itself). To be sure, other terms and phrases could be enlisted to understand this assortment of elements and their relationships to one another (*resignification* and *repetition with difference* come readily to mind, as does *parody* in its broad (re)definition by Linda Hutcheon),[83] but I incline rather to remixing for two key reasons.

First, remixing retains the sexual and racial specificities of Juzwiak's project and the histories that it carries forward, given the centrality of DJs' remixes to the predominantly queer disco and house music cultures and to the predominantly African-American hip hop cultures that, in his allegiance to them, animate Juzwiak's initial desire to blog: cultures, moreover, that have often been thought as separate and even inimical to each other but that, as Tim Lawrence charts so thoughtfully, have informed, overlapped with, and sometimes tenderly regarded each other over the course of their evolutions.[84] As a fan of all three musics (and more, including the "contemporary R&B" that he cites in his first blog post), Juzwiak writes personally driven music criticism that manifests such criss-crossing—and, more provocatively, incarnates that criss-crossing through the risky disidentification with whiteness (measured in part in stylistic gestures and lexical borrowings from vernaculars associated chiefly with African-American life) that fuels his self-identification as queer. Following Dagmawi Woubshet's careful assessment of Keith Haring's work, I would assert that Juzwiak performs, with a slightly different historical inflection, a version of Haring's "reiterated disidentifications with whiteness, which enabled him to hone a . . . vernacular largely inspired by

5.2 The magic of the remix marks *fourfour*'s recaps of *America's Next Top Model* installments.

the budding hip hop culture of the late 1970s and early '80s"—with Juzwiak largely taking up instead hip hop (and other) musics of the late 1980s and early 1990s. And like Haring, Juzwiak does not "succumb to easy white exploitation and appropriation of that art" but rather "*sees* race, recognizes the blinding power of race," in a way that enables him to "begin to identify with African American culture and life."[85] Moreover, Juzwiak extends this vision from his occasional entries about music to his more sustained recaps of *America's Next Top Model*, a series that, in Mary Thompson's sound evaluation, "participates in emerging, neoliberal understandings of racial and gendered identities, which, characterized by a hegemonic postfeminist and postrace worldview, obscure the operating of privilege in . . . young women's 'choices' of how and when to perform their ethnicities."[86] In working thus, ANTM, an "older" television product made in the moment of television's powerful convergence with Web 2.0, manifests the racialized logics that Lisa Nakamura identifies as guiding many mass cultural efforts of the early 2000s (including "televisual" music videos that circulate mostly online): efforts that "sell . . .

multiple ways of seeing and surveilling that are framed as exactly that, exploiting the [Web or allied] interface as a visual culture that purveys an ideal and mutable female body of color, perpetually and restlessly shifting 'just in time' to meet fickle audience preferences."[87] Painfully aware of the ways in which, for instance, the ostensibly "mutable female bod[ies] of color" that appear on ANTM are performing not "optional" but highly constrained versions of fetishized race, normative beauty, neoliberal competitiveness, and their coconstitution, Juzwiak champions the often assailed yet fascinating contestants of color (especially as they fail to become champions in the reality competition) *as* contestants of color and thus marks what ANTM would wish to leave unmarked: the extent to which race, however historically constructed and changeable its categories, sticks to certain subjects more than others. In this way—and, along the way, hilariously excoriating the series for related blindnesses and opacities—Juzwiak (re)mixes ANTM in the "obsolete" and "poetic" sense that the OED identifies with the term: "meet[ing]" the marginalized in a series of "glances" that figures a form of "clasp[ing] hands" with them,[88] he "*sees* race, recognizes the blinding power of race," in order to touch, in turn, his blog's readers with that recognition.

To claim as much about Juzwiak's navigation of racialization is to suppose that he is not (merely), as a white gay man fascinated by displays of black femininity, appropriating that femininity for a project of queer (re)self-fashioning. And to meditate on these issues with reference to a blogger feels particularly freighted after the going viral in summer 2014 of then-college senior Sierra Mannie's essay, "Dear White Gays: Stop Stealing Black Female Culture,"[89] which incited a wide array of largely well-meaning, if, as Aaron C. Thomas correctly diagnoses, also largely unhelpful and reductive responses in the blogosphere.[90] To digress away from this distracting discourse, we may more valuably revisit Brian Currid's now twenty-year-old but still fresh and timely essay on the complex knotting together of racialized, gendered, and sexualized subjectivations in the scenes of house music's circulation, with particular attention paid to the club dance floor. Ideology critique, and what is—usefully—tautological about its approach to understanding culture is a necessary part of the mix, in Currid's view (say, of the dance floor), yet so too is a remixing that torques away from the lessons of such critique and toward the manner in which club scenes produce "fields . . . of . . . unstable oscillation, whereby the [black] diva becomes spectacle to the queer boy spectator, but simultaneously the very spectatorship of the queer boy can be reinterpreted as spectacular."[91] An interpretation very like this one could animate our sense of *fourfour*, where Juzwiak's disidentification with whiteness is neither an unmarking or rendering invisible of that whiteness nor a simple theft of blackness but a making "spectacular"—and an aggressively reflexive making spectacular—of his own embodied positionality, which he literally images (with photographs) and underlines (with captions) in winking ways, avowing his implantation in a social grid that binds together such subjects as viewer-writers and contestant-performers in messy, "unstable oscillation."

As the uptake of Currid and the coconsideration of the optic and the haptic begin to intimate, a second reason to route the present ruminations through the rubric of remixing stems from the impact with which remixing may underscore, because of its turntable associations with scratching and spinning, the tactile—and not simply verbal and visual—work that Juzwiak performs as a blogger. This tactility is a quality of Juzwiak's cultural work toward which the blog itself otherwise points, as it were, in its repeated textual and imagistic emphases on hands and their motions: repetitions bordering in their frequency on an obsessive fixation. To name just a few of many examples (alongside the riff on Madonna, "Touched for the Very Second Time," already identified above), we may consider (1) Juzwiak's pithy yet multireferential answer to Typepad's call, "About Me": "One-Line Bio: I can't even thread a needle," to which he adds, "New rule: If you say, 'You have a lot of time on your hands,' to someone who's creating things, you have to prove what you've done with your life so far" (about which, more below);[92] (2) the suggestive titles of posts, including, "Hands Off" and "Finger and Mouth Exercises"; (3) the yet more suggestive meditations within such posts on others' hands (is their largeness uncanny?) and fingers (do they look like penises?); and (4) reflexive and allusive equations of his blogging practice with (other) forms of manual work ("and knitting, and knitting . . .").[93] One mundane—but for that, no less touching—reason why Juzwiak may not be able to get hands off his mind (and vice versa) is surely to be found in his suffering from carpal tunnel syndrome: a particularly unfortunate condition for a writer whose vocation and related avocations demand that he bang away on his computer keyboard for extended periods of time—and one to which Juzwiak himself calls conspicuous attention in a series of notes appended to an ANTM recap that was judged by fans to appear "late":

(Note: I will be recapping, to whatever extent, the clips show that aired after this episode. That should be up on Monday. . . .

(Note 2: ~~I don't mean to sound like an asshole, because I appreciate being appreciated, but seriously, y'all, get off my dick.~~ I never post recaps before Friday morning because ~~it takes that much time to generate them. Sad, I know, but my carpal tunnel~~

can attest to that being true. I work as fast as I can, and really, I'm the only source of pressure that I need. I don't go out on Thursdays *ever* because of this shit and I really, really don't need people breathing down my neck and getting all, "Jet-SON!!!" on me. Pissing me off slows me down. Even though I know that asking where the recap is comes from a place of love, it sounds pretty fucking rude from over here. Thank you for understanding.)

(**Note 3:** In retrospect, the note above seems too cantankerous. The last thing I want to come across as is an ingrate. "Oh, poor me! People want to read what I have to say! What will I ever do?" That's gross. Anyway, just rest assured that, as Joanie might say, the fire I have lit under my own ass burns the midnight oil.)[94]

Wishing ambivalently both to retract and to let stand writing about the physical tolls of his labor that "seems too cantankerous," Juzwiak takes the measure of a larger, more diffuse ambivalence about the competing calls of work and play—or, rather, the hopeless blurring of the two for the cultural workers that the information economy hails, in one of neoliberalism's signature examples of zombie-speak, as "content creators." More basically, yet with complex implications to be unpacked further, the notes bring boldly into view how fundamentally Juzwiak's remixing entails digitization meeting digitation: his artistic handiwork is also artisanal handwork.

To remark as much is also to gesture toward the ways in which work, like Juzwiak's, of taste (re)making, is also a form of tact-negotiating (the latter a matter highlighted in the care with which he aims to handle, as it were, his readers in "Note 3" above): that is, to comprehend, with critics like Laurent Milesi (in a reading of Derrida on Nancy), "how touch as proximity and auto-affection (that of a *se toucher* . . .) connects with taste."[95] Juzwiak also intuits this "connect[ion]" when he cites seamstress Molly Abrams's memorably tasteless line in *Showgirls*, "I can't even thread a needle" (the result, it is implied in the film, of excessive masturbation) as an autodescription that touches with shameless insouciance on autoaffection. Yet the shameless and the shameful—or at least the anticipatorily defensive—go hand in hand when Juzwiak, adapting a rhetorical device from television's *Real Time with Bill Maher*, appends the "New Rule" that he shouldn't be judged as a narcissist with too much "time on" (and self in) his "hands." Taken together, the opposed statements prompt tricky questions: Is blogging a masturbatory exercise in solipsism or a valuable form of "creating things" for others' pleasure and instruction; an indulgence in bad taste touching *Showgirls*' own or a refinement thereupon because of the remixing—the re-flexing—with which the avowal of bad taste is rendered? Juzwiak's "About Me" only poses rather than answers these questions, but the blog, experienced cumulatively and over time, suggest that "bad" taste—the kind, say, that would prompt a blogger to recap ANTM obsessively—may be touching, may touch others, precisely because of the ways in which that taste is anatomized: namely, in an ongoing camp maneuver whose relationship to temporality, indeed to what Chun calls the "enduring ephemeral," needs to be considered further. Yet the maneuver, far from delimited to its camp dimensions, may also touch others because of what it discloses poignantly about capital, of whose relationship to texture and touch Renu Bora has written so thoughtfully:

> Glimmering smoothness seems linked to a TEXXTURE that is quite mysterious, both of which textural properties will seem to make gold fetishistic in the commodity sense. I argue this to identify the perception of its value, without engaging whether Marx's labor theory is wrong or should be changed. Even more complicated, the shine of manufactured products (gold might be included), because they are dazzling and often produced by assembly lines or machines, marks commodity fetishes because such products have little trace of manual (social) labor/production process in them, no Benjaminian aura. There are dialectics here of a fractal order, of smoothness/roughness, of shine/color, of gleam/volume, where the former term must scintillate to erupt from the latter. In fact, the very maintenance of these valorized material properties and the ideology of the new, the white, the smooth, the shiny, the clean, can involve a ritualistic fetishism where the distinction between production and consumption might be encapsulated by the concept of reproduction.[96]

Computers are the new gold. And what the hand of carpal tunnel syndrome's sufferer, coming into contact with the hard, shiny keyboard, feels—and has the potential to reveal, sensibly and sensuously to others—is the toll of productive labor. It is a toll that commodities like smooth, gleaming computers tend to occlude in their capacities not just as the vehicles for our practices and patterns of consumption but as the reified totems or idols, the fetishes, of such consumption. (It is also a toll occluded from dewily celebratory and naïve accounts, like Clay Shirky's in *Cognitive Surplus*, to which this reading is opposed, of how Web-based projects demonstrate the expenditure of supposedly abundant, somehow globally shared "free time.")[97] As a "manual (social) labor[er]" who is also a remixer or re-producer, working at the site "where the distinction between production and consumption" becomes blurred (*smudged* might be better), Juzwiak doesn't merely "maint[ain] . . . the . . . valoriz[ation] [of] material properties" like newness, shininess, and whiteness; rather, and precisely because he is an agential re-producer—not a passive avatar of an ideology of reproduction, in Bora's sense—his blog brings into view and into hand the "roughness" (both "rough" or unpolished work, televisual and meta-televisual, done quickly and the "rough" abrasions with which it marks cultural workers), the "volume" (of material churned out in this rough manner), and the "color" (of nonwhite subjects, often spat out of the machinery that uses them in the churning out of such rough work) that could all too easily disappear and, in so disappearing, fail to touch us.

And with that rhetorical touch, I must come here to the end of a lengthy digression; for how else to characterize these pages on *fourfour* that have veered away from, rather than toward, the "pressing questions" in their relationship to digressiveness and encyclopedism whose engagement I promised at the end of this chapter's last section? Yet, just as Diderot's digressions on dictionaries and style, for instance, became structurally necessary to the eccentric version of encyclopedism that he produced—and that, in the process, he theorized—so, too, has this digressive consideration of Juzwiak's remixing and its haptics constituted a nonincidental precondition for what (and how) I can know in turn. Regarding such knowing, I might just as well have written above of "what the hand knows" as of "what the hand feels"— inseparable matters of inquiry in Vivian Sobchack's phenomelogical-cum-epistemological project of theorizing the "cinesthetic subject" in her essay, "What My Fingers Knew":

> Our vision is always already "fleshed out"—and even at the movies it is "in-formed" and given meaning by our other sensory means of access to the world: our capacity not only to hear, but also to touch, to smell, to taste, and always to proprioceptively feel our dimension and movement in the world. In sum, the film experience is meaningful *not to the side of my body, but because of my body.*
>
> Here, in an attempt not only to acknowledge but also to explicate the way in which the cinema is somatically intelligible and, moreover, richly meaningful in this register, I want to alter the binary structure suggested by previous formulations and, instead, posit the film viewer's lived body as a carnal "third term" that chiasmatically mediates vision and language, experience and image.[98]

In response to this enlivening account, we might ask what happens when one is not "at the movies" but otherwise sensuously engaging "vision and language" in their form as moving "image": what happens, that is (for instance), when a television recapper working a deadline watches moving images on television and has "carnal" thoughts about them in the way that Sobchack describes—and then *remixes* those carnal thoughts in an equally embodied way, quite closely on the heels of experiencing those moving images . . . or sometimes remixes those moving images *while* experiencing them for the first time in real time, and so forth? These versions of "cinesthetic" experience, with their greater haptic portion, are arguably fuller and more amplified than the one "at the movies"—more *encyclopedic*—because of what the fingers punch (typing) or grab (screen capturing); at the same time, these experiences are more diffused or dispersed—more *digressive*, in their way—because of the sheer number of bodily zones that are aggressively and not just "chiasmatically" activated. In other words, haptic remixing *is* (one key part of) Juzwiak's contemporary, media-specific version of digressive encyclopedism.

This much in the name of difference: and as for sameness? For there are powerful resonances that invite an examination of the ways in which Juzwiak's digressive encyclopedism touches (perhaps queerly, and perhaps queerly in Carolyn Dinshaw's sense) Diderot's, even as his blogging departs picquantly from the norms and standards that Diderot affirms in his *Encyclopédie* entry for "Journalist."[99] For one thing, the two writers share a penchant for digressiveness enacted both at the level of style and at the level of structure. In Juzwiak's case, the ANTM recap, "Bre's on Down the Road," provides a paradigmatic example, moving digressively through a series of "And now"s and "And then"s away from the "point" of the episode, as he understands it—and metacommenting on the digressiveness along the way—only for that "point" to emerge as one discernible precisely because of the manner in which the paratactic digressions accreted, encyclopedically charting the episode's own movements, and because of the matter toward which they thereby pointed.[100] (To boot, the recap's Wiz-allusive title also conjures the roads, streets, and avenues down which Diderot strolls breezily.) For another thing, recaps of television episodes are like the *Encyclopédie*'s much-celebrated (and critiqued) articles on machines and machinic processes. Almost always, readers of both don't have the original, technical objects and processes at hand but rather confront digressive essays to which other elements are complexly stitched (*Encyclopédie* texts plus plates; blog texts plus captures, GIFs, and MP3s)—and to which those readers have to respond with their own, likely digressive comprehensions. (It may also be the case that television recaps, like *Encyclopédie* accounts of machines and the occupations they serve, "shift. . . the balance" of cultural commentary "away from the . . . great towards humble, often anonymous, manual work.")[101] And for yet another, most sobering thing, Diderot, once "the *Encyclopédie* was finished and published, . . . looked back on all the years of work with . . . bitterness and disappointment" because of his conviction that he "wasted his life on a work he now considered almost entirely bad"—in this anticipating the "bitterness and disappointment" similarly suffusing Juzwiak's renunciation of his work on ANTM, "Tune In, Recap, Drop Out: Why I'll Never Recap a TV Show Again" (a piece written for *Gawker*, where in 2012 Juzwiak secured a position as a staff writer largely on the basis of the quality and popularity of his—since arrested—blog):

> I'll never stop writing about tv. I'll never get over my love of minutiae and I'll never stop attempting to capture and describe the bigger picture. Recapping found me reveling in the former and unable to focus on the latter. It made me an unbalanced writer. The grind's minor rewards do not outweigh its burden.
>
> I cannot deny that my recapping built me an audience and had a hand in career opportunities. I always said that I worked so much on my blog, eschewing socializing on weeknights, because I preferred to have something to show for my time. My archives haven't gone anywhere, and while the idea of them is soothing, the actual contents are not. Those thousands and thousands of words I wrote are largely meaningless, pulled away from whatever significance they had by the tides of time. This is what it feels like from the rocks, beaten by my beat.[102]

The resignation and weariness in this account palpate on my ear drum—but I also hear the persistent "beat" of the "4/4 stomp" underneath the "beaten" declaration, the siren call to revisit *fourfour* and see, hear, and touch in it something that Juzwiak can't when he equates the "actual contents" of the blog, rather, with nothing. More than "ha[ving] a hand in [his] career opportunities," the blog has a hand that reaches up from the grave to which he would consign its entries and pulls me back, attentively—not distractedly or distractingly—to its world. How is it (to return, finally, to Chun) that this ephemeral endures, pace Juzwiak's own assertion that its "significance" has been eroded "by the tides of time"? In part, the endurance comes from a special, underremarked quality of camp, which tends to be thought along two axes—camp about superannuated objects and camp about objects *du jour*— that can't quite account for the phenomenon of camp about objects *du jour* that *itself* grows superannuated, but that in turn grows, paradoxically, in its charm even as (and to some extent because) it loses its so-called relevance, freed from that banality to exercise other, more idiosyncratic, more (touch) tonal magics on its afterlife-ly, but lively, receivers. This charm is the sort that Juzwiak himself ascribes to "the post-acid period of '89-'94" in his very first blog foray, and he undervalues his own gifts as a writer to suppose that his words and images cannot prompt similar—in (almost) every sense of the word—fondness.

Such an undervaluation indicates the extent to which Juzwiak embodies an updated, remixed, yet thoroughly Diderotian modesty for which, alongside his purportedly outdated blog, we ought yet to have time. Less creditable is his claim that "attempting to capture" the "minutiae" of television programming obstructed his capacity to "describe the bigger picture." Quite to the contrary, *a* bigger picture is there—emphatic, if also eccentric and idiosyncratic, and all the more congenial for the eccentricity and idiosyncrasy (at odds with the putative mastery connoted by "*the*" *bigger picture*)—in the form of the *Encyclopédie of America's Next Top Model* that he wrought by letting himself be admirably, which is to say digressively, guided from sensation(s) to reflection(s) rather than from assumption, conviction, or premise to deduction. The persisting document that attests to this embrace of digressive obstruction is, like the earlier *Encyclopédie* to which I liken it, one wildly dimensional node in a larger networked ecology, and it invites equally wild, dimensional (if nonetheless partial) footsteps with—and beyond—its many interconnected, and otherwise connected, pieces, as readers track Mariah Carey down one byway, swerve with Bobby Brown across several highway lanes, and tail Juzwiak's cats into their gridlock- (also yarn ball-) like knottedness with any number of the other felines yawning, stretching, and mewing their way across the Web. For some Diderotian—by which I now mean, too, Juzwiakian—audiences, the engagement will perhaps be more parts dimensional, fewer wild, as they take stock of and pleasurable instruction in the value of the stroll, leading them away from but back, sweetly, to the "broad, vast avenue" of *fourfour* and its own stroll along, as well as away from and back to, the broad, vast avenue of ANTM recapping. More particularly, the scholar-digressers among that constituency may take from such a stroll, or at least from my stroll with, through, and alongside it, the value in following "astray" our proverbial noses—read: our pricked ears; remix: our prodding hands—without worrying about losing our way but confident, modestly confident, that our ears will hear the four-four in the din and that our hands will touch their keys (supercut to the abiding cliché, and step aside from it) once more, with crazy feeling.

Conclusion.   Sober Futurity

At the end of the last chapter, I quoted at some length Rich Juzwiak's renunciation of his efforts as a television recapper, in part because I wanted to contest
the renunciation's account of the lack of value obtaining in those efforts. Another aspect of the account worth considering in a less skeptical way lies in its
emphasis on the physical and mental toll that recapping took on Juzwiak: "I
want to be a normal person who's watching TV, not some frantic note-taking
instant replayer. No more regularly scheduled forced digestion in a period of
time that gives my brain and writing cramps. It's fatigue, plain and simple,
that comes from within but is informed from without. The limitless ubiquity
of recaps makes writing them a challenge."[1] While Juzwiak responded, as I
demonstrate, to the "challenge" of recapping with digressive ingenuity, any
reckoning of that response that doesn't at least briefly measure the digest
made through its acts of "digestion" against the "fatigue, plain and simple"
that accompanied those acts would be a misleadingly incomplete one. Recalling what Chun writes in her resistance to the "dictatorship of speed,"[2]
I may likewise have the capacity to resist that dictatorship in my digressive
stroll to, with, and through *fourfour* (and linked assays), but Juzwiak didn't
and perhaps couldn't, even as a digresser in his approach to recapping,
perform such a challenge to speed's hegemony; the demand of punctual digressing in a "regularly scheduled" way whose regularity also constitutes its
"frantic[ness]" and near "instant[aneity]" comes with a cost—the debility
of exhaustion—that digressing in the rhythms of my scholarly pace did not
demand and that Juzwiak finally, reasonably refused to keep paying.

   I linger over Juzwiak's exhaustion not only to make my account of his
blogging less partial (in both senses)—nor even, more simply, to honor his
work in as fully textured a way as he honors the work of artists, particularly

musicians, about whom he writes with critical admiration—but also by way of ambling toward an admission that exhaustion was, in an early imagining of *Obstruction*, an experiential phenomenon that I planned to situate alongside the book's five obstructions in a conclusion that would affirm exhaustion's value. More specifically, I thought that the dialectical interplay of the exhausting and the exhaustive—distinct from the modestly encyclopedic ambitions that I identify as animating Diderot's and Juzwiak's projects, and constitutive of a valuably loopy rigor (the loopiness stemming from exhausting work, the rigor from its exhaustive results)—would disclose an excitingly different dimension of the eccentricity that I name in this book's introduction and that attends each of the obstructive efforts explored in the pages that follow. And, allied with the case studies invoked in those pages, an illustrative example had powerfully suggested itself to me as a model for the exhaustion that I would assess: experimental theater troupe Elevator Repair Service's *Gatz*, a seven-hour-long extravaganza in which actor Scott Shepherd recites *The Great Gatsby* from start to finish, a recitation kaleidoscopically accompanied by his E.R.S. colleagues' fantastical re-creations of elements of the novel's action. Simultaneously exhausting (for Shepherd, but also for audiences) and exhaustive (in its re-presentation of Fitzgerald's prose—and of so much besides), the piece would, I thought, teach me how to do something better with "fatigue" than "give . . . my brain and writing cramps" in the way that Juzwiak describes.

In a related maneuver, I also imagined, right around the same time in this project's development, that I would write a standalone essay, closely in dialogue with *Obstruction* but not to be included as one of its chapters, on the paradoxical boons of worrying. To some extent, that effort was conceived to work as an obverse to the chapter on "Laziness," whose location of value in a liquid, relaxed mode of intellection would have a Janus-faced counterpart in the torn but tender "quarry" that worry's rending renders, the weirdly lively because deathly processes that its "morbid stimulation" excites.[3] The essay would have also provided a counterpart to the chapter on "Embarrassment" and its account of popular music composed and performed by Tori Amos, as the worrier through an examination of whose work I would have routed my remarks is Gillian Welch, the alt-folk singer-songwriter who, among other fascinating efforts marked by a preoccupation with worrying, leveraged a years-long bout with writer's block (fueled by her worry about not rising to her own, exacting standard of artistry) to produce an album titled, fittingly enough, *The Harrow and the Harvest*. To be distinguished from the anxiety that has been theorized in a multipronged critical tradition, dating back at least to Harold Bloom's influential *The Anxiety of Influence* (a tradition whose scale is so massive that any attempt to comprehend it is now poised itself to produce anxiety), worry would have, in this account, contrasted in its discrete deployments as a series of generative activities with the weight and freight of anxiety, a pervasive and arresting state; and an analysis of the choked or strangled quality of Welch's singing, as well as of partner Dave Rawling's distinctive, sometimes agitated playing of his fretted instruments, would have lent itself with a full materiality to a meditation on worry's own choking and fretting.

In the end, both of these ideas were shed—indeed, had to be shed in order for me to theorize obstruction's embrace as a carefully and caringly delimited phenomenon, one that must give at least as much as it takes. The more I read about sleep and fatigue—and thought about the ups and downs in my own relationship to sleep—the more convinced I became that there is simply not a recuperation of exhaustion that jibes with my particular way of locating value in obstructions (thinking back to and reinvoking Wood's language on distraction, I would venture that some creativity might erupt in exhaustion, but not enough to make it "respectable" or to compensate for its destructive effects on mind and body).[4] Likewise, whatever value may be extracted from worry does not match or exceed what worrying corrodes, however much less corrosive it may be than sister states—that is, the stases—of anxiety. This is not to say that there is not a great deal to praise in and learn from artistic endeavors like E.R.S.'s and Gillian Welch's—there most emphatically is— just that the praise may more usefully be lavished on the work with different accents than those identified briefly above (for example, with direction to the sheer virtuosity of E.R.S.'s devisements, or to the slyly deceptive simplicity of Welch's compositions), the learning responsive to otherwise inflected lessons inherent in their theater and music-making (ditto, lessons imbibed from the robust athleticism of E.R.S.'s movements and voicings, or from the understated but all the same beguiling wiliness of Welch's performances). In short, and from my perspective, exhaustion and worry really are boring (in the sense of wearying), because boring (in the sense of wounding), impediments to the modes of intellection that I have saluted and aimed to enact performatively in *Obstruction*. Some blockages that remain dogged blockages perhaps ought to be marked—and left—as such.

Of course, there are ways unlike the approach that I have deployed in these pages to find value in phenomena like worry and exhaustion. Where the latter is concerned, for instance, Berardi predicates one of his more polemical rallying cries on exhaustion's uptake in a passage worth quoting at some length:

In the activist view, exhaustion is seen as the inability of the social body to escape the vicious destiny that capitalism has prepared: deactivation of the social energies that once upon a time animated democracy and political struggle. But exhaustion could also become the beginning of a slow movement toward a "wu wei" civilization, based on . . . withdrawal and frugal expectations for life and consumption. Radicalism could abandon the mode of activism, and adopt the mode of passivity. A radical passivity would definitely threaten the ethos of relentless productivity that neoliberal politics has imposed. . . .

Is it possible to divert [ourselves away] from the direction of death, murder, and suicide, toward a new kind of autonomy, of social creativity and of life?

I think that it is possible only if we start from exhaustion, if we emphasize the creative side of withdrawal. The exchange between life and money could be abandoned, and exhaustion could give way to a huge wave of withdrawal from the sphere of economic exchange. A new refrain could emerge in that moment and wipe out the law of economic growth. The self-organization of the general intellect could abandon the law of accumulation and growth, and start a new concatenation, where collective intelligence is only subjected to the common good.[5]

Berardi's vision will and ought to strike many as a rousing, indeed inspiring one, yet it rouses and inspires precisely to the extent that it only "start[s] from exhaustion" and then abandons exhaustion in an affirmation of "a new kind of autonomy," "social creativity," and "collective intelligence . . . subjected to the common good." To use an obstruction like exhaustion as a lever whose turning leads to the supersession of that obstruction differs markedly from the way in which I have pressed on and pressed with my obstructions—an embrace of them that is not fleeting but clinging—in order to locate the value they have to disclose (admittedly much more limited in scope and scale than the wholesale renovation of social and economic life that Berardi imagines).

A few further points remain to be made about this strategy for cleaving to rather than from obstructions. First, as I hope that the foregoing chapters of the book have demonstrated, this cleaving is genuine, not dodged through rhetorical sleights of hand, so that, for instance, lazing really is a form of laziness, encyclopedic digressiveness really retains its digressive character, and so forth. Yet—and this second point is more key—the five obstructions that I have presented here, that is, *as* I have presented them here, work because I have endeavored to find qualities or strains in them worth endorsing. To be sure, each of these obstructions could be framed in a darker light and experienced in a more debilitating way, to the extent that they would not disclose value as they have here but block the good, as for instance when acute cynicism makes subjects indifferent to moral or ethical imperatives that should be urgent or when extreme embarrassment leads to suicide (a disturbingly regularized action, motivated variously, that Berardi identifies as an "implosive trend" in a number of contemporary social and political scenes).[6] A useful project could linger over obstructions that more narrowly hurt, damage, or impede activity, especially intellective activity, but its aims and premises would differ pointedly from this one's; perhaps such a project would be likelier to inhabit a diagnostic rather than a pedagogical mode, wherein learning about the tolls rather than from the possibilities inherent in obstructions would be the signal gesture.

At the same time, the likelihood that some other meditation on obstruction would emphasize diagnosis is just that—a likelihood, not a certainty. Indeed, it would also be possible to imagine a third way, a meditation on obstruction that leveraged either tonal and temperamental negativity or a methodology of negation—or both—in order to find the animating, even motoring dimensions in obstructions experienced bluntly as failures or breaks. Perhaps such a meditation would draw nearer than this book does to work in queer theory, such as Heather Love's or Lee Edelman's, or to work in Afro-pessimism, for instance by Jared Sexton or Frank B. Wilderson III, which in very different but nonetheless related ways are marked by refusals, renunciations, the downward, the backward, stigmatization, and abjection. Precisely because I read such work with great interest and sympathy, I want to echo and repurpose a question of Fred Moten's in a recent reassessment of his earlier position on Afro-pessimism, contradistinct in its principles from what Moten names a method of celebration galvanizing his own work: "Is it just a minor internal conflict [in black studies], this intimate nonmeeting [of black optimism and Afro-pessimism], this impossibility of touching in mutual radiation and permeation? Can pessimists and optimists be friends? I hope so. Maybe that's what friendship is, this bipolarity, which is to say, more precisely, the commitment to it."[7] While I would, with a slight semantic distinction, characterize my own position not as optimistic but rather as angling toward the hopeful (about which, more below), I do wonder with Moten about the prospect that a project like *Obstruction* and others in a critical tradition of negation may "touch . . . in mutual radiation and permeation." To name just one way in which I see that prospect, that touch, materialize, I think of the manner in which each of the five obstructions named here becomes, in the naming, something like the critical "catchwords" in the late writing of Adorno, for whom rigorous, relentless negation was the sine qua non. Not entirely like Adorno, and yet not entirely unlike Adorno, who "fear[s] for the reification of language" and thus "use[s] catchwords to catch catchwords out"[8] (perhaps most vividly in the instances in which he exerts critical pressure on phrases like *minor age* and *working through the past*),[9] I have torqued and retorqued keywords like *cynicism* so that the givenness with which they appear as mere obstructions in common currency can no longer be so given or taken for granted. If that makes Adorno available to me, and I to him, in what Moten calls "friendship," albeit a friendly relation marked by "bipolarity" or at least by bifurcation, then *Obstruction* will have moved in a certain current but also with a cross-current whose remembrance—and acknowledgment here—may serve the work of complicating what perspective can obtain regarding the book's claims.

To speak of some more prosaically present friends than Adorno, I want to circle back to the issue of this book's passed-over impediments, which have included not just the contenders for *Obstruction* whose consideration more or less originated with "me," but also those that have been recommended to me by a variety of interlocutors with whom I have discussed this project over the years of its cultivation. Most scholars have dialogic experiences like the ones to which I refer, sometimes spurring a new, unexpected, and genuinely rousing approach to an intellective question or problematic—and perhaps just as often inspiring the thought, "Uh . . . no," one that politeness and, what's better, generosity instruct us to bracket as we greet such recommendations with more gentle and genial responses. "Uh . . . no" was certainly the response on my mind, if not my lips, when a convivial friend with a completely different professional orientation from my own asked me, at a holiday party, whether housekeeping was an obstruction to work (though now I may need to eat those unspoken words, having had to stop writing the first draft of this very conclusion in order to hang laundry on a terrace's line—and in the process having confronted a literally obstructed door to said terrace, whose stuck lock's prying took me more minutes than I cared to spend on such a task). As the conversation with this friend proceeded, and as he grew more happily tipsy, he wondered aloud whether the obstruction of drunkenness could be mobilized in the service of, instead of only shutting down, work. That wondering might prompt our recall of the drunken, injured worker given poignant attention in *The Dream Express* and the other, brief mentions of alcohol consumption in the chapter on "Laziness"; it might also direct us to pieces of scholarship by Michael Warner and Marty Roth, which highlight, respectively, the ways in which drunkenness may lead not only to "lost labor" but also to "expressive" possibilities for "self-contemplation"[10]—and the ways in which an "[a]esthetic" may be "driven" not "by individual genius or the imagination, but rather by intoxication" (an intoxication distinguished historically and theoretically from the alcoholism pathologized with remarkably consistent logic from the ascendancy of the American temperance movement through the invention of Alcoholics Anonymous).[11]

Though pleasurable drinking encouraged at the theater (and as discussed in chapter 2) accompanied only my watching of The Dream Express: Set III and not my writing about the piece, and though my "aesthetic" is not one "driven" by "intoxication"—in short, though "Uh . . . no" could still serve as a rejoinder to my friend's wondering about alcohol and obstruction (or Obstruction)— our conversation did eventually make me think about a contemporary project, unlike this one's meditation on contemporaneity, that is in fact driven by drunkenness as a generative obstruction. That project, Drunk History, a highly viral series of six shorts posted to the website Funny or Die in 2007,[12] features a set of monologists whose intensely drunk, semi-coherent, and error-laden speeches about noteworthy events in American history are hilariously dramatized in scenes of mock seriousness or "sobriety"—scenes given a frisson in their cross-cutting to and from video recordings of the monologues as initially spoken (usually slurred). In the process, Drunk History yields a parody both of the failed earnestness that saturates populist costume documentaries, staple programming on television networks like A&E and The History Channel, and of the equal and yet creepier earnestness of historical reenactors, who perform live versions of Civil War battles, colonial trades and chores, and a host of related activities that aspire to "accuracy" (guided by highly fraught ideologies of fidelity and authenticity). I have been seduced to figure a brief but pressurized look at Drunk History in this conclusion in part because of how consistently and pointedly the webisodes showcase the very phenomena studied in Obstruction, as its monologists inspire embarrassed feeling in (less drunk) viewers, think lazily about historical actors and events, speak more and more slowly as they grow increasingly blitzed, offer cynical interpretations of the histories that they (mis)narrate, and give digressive voice to those narrations while their deranged minds follow a series of detours. On one view, Drunk History discloses not only what happens when an obstruction like drunkenness gets torqued into the production of value—as entertainment, as commerce—but also how the five obstructions that I have argued are central to contemporaneity may be stirringly acknowledged, yet made less disquieting in that acknowledgment, as they are rendered pliable to the conventions of silly (yet nonetheless saleable) diversion. And, again, on this view, the—not drunk—makers of the series, firmly in control of both their faculties and the commercial apparatus on which they capitalize, can make these usually more troubling obstructions tractable to whatever appetite we sustain for trivial entertainment precisely because of the shaping control that they exert over the wilder, darker energies of their drunk collaborators.

Yet if that were the only history of Drunk History to offer, it would not merit its privileged treatment here—nor, I suspect, would it have become as popular as it did, taking stock of the moment of its making in ways irreducible to its status as a six-times-repeated gimmick. To take adequate stock of the series in turn requires a consideration of the most curious aspect of the supposed gimmick: as monologic scenes of rambling give way to costume-dramatic reenactments of the "histories" that the ramblings recount, the monologists' words are carried forth in voiceovers that suture the former scenes to the latter—and those voiceovers, with all of their drunken stammering, hiccoughs, garbling or mangling of words, anachronisms, and related tics and solecisms, are hypermeticulously lip-synced by the costumed actors in the reenactments (the best of whom, like Michael Cera as Alexander Hamilton and Don Cheadle as Frederick Douglass, also find comic gold in reflexive facial expressions that simultaneously make "sense," within the strained diegeses of the historical scenes, of these vocal and verbal idiosyncrasies and mark as absurd such sense-making). In these moments, Drunk History moves adventurously beyond the parody of television documentaries and of live, site-specific reenactments as it likewise parodies—with great sophistication— the similar, more sober hypermimesis of earlier recorded footage that animates virtuosic experiments like The Wooster Group's Poor Theatre. Not coincidentally, a deft reading of Poor Theatre enjoys a pride of place in Rebecca Schneider's recent book Performing Remains, which also surveys Civil War battle re-creations and other, far-from-avant practices as it makes the case that, across a wide range of aesthetic and political registers, reenactment has become a dominant contemporary mode for reckonings with history, memory, trauma, and related forms of loss and preservation (and their vexed interinanimation).[13] In line with Schneider's smart, principled refusal to predict in advance what meanings will attach to or emerge from any of the turbulently various performances that she arrays, we might ask: what if Drunk History's comic translation of tactics that we expect to limn more highminded projects like Poor Theatre has, for all of the comedy, a similarly serious message to convey about affect, iteration, legacy, and more? Because of the Brechtian split vision with which it labors both to redouble muddy accountings of the

C.1 and C.2 In *Drunk History*, an incapacitated woman mangles her tale of Frederick Douglass's life, which Don Cheadle reenacts with reflexive bemusement.

past's immanence to the present and, winkingly, to belabor that labor, *Drunk History* may inspire no simple giggling but rather a critically nervous laughter about all that it lets go "uncorrected" yet underlines as such—with exacting correctness. Giving us all at once a palpable sense of how much abandon to feeling—and, what's more, how much abandoned feeling—is the locus of contemporary living with the dead; how inadequate such feeling is to the registration of the dead's import; how lively but nonetheless deathly, caught in a feedback loop, the appraisal of such inadequacy may be in its turn; and how quickened (deadened, enlivened) we are to appraise as much in our own turns, the series obstructs like no other, Web-based or otherwise, that I have

encountered. That is, Drunk History makes central to its proceeding an obstruction (drunk feeling), alters the obstruction by framing it (thinking the
feeling), obstructs easy comprehension of that alteration by embellishing the
framing (touching thinking feeling), and, through citational estrangement,
obstructs yet again any ease in assessing the change rung on the change
(smarting touching thinking feeling). The key value of the endeavor lodges
in its quixotic, insistent obstruction to knowing stably how to valuate—and
thus precisely how to value—such endeavors as Drunk History itself; and, now
that it has been wrapped into this book, that obstruction may also, valuably,
temper any blithe comfort to be taken from Obstruction's own insistences.

At the same time, Drunk History has a more mundane value as an artifact
well situated to attest to the relationship of the recent past to the present and
near future. The 2007 Web shorts have inspired a 2013 Comedy Central series
that in most ways is very much like the original work and in other, smaller
ways deviates from its Web model. (On the one hand, actors like Winona Ry-
der bring just as much wicked sharpness to their lip-syncing as did predecessors Cera and Cheadle. On the other hand, the much slicker production values brought to bear when Drunk History is made for cable television defang the
parody of other cable television endeavors, to which the series' own aesthetic
has perhaps drawn too uncritically near.) The continuing fascination exerted
by this experiment suggests that Drunk History meets a desire or demand that
hangs over, as it were, from the moment right before the Great Recession in
which the first version of the series was imagined: a moment when drinking
to excess could very well have seemed like an appropriate response to a woeful world alit with signs that the woe would only intensify—and one still alit
with signs that the woe may yet intensify further.

Hovering over Drunk History to think about not just where we are but also
where we may be headed, I do not advocate a sober future, exactly—drinking
may still seem to some like a warranted way to lubricate livability under the
conditions of neoliberal capitalism—but rather a sober futurity; that is, a
careful and clear-eyed orientation toward the horizon, one animated not, for
instance, by the audacious hope that Barack Obama claims and proclaims but
rather by an obversely humble hope. As Hirokazu Miyazaki underscores in
his elegant anatomization of the feeling, humble would not strictly make sense
as a qualifier of hope were we to adhere to the definitions of hope proffered by
philosophers like Richard Rorty, whose "self-consciously aggrandizing concept of human agency explicitly rejects humility as instrumental to the production of hope."[14] Yet humility—sometimes named with flickering explic-
itness, mostly implied—is exactly what motors hope in an alternative critical

tradition, most recently embraced and vividly advanced by queer theorists of performance like Jill Dolan and José Esteban Muñoz.[15] As Muñoz says in a moving dialogue with Lisa Duggan, made all the more moving and precious in the wake of his recent, untimely passing, "a certain practice of hope helps [us] escape from a script in which human existence is reduced," yet in order to engage that practice requires care and "education," as well as an alertness not to presume too much, so that we avoid the danger of sliding into the alternative, toxic "mode of hope that simply keeps one in place within an emotional situation predicated on control" (that is, the situation that Berlant describes as cruel optimism).[16]

Far from hobbling hope, we may infer from a reading of critics like Muñoz, humility charts a trajectory for hope's sustainability and the inevitable, punctual interruptions of that sustainability. By so averring, I follow yet another queer theorist, Gayle S. Rubin, whose short yet far from minor essay, "A Little Humility," lays out the stakes of thinking in this way about humility and its processual unfolding in time:

> Along with pride and shame, we should be giving due consideration to humility: humility about the inevitability of change; humility about the imperfection of our formulations; and humility toward the decisions of the past, which were made in different circumstances and under different conditions to meet a different set of needs. Moreover, what we do today will be critically assessed when it becomes part of the past (if not before). History makes fools of us all, sooner or later. We can only hope that it is later, and do our best to ensure that the positive contributions outweigh the collateral damage.[17]

If "history makes fools of us all, sooner or later"—and Drunk History makes us keen witnesses to such folly—then we should not only hope, humbly, that our "positive contributions outweigh the collateral damage" of our acting in the world, as Rubin affirms outright, but also humble our hope, as her remarks suggest with more obliquity, that "the inevitability of change" will also inevitably constitute a progressive movement forward rather than a slide backward, a deflection sideward, or an obstruction, tucked. If it is to be obstruction, then may value be held in its folds, as I have held humbly of the obstructions enfolded in these pages; and if otherwise, then may we not worry the change, nor be exhausted by it, but stay calm before the storm.

Notes

Introduction

1 See, for instance, Gayatri Chakravorty Spivak, "Scattered Speculations on the Question of Value," 73–93; Amy Villarejo's reading of Spivak in *Lesbian Rule: Cultural Criticism and the Value of Desire*, 31–36; and Christopher Nealon, "Value | Theory | Crisis," 101–6.

2 A sanguine approach to these issues—one that pulls back from the excesses of crisis rhetoric—is to be found in Kathleen Fitzpatrick's *Planned Obsolescence: Publishing, Technology, and the Future of the Academy*. For an equally sanguine survey of the field of "critical university studies" in which Fitzpatrick participates, see Jeffrey J. Williams, "Deconstructing Academe: The Birth of Critical University Studies."

3 See, for instance, Stanley Aronowitz and Jonathan Cutler, eds., *Post-Work: The Wages of Cybernation*; and Kathi Weeks, *The Problem with Work: Feminism, Marxism, Antiwork Politics, and Postwork Imaginaries*.

4 William Shakespeare, *The Merchant of Venice*.

5 Tammy Wynette, "Stand by Your Man."

6 Intersecting queer studies and disability studies, Jasbir Puar confronts prevailing assumptions about capacity and debility in her recent essay, "The Cost of Getting Better." With acknowledgment of that work's insights, I mobilize the word *capacities* rather in a sense nearer to Judith Butler's when she celebrates Eve Kosofsky Sedgwick's writing for bringing "into theoretical regions precisely that ethically capacious sensibility which affirms the necessity of the incongruous, and where the trajectory of desire requires a detour from the logic of either/or in order to thrive and—in whatever way—become known" (119). See Puar, "Coda: The Cost of Getting Better. Suicide, Sensation, Switchpoints"; and Butler, "Capacity." This note anticipates as well my working with and to the side of Agamben's deployment of *capacity*, which features in a later section of this introduction.

7 Judith Halberstam, *The Queer Art of Failure*, 5.

8 Lauren Berlant, *Cruel Optimism*, 95.

9 Paul H. Fry, *A Defense of Poetry*, 92, 94.

10 See, for instance, Berlant, *Cruel Optimism*, and Ann Cvetkovich, *Depression: A Public Feeling*.

11 Matthew E. May, *In Pursuit of Elegance*, 53.

12 *The Five Obstructions*.

13 In this aspect of my interpretation, I depart from the otherwise fine reading of Claire Perkins, who asserts that "it is the documentary-style sections depicting the two filmmakers in conversation that are most important, not the closed 'interpretations' of the remakes themselves" (155). See Perkins, "In Treatment: *The Five Obstructions*."

14 "In Treatment: *The Five Obstructions*," 157.

15 *The Five Obstructions*. In writing, as I do here, of pathos and its (non) feeler, I look ahead to chapter 1's fuller discussion of emotion and subjectivity.

16 *OED Online*, entry for "ob-."

17 *OED Online*, entry for "structure."

18 Martin Heidegger, *Being and Time*, 68–71.

19 For a fuller unpacking of some of these issues (if one that is slightly imprecise in its characterization of von Trier's "postmodernism"), see Benjamin Ogden, "How Lars von Trier Sees the World."

20 Fredric Jameson, *Postmodernism; or, The Cultural Logic of Late Capitalism*.

21 José López and Garry Potter, eds., *After Postmodernism*.

22 Terry Smith, "Introduction: The Contemporaneity Question," 16.

23 Smith, Okwui Enwezor, and Nancy Condee, "Preface," xiii. Italics in the original.

24 Smith, "Introduction," 16–17.

25 Smith, "Introduction," 9.

26 Natalie Melas, "Comparative Noncontemporaneities," 61, 59.

27 Paul Rabinow, *Marking Time*, 2, 29. Italics in the original.

28 See, for instance, Neil Brooks and Josh Toth, eds., *The Mourning After*; and John Rajchman, "The Contemporary: A New Idea?"

29 Giorgio Agamben, "What Is the Contemporary?" 46, 41.

30 Agamben, "What Is the Contemporary?" 41, 42.

31 Osip Mandelstam, "The Age."

32 Agamben, "What Is the Contemporary?" 43.

33 Agamben, "What Is the Contemporary?" 42, 39.

34 I thank my dear friend and colleague Masha Raskolnikov for sitting with me and reading Mandelstam's poem in Russian, alongside its English translation, with painstaking care in order to help me formulate the ideas about the poem expressed here and above.

35 Mandelstam, "The Age."

36 Melas, "Comparative Noncontemporaneities," 72.

37 Jane Gallop, *Anecdotal Theory*.

38 Villarejo, *Lesbian Rule*, 9.

39 *OED Online*, entry for "obstruction."

40 Eve Kosofsky Sedgwick and Michael Moon, "Divinity," 217–18.

41 See, for instance, Diana Fuss, ed., *Inside/Out*; and, in a more recent inside/out turn, Sara Ahmed, *The Cultural Politics of Emotion*.

42 Rebecca Schneider, "It Seems As If . . . I Am Dead." See also Chris Harman, *Zombie Capitalism*.

43 Hortense J. Spillers, "'All the Things You Could Be by Now, If Sigmund Freud's Wife Was Your Mother': Psychoanalysis and Race," 399–400.

44 Fred Moten and Stefano Harney, *The Undercommons*.

45 See, for instance, Louis Menand, *The Marketplace of Ideas*; and Cary Nelson, *No University Is an Island*.

46 Heidegger, *Being and Time*, 166.

47 Mark Fisher, *Capitalist Realism*, 4.

Chapter 1. Embarrassment

1 Mark Greif, "Radiohead, or the Philosophy of Pop," 23.

2 Greif, "Radiohead," 24.

3 Russell Nye, *The Unembarrassed Muse*.

4 Greif, "Radiohead," 28, 36.

5 Greif, "Radiohead," 36, 38.

6 Nye, *Unembarrassed Muse*, 421.

7 Henry Jenkins, *Textual Poachers*; Jane Tompkins, *West of Everything*, 3.

8 Joseph Litvak, *Strange Gourmets*, 18. See, for example, Lauren Berlant's *The Queen of America Goes to Washington City*, published contemporaneously with *Strange Gourmets*, or essays in the more recent *Fandom*, edited by Jonathan Gray, Cornel Sandvoss, and C. Lee Harrington. In their introduction to *Fandom*, the editors take stock of a return to and reimagining of Adornian concerns in (by their count) a third generation of fandom studies when they note that "contemporary research on fans (like its predecessors) acknowledges that fans' readings, tastes, and practices are tied to wider social structures, yet extends the conceptual focus beyond questions of hegemony and class to the overarching social, cultural, and economic transformations of our time, including the dialectic between the global and the local . . . and the rise of spectacle and performance in fan consumption" (8).

9 Litvak, *Strange Gourmets*, 3, 18. Litvak notes that egalitarian class politics animating critiques of sophistication often provide an alibi for underexamined homophobia directed at the purportedly elitist (queer) critic; one impoverishing result is the typical failure to recognize that "embarrassment provoked by sophistication has as much to do with sex as with class" (3).

10 Not every critic is equally susceptible to this double bind. As Litvak shrewdly points out, in a passage that resonates with the work of Jeffrey Sconce, "many members of the academy *are* nonelite others. Or at least, *were*" (115), in contradistinction to whom we might consider the kind of critic who, in

Tompkins's account, not only loves and writes about Westerns but also "lived for the summers when [she] took riding lessons" (16). See also Sconce, "'Trashing' the Academy." Also, see Litvak, 117, 115. Tellingly, a preoccupation with sophistication—and an unapologetic use of the words *sophisticated* and *sophistication*—saturates Nye's *The Unembarrassed Muse*, just as, according to Litvak, a recurrent but mostly unacknowledged "*méchanceté*," likewise predicated on a sense of sophistication, haunts more recent efforts in cultural studies (117).

11 Eve Kosofsky Sedgwick, *Epistemology of the Closet*, 143; and Rei Terada, *Feeling in Theory*, 46.

12 See Anthony Balderama, "Album Review: Tori Amos—*Midwinter Graces*."

13 Tori Amos and Ann Powers, *Tori Amos: Piece by Piece*, 11.

14 Simon Reynolds and Joy Press, *The Sex Revolts*.

15 Bonnie Gordon, "Tori Amos's Inner Voices."

16 Sheila Whiteley, *Women and Popular Music*.

17 Lori Burns, "Analytic Methodologies for Rock Music"; and Mélisse Lafrance, "The Problems of Agency and Resistance in Tori Amos's 'Crucify.'"

18 Sady Doyle, "Birth of the Uncool."

19 Sianne Ngai, *Ugly Feelings*.

20 Luke Purshouse, "Embarrassment," 519.

21 Rowland S. Miller, *Embarrassment*, 157, 158, 183 (italics in original).

22 Christopher Ricks, *Keats and Embarrassment*, 1.

23 Ricks, *Keats and Embarrassment*, 1.

24 See David M. Halperin and Valerie Traub, eds., *Gay Shame*. In his recent work on humiliation, Wayne Koestenbaum does not make fully consistent or thoroughly careful delineations among humiliation, shame, embarrassment, and related affects or feelings, though he does offer a provisional distinction between humiliation and shame that consonates with my (and others') related distinction between embarrassment and shame. He writes, "Humiliation is external, though it registers internally. Shame, on the other hand, can arise simply internally, without any reference to outside circumstances. Humiliation, I believe, must arise (if only in imagination) from outside. Humiliation is an observable lowering of status and position. One can be humiliated without being ashamed, or even without being sad. Humiliation pertains not merely to internal affect but to external climate, context, scenario." See Koestenbaum, *Humiliation*, 9–10.

25 Eve Kosofsky Sedgwick, "Shame, Theatricality, and Queer Performativity," in *Touching Feeling*, 36, 63, 37.

26 Andre Modigliani, "Embarrassment and Embarrassability," 314.

27 Dacher Keltner and Cameron Anderson, "Saving Face for Darwin: The Functions and Uses of Embarrassment," 187.

28 Douglas Crimp, "Mario Montez, For Shame," 71.

29 Crimp, "Mario Montez, For Shame," 71.

30 Joe Vallese, email to the author.

31 "Just Me," email to the author.
32 See Max Black, "Definition, Presupposition, and Assertion," and "How Do Pictures Represent?"; and Ben Singer, *Melodrama and Modernity*.
33 Singer, *Melodrama and Modernity*, 44.
34 Ricks, *Keats and Embarrassment*, 10, 12.
35 Miller, *Embarrassment*, 1, 2.
36 Miller, *Embarrassment*, 87, 97. Italics in the original.
37 Purshouse, "Embarrassment," 532, 530–31.
38 Erving Goffman, "Embarrassment and Social Organization," 269.
39 Goffman, "Embarrassment and Social Organization," 265, 264.
40 Miller, *Embarrassment*, 137.
41 Ira Glass, "Cringe."
42 Crimp, like other theorists of gay or queer shame, attempts to imagine conditions for communities of the shamed, but that effort is shadowed (and, indeed, contraindicated) by his avowal of shame's piercing delineations of selves from their others.
43 Terada, *Feeling in Theory*, 21, 46, 7.
44 Terada, *Feeling in Theory*, 7.
45 Terada, *Feeling in Theory*, 23, emphasis added.
46 For a related perspective, see Nicholas Ridout, "Embarrassment: The Predicament of the Audience," in which Ridout claims suggestively, though in passing (and in the context of a to my mind counterproductive confusion of shame and embarrassment), "Embarrassment might . . . be the appearance of . . . a desubjectified subject" (92).
47 In the final pages of *West of Everything* (229–33), Tompkins offers a poignant and bracing account of how much violence and aggression—including her own—fuels activity in professional academic spheres.
48 Henry James, "Preface," vii (emphasis added).
49 See Eric Savoy, "Embarrassments: Figure in the Closet." As Savoy himself nearly concedes, his underdetermined definition of embarrassment "as a peculiar conflation of 'too much' and 'too little,' of excess and impoverishment" (228) is, in fact, a definition of the "mode of ludic self-parody" commonly, and rather, called camp (230). In the guise of investigating embarrassment— but in fact tracing the contours of Jamesian camp—Savoy, like so many other readers, searches for James's "secret" and finds it, queerly, in the "intense realization of shame produced by the visibility of the closet" (232). I will return to the distinction between embarrassment and camp later in this chapter.
50 Henry James, "The Figure in the Carpet," in *Embarrassments*, 15, 17, 29, 33.
51 In a fine reading of Lacan, Eugenie Brinkema explores this etymological connection—and with a semirandom reference to pop music, no less—when she asserts, "Embarras 'is very exactly the subject S invested with the bar' from the etymological root *imbarrare* that evokes the bar (*bara*). The putting in place of the bar evokes 'the most direct lived experience of embarrassment.'

In perhaps the only phrasal connection between Lacan and Burt Bacharach, anxiety creates a situation 'when you no longer know what to do with yourself.' Embarrassment is the experience of the bar, but a flimsy or segmented barrier behind which one cannot barricade or block oneself, a bar or obstacle put into place, but not enough to prevent shameful exposure." See Brinkema, *The Forms of the Affects*, 204–5.

52 See Avital Ronell, *Stupidity*, 5.

53 E. S. Burt, "Regard for the Other," 59.

54 Goffman, "Embarrassment and Social Organization," 270–71.

55 Amos, "All Through the Night."

56 See Sedgwick and Moon, "Divinity."

57 Quoted in Amos and Powers, *Tori Amos: Piece by Piece*, 276.

58 Amos, quoted in "The Power and the Passion," 68.

59 Amos and Powers, *Tori Amos: Piece by Piece*, 337.

60 For instance, the album is carefully expunged from the discography available at Amos's official website; see www.toriamos.com/go/music.

61 See, among other accounts, Amos and Powers, *Tori Amos: Piece by Piece*, 48–50.

62 Amos, "Precious Things."

63 Amos, "Liquid Diamonds."

64 Amos, "Glory of the 80s."

65 Amos, "Cornflake Girl."

66 Amos, "Your Cloud."

67 Amos, "Tear in Your Hand."

68 Amos, "When a Star Falls Down."

69 Jacques Derrida, "Otobiographies," 33.

70 Derrida, "Otobiographies," 33, 38.

71 Susan Sontag, "Notes on Camp," 275. Despite all the ways in which Sontag's account of camp has been—rightly—contested and superseded, I still find striking this phrase's manner of conveying camp's potential for the galvanizing of community or collectivity.

72 Camp mobilizes one version of sophistication by offering its practitioners what Litvak describes in *Strange Gourmets* (though not, in his account, with direct reference to camp) as "a certain compound of luxury and sadism, a volatile . . . mixture of intoxicating vengefulness, on the one hand, and something like the intellectual equivalent of conspicuous consumption, on the other" (121).

73 For a further elaboration of this understanding of camp, see Nick Salvato, "Tramp Sensibility and the Afterlife of *Showgirls*," and *Uncloseting Drama*, 180–83.

74 OED *Online*, entry for "comment."

75 I refer here to the opening lyrics of "Cornflake Girl": "Never was a cornflake girl / thought that was a good solution / hangin' with the raisin girls."

76 See, for instance, the entry "ears with feet," *Urban Dictionary*.

77 Sinéad O'Connor, "Open Letter to Miley Cirus."

78 As Lynne Joyrich directs us in a footnote for "Tubular Visions: The Ins and Outs of Television Studies" (an essay forthcoming in the revised and expanded anthology *New Media, Old Media*), see "Janet Jackson Bares All in GENRE Interview; Entertainer Says President Bush Used 'Nipplegate' to Divert Attention from War Woe," PR *Newswire* (October 2004), http://www .prnewswire.com/news-releases/janet-jackson-bares-all-in-genre-interview -entertainer-says-president-bush-used-nipplegate-to-divert-attention-from -war-woes-73857172.html. See also Jackson's quote, "I truly feel in my heart that the president wanted to take the focus off of him at that time, and I was the perfect vehicle to do so at that moment" at "On the Trail," *The Economist* (August 2004), http://www.economist.com/node/3139109.

79 Joyrich, "Tubular Visions."

80 Joyrich, "Tubular Visions."

81 For further details on such aspects of Amos's professional trajectory as a musician and businessperson, see Amos and Powers, *Tori Amos: Piece by Piece*.

82 See Sedgwick, "Paranoid Reading and Reparative Reading," in *Touching Feeling*.

83 Doyle, "Birth of the Uncool."

84 Amos, "Cooling."

85 Representative performances that conform to this description include Amos, "Cooling," QPAC Concert Hall, Brisbane, AU, November 24, 2009; and Amos, "Cooling," Bonnaroo, Manchester, TN, June 11, 2010.

86 This account of the parodist's work is indebted to Linda Hutcheon's thinking in *A Theory of Parody*.

Chapter 2. Laziness

1 Karen Finley, "Introduction," *Make Love*, 51.

2 Association for Theater in Higher Education, "Keynote Performance," 12.

3 Lucas Hilderbrand, "'More Than One Way to Love,'" 179, 181.

4 Tom Lutz, *Doing Nothing*.

5 For an alternative historical frame of reference, see, for instance, James Simpson, "The Economy of Involucrum." Simpson, as quoted less fully in the epigraph to this chapter's first section, "argue[s] that *otium* is an essential part of a mental economy, as ancient and medieval materials long recognized" (390); investigates "the boundary between wasteful and productive idleness . . . fought over with great intensity in economic and spiritual terms" in the Middle Ages (390); points to prominent medieval poets like Langland, who "finds himself drawn powerfully to 'idleness,' as Piers [Plowman] abandons work in the world" (391); and traces the ways in which, "by the early sixteenth century [in Europe,] the gravity of the issue [of idleness] is unmistakable, as the principal charge launched by evangelical polemicists against the regular religious is their idleness" (391). He also calls for the inauguration of "a medieval and early modern sub-branch of Idleness Studies" (391), a call that presupposes that such a field already exists (and it does, to some extent, waiting [idly?] to

be recognized and named as such or by some alternative moniker like Laziness Studies—about which more to come).

6 Here I take a cue from Ngai, who in *Ugly Feelings* identifies that "what seems intolerable about Bartleby is how paradoxically visible he makes his social invisibility" (333).

7 As Lutz notes in *Doing Nothing*, "Johnson's first major essay series in the early 1750s . . . published under the pseudonym the Rambler" also entails "a certain lackadaisical lassitude" (68).

8 Lutz, 69.

9 Samuel Johnson, "The Idler's Character," 4.

10 Johnson, "The Idler's Character,"5, 4 (emphasis added).

11 Johnson, "The Idler's Character,"3.

12 Johnson, "The Idler's Character,"4 (emphasis added), 5.

13 As Johnson writes in "The Idler's Character," "I think it necessary to give notice, that I make no contract, nor incur any obligation. If those who depend on the Idler for intelligence and entertainment, should suffer the disappointment which commonly follows ill-placed expectations, they are to lay the blame only on themselves" (5). At the same time, and as Lutz rightfully reminds us in *Doing Nothing*, Johnson had at best an ambivalent rather than robustly adversarial relationship to the market, "his understanding of [whose] 'degredations'" did not preclude "his obviously deep need to produce for that market" (*Doing Nothing*, 72).

14 Of course, neither Lafargue nor his translator could predict the complex evolution of leisure in the first half of the twentieth century nor the Adornian critique thereof. We could also profitably contemplate a definition of leisure provided by Sebastian de Grazia, who comprehends it as "a state of being in which activity is performed for its own sake or as its own end" and thus distinguishes it from an occupation that is "activity pursued for a purpose. If the purpose were not necessary, the activity would not occur." See de Grazia, *Of Time, Work and Leisure*, 15.

15 Paul Lafargue, "The Right to Be Lazy," 57, 29, 49, 36.

16 Lafargue, "The Right to Be Lazy," 13.

17 Oscar Wilde, "The True Function and Value of Criticism," 128.

18 Wilde, "The True Function and Value of Criticism," 137, 443.

19 Wilde, "The True Function and Value of Criticism," 451, 441. Italics in the original.

20 Wilde, "The True Function and Value of Criticism," 451 (emphasis added).

21 Robert Louis Stevenson, "An Apology for Idlers."

22 Stevenson, "An Apology for Idlers."

23 Stevenson, "An Apology for Idlers."

24 Stevenson, "An Apology for Idlers."

25 Roland Barthes, *The Neutral*, 9. Here, Barthes may recall for us Johnson's Idler, "who habituates himself to be satisfied with what he can most easily obtain."

26 Barthes, *The Neutral*, 9. Italics in the original.

27 Barthes, *The Neutral*, 19.

28 One could trace a complex lineage of cultural constructions of laziness's waters, with highlights ranging (for instance) from the "fishing-boats" with "no rigging" made for fishermen who "got their living entirely by looking at the ocean" in Collins and Dickens's *The Lazy Tour of Two Idle Apprentices* to the sleep-inducing sounds of the "downward stream" in Tennyson's "The Lotos-Eaters" to the swimming pool and hot tub in *Ferris Bueller's Day Off*.

29 Wendy Wasserstein, *Sloth*, 15, 14, 100, 101.

30 Pierre Saint-Amand, *The Pursuit of Laziness*, 12. Curiously, though Saint-Amand addresses "Barthes' Laziness" in an article whose stakes are intimately tied to those of *The Pursuit of Laziness*, he does not, in either work, address *The Neutral* explicitly, though he does address the concept of "the neutral" as it animates Barthes's other work (though never, to my mind, animating it in quite so lazing a fashion as in that late lecture course).

31 Lutz, *Doing Nothing*, 39, 38, 39.

32 Lutz, *Doing Nothing*, 39.

33 Ellen Schrecker, *The Lost Soul of Higher Education*, 193.

34 Anonymous interview respondent, quoted in William G. Tierney and Estela Mara Bensimon, *Promotion and Tenure*, 62; requoted in Schrecker, *The Lost Soul of Higher Education*, 193.

35 Stanley Aronowitz, "The Last Good Job in America," in Aronowitz and Jonathan Cutler, eds. *Post-Work*, 208.

36 Eve Kosofsky Sedgwick observes shrewdly of the *ressentiment* directed at university professors, as she advocates for opportunities like ours to be afforded more regularly and robustly to others, "Millions of people today struggle to carve out—barely, at great cost to themselves—the time, permission, and resources, 'after work' or instead of decently-paying work, for creativity and thought that will not be in the service of corporate profit, nor structured by its rhythms. Many, many more are scarred by the prohibitive difficulty of doing so. . . . I see that some must find enraging the spectacle of people for whom such possibilities are, to a degree, built into the structure of our regular paid labor. Another way to understand that spectacle, though, would be as one remaining form of insistence that it is not inevitable—it is not a simple fact of nature—for the facilities of creativity and thought to represent rare or exorbitant privilege. Their economy should not and need not be one of scarcity." See Sedgwick, "Queer and Now," in *Tendencies*, 19.

37 Stanley Aronowitz, Dawn Esposito, William DiFazio, and Margaret Yard, "The Post-Work Manifesto," in *Post-Work*, eds. Aronowitz and Cutler, 59.

38 In "The Last Good Job in America," Aronowitz himself makes clear how his thinking dovetails with that of laziness's theorists when he writes approvingly of academic work that "much of it is useful, in the direct sense, neither for the economy nor for the political system and may even be opposed to . . . institutional requirements" (212). Also see Weeks, *The Problem with Work*. Weeks shares with Aronowitz and with many of the theorists of laziness cited here a

desire not to devalue work but to revalue it in ways that challenge the numbing norms of (in her era, neoliberal, corporate) capitalism; as she writes forcefully, "Let me be clear: to call these traditional work values into question is not to claim that work is without value. It is not to deny the necessity of productive activity or to dismiss the likelihood that, as William Morris describes it, there might be for all living things 'a pleasure in the exercise of their energies.' . . . It is, rather, to insist that there are other ways to organize and distribute that activity and to remind us that it is also possible to be creative outside the boundaries of work. It is to suggest that there might be a variety of ways to experience the pleasure that we may now find in work, as well as other pleasures that we may wish to discover, cultivate, and enjoy. And it is to remind us that the willingness to live for and through work renders subjects supremely functional for capitalist purposes" (12).

39 Michael Hardt and Antonio Negri, Empire, 290–91.

40 Tiziana Terranova, Network Culture, 73–97.

41 Paolo Virno, A Grammar of the Multitude, 102.

42 Franco "Bifo" Berardi, The Soul at Work, 192.

43 Berardi, The Soul at Work, 192.

44 Hannah Arendt, The Human Condition. As Arendt explains early in the book, "Labor is the activity which corresponds to the biological process of the human body. . . . Work is the activity which corresponds to the unnaturalness of human existence [and] provides an 'artificial' world of things, distinctly different from all natural surroundings. . . . Action, the only activity that goes on directly between men without the intermediary of things or matter, corresponds to the human condition of plurality, to the fact that men, not Man, live on the earth and inhabit the world. While all aspects of the human condition are somehow related to politics, this plurality is specifically the condition—not only the conditio sine qua non, but the conditio per quam—of all political life" (7).

45 Arendt, The Human Condition, 169.

46 Arendt, The Human Condition, 169 (emphasis added).

47 Miguel Balsa, "Recourse to Action," 24.

48 Villarejo, Lesbian Rule, 4.

49 Lutz, Doing Nothing, 14, 76–77, 77–78.

50 The second oldest entry in Lounge, dating to 1760, associates the phrase "lounge bar" with a pub in Havant; and, according to the same source, a publication of "Tavern Anecdotes and Reminiscences" could, as early as 1825, identify itself "as a lounge-book for Londoners and their country cousins." Similarly, the Oxford English Dictionary notes that a cluster of usages of lounge to mean "a place for lounging; a gathering of loungers" dates to the late eighteenth and early nineteenth centuries. See Philip M. Parker, ed., Lounge, 5, 6; and OED Online, entry for lounge.

51 Andrew K. Sandoval-Strausz, Hotel: An American History, 171–72, 168.

52 The OED attributes the earliest uses of this slang term, meant to describe "a man who spends his time idling in fashionable society, esp. in search of

a wealthy patroness," to the late 1910s and 1920s. See OED *Online*, entry for
lounge.

53 Sandoval-Strausz, *Hotel: An American History*, 211.

54 In so capaciously defining the lounge idiom, I depart, in the spirit of lazing, with deliberate loosening or relaxation from the definition of lounge
music offered by Melissa Ursula Dawn Goldsmith, who asserts, "The genre
designation 'lounge' describes a complex network of music ranging from
light instrumentals (easy listening) to experimental uses of instruments and
cutting-edge technology (not-so-easy listening)." That designation means to
cordon off "the 'lounge' designation" from "Las Vegas-style lounge singing."
See Goldsmith, "Lounge Caravan," 1060, 1069.

55 Lynn Spigel, *Make Room for TV*, 41.

56 Litvak, *Strange Gourmets*, 15. Litvak develops the notion of "expansive sophistication" in order to discuss the double-hinged leveraging of middle-class
embodiment typified by Elizabeth Bennet in *Pride and Prejudice*, but I find that
the concept works equally well, indeed elegantly, to diagnose "a persistent,
perhaps inexhaustible, middle-class desire for instruction in the hermeneutics
of social performance"; in the 1950s and 1960s, this desire sometimes takes
the form of how to make the perfect cocktail or throw the perfect tiki party,
sometimes how to emulate or aspire to Rat Pack sophistication—which,
weirdly enough, shows, like the sophistication of Elizabeth Bennet, "how
much a school for sophistication can resemble a school of hard knocks" (15).

57 When I write here of lounge style's rapid descent from coolness to its obverse,
I am thinking chiefly of its disrepute in the 1970s and 1980s and bracketing
its resuscitation in the 1990s and 2000s—precisely because that resuscitation
required strategies of citation, irony, and critical distancing that made the
thing taken up "again" not quite the same thing as I describe it in these pages.
As Francesco Adinolfi writes helpfully of the distinction between lounge
and something like metalounge, "Precisely when alternative rock became a
mainstream chart staple, the sound that once represented the very essence of
mainstream (Frank Sinatra, Yma Sumac, Carla Boni, etc.) became profoundly
alternative. . . . In particular, new dance electronica (trip-hop, techno, drum
and bass, house, and various derivatives)—perhaps the true contemporary
rock in terms of its mass impact, deviance, and antagonism (demonstrated
in venues such as illegal raves)—drew upon the sounds of space-age pop
for new lifeblood and inspiration. . . . Certainly, it was a good starting point
for vibrant, new musical futures. But the key is to prevent each future revival from going back and rekindling that boorish, racist exoticism that had
characterized the genre, an exoticism that some fifty years later can perhaps
be obliterated by means of a conscious detachment and proper irony. For us,
that is, irony lies in the fact that like our parents, we can delight in longing for
different worlds, appropriating styles and modes. Our parents might have put
on Hawaiian shirts and served up canned pineapple at a backyard barbecue
without a second thought. Unlike them, we came to knowledge that behind

the appropriation of other cultures—however playful and pleasurable—lies a certain form of denigration." See Adinolfi, *Mondo Exotica*, 20–21.

58 For an evocation of the feeling of tony lounges in Las Vegas casinos—within the context of a larger, thoughtful history of mid-twentieth-century lounge culture (and the Orientalist coordinates of its exotica)—see Adinolfi, *Mondo Exotica*, 87–88.

59 Wilde, "The True Function and Value of Criticism," 443. See also "Dean Martin: Quotes from the Man Himself." I am well aware of the laziness entailed by citing this source for Martin's witty remark about Berle.

60 Sigfried Kracauer, "The Hotel Lobby," 293, 291, 292, 295, 291, 293.

61 Kracauer, "The Hotel Lobby," 295, 292.

62 Villém Flusser, *Into the Universe of Technical Images*, 143. Flusser's praise is cautious: he posits that this idealized life of leisurely contemplation may come at the price of "all effects (politics) becom[ing] subhuman" and all knowledge of "suffering and . . . death" forgotten (144). And, of course, though we do live in something like the "telematic" or "cybernetic society" that Flusser conjures (143), its fruits are not, by a long shot, distributed evenly or equitably, and nowhere near "everyone" is situated to "live . . . at leisure."

63 Flusser, *Into the Universe of Technical Images*, 152–53.

64 Perry Como, quoted in Gilbert Millstein, "How to Relax: The Como Way," 19.

65 Shawn Levy, *Rat Pack Confidential*, 46, 124.

66 Nick Salvato, Review of *Amore: The Story of Italian American Song*, *Italian Americana* 30:2, 239. To return here to *Pride and Prejudice*, whose bizarrely uncanny resonances with lounge culture are becoming something more than a joke and, I hope, less than an obsession for me, I think of a fleeting moment in its television adaptation. In her account of Mr. Darcy (whom she is surprised not to find proud, as she had expected after conversation with her niece, Elizabeth), Mrs. Gardiner utters a line that a circle of old friends and I have long considered—for reasons that are only now becoming clear to me because of this work on lounging—one of the best of the miniseries: "His manners are all ease." Far from "eas[y]," manners are studied, acquired, and cultivated: to make them seem effortless, and thus to be charming, is to practice a talent intimately related to Martin's when he makes his work as an entertainer seem likewise easy, effortless, and charmed. See *Pride and Prejudice*.

67 Salvato, Review of *Amore*, 239.

68 Vivian Sobchack, "'Lounge Time,'" 156–58.

69 Michael Freedland, *Dean Martin*, 123.

70 Levy, *Rat Pack Confidential*, 47. If anyone worked hard, in a more conventional sense, on *Sleep Warm*, it was conductor Frank Sinatra, who chose not only the theme and songs for the concept album but also their arranger, whose "sympathetic string arrangements supported [Martin's] romantic vocals"; see William Ruhlmann, Review of *Sleep Warm*.

71 Freedland, *Dean Martin*, 144, 148, 149, 151.

72 I am grateful to the *Oxford English Dictionary*'s compilers for steering me to this epigraph and the preceding one. See the OED *Online*, entry for *unlocal*.

73 Deirdre O'Connell, telephone interview with the author.

74 O'Connell, telephone interview with the author.

75 Len Jenkin, quoted in Gary Winter, "Len Jenkin's *The Dream Express*."

76 Winter, "Len Jenkin's *The Dream Express*."

77 Jenkin, *The Dream Express: Set I*, 1, 2, 5, 15.

78 Jenkin, *The Dream Express: Set I*, 2.

79 Winter, "Len Jenkin's *The Dream Express*."

80 Jenkin, *The Dream Express: Set I*, 4.

81 Sven A. Kirsten, *The Book of Tiki*, 53, 52.

82 Kirsten, *The Book of Tiki*, 52–53.

83 See www.myspace.com/thedreamexpress.

84 Jenkin, *The Dream Express: Set I*, 6–8.

85 Jenkin, *The Dream Express: Set I*, 22.

86 Jenkin, *The Dream Express: Set I*, 26. In performance, audiences don't see these contrasts directly, though they are instructed by Spin and Marlene to visualize them ("Picture this"). And they do occasionally hear, as if on the other end of a telephone call, Uncle Wolfie's disembodied, booze-soaked, cigarette-coarsened (and prerecorded) voice, vividly provided by the late actor John Nesci (O'Connell, interview).

87 Jenkin, *The Dream Express: Set I*, 26, 27.

88 Jenkin, *The Dream Express: Set I*, 28.

89 Jenkin, *The Dream Express: Set I*, 3, 42.

90 Jenkin, *The Dream Express: Set I*, 22, 29.

91 Jenkin, *The Dream Express: Set I*, 1.

92 O'Connell, interview.

93 Moten and Harney, *The Undercommons*, 58–69.

94 Jenkin, *The Dream Express: Set I*, 11.

95 O'Connell, interview.

96 Adinolfi, *Mondo Exotica*, 79–80.

97 Saint-Amand, "Barthes' Laziness," 520.

98 Eve Kosofsky Sedgwick, *The Weather in Proust*, 83.

99 Jenkin, *The Dream Express: Set I*, 2, 8.

100 Jenkin, *The Dream Express: Set I*, 43.

101 *River of Grass*.

102 Todd Haynes, "Kelly Reichardt."

Chapter 3. Slowness

1 Editorial note in *Echographies of Television*, 30.

2 Derrida, "Echographies of Television," 70–71.

3 For a recent, insightful reading of Bergsonian "pure duration," see Bliss Cua Lim, *Translating Time*, 46–49. As Lim, following Bergson, suggests, temporal

heterogeneity does not inhere only in the varying rhythms of our responses to objects but also in the differences between our rhythmic perceptions of the objects and the rhythmic qualities of the objects themselves (66–67).

4 For an account of this historical imposition, see Lim, *Translating Time*, 44–45.

5 Whether one understands, in a commonsense way, slowness as a modifier of measurable duration or, in a Bergsonian way, measurable duration as a veil between us and such phenomenal experiences of time as slowness is less important to this analysis than offering a thick description of slowness and a theorization of its value—a theorization that would potentially confuse or alienate the maximal number of readers for whom I hope it will have purchase if I subordinated its unfolding to a Bergsonism with which either they are unfamiliar or they find inimical. Turning to Heidegger rather than Bergson, Stiegler offers an implicit way to understand why we might conceive the phenomenal experience of time as a quality or aspect of duration when he writes, "When Heidegger says that the clock is the time of the with-one-another, he means that technological time is public time. Now, it is in this common, public time, according to its possibilities, that a time is constituted that is not 'private' but *deferring and differing* [*différant*]. The calculation of time is thus not a falling away from primordial time, because calculation, *qua* the letter-number, also *actually* gives access in the history of being to any différance." See Stiegler, *Technics and Time*, 1, 237.

6 See, for instance, the third section of this interview, "Acts of Memory: Topolitics and Teletechnology," 56–67.

7 I borrow Derrida's (translator's) word for the critical intervention that cannot be understood as a wholesale reappropriation of power and meaning but that at the same time is not wholly collusive with, for instance, the mystifications of capital and the technical apparatuses through which these mystifications are propagated. As Derrida says in the filmed interview, "This mirage, that the addressee [of technics] might reappropriate what reaches him, is a fantasy. But this is no reason to abandon the addressee to passivity and not to militate for all forms, summary or sophisticated, of the right of response, right of selection, right of interception, right of intervention. . . . It's taking place, it's happening, this relative reappropriation is under way. . . . Above all, we should not be saying 'reappropriation' here, nor even relative reappropriation, but analyze another structure of what I have proposed to call exappropriation" (58).

8 Sam See, "Fast Books Read Slow," 342–43. The phrase *cult of speed* is Kern's; see *The Culture of Time and Space*, 111.

9 Paul Virilio, *Speed and Politics*, 46.

10 As Ulrik Ekman observes, though Stiegler does not explicitly acknowledge the debt, his work owes a great deal to Virilio's precedential example; in Ekman's words, "Stiegler's insistent call for a mode of critique responsive to the current condition of temporalization and territorialization, a new politics of memory, is not dissimilar in tone and motivation from at least three traits in Virilio:

technology as rapidly transformative in terms of transport or transmission; the speed of technology as anthropologically denaturing; technology today moving tendentially towards the absolute speed of light." See Ekman, "Of Transductive Speed—Stiegler," 54.

11 Ekman, "Of Transductive Speed—Stiegler," 46.

12 Stiegler, *Technics and Time, 1*, 276.

13 Ekman, "Of Transductive Speed—Stiegler," 54.

14 Virilio, *Speed and Politics*, 62.

15 Virilio, *Speed and Politics*, 67, 142. Italics in the original.

16 Stiegler, *Technics and Time, 2*, 7.

17 Virilio, *Speed and Politics*, 142.

18 In recent work, Stiegler raises this possibility in more explicit and emphatic terms. For instance, in the third chapter of *Mécréance et Discrédit*, an adaptation of which has been rendered in English, Stiegler contrasts the salutary "slow time of a true artistic experience," celebrated alongside "the primary affective solicitations of the greenery, of flowers, animals, the elements, solitude, of the village market, of silence and of slow time," with the baleful experience of the landscape "of urban congestion engendered by the excess of automobile traffic, of which bottlenecks are the most banal experience, and where the automobile, thought to facilitate mobility, produces on the contrary a noisy and polluting—that is, toxic—slowing down and paralysis." See Stiegler, "The Disaffected Individual in the Process of Psychic and Collective Disindividuation."

19 Eriksen writes, "A lot of what we do are [sic] hybrid activities that mix speed with slowness," and he adds, "It is necessary to switch consciously between fast and slow time. . . . Opposing (or complementary) tendencies exist side by side: a restlessness caused by the slowness of others, and frustration over external demands for speed and efficiency." See Eriksen, *Tyranny of the Moment*, 155, 159. In a similar fashion, John Tomlinson weighs the relative merits of speed and slowness against each other when he advocates, "Not uniform deceleration then, but the scope to intervene, to apply deliberate pressure to either pedal. . . . Proportion . . . has to be applied to our critical understanding of acceleration itself: that there may be *intrinsic value* in speed which should be preserved within any potential intervention in the rhythms of modernity." See Tomlinson, *The Culture of Speed*, 154.

20 Eriksen, *Tyranny of the Moment*, 147, 156–57, 160–64.

21 William E. Connolly, *Neuropolitics*, 143. Connolly's caution not to romanticize a slower and ostensibly more sanguine, pleasurable past is a welcome corrective to the nostalgic impulses animating works like Milan Kundera's *Slowness*.

22 John Urry, *Sociology beyond Societies*, 158, 159, 158.

23 Wendy Parkins and Geoffrey Craig, *Slow Living*, 50, 59.

24 Parkins and Craig, *Slow Living*, 3.

25 Robert Levine, *A Geography of Time*, 24, 25.

26 See Giorgio Agamben, *The Open*.

27 Karen Wendy Gilbert, "Slowness," 85.

28 Mihaly Csikszentmihalyi, *Flow*, 20.

29 Lama Surya Das, *Buddha Standard Time*, 129.

30 Csikszentmihalyi, *Flow*, 5, 4.

31 Csikszentmihalyi, *Flow*, 49.

32 Das, *Buddha Standard Time*, 6.

33 Das, *Buddha Standard Time*, 8–9.

34 Eve Kosofksy Sedgwick, "The Pedagogy of Buddhism," in *Touching Feeling*, 156.

35 Eihei Dōgen, *Shōbōgenzō: The Treasure House of the Eye of the True Teaching*, 109.

36 Kenneth K. Inada, "Time and Temporality," 176.

37 See, for instance, Zhihua Yao, "Four-Dimensional Time in Dzogchen and Heidegger."

38 Hubert Nearman, "Translator's Introduction: Uji," Dōgen, *Shōbōgenzō*, 106.

39 Inada, "Time and Temporality," 177.

40 Das, *Buddha Standard Time*, 6, 101.

41 Das, *Buddha Standard Time*, 118, 159.

42 Csikszentmihalyi, *Flow*, 66–67.

43 Csikszentmihalyi, *Flow*, 97 (emphasis added).

44 Csikszentmihalyi, *Flow*, 129.

45 The "temporarily . . . enjoyable" "loss of self-consciousness" that Csikszentmihalyi identifies with the flow experiences of the violinist and the rock climber (64), as well as his endorsement of the "enjoyment one gets from looking at a painting or sculpture," an enjoyment that "depends on the challenges that the work of art contains" (51), resonate powerfully with myriad descriptions of how cinema works on its audiences.

46 Das, *Buddha Standard Time*, 195.

47 In "The Time of Affect, or Bearing Witness to Life," Mark Hansen observes astutely of Stiegler's privileging of the identity between cinema and consciousness that "Stiegler generalizes" about consciousness on the basis of a medially "specific situation" and thereby "transforms what, for Husserl," of whom Stiegler's account comprises a reading and revision, "was a theoretically useful, but by no means typical, situation into a universal model of perception." While Hansen is right to critique the generalizing and universalizing tendency of Stiegler's argumentation, I would nonetheless submit that cinema provides a vibrantly occasional model for certain versions of consciousness. See Hansen, "The Time of Affect, or Bearing Witness to Life," 600.

48 Though Stiegler's turn to cinematic time is inextricably bound up with his investigation of lethargy, malaise, and the loss of individuation, he does allow of cinematic viewership, in a short burst of charity, that "if the film is good, we come out of it less lazy, even re-invigorated, full of emotion and the desire to do something, or else infused with a new outlook on things: the cinematographic machine, taking charge of our boredom, will have transformed it into new energy, transubstantiated it, made something out of nothing—the

nothing of that terrible, nearly fatal feeling of a Sunday afternoon of nothingness." See Stiegler, *Technics and Time, 3*, 10.

49 Csikszentmihalyi distinguishes pleasure from happiness when, for example, he writes, "Pleasure is an important component of the quality of life, but by itself it does not bring happiness. Sleep, rest, food, and sex provide restorative *homeostatic* experiences that return consciousness to order after the needs of the body intrude and cause psychic entropy to occur. But they do not produce psychological growth. They do not add complexity to the self. Pleasure helps to maintain order, but by itself cannot create new order in consciousness." Similarly, Das asserts of the difference between fleeting pleasure and sustained, blissful enlightenment, "You can exercise, nap, luxuriate in bed with a good book, get a massage, take a walk, work on a favorite project, take a long, hot bath, make love—and after such experiences, there's no doubt you can go back into the fray with more resolve, determination, and peace of mind. But these restorative activities do not always result in deep renewal, long-lasting regeneration, and spiritual liberation. They are the equivalent of profane time, experienced by the small self." See Csikszentmihalyi, *Flow*, 46; and Das, *Buddha Standard Time*, 163. Given Foucault's still-urgent rallying cry for an opposition to neoliberal biopolitics rooted in bodies and their pleasures—and given the precarity with which so many marginalized bodies move through the world and the fragility, if not foreclosure, of those bodies' pleasures—any discourse that brackets or refutes the value of pleasure must at least be subject to careful, skeptical scrutiny.

50 Adam Sternbergh explains that "on May 1 [2011]—almost seven weeks ago, or several eons in Internet time—the [*New York Times*] magazine published a Riff by Dan Kois titled 'Reaching for Culture That Remains Stubbornly Above My Grasp.' The shorter online headline is 'Eating Your Cultural Vegetables.' The tonal distinction between these two headlines may be crucial" as a force in unleashing the debate that followed these appearances of Kois's article. See Sternbergh, "How a Confession about Cultural Vegetables Turned into a Film-Critic Food Fight."

51 Dan Kois, "Eating Your Cultural Vegetables."

52 Manohla Dargis, "In Defense of the Slow and the Boring."

53 Sternbergh, "Food Fight."

54 Dargis, "In Defense of the Slow and the Boring."

55 Gilles Deleuze, *Cinema 2*, 100.

56 Ann Hornaday, "Director Kelly Reichardt on 'Meek's Cutoff' and Making Movies Her Way."

57 Vicente Rodriguez-Ortega, "An Interview with Kelly Reichardt."

58 Ryan Stewart, "Redefining Success: An Interview with Kelly Reichardt."

59 Kelly Reichardt, quoted in Gus Van Sant, "Kelly Reichardt."

60 Stewart, "Redefining Success."

61 Reichardt, quoted in Van Sant, "Kelly Reichardt."

62 Reichardt, quoted in Stewart, "Redefining Success."

63 Reichardt, quoted in Michael Joshua Rowin, "Q&A: Kelly Reichardt, Director of *Old Joy*."
64 Reichardt, quoted in James Ponsoldt, "Sound of Silence."
65 Reichardt, quoted in Rodriguez-Ortega, "An Interview."
66 *Old Joy*.
67 Rodriguez-Ortega, "An Interview."
68 Dargis, "In Defense of the Slow and Boring."
69 Vivian Sobchack, "Breadcrumbs in the Forest," 21–29.
70 Reichardt, quoted in Rodriguez-Ortega, "An Interview."
71 Reichardt, quoted in Ponsoldt, "Sound of Silence."
72 *Wendy and Lucy*.
73 Lim, *Translating Time*, 75.
74 Sarah Sharma, *In the Meantime*, 14.
75 Susan Stewart, *On Longing*, 13.
76 Reichardt, quoted in Ponsoldt, "Sound of Silence."
77 Reichardt, quoted in Ponsoldt, "Sound of Silence."
78 Reichardt, quoted in Alison Willmore, "Interview: Kelly Reichardt on 'Wendy and Lucy.'"
79 Reichardt, quoted in Sam Adams, "Kelly Reichardt and Jon Raymond."
80 Jon Raymond, quoted in Sam Adams, "Kelly Reichardt and Jon Raymond." For a detailed account of Raymond's collaboration with Reichardt, see J. J. Murphy, "A Similar Sense of Time."
81 Ponsoldt, "Sound of Silence."
82 Reichardt, quoted in Willmore, "Interview."
83 Reichardt, quoted in Rowin, "Q&A."
84 Reichardt, quoted in Willmore, "Interview."
85 Reichardt, quoted in Stewart, "Redefining Success."
86 Berlant, *Cruel Optimism*, 100, 106.
87 Berlant, *Cruel Optimism*, 113.
88 Berlant, *Cruel Optimism*, 114.
89 *12 Years a Slave*.
90 Csikszentmihalyi, *Flow*, 160.
91 Fred Moten and Stefano Harney, "The Academic Speed-Up."
92 Moten and Harney, "The Academic Speed-Up."
93 Moten and Harney, "The Academic Speed-Up."

Chapter 4. Cynicism

1 Traci Carroll, "Talking Out of School," 216–17.
2 See, among other exemplary texts in this field, Jacques Derrida, "The Animal That Therefore I Am (More to Follow)"; Cora Diamond, "The Difficulty of Reality and the Difficulty of Philosophy"; and Donna Haraway, *The Companion Species Manifesto*.
3 Carl Elliott, "How to Be an Academic Failure."

4 Elliott, "How to Be an Academic Failure."

5 Pierre Bourdieu, *On Television*, 5, 9.

6 Luis E. Navia, *Classical Cynicism*, 7.

7 William Chaloupka, *Everybody Knows*, 103.

8 Entry for "what evs," *Urban Dictionary*.

9 Chaloupka, *Everybody Knows*, xiv.

10 Timothy Bewes, *Cynicism and Postmodernity*, 7.

11 See, for instance, Ian Cutler, *Cynicism from Diogenes to Dilbert*, 8; William Desmond, *Cynics*, 2–3; and Navia, *Classical Cynicism*, viii.

12 David Mazella, *The Making of Modern Cynicism*, 8–11. Mazella, who adapts his three master terms from Alan Keenan's *Democracy in Question*, also makes frequent use of terms like *deadlock* and *impasse* to describe the cynical scenarios from which he hopes contemporary subjects might escape; and the regular appearance of these terms signals the gap between the cynicism imaginable only as a deadening position and the one constituting an enlivening obstruction, so different from an impasse, that I consider here.

13 Alan Liu, *The Laws of Cool*, 77–78.

14 Peter Sloterdijk, *Critique of Cynical Reason*, 5.

15 Liu, *The Laws of Cool*, 293–94.

16 Sloterdijk, *Critique of Cynical Reason*, xxxii.

17 Sloterdijk, *Critique of Cynical Reason*, 5.

18 Sloterdijk, *Critique of Cynical Reason*, 106.

19 Leslie Adelson, "Against the Enlightenment," 630.

20 Navia, for instance, is exceptional for claiming that modern cynicism is "the antithesis of classical Cynicism" (viii).

21 Epictetus, *The Discourses*, 278.

22 Desmond, *Cynics*, 2.

23 See Louisa Shea, *The Cynic Enlightenment*, xii.

24 Sharon A. Stanley, *The French Enlightenment and the Emergence of Modern Cynicism*, 12. Stanley is also invested in the possibility that accommodational cynicism— in her language, "cynical complicity" with the parts of the world that "appear mired in corruption and vice" (154)—could be a viable tactic in the arsenal of tools for navigating such a world; she is less interested than I am in distinguishing such accommodational cynicism from the critical cynicism with which it has an admittedly knotty relationship, and she claims that "diagnosis of constitutive social hypocrisy, dissimulation, and corruption," that is, critical cynicism, tends to lead the diagnosticians to "choose . . . complicity," that is, accommodational cynicism, "as the only viable mode of acting in concert with others" (12).

25 Stanley, *The French Enlightenment and the Emergence of Modern Cynicism*, 21.

26 Stanley, *The French Enlightenment and the Emergence of Modern Cynicism*, 12, 17.

27 Stanley, *The French Enlightenment and the Emergence of Modern Cynicism*, 154, 17, 154.

28 Berlant, *Cruel Optimism*, 1.

29 Berlant, *Cruel Optimism*, 2.
30 Stanley, *The French Enlightenment*, 17, 197.
31 Berlant, *Cruel Optimism*, 222, 28.
32 Berlant, *Cruel Optimism*, 117.
33 Michel Foucault, *The Government of Self and Others*, 43, 133, 56.
34 Foucault, *The Government of Self and Others*, 286–87.
35 See Sanford F. Schram, *After Welfare*, 178–80.
36 Schram, "The Praxis of Poor People's Movements," 716.
37 John L. Moles, "Cynic Cosmopolitanism," 119.
38 Navia, *Classical Cynicism*, 141.
39 Eric J. Brandenberg, interview with John Andrews.
40 Brandenberg, Interview with John Andrews.
41 Carol A. Stabile and Mark Harrison, "Introduction: Prime Time Animation— An Overview," 10.
42 "Cast and Crew Interviews," *Daria: The Complete Animated Series*.
43 "Cast and Crew Interviews," *Daria: The Complete Animated Series*.
44 Linda Simensky, "The Revival of the Studio-Era Cartoon in the 1990s."
45 In work produced in the 1980s and early 1990s, Andrew Goodwin developed an economic and material history of MTV that described three different periods at the network, each distinguished by different strategies for monetization and correspondingly different kinds of programming forms and decisions. Building on this instructive but now dated work—and drawing on more recent histories, like *I Want My MTV: The Uncensored Story of the Music Video Revolution*—I would embroider the account offered in the body of this book chapter and identify five distinct periods of the MTV project: a first lasting from the network's inception to the "*Thriller* moment," when big budgets for videos and the inclusion of African-American artists' videos in the programming lineup first made their presence impactfully felt; a second marked by the consolidation of big-budget video making as a norm, coinciding with the financial revitalization of the music industry, expanding markets for MTV, the network's purchase by Viacom, and changing corporate personnel at MTV; a third in which Sumner Redstone's takeover of Viacom stabilized personnel and inaugurated another shift in programming strategy at MTV, notably reflected in the development of original series, many of them ironically reflexive—the most network-referential and culturally influential examples of this kind of programming consisting in *The Real World* and *Beavis and Butt-head*; a fourth, the focus of this chapter's investigation of *Daria*, that we could call "MTV without music" and in which the exhaustion and abandonment of "original" programming ideas, in favor of spinoffs and sequels, coincided with the network's waning commitment to music (a waning occasionally but never fully interrupted or preempted by the network's responses to criticism of this shift) and thus sharp reduction in programming hours committed to airing music videos; and a fifth, ongoing at the time of this writing, whose intensification of the fourth period's trends are indexed by the cancellation of *Total Request Live*,

the rise of YouTube and Vevo as platforms for music videos' wide distribution and MTV's own more aggressive Web presence, and the network's new music-free logo and corporate name (MTV, akin to KFC before it, no longer officially abbreviating "Music Television"). See Andrew Goodwin, *Dancing in the Distraction Factory*; and Rob Tannenbaum and Craig Marks, *I Want My MTV*.

46 Kara Wild, "Glenn Eichler Interview."

47 Wild, "Glenn Eichler Interview."

48 Bill Hanna and Tom Ito, "Commercial Breaks," in *Animation: Art and Industry*, 181.

49 Scott Bukatman, *The Poetics of Slumberland*, 2.

50 For one of many examples, see Glenn Eichler, "Café Disaffecto." The episode concludes with Daria's public reading of an original short story, which is a parody of romance novels and spy thrillers and whose length breaks TV rules, especially those governing the family sitcoms that *Daria* resembles superficially, about how much uninterrupted listening to a monologue viewers—or rather auditors—will tolerate.

51 George Griffin, "Cartoon, Anti-Cartoon," in *Animation: Art and Industry*, 191–92.

52 Griffin, "Cartoon, Anti-Cartoon," 191.

53 Thomas Lamarre, *The Anime Machine*, xxv.

54 Lamarre, *The Anime Machine*, xxiv, 27, 110, 111, 38, 27.

55 "Transcript: Episode #102—'The Invitation,'" *Outpost Daria*. See also Anne D. Bernstein, "The Invitation."

56 Kathy M. Newman, "'Misery Chick': Irony, Alienation, and Animation in MTV's *Daria*," in *Prime Time Animation*, 192, 193.

57 In the episode "Arts 'n Crass," for instance, Helen admonishes Daria for "be[ing] so cynical all the time"; more substantively, in the episode "Write Where It Hurts," Daria has writer's block and confides as much to Helen, who responds, "What's hard for you is being honest about your wishes. About the way you think things should be, not the way they are. You gloss over it with a cynical joke and nobody finds out what you really believe in." On the other side of this conversation, Daria writes a story about an imagined future in which the members of her family have all cultivated the best versions of themselves. Helen's observation rings in time with the routine (and inaccurate) charge not just of cynics but indeed of Cynics that their vision is negative (in the sense of substractive) and offers no positive value, ideal, or system to affirm, whereas Daria's story jibes with Diogenes' interest in better approaching the perfectability of human nature, as well as with the ethical imperative to care for self and other that animates Foucault's reading of Cynical parrēsia. See Glenn Eichler, "Arts 'n Crass" and "Write Where It Hurts."

58 When looking to the representation of Daria (rather than to the conditions of *Daria*'s production or distribution), I tend to focus more, due to the constraints of space, on the character's critical cynicism and renovated Cynicism than on her ultimately less interesting accommodational cynicism. Nonetheless, they are all of a piece with one another, and in thinking through as much and

demonstrating as much in a more catalogic way, one could look further to numerous episodes, including "Lucky Strike," in which Daria-as-scab breaks the picket line to teach her own classmates while her teachers strike—but uses the occasion to excuse from class talented artist friend Jane Lane, who then helps the teachers design the signs for their picket; or "College Bored," in which Daria turns a healthy profit ghostwriting essays for college students—only, we later learn, to spend the money from this and related scams, bribes, and deals on such bizarre items for intellective contemplation (and thus singular self-cultivation) as a replica of a hydrocephalic skull ("The F Word"). See Peter Elwell, "Lucky Strike"; Sam Johnson and Chris Marcil, "College Bored"; and Rachelle Romberg, "The F Word."

59 Andreas Huyssen, "Foreword," in *Critique of Cynical Reason*, xx.

60 Desmond, *Cynics*, 122, 127.

61 Desmond, *Cynics*, 123.

62 Also memorable are a series of smirks and half-smiles that become all the more vivid than wide grins would be because of the way in which they break the relative singularity—the so-called "lack" of animation—of the deadpan (not the same as absent or blank) facial expressions with which Daria's deadpan voice is matched. The smirks contradict the typical journalistic claim that "Daria has never cracked a smile," and their paucity is glossed by Daria when, in response to her mother's prodding that "people judge you by your expressions," she retorts, "I don't like to smile unless I have a reason. . . . I believe there is something intrinsically wrong with that system [of judging] and have dedicated myself to changing it." See Anita Gates, "In Praise of the Most Unpopular Girl at Lawndale"; and Eichler, "The Misery Chick."

63 Eichler, "Esteemsters."

64 See Elwell, "Legends of the Mall."

65 Anton Chekhov, letter to Alexander Tikhonov (1902), quoted for instance in Geoffrey Borny, *Interpreting Chekhov*, 23.

66 Newman, "Misery Chick," 186. The quotation within this quotation originally appeared in Walter Belcher, "It's Time to Fall for 'Daria' and Gang," 4.

67 Neena Beeber, "The Lost Girls."

68 On May 24, 2010, then fourteen-year-old Tavi Gevinson, a precocious fashionista and already influential blogger-cum-tastemaker, gave an L2 Generation Next Forum talk, "The Unpredictability of Gen Y," in which she lovingly cited Daria's *edgy* monologue—and in which she also served "market research and . . . corporate master plan[ning]" by explaining to her industrial audience how best to brand clothing, social media, and related goods to tweens and teens. The beyond-ironic cynicism of making the reference in this context seems to have been lost on Gevinson. See Gevinson, "The Unpredictability of Gen Y."

69 In the episode "Prize Fighters," for instance, Daria writes a scathing essay when applying cynically for a college scholarship sponsored by a corporation with a discriminatory hiring record; but when she surprisingly gets an

interview for the prize, she learns that her parrēsiastic effort was construed as a "light-hearted spoof" rather than a serious critical intervention. See Neena Beeber, "Prize Fighters."

70 Laura Kightlinger and Glenn Eichler, "This Year's Model."

71 Eichler, "Fizz Ed."

72 Romberg, "The F Word."

73 Bernstein, "That Was Then, This Is Dumb."

74 Desmond, Cynics, 208.

75 See again, for instance, "Café Disaffecto," in which Daria questions the stated goals of an Internet café: "Come together with the planet? By staring at a screen for hours? Sitting in a room full of people you never say a word to?" Similarly, in the next episode, she satirizes sister Quinn's "interest . . . in what's new and attractive and popular"—that is, Quinn's desire to go to a nearby mall opening—when she quips, "Oh, I'm interested. But why go a mere 100 miles away? I bet they have some fascinating malls in Southeast Asia." Implicitly animating her barbs and jokes is a more capacious interest in global communities and their particularities than she finds among others in Lawndale. See Beeber, "Malled."

76 Kwame Anthony Appiah, Cosmopolitanism, xv.

77 Lamarre, The Anime Machine, 126.

78 Such an interpretation could jibe, more or less, with Lawrence Grossberg's take on the logic that obtains in cynically orchestrated popular cultures. As he writes, "If every identity is equally fake, a pose taken, then authentic inauthenticity celebrates the possibilities of poses without denying that that is all they are. It is a logic which seeks satisfactions knowing that they can never be satisfied, and that any particular pleasure is likely, in the end, to be disappointing. For even if all images are equally artificial, and all satisfactions equally unsatisfying, people still need some images, still seek some satisfactions. Although no particular pose can make a claim to some intrinsic status, any pose can gain a status by virtue of the [temporary and reflexive] commitment to it." See Grossberg, "Rock, Postmodernity and Authenticity," in We Gotta Get Out of This Place, 226.

79 "Daria Voice for GPS," NavTones.

80 Bernstein, "Pinch Sitter."

81 The series offers its own best summation of the cynical contours of Daria's and Jane's relationship when the characters exchange the following dialogue. Daria: "Sometimes I wonder if you're too cynical, even for me." Jane: "Really? You think?" Daria: "No. I was being sarcastic." See Sam Johnson and Chris Marcil, "Depth Takes a Holiday."

82 Eichler, "Boxing Daria."

83 Eichler, "Dear Beloved Consumer."

84 Bernstein, "Road Worrier."

85 Bernstein, "The Invitation," Daria.

86 Johnson and Marcil, "Depth Takes a Holiday."

87 Bernstein, "Road Worrier."

88 Jonathan Greenberg, "Groped by an Angel."

89 Manuel DeLanda, *Intensive Science and Virtual Philosophy*, 47, 117.

Chapter 5. Digressiveness

1 Anne Cotterill, *Digressive Voices in Early Modern English Literature*, 3.

2 Cotterill, *Digressive Voices in Early Modern English Literature*, 3.

3 Thomas M. Kavanaugh, "*Jacques le fataliste*," in *Diderot, Digression, and Dispersion*, 50.

4 Alan Liu, "The End of the End of the Book," 514.

5 Damon Young, *Distraction*, 2.

6 Young, *Distraction*, 3.

7 Nicholas Carr, *The Shallows*, 77, 118, 119.

8 Sven Birkerts, "Reading in the Digital Age."

9 Carr, *The Shallows*, 119.

10 Johann Hari, "How to Survive the Age of Distraction."

11 Robert Hassan, *The Age of Distraction*, xiv.

12 Thomas L. Friedman, "The Age of Interruption." Friedman borrows the phrase *continuous partial attention* from Linda Stone, "Continous Partial Attention."

13 Michael Wood, "Distraction Theory," 583.

14 Hanif Kureishi, "The Art of Distraction."

15 Joshua Foer, "The Adderall Me."

16 See, for instance, Cory Doctorow, "Writing in the Age of Distraction."

17 Joseph R. Urgo, *In the Age of Distraction*, 14, 8.

18 Urgo, *In the Age of Distraction*, 8.

19 Cathy N. Davidson, *Now You See It*, 5.

20 Davidson, *Now You See It*, 5 (emphasis added), 55–56.

21 Davidson, "Collaborative Learning for the Digital Age."

22 Urgo, *In the Age of Distraction*, 8.

23 Jonathan Crary, *Suspensions of Perception*, 1.

24 N. Katherine Hayles, *How We Think*, 69.

25 Hayles, *How We Think*, 250.

26 Hayles, *How We Think*, 69.

27 Hayles, *How We Think*, 73, 61.

28 Cotterill, *Digressive Voices in Early Modern English Literature*, 6, 7, 23, 22.

29 Jack Undank, "Preface," *Diderot, Digression, and Dispersion*, 7.

30 Undank, "Preface," *Diderot, Digression, and Dispersion*, 10.

31 *OED Online*, entries for *scroll* and *troll*.

32 Leslie Adelson, "Against the Enlightenment," 626.

33 Max Horkheimer and Theodor W. Adorno, *Dialectic of Enlightenment*, xv.

34 Horkheimer and Adorno, *Dialectic of Enlightenment*, xvi.

35 Horkheimer and Adorno, *Dialectic of Enlightenment*, 4, 2, 6.

36 Horkheimer and Adorno, *Dialectic of Enlightenment*, xviii, xvi.

37 Herbert Josephs, "Preface," *Diderot, Digression, and Dispersion*, 15–16.

38 Andrew H. Clark, "Diderot's Encyclopedic Poetics," 101. Again, what distinguishes my effort is a focus on the *Encyclopédie*, which Clark does not discuss explicitly even as he develops an account of Diderot's "encyclopedic counter poetics" (107).

39 Richard Yeo, "Lost Encyclopedias," 50.

40 Kavanaugh, "*Jacques le fataliste*," 161–62.

41 See DeLanda, *Intensive Science and Virtual Philosophy*. DeLanda distinguishes between "an ontology based on relations between general types and particular instances [that] is *hierarchical*, each level representing a different ontological category (organism, species, genera)," and an alternative "approach," which he advocates, rendered "in terms of interacting parts and emergent wholes lead[ing] to a *flat ontology*, one made exclusively of unique, singular individuals, differing in spatio-temporal scale but not in ontological status" (47).

42 David S. Ferris, "Post-Modern Interdisciplinarity," 1261.

43 Robert Darnton, "Philosophers Trim the Tree of Knowledge," in *The Great Cat Massacre*, 195 (emphasis added).

44 Denis Diderot, "Encyclopedia."

45 Daniel Brewer, *The Discourse of Enlightenment in Eighteenth-Century France*, 41.

46 Meditating thoughtfully on the linkage between the writerly and readerly positions established by the *Encyclopédie* (of which, I argue, the avenue passage provides one key manifestation via metaphorization), Brewer writes, "Unable to escape the arbitrary, the encyclopedic text figures an *arbiter*, marking out the reader's place in the interpretive act, demanding his or her participation, indeed justifying and legitimating it. And with this intervention, the fixed geometric point that previously grounded representation becomes plural. That single point, occupied by the transcendent observer of the Cartesian eye/I, multiplies into an infinite number of points of view. This is why the encyclopedists invent the crucial notion of *enchaînement* or linkage, a way of representing knowledge continuously, the linkage occurring in the act of reading" (Brewer, 53).

47 Of the relationship of a part like the "Encyclopedia" entry to the "whole, but one that is open," constituted by a work like the *Encyclopédie*, Clark writes, "Only by perceiving the inherent autonomy of the *parts*, their 'surreal monstrosity' as Barthes calls it, which is unleashed in the . . . order [of Diderot's encyclopedic counter poetics], can the [reader] gain any insight into the *whole*." In other words, apprehending the way in which the avenue metaphorizes the entry is necessary to apprehending how the avenue simultaneously metaphorizes the encyclopedia as such. See Clark, "Diderot's Encyclopedic Poetics," 108; and Roland Barthes, "The Plates of the *Encyclopedia*," 38.

48 Philipp Blom, *Enlightening the World*, 151, 152.

49 Yeo, "Lost Encyclopedias," 56.

50 Yeo, "Lost Encyclopedias," 62.

51 Joanna Stalnaker, *The Unfinished Enlightenment*, 214, 215. See also Philippe Roger and Robert Morrissey, eds., *"L'Encyclopédie."*

52 For a thick description of these design elements, their interactions, and the reasons for their invention and implementation, see Leonid Andreev, Jack Iverson, and Mark Olsen, "Re-Engineering a War Machine," 11–28.

53 Diderot, "Encyclopedia."

54 Berlant, "Introduction: The Intimate Public Sphere," *The Queen of America Goes to Washington City*, 9.

55 Stalnaker, *The Unfinished Enlightenment*, 214.

56 Wendy Hui Kyong Chun, "Introduction: Did Somebody Say New Media?" in Chun and Thomas Keenan, eds. *New Media, Old Media*, 2.

57 Chun, "Introduction: Did Somebody Say New Media?" in Chun and Keenan, eds. *New Media, Old Media*, 3.

58 Wolfgang Ernst, "Dis/Continuities," in *New Media, Old Media*, 107.

59 Peter Krapp, *Noise Channels*, 2.

60 Krapp, *Noise Channels*, 2.

61 Michael Zimmer, "*Renvois* of the Past, Present and Future," 96, 98.

62 In *Enlightening the World*, Blom also invites us implicitly to think along these lines when he writes of the cross-reference to a "nonexistent entry" in a way that jibes with similar, contemporary accounts of broken links: "An alphabetical order had seductive advantages: it democratized all forms of knowledge and avoided from the beginning the necessity to devote entire sections to subjects like theology. It also conformed with the fundamental ambition of the Encyclopedists to order the world according to rational criteria alone. It did, however, require a great deal of additional work. . . . Cross-references had to be agreed upon . . . binding the articles together in a network of interrelations; and then they had to be noted and remembered, making certain that a reference in a word beginning with 'A' to one beginning with 'Z' would not point to a nonexistent entry (inevitably, it did at times, as enraged subscribers were to point out)" (43–44).

63 Chun, "Introduction," 9.

64 Ernst Bloch, *The Principle of Hope*, 4–5.

65 Collin Gifford Brooke, "Revisiting the Matter and Manner of Linking in New Media," 73.

66 Dave Ciccoricco, "Network Vistas."

67 Ernst, "Dis/Continuities," 106.

68 Tara McPherson, "Reload," in *New Media, Old Media*, 205–6.

69 Alexander R. Galloway, "Protocol vs. Institutionalization," in *New Media, Old Media*, 195, 196.

70 Liu, "The End of the End of the Book," 508.

71 McPherson, "Reload," 206.

72 Zimmer, "*Renvois* of the Past, Present and Future," 96–97.

73 Chun, "The Enduring Ephemeral, or The Future Is a Memory," 148, 164, 171.

74 Chun, "The Enduring Ephemeral, or The Future Is a Memory," 170, 171.

75 Aimée Morrison, "Blogs and Blogging: Text and Practice," 370–72.

76 Eugenia Williamson, "Rich Juzwiak, the Superman of Supercuts, Waxes Philosophical about His Métier."

77 Tom McCormack, "Compilation Nation."

78 For a detailed and thoughtful history of the practice of television recapping, see Rich Juzwiak, "Tune In, Recap, Drop Out."

79 Rich Juzwiak, "Check It Out, Party People, While I Rock the Mic."

80 For an insightful account of the MP3 as container format, see Jonathan Sterne, "The MP3 as Cultural Artifact."

81 Juzwiak, "Waiting for Tonight."

82 Juzwiak, "Touched for the Very Second Time."

83 See Linda Hutcheon, A Theory of Parody.

84 Tim Lawrence, "Disco Madness."

85 Dagmawi Woubshet, Looking for the Dead.

86 Mary Thompson, "'Learn Something from This!'" 336.

87 Lisa Nakamura, Digitizing Race, 27.

88 OED Online, entry for mix.

89 Sierra Mannie, "Dear White Gays."

90 Aaron C. Thomas, "In Search of a Culture That Isn't Appropriate/d."

91 Brian Currid, "'We Are Family,'" 188.

92 Juzwiak, "About Me."

93 Juzwiak, "Check It Out."

94 Juzwiak, "And Back to Africa She Goes!"

95 Laurent Milesi, "Taste, Tastare, Tact," 322.

96 Renu Bora, "Outing Texture," 103–4.

97 Clay Shirky, Cognitive Surplus, 27–28.

98 Vivian Sobchack, "What My Fingers Knew."

99 See Carolyn Dinshaw, Getting Medieval; and Denis Diderot, "Journalist."

100 Juzwiak, "Bre's on Down the Road."

101 Blom, Enlightening the World, 46.

102 Juzwiak, "Tune In, Recap, Drop Out."

Conclusion. Sober Futurity

1 Juzwiak, "Tune In, Recap, Drop Out."

2 Chun, "The Enduring Ephemeral," 170.

3 OED Online, entry for "worry."

4 Wood, "Distraction Theory," 583.

5 Franco Berardi, After the Future, 138–39.

6 Berardi, After the Future, 139.

7 Fred Moten, "Blackness and Nothingness (Mysticism in the Flesh)," 779.

8 Lydia Goehr, "Reviewing Adorno," in Critical Models, ed. Goehr, trans. Henry W. Pickford, xxxiii.

9 Adorno, Critical Models, 80–81, 89.

10 Michael Warner, "Whitman's Drunkenness," 31, 37–38.

11 Marty Roth, "Carnival, Creativity, and the Sublimation of Drunkenness," 18. See also Roth, *Drunk the Night Before*. For further discussion of the continuities between nineteenth- and twentieth-century ideologies of drinking, see Harry Gene Levine, "The Alcohol Problem in America," 109–19.

12 Derek Waters and Jeremy Konner, *Drunk History*.

13 Rebecca Schneider, *Performing Remains*.

14 Hirokazu Miyazaki, *The Method of Hope*, 16.

15 See Jill Dolan, *Utopia in Performance*; and José Esteban Muñoz, *Cruising Utopia*. Like Miyazaki, both Dolan and Muñoz draw on Ernst Bloch's work in the magisterial, three-volume *The Principle of Hope*.

16 Lisa Duggan and José Esteban Muñoz, "Hope and Hopelessness: A Dialogue," 278.

17 Gayle S. Rubin, "A Little Humility," 371.

Bibliography

Books and Periodicals

Adams, Sam. "Kelly Reichardt and Jon Raymond." *The A.V. Club*. April 26, 2011. http://www.avclub.com/articles/kelly-reichardt-and-jon-raymond,55095/. Accessed October 5, 2012.

Adelson, Leslie. "Against the Enlightenment: A Theory with Teeth for the 1980s." *German Quarterly* 57:4 (autumn 1984): 625–31.

Adinolfi, Francesco. *Mondo Exotica: Sounds, Visions, Obsessions of the Cocktail Generation*. Ed. and trans. Karen Pinkus with Jason Vivrette. Durham, NC: Duke University Press, 2008.

Adorno, Theodor W. *Critical Models: Interventions and Catchwords*. Introduction by Lydia Goehr. Trans Henry W. Pickford. New York: Columbia University Press, 2005.

Agamben, Giorgio. *The Open: Man and Animal*. Trans. Kevin Attell. Stanford, CA: Stanford University Press, 2003.

———. "What Is the Contemporary?" In *"What Is an Apparatus?" and Other Essays*. Trans. David Kishik and Stefan Pedatella, 39–54. Stanford, CA: Stanford University Press, 2009.

Ahmed, Sara. *The Cultural Politics of Emotion*. Edinburgh: Edinburgh University Press, 2004.

Amos, Tori, and Ann Powers. *Tori Amos: Piece by Piece*. New York: Broadway Books, 2005.

Anderson, Sam. "In Defense of Distraction." *New York Magazine*. May 17, 2009. http://nymag.com/news/features/56793. Accessed September 16, 2013.

Andreev, Leonid, Jack Iverson, and Mark Olsen. "Re-Engineering a War Machine: ARTFL's *Encyclopédie*." *Literary and Linguistic Computing* 14:1 (1999), 11–28.

Appiah, Kwame Anthony. *Cosmopolitanism: Ethics in a World of Strangers*. New York: W. W. Norton, 2007.

Arendt, Hannah. *The Human Condition*. Chicago: University of Chicago Press, 1958.

Aronowitz, Stanley, and Jonathan Cutler, eds. *Post-Work: The Wages of Cybernation.* New York: Routledge, 1997.

Association for Theater in Higher Education. "Keynote Performance." *Performance Remains, Global Presence: Memory, Legacy, and Imagined Futures,* 12. Conference of the Association for Theater in Higher Education, 2011, Chicago, IL.

Balderama, Anthony. "Album Review: Tori Amos—*Midwinter Graces.*" *Consequence of Sound,* November 9, 2009. consequenceofsound.net/2009/11/album-review -tori-amos-midwinter-graces. Accessed March 23, 2011.

Balsa, Miguel. "Recourse to Action: The Renewal of Politics and Theater in Hannah Arendt, Antonin Artaud, and Augusto Boal." *Gestos* 23 (November 2008): 21–42.

Barthes, Roland. *The Neutral: Lecture Course at the Collège de France (1977–1978).* Trans. Rosalind E. Krauss and Denis Hollier. New York: Columbia University Press, 2005.

———. "The Plates of the *Encyclopedia.*" *New Critical Essays.* Trans. Richard Howard, 23–39. New York: Hill and Wang, 1980.

Belcher, Walter. "It's Time to Fall for 'Daria' and Gang." *Tampa Tribune.* August 27, 2000, 4.

Berardi, Franco "Bifo." *After the Future.* Trans. Arianna Bove, Melinda Cooper, Erik Empson, Enrico, Giuseppina Mecchia, and Tiziana Terranova. Oakland, CA: AK Press, 2011.

———. *The Soul at Work: From Alienation to Autonomy.* Trans. Francesca Cadel and Giuseppina Mecchia. New York: Semiotext(e), 2009.

Berlant, Lauren. *Cruel Optimism.* Durham, NC: Duke University Press, 2011.

———. *The Queen of America Goes to Washington City: Essays on Sex and Citizenship.* Durham, NC: Duke University Press, 1997.

Bewes, Timothy. *Cynicism and Postmodernity.* New York: Verso, 1997.

Birkerts, Sven. "Reading in the Digital Age." *American Scholar* (spring 2010). http:// theamericanscholar.org/reading-in-a-digital-age/#.Uiio2oD3Dfg. Accessed September 15, 2013.

Black, Max. "Definition, Presupposition, and Assertion." *Problems of Analysis: Philosophical Essays,* 25–54. Ithaca, NY: Cornell University Press, 1954.

———. "How Do Pictures Represent?" In *Art, Perception, and Reality,* ed. E. H. Gombrich, Julian Hochberg, and Black, 95–129. Baltimore, MD: Johns Hopkins University Press, 1972.

Bloch, Ernst. *The Principle of Hope.* Vol. 1. Trans. Neville Plaice, Stephen Plaice, and Paul Knight. Cambridge, MA: MIT Press, 1986.

Blom, Philipp. *Enlightening the World: Encyclopédie, The Book that Changed the Course of History.* New York: Palgrave, 2005.

Bora, Renu. "Outing Texture." In *Novel Gazing: Queer Readings in Fiction.* Ed. Eve Kosofsky Sedgwick, 94–127. Durham, NC: Duke University Press, 1997.

Bourdieu, Pierre. *On Television.* Trans. Priscilla Parkhurst Ferguson. New York: New Press, 1999.

Brandenberg, Eric J. Interview with John Andrews. *Animation Magazine,* May 4,

2005. www.animationmagazine.net/people/john-andrewssenior-vp
-creative—directorkachew. Accessed November 29, 2012.

Brewer, Daniel. *The Discourse of Enlightenment in Eighteenth-Century France: Diderot and the Art of Philosophizing*. New York: Cambridge University Press, 1993.

Brinkema, Eugenie. *The Forms of the Affects*. Durham, NC: Duke University Press, 2014.

Brooke, Collin Gifford. "Revisiting the Matter and Manner of Linking in New Media." In *Small Tech: The Culture of Digital Tools*, ed. Byron Hawk, David M. Reider, and Ollie Oviedo, 69–79. Minneapolis: University of Minnesota Press, 2008.

Brooks, Neil, and Josh Toth, eds. *The Mourning After: Attending the Wake of Postmodernism*. New York: Rodopi, 2007.

Bukatman, Scott. *The Poetics of Slumberland: Animated Spirits and the Animating Spirit*. Berkeley: University of California Press, 2012.

Burns, Lori. "Analytic Methodologies for Rock Music: Harmonic and Voice-Leading Strategies in Tori Amos's 'Crucify.'" In *Expression in Pop-Rock Music: A Collection of Critical and Analytical Essays*, ed. Walter Everett, 63–92. New York: Routledge, 1999.

Burt, E. S. "Regard for the Other: Embarrassment in the *Quatrième promenade*." *L'Esprit Créateur* 39:4 (winter 1999): 54–67.

Butler, Judith. "Capacity." In *Regarding Sedgwick: Essays on Queer Culture and Critical Theory*, ed. Stephen M. Barber and David L. Clark, 109–19. New York: Routledge, 2002.

Carr, Nicholas. *The Shallows: What the Internet Is Doing to Our Brains*. New York: W. W. Norton, 2010.

Carroll, Traci. "Talking Out of School: Academia Meets Generation X." In *GenXegesis: Essays on "Alternative" Youth (Sub)Culture*, ed. John M. Ulrich and Andrea L. Harris, 199–220. Madison: University of Wisconsin Press, 2003.

Chaloupka, William. *Everybody Knows: Cynicism in America*. Minneapolis: University of Minnesota Press, 1999.

Chekhov, Anton. Letter to Alexander Tikhonov (1902). Quoted in Geoffrey Borny, *Interpreting Chekhov*, 23. Canberra, AU: ANU E Press, 2006.

Chun, Wendy Hui Kyong. "The Enduring Ephemeral, or The Future Is a Memory." *Critical Inquiry* 35:1 (autumn 2008): 148–71.

Chun, Wendy Hui Kyong, and Thomas Keenan, eds. *New Media, Old Media: A History and Theory Reader*. New York: Routledge, 2006.

Ciccoricco, Dave. "Network Vistas: Folding the Cognitive Map." *Image [and] Narrative* 8 (May 2004). http://www.imageandnarrative.be/inarchive/issue08/daveciccoricco.htm. Accessed September 22, 2013.

Clark, Andrew H. "Diderot's Encyclopedic Poetics." *The Eighteenth Century* 53:1 (spring 2012): 99–111.

Collins, Wilkie, and Charles Dickens. *The Lazy Tour of Two Idle Apprentices*. www.authorama.com/the-lazy-tour-or-two-idle-apprentices-1.html.

Connolly, William E. *Neuropolitics: Thinking, Culture, Speed*. Minneapolis: University of Minnesota Press, 2002.

Cotterill, Anne. *Digressive Voices in Early Modern English Literature.* New York: Oxford University Press, 2004.

Crary, Jonathan. *Suspensions of Perception: Attention, Spectacle, and Modern Culture.* Cambridge, MA: MIT Press, 2001.

Crimp, Douglas. "Mario Montez, For Shame," In *Gay Shame*, ed. David M. Halperin and Valerie Traub, 63–75. Ann Arbor: University of Michigan Press, 2010.

Csikszentmihalyi, Mihaly. *Flow: The Psychology of Optimal Experience.* New York: HarperPerennial, 1991.

Currid, Brian. "'We Are Family': House Music and Queer Performativity." In *Cruising the Performative: Interventions into the Representation of Ethnicity, Nationality, and Sexuality*, ed. Sue-Ellen Case, Philip Brett, and Susan Leigh Foster, 162–96. Bloomington: Indiana University Press, 1995.

Cutler, Ian. *Cynicism from Diogenes to Dilbert.* Jefferson, NC: McFarland, 2005.

Cvetkovich, Ann. *Depression: A Public Feeling.* Durham, NC: Duke University Press, 2012.

Dargis, Manohla. "In Defense of the Slow and the Boring." *New York Times.* June 3, 2011. http://www.nytimes.com/2011/06/05/movies/films-in-defense-of-slow-and-boring.html. Accessed October 5, 2012.

"Daria Voice for GPS." *NavTones.* www.navtones.com/daria-voice-for-gps.html. Accessed December 2, 2012.

Darnton, Robert. *The Great Cat Massacre and Other Episodes in French Cultural History.* New York: Basic Books, 1984.

Das, Lama Surya. *Buddha Standard Time: Awakening to the Infinite Possibilities of Now.* New York: HarperOne, 2011.

Davidson, Cathy N. "Collaborative Learning for the Digital Age." *The Chronicle of Higher Education.* August 26, 2011. http://chronicle.com/article/Collaborative-Learning-for-the/128789. Accessed September 17, 2013.

———. *Now You See It: How Technology and Brain Science Will Transform Schools and Business for the 21st Century.* New York: Viking, 2011.

De Grazia, Sebastian. *Of Time, Work and Leisure.* New York: Twentieth Century Fund, 1962.

DeLanda, Manuel. *Intensive Science and Virtual Philosophy.* New York: Continuum, 2002.

Deleuze, Gilles. *Cinema 2: The Time-Image.* Trans. Hugh Tomlinson and Robert Galeta. Minneapolis: University of Minnesota Press, 1986.

Derrida, Jacques. "The Animal that Therefore I Am (More to Follow)." Trans. David Wills. *Critical Inquiry* 28:2 (winter 2002): 369–418.

———. "Otobiographies: The Teaching of Nietzsche and the Politics of the Proper Name." Trans. Avital Ronell. In *The Ear of the Other: Otobiography, Transference, Translation*, ed. Christie McDonald, 3–38. Lincoln: University of Nebraska Press, 1985.

Derrida, Jacques, and Bernard Stiegler. *Echographies of Television: Filmed Interviews.* Trans. Jennifer Bajorek. Malden, MA: Polity Press, 2002.

Desmond, William. *Cynics.* Berkeley: University of California Press, 2008.

Diamond, Cora. "The Difficulty of Reality and the Difficulty of Philosophy." *Philosophy and Animal Life*, 43–90. New York: Columbia University Press, 2008.

Diderot, Denis. "Encyclopedia." *The Encyclopedia of Diderot and d'Alembert Collaborative Translation Project*. Trans. Philip Stewart. Ann Arbor: MPublishing, University of Michigan Library, 2002. http://hdl.handle.net/2027/ spo.did2222.0000.004. Accessed September 20, 2013. Originally published as "Encyclopédie." *Encyclopédie ou Dictionnaire raisonné des sciences, des arts et des métiers*. Paris, 1755. 5:635–648A.

———. "Journalist." *The Encyclopedia of Diderot and d'Alembert Collaborative Translation Project*. Trans. Ethan Kent. Ann Arbor, MI: MPublishing, University of Michigan Library, 2005. http://hdl.handle.net/2027/spo.did2222.0000.536. Accessed September 20, 2013. Originally published as "Journaliste." *Encyclopédie ou Dictionnaire raisonné des sciences, des arts et des métiers*. Paris, 1765. 8:897–98.

Dinshaw, Carolyn. *Getting Medieval: Sexualities and Communities, Pre- and Postmodern.* Durham, NC: Duke University Press, 1999.

Doctorow, Cory. "Writing in the Age of Distraction." *Locus Magazine* (January 2009). http://www.locusmag.com/Features/2009/01/cory-doctorow-writing -in-age-of.html. Accessed September 16, 2013.

Dōgen, Eihei. *Shōbōgenzō: The Treasure House of the Eye of the True Teaching*. Trans. Hubert Nearman. Mount Shasta, CA: Shasta Abbey Press, 2007.

Dolan, Jill. *Utopia in Performance: Finding Hope at the Theater*. Ann Arbor: University of Michigan Press, 2005.

Doyle, Sady. "Birth of the Uncool: In Defense of the Tori Amos Fan." *Bitch* (spring 2011), bitchmagazine.org/article/birth-of-the-uncool. Accessed March 21, 2011.

"The Dream Express." *MySpace*. www.myspace.com/thedreamexpress. Accessed June 9, 2012.

Duggan, Lisa, and José Esteban Muñoz. "Hope and Hopelessness: A Dialogue." *Women and Performance: A Journal of Feminist Theory* 19:2 (July 2009): 275–83.

"Ears with Feet." *Urban Dictionary*. www.urbandictionary.com/define.php?term =ears%20with%20fe. Accessed April 27, 2011.

Ekman, Ulrik. "Of Transductive Speed—Stiegler." *Parallax* 13:4 (2007): 46–63.

Elliott, Carl. "How to Be an Academic Failure: An Introduction for Beginners." www.whitecoatblackhat.com/academicfailure. Accessed November 16, 2012.

Epictetus. *The Discourses*. Trans. George Long. New York: A. L. Burt, 1900.

Eriksen, Thomas Hylland. *Tyranny of the Moment: Fast and Slow Time in the Information Age*. Sterling, VA: Pluto Press, 2001.

Ferris, David S. "Post-Modern Interdisciplinarity: Kant, Diderot, and the Encyclopedic Project." MLN 118:5 (December 2003): 125–177.

Feuerbach, Ludwig. *The Essence of Christianity*. Trans. George Eliot. London: J. Chapman, 1854.

Finley, Karen. "Introduction." *Make Love: A Performance*. TDR: The Drama Review 47:4 (winter 2003): 51–53.

Fisher, Mark. *Capitalist Realism: Is There No Alternative?* Ropley, UK: Zero Books, 2009.

Fitzpatrick, Kathleen. *Planned Obsolescence: Publishing, Technology, and the Future of the Academy.* New York: NYU Press, 2011.

Flusser, Villém. *Into the Universe of Technical Images.* Trans. Nancy Ann Roth. Minneapolis: University of Minnesota Press, 2011.

Foer, Joshua. "The Adderall Me: My Romance with ADHD Meds." *Slate.* May 10, 2005. http://www.slate.com/articles/health_and_science/medical_examiner /2005/05/the_adderall_me.html. Accessed September 16, 2013.

Foucault, Michel. *The Government of Self and Others: Lectures at the Collège de France, 1982–1983.* Trans. Graham Burchell. New York: Palgrave Macmillan, 2010.

Freedland, Michael. *Dean Martin: King of the Road.* London: Robson Books, 2005.

Friedman, Thomas L. "The Age of Interruption." *New York Times.* July 5, 2006. http://www.nytimes.com/2006/07/05/opinion/05friedman.html?_r=0. Accessed September 15, 2013.

Fry, Paul H. *A Defense of Poetry: Reflections on the Occasion of Writing.* Stanford, CA: Stanford University Press, 1995.

Furniss, Maureen, ed. *Animation: Art and Industry.* Hertfordshire: John Libbey, 2009.

Fuss, Diana, ed. *Inside/Out: Lesbian Theories, Gay Theories.* New York: Routledge, 1991.

Gallop, Jane. *Anecdotal Theory.* Durham, NC: Duke University Press, 2002.

Gates, Anita. "In Praise of the Most Unpopular Girl at Lawndale." *New York Times.* May 16, 1999. www.nytimes.com/1999/05/16/arts/television-radio-in-praise -of-the-most-unpopular-girl-at-lawndale.html. Accessed December 3, 2012.

Gilbert, Karen Wendy. "Slowness: Notes toward an Economy of Différancial Rates of Being." In *The Affective Turn: Theorizing the Social,* ed. Patricia Ticineto Clough and Jean Halley, 77–105. Durham, NC: Duke University Press, 2007.

Goffman, Erving. "Embarrassment and Social Organization." *The American Journal of Sociology* 62:3 (November 1956): 264–71.

Goldsmith, Melissa Ursula Dawn. "Lounge Caravan: A Selective Discography." *Sound Recording Reviews* (June 2005): 1060–83.

Goodwin, Andrew. *Dancing in the Distraction Factory: Music Television and Popular Culture.* Minneapolis: University of Minnesota Press, 1992.

Gordon, Bonnie. "Tori Amos's Inner Voices." In *Women's Voices across Musical Worlds,* ed. Jane A. Bernstein, 187–207. Boston: Northeastern University Press, 2003.

Gray, Jonathan, Cornel Sandvoss, and C. Lee Harrington, eds. *Fandom: Identities and Communities in a Mediated World.* New York: NYU Press, 2007.

Greif, Mark. "Radiohead, or the Philosophy of Pop." *n+1* (fall 2005): 23–39.

Grossberg, Lawrence. *We Gotta Get Out of This Place: Popular Conservatism and Postmodern Culture.* New York: Routledge, 1992.

Halberstam, Judith. *The Queer Art of Failure.* Durham, NC: Duke University Press, 2011.

Hansen, Mark. "The Time of Affect, or Bearing Witness to Life." *Critical Inquiry* 30:3 (spring 2004): 584–626.

Haraway, Donna. *The Companion Species Manifesto: Dogs, People, and Significant Otherness*. Chicago: Prickly Paradigm Press, 2003.

Hardt, Michael, and Antonio Negri. *Empire*. Cambridge, MA: Harvard University Press, 2000.

Hari, Johann. "How to Survive the Age of Distraction." *The Independent*. June 24, 2011. http://www.independent.co.uk/voices/commentators/johann-hari /johann-hari-how-to-survive-the-age-of-distraction-2301851.html. Accessed September 15, 2013.

Harman, Chris. *Zombie Capitalism: Global Crisis and the Relevance of Marx*. Chicago: Haymarket Books, 2010.

Hassan, Robert. *The Age of Distraction: Reading, Writing, and Politics in a High-Speed Networked Economy*. New Brunswick, NJ: Transaction, 2011.

Halperin, David M., and Valerie Traub, eds. *Gay Shame*. Ann Arbor: University of Michigan Press, 2010.

Hayles, N. Katherine. *How We Think: Digital Media and Contemporary Technogenesis*. Chicago: University of Chicago Press, 2012.

Haynes, Todd. "Kelly Reichardt." BOMB *Magazine* 53 (fall 1995). http://bombsite .com/issues/53/articles/1891. Accessed October 8, 2012.

Heidegger, Martin. *Being and Time*. Trans. Joan Stambaugh. Albany: State University of New York Press, 1996.

Hilderbrand, Lucas. "'More Than One Way to Love': On Kiki and Herb (But Mostly Kiki)." *Camera Obscura* 67 (spring 2008): 178–83.

Horkheimer, Max, and Theodor W. Adorno. *Dialectic of Enlightenment: Philosophical Fragments*. Ed. Gunzlein Schmid Noerr and trans. Edmund Jephcott. Stanford, CA: Stanford University Press, 2002.

Hornaday, Ann. "Director Kelly Reichardt on 'Meek's Cutoff' and Making Movies Her Way." *The Washington Post*. May 19, 2011. http://www.washingtonpost .com/lifestyle/style/director-kelly-reichardt-on-meeks-cutoff—and-making -movies-her-way/2011/05/08/AFo1oK7G_story.html. Accessed October 5, 2012.

Hutcheon, Linda. *A Theory of Parody: The Teachings of Twentieth-Century Art Forms*. New York: Methuen, 1985.

Inada, Kenneth K. "Time and Temporality: A Buddhist Approach." *Philosophy East and West* 24:2 (April 1974): 171–79.

James, Henry. *Embarrassments*. New York: Macmillan, 1896.

———. *The Novels and Tales of Henry James*. Vol. 15. New York: Scribner's, 1909.

Jameson, Fredric. *Postmodernism; or, The Cultural Logic of Late Capitalism*. Durham, NC: Duke University Press, 1991.

Jenkins, Henry. *Textual Poachers: Television Fans and Participatory Culture*. New York: Routledge, 1992.

Johnson, Samuel. "The Idler's Character." In *Yale Edition of the Works of Samuel Johnson*. Vol. 2. *The Idler* and *The Adventurer*. Ed. W. J. Bate, John M. Bullitt, and L. F. Powell. New Haven, CT: Yale University Press, 1963.

Jones, Daniel. *My Friend Dylan Thomas*. London: Dent, 1977.

Joyrich, Lynne. "Tubular Visions: The Ins and Outs of Television Studies." Unpublished essay (2014).

"Just Me." Email to the author. March 21, 2011.

Juzwiak, Rich. "About Me." *fourfour*. http://fourfour.typepad.com/about.html. Accessed September 17, 2013.

———. "And Back to Africa She Goes!" *fourfour*. April 28, 2006. http://fourfour.typepad.com/fourfour/2006/04/and_back_to_afr.html. Accessed September 17, 2013.

———. "Bre's on Down the Road." *fourfour*. October 24, 2011. http://fourfour.typepad.com/fourfour/2011/10/bres-on-down-the-road.html. Accessed September 18, 2013.

———. "Check It Out, Party People, While I Rock the Mic." *fourfour*. May 31, 2005. http://fourfour.typepad.com/fourfour/2005/05/check_it_out_pa_1.html. Accessed September 15, 2013.

———. "Touched for the Very Second Time." *fourfour*. November 13, 2011. http://fourfour.typepad.com/fourfour/2011/11/touched-for-the-very-second-time.html. Accessed September 16, 2013.

———. "Tune In, Recap, Drop Out: Why I'll Never Recap a TV Show Again." *Gawker*. March 22, 2012. http://gawker.com/5895232/tune-in-recap-drop-out-why-ill-never-recap-a-tv-show-again. Accessed September 15, 2013.

———. "Waiting for Tonight." *fourfour*. September 17, 2007. http://fourfour.typepad.com/fourfour/2007/09/waiting-for-ton.html. Accessed September 16, 2013.

Keenan, Alan. *Democracy in Question*. Stanford, CA: Stanford University Press, 2003.

Keltner, Dacher, and Cameron Anderson. "Saving Face for Darwin: The Functions and Uses of Embarrassment." *Current Directions in Psychological Science* 9:6 (December 2000): 187–92.

Kern, Stephen. *The Culture of Time and Space, 1880–1918*. Cambridge, MA: Harvard University Press, 1986.

Kirsten, Sven A. *The Book of Tiki: The Cult of Polynesian Pop in Fifties America*. New York: Taschen, 2003.

Koestenbaum, Wayne. *Hotel Theory*. Brooklyn, NY: Soft Skull Press, 2007.

———. *Humiliation*. New York: Picador, 2011.

Kois, Dan. "Eating Your Cultural Vegetables." *New York Times*. April 29, 2011. http://www.nytimes.com/2011/05/01/magazine/mag-01Riff-t.html?pagewanted=all. Accessed October 5, 2012.

Kracauer, Sigfried. "The Hotel Lobby" (1963). Trans. Thomas Y. Levin. *Postcolonial Studies* 2:3 (1999): 289–97.

Krapp, Peter. *Noise Channels: Glitch and Error in Digital Culture*. Minneapolis: University of Minnesota Press, 2011.

Kundera, Milan. *Slowness: A Novel*. Trans. Linda Asher. New York: HarperCollins, 1996.

Kureishi, Hanif. "The Art of Distraction." *New York Times*. February 18, 2012. http://

www.nytimes.com/2012/02/19/opinion/sunday/the-art-of-distraction.html
?pagewanted=all. Accessed September 16, 2013.

Lafargue, Paul. *The Right to Be Lazy and Other Studies.* Trans. Charles H. Kerr. Chicago: Charles H. Kerr, 1907.

Lafrance, Mélisse. "The Problems of Agency and Resistance in Tori Amos's 'Crucify.'" In *Disruptive Divas: Feminism, Identity and Popular Culture,* ed. Lori Burns and Mélisse Lafrance, 63–72. New York: Routledge, 2001.

Lamarre, Thomas. *The Anime Machine: A Media Theory of Animation.* Minneapolis: University of Minnesota Press, 2009.

Lawrence, Tim. "Disco Madness: Walter Gibbons and the Legacy of Turntablism and Remixology." *Journal of Popular Music Studies* 20:3 (2008): 276–329.

Levine, Harry Gene. "The Alcohol Problem in America: From Temperance to Alcoholism." *British Journal of Addiction* 79 (1984): 109–19.

Levine, Robert. *A Geography of Time.* New York: Basic Books, 1997.

Levy, Shawn. *Rat Pack Confidential.* New York: Broadway Books, 1998.

Lim, Bliss Cua. *Translating Time: Cinema, the Fantastic, and Temporal Critique.* Durham, NC: Duke University Press, 2009.

Litvak, Joseph. *Strange Gourmets: Sophistication, Theory, and the Novel.* Durham, NC: Duke University Press, 1997.

Liu, Alan. "The End of the End of the Book: Dead Books, Lively Margins, and Social Computing." *Michigan Quarterly Review* 48:4 (fall 2009): 499–520.

———. *The Laws of Cool: Knowledge Work and the Culture of Information.* Chicago: University of Chicago Press, 2004.

López, José, and Garry Potter, eds. *After Postmodernism: An Introduction to Critical Realism.* New York: Continuum, 2005.

Lutz, Tom. *Doing Nothing: A History of Loafers, Loungers, Slackers, and Bums in America.* New York: Farrar, Straus and Giroux, 2006.

Mandelstam, Osip. "The Age." Trans. James McGavran. "4 Poems by Osip Mandelstam." *Tropics of Meta: Historiography for the Masses.* July 18, 2013. tropicsofmeta .wordpress.com/2013/07/18/4-poems-by-osip-mandelstam. Accessed December 28, 2014.

Mannie, Sierra. "Dear White Gays: Stop Stealing Black Female Culture." *Daily Mississippian.* July 8, 2014. http://thedmonline.com/dear-white-gays. Accessed January 5, 2014.

Martin, Dean. "Dean Martin: Quotes from the Man Himself." *Coolness Is Timeless.* March 16, 2009. www.coolnessistimeless.blogspot.com/2009/03/dean-martin -quotes-from-man-himself.html. Accessed June 5, 2012.

May, Matthew E. *In Pursuit of Elegance: Why the Best Ideas Have Something Missing.* New York: Broadway Books, 2009.

Mazella, Dave. *The Making of Modern Cynicism.* Charlottesville: University of Virginia Press, 2007.

McCormack, Tom. "Compilation Nation: The History and the Rise of the Supercut." *Moving Image Source.* April 25, 2011. http://www.movingimagesource.us /articles/compilation-nation-20110425. Accessed September 23, 2013.

Melas, Natalie. "Comparative Noncontemporaneities: C.L.R. James and Ernst Bloch." In *Theory Aside*, ed. Jason Potts and Daniel Stout, 56–77. Durham, NC: Duke University Press, 2014.

Menand, Louis. *The Marketplace of Ideas: Reform and Resistance in the American University*. New York: W. W. Norton, 2010.

Milesi, Laurent. "Taste, Tastare, Tact: A Deconstructive Touch of Digital Theory." In *Technicity*, ed. Arthur Bradley and Louis Armand, 317–45. Prague: Litteraria Pragensia, 2006.

Miller, Rowland S. *Embarrassment: Poise and Peril in Everyday Life*. New York: Guilford Press, 1996.

Millstein, Gilbert. "How to Relax: The Como Way." *New York Times*. January 29, 1956. 19, 22.

Miyazaki, Hiro. *The Method of Hope: Anthropology, Philosophy, and Fijian Knowledge*. Stanford, CA: Stanford University Press, 2004.

Modigliani, Andre. "Embarrassment and Embarrassability." *Sociometry* 31:3 (September 1968): 313–26.

Moles, John L. "Cynic Cosmopolitanism." In *The Cynics: The Cynic Movement in Antiquity and Its Legacy*, ed. R. Bracht Branham and Marie-Odile Goulet-Cazé, 105–20. Berkeley: University of California Press, 1996.

Morrison, Aimée. "Blogs and Blogging: Text and Practice." In *A Companion to Digital Literary Studies*, ed. Ray Siemens and Susan Schreibman, 369–87. Malden, MA: Blackwell, 2013.

Moten, Fred. "Blackness and Nothingness (Mysticism in the Flesh)." *South Atlantic Quarterly* 112:4 (fall 2013): 737–80.

Moten, Fred, and Stefano Harney. "The Academic Speed-Up." *Workplace: A Journal for Academic Labor* 4 (1999): http://louisville.edu/journal/workplace/issue4/harneymoten.html. Accessed October 5, 2012.

————. *The Undercommons: Fugitive Planning and Black Study*. New York: Autonomedia, 2013.

Muñoz, José Esteban. *Cruising Utopia: The Then and There of Queer Futurity*. New York: NYU Press, 2009.

Nakamura, Lisa. *Digitizing Race: Visual Cultures of the Internet*. Minneapolis: University of Minnesota Press, 2007.

Navia, Luis E. *Classical Cynicism: A Critical Study*. Westport, CT: Greenwood Press, 1996.

Nealon, Christopher. "Value | Theory | Crisis." PMLA 127:1 (January 2012): 101–6.

Nelson, Cary. *No University Is an Island: Saving Academic Freedom*. New York: NYU Press, 2010.

Ngai, Sianne. *Ugly Feelings*. Cambridge, MA: Harvard University Press, 2005.

Nye, Russell. *The Unembarrassed Muse: The Popular Arts in America*. New York: Dial Press, 1970.

O'Connell, Deirdre. Telephone interview with the author. May 27, 2012.

O'Connor, Sinéad. Open Letter to Miley Cyrus. October 2013. www.theguardian

.com/music/2013/oct/03/sinead-o-connor-open-letter-miley-cyrus. Accessed January 2, 2014.

OED Online. Entry for "comment," *v*. www.oedonline.com. Accessed October 10, 2013.

———. Entry for "lounge," *n*. www.oedonline.com. Accessed June 5, 2012.

———. Entry for "mix," *v*. www.oedonline.com. Accessed September 24, 2013.

———. Entry for "ob-," *prefix*. www.oedonline.com. Accessed October 1, 2013.

———. Entry for "obstruction," *n*. www.oedonline.com. Accessed October 3, 2013.

———. Entry for "scroll," *v*. www.oedonline.com. Accessed September 18, 2013.

———. Entry for "structure," *n*. www.oedonline.com. Accessed October 1, 2013.

———. Entry for "troll," *v*. www.oedonline.com. Accessed September 18, 2013.

———. Entry for "unlocal," *adj*. www.oedonline.com. Accessed June 7, 2012.

———. Entry for "worry," *n*. www.oedonline.com. Accessed October 7, 2013.

Ogden, Benjamin. "How Lars von Trier Sees the World: Postmodernism and Globalization in *The Five Obstructions*." *Quarterly Review of Film and Video* 27 (2010): 54–68.

Parker, Philip M., ed. *Lounge: Webster's Timeline History, 1466–2007*. San Diego: ICON Group International, 2009.

Parkins, Wendy, and Geoffrey Craig. *Slow Living*. New York: Berg, 2006.

Perkins, Claire. "In Treatment: *The Five Obstructions*." *Studies in Documentary Film* 4:2 (2010): 149–58.

Phillips-Fein, Kim. "Seattle to Baghdad." *n+1*, February 14, 2005, http://nplusonemag.com/seattle-baghdad. Accessed October 2, 2013.

Ponsoldt, James. "Sound of Silence." *Filmmaker* 15:1 (fall 2006). http://www.filmmakermagazine.com/issues/fall2006/features/sound_silence.php. Accessed October 5, 2012.

Puar, Jasbir. "Coda: The Cost of Getting Better. Suicide, Sensation, Switchpoints." *GLQ: A Journal of Lesbian and Gay Studies* 18:1 (2011): 149–58.

Purshouse, Luke. "Embarrassment: A Philosophical Analysis." *Philosophy* 76:298 (October 2001): 515–40.

Rabinow, Paul. *Marking Time: On the Anthropology of the Contemporary*. Princeton, NJ: Princeton University Press, 2008.

Rajchman, John. "The Contemporary: A New Idea?" *Passagens* 7 (January 2011): 4–21.

Reynolds, Simon, and Joy Press. *The Sex Revolts: Gender, Rebellion, and Rock 'n' Roll*. Cambridge, MA: Harvard University Press, 1996.

Ricks, Christopher. *Keats and Embarrassment*. New York: Oxford University Press, 1984.

Ridout, Nicholas. "Embarrassment: The Predicament of the Audience." In *Stage Fright, Animals, and Other Theatrical Problems*. Cambridge: Cambridge University Press, 2006.

Rodriguez-Ortega, Vicente. "An Interview with Kelly Reichardt." *Reverse Shot* 18 (fall 2006): http://www.reverseshot.com/article/reichardt_interview. Accessed October 5, 2012.

Roger, Philippe, and Robert Morrissey, eds. *L'Encyclopédie: Du réseau au livre et du livre au réseau.* Paris: Honoré Champion, 2001.

Ronell, Avital. *Stupidity.* Chicago: University of Illinois Press, 2002.

Roth, Marty. "Carnival, Creativity, and the Sublimation of Drunkenness." *Mosaic: A Journal for the Interdisciplinary Study of Literature* 30:2 (June 1997): 1–18.

———. *Drunk the Night Before: An Anatomy of Intoxication.* Minneapolis: University of Minnesota Press, 2005.

Rowin, Michael Joshua. "Q&A: Kelly Reichardt, Director of *Old Joy.*" *Stop Smiling.* September 22, 2006. http://www.stopsmilingonline.com/story_detail.php?id=655. Accessed October 5, 2012.

Rubin, Gayle S. "A Little Humility." In *Gay Shame,* ed. Halperin and Traub, 369–73.

Ruhlmann, William. Review of *Sleep Warm.* www.allmusic.com/album/sleep–warm–mw0000186071. Accessed June 7, 2012.

Saint-Amand, Pierre. "Barthes' Laziness." Trans. Jennifer Curtiss Gage. *Yale Journal of Criticism* 14:2 (fall 2001): 519–26.

———. *The Pursuit of Laziness: An Idle Interpretation of the Enlightenment.* Trans. Jennifer Curtiss Gage. Princeton, NJ: Princeton University Press, 2011.

Salvato, Nick. Review of *Amore: The Story of Italian American Song* by Mark Rotella. *Italian Americana* 30:2 (summer 2012): 239.

———. "Tramp Sensibility and the Afterlife of *Showgirls.*" *Theatre Journal* 58:4 (2006): 633–48.

———. *Uncloseting Drama: American Modernism and Queer Performance.* New Haven, CT: Yale University Press, 2010.

Sandoval-Strausz, Andrew K. *Hotel: An American History.* New Haven, CT: Yale University Press, 2008.

Savoy, Eric. "Embarrassments: Figure in the Closet." *The Henry James Review* 20:3 (fall 1999): 227–36.

Schneider, Rebecca. "It Seems As If . . . I Am Dead: Zombie Capitalism and Theatrical Labor." *TDR: The Drama Review* 56:4 (winter 2012): 150–62.

———. *Performing Remains: Art and War in Times of Theatrical Reenactment.* New York: Routledge, 2011.

Schram, Sanford F. *After Welfare: The Culture of Postindustrial Social Policy.* New York: NYU Press, 2000.

———. "The Praxis of Poor People's Movements: Strategy and Theory in Dissensus Politics." *Perspectives on Politics* 1:4 (December 2003): 715–20.

Schrecker, Ellen. *The Lost Soul of Higher Education: Corporatization, the Assault on Academic Freedom, and the End of the American University.* New York: New Press, 2010.

Sconce, Jeffrey. "'Trashing' the Academy: Taste, Excess, and an Emerging Politics of Cinematic Style." *Screen* 36:4 (1995): 371–93.

Sedgwick, Eve Kosofsky. *Epistemology of the Closet.* Berkeley: University of California Press, 1990.

———. *Tendencies.* Durham, NC: Duke University Press, 1993.

———. *Touching Feeling: Affect, Pedagogy, Performativity*. Durham, NC: Duke University Press, 2002.

———. *The Weather in Proust*. Durham, NC: Duke University Press, 2011.

Sedgwick, Eve Kosofsky, and Michael Moon. "Divinity: A Dossier, A Performance Piece, A Little Understood Emotion." In Sedgwick, *Tendencies*.

See, Sam. "Fast Books Read Slow: The Shapes of Speed in *Manhattan Transfer* and *The Sun Also Rises*." *JNT: Journal of Narrative Theory* 38:3 (fall 2008): 342–77.

Shakespeare, William. *The Merchant of Venice* (1596). OpenSource Shakespeare, http://www.opensourceshakespeare.org/views/plays/playmenu.php?WorkID=merchantvenice. Accessed October 4, 2013.

Sharma, Sarah. *In the Meantime: Temporality and Cultural Politics*. Durham, NC: Duke University Press, 2014.

Shea, Louisa. *The Cynic Enlightenment: Diogenes in the Salon*. Baltimore, MD: Johns Hopkins University Press, 2009.

Shirky, Clay. *Cognitive Surplus: Creativity and Generosity in a Connected Age*. New York: Penguin, 2010.

Simensky, Linda. "The Revival of the Studio-Era Cartoon in the 1990s." In *Funny Pictures: Animation and Comedy in Studio Era Hollywood*, ed. Daniel Goldmark and Charlie Keil, 272–91. Berkeley: University of California Press, 2011.

Simpson, James. "The Economy of Involucrum: Idleness in *Reason and Sensuality*." In *Through a Classical Eye: Transcultural and Transhistorical Visions in Medieval English, Italian, and Latin Literature in Honour of Winthrop Wetherbee*, ed. Andrew Galloway and R. F. Yeager, 390–412. Toronto: University of Toronto Press, 2009.

Singer, Ben. *Melodrama and Modernity: Early Sensational Cinema and Its Contexts*. New York: Columbia University Press, 2001.

Sloterdijk, Peter. *Critique of Cynical Reason*. Trans. Michael Eldred. Minneapolis: University of Minnesota Press, 1987.

Sobchack, Vivian. *Carnal Thoughts: Embodiment and Moving Image Culture*. Berkeley: University of California Press, 2004.

———. "'Lounge Time': Post-War Crises and the Chronotope of Film Noir." In *Refiguring American Film Genres: History and Theory*, ed. Nick Browne, 129–70. Berkeley: University of California Press, 1998.

———. "What My Fingers Knew: The Cinesthetic Subject, or Vision in the Flesh." *Senses of Cinema* 5 (April 2000). http://sensesofcinema.com/2000/5/fingers. Accessed September 19, 2013.

Sontag, Susan. *Against Interpretation and Other Essays*. New York: Farrar, Straus & Giroux, 1966.

Smith, Terry, Okwui Enwezor, and Nancy Condee, eds. *Antinomies of Art and Culture: Modernity, Postmodernity, Contemporaneity*. Durham, NC: Duke University Press, 2008.

Spigel, Lynn. *Make Room for TV: Television and the Family Ideal in Postwar America*. Chicago: University of Chicago Press, 1992.

Spillers, Hortense J. "'All the Things You Could Be by Now, If Sigmund Freud's

Wife Was Your Mother': Psychoanalysis and Race." In *Black, White, and in Color: Essays on American Literature and Culture*, 376–427. Chicago: University of Chicago Press, 2003.

Spivak, Gayatri Chakravorty. "Scattered Speculations on the Question of Value." *Diacritics* 15:4 (winter 1985): 73–93.

Stabile, Carol A., and Mark Harrison, eds. *Prime Time Animation: Television Animation and American Culture*. New York: Routledge, 2003.

Stalnaker, Joanna. *The Unfinished Enlightenment: Description in the Age of the Encyclopedia*. Ithaca, NY: Cornell University Press, 2010.

Stanley, Sharon A. *The French Enlightenment and the Emergence of Modern Cynicism*. New York: Cambridge University Press, 2012.

Sternbergh, Adam. "How a Confession about Cultural Vegetables Turned into a Film-Critic Food Fight." *New York Times*. June 9, 2011. http://6thfloor.blogs .nytimes.com/2011/06/09/how-a-confession-about-cultural-vegetables -turned-into-a-film-critic-food-fight. Accessed October 5, 2012.

Sterne, Jonathan. "The MP3 as Cultural Artifact." *New Media and Society* 8:5 (2006): 825–42.

Stevenson, Robert Louis. "An Apology for Idlers." www.library.wisc.edu/projects /glsdo/feraca/idlers.html. Accessed June 4, 2012.

Stewart, Ryan. "Redefining Success: An Interview with Kelly Reichardt." *Slant*. December 5, 2008. http://www.slantmagazine.com/film/feature/redefining -success-an-interview-with-kelly-reichardt/44. Accessed October 5, 2012.

Stewart, Susan. *On Longing: Narratives of the Miniature, the Gigantic, the Souvenir, the Collection*. Baltimore, MD: Johns Hopkins University Press, 1984.

Stiegler, Bernard. "The Disaffected Individual in the Process of Psychic and Collective Disindividuation." Trans. Patrick Rogan and Daniel Cross. *Ars Industrialis*. August 19, 2006. http://arsindustrialis.org/disaffected-individual -process-psychic-and-collective-disindividuation. Accessed October 11, 2013.

———. *Technics and Time, 1: The Fault of Epimetheus*. Trans. Richard Beardsworth and George Collins. Stanford, CA: Stanford University Press, 1998.

———. *Technics and Time, 2: Disorientation*. Trans. Stephen Barker. Stanford, CA: Stanford University Press, 2008.

———. *Technics and Time, 3: Cinematic Time and the Question of Malaise*. Trans. Stephen Barker. Stanford, CA: Stanford University Press, 2011.

Stone, Linda. "Continous Partial Attention." http://lindastone.net/qa/continuous -partial-attention/. Accessed September 15, 2013.

Tannenbaum, Rob, and Craig Marks. *I Want My MTV: The Uncensored Story of the Music Video Revolution*. New York: Plume, 2012.

Tennyson, Alfred. "The Lotos-Eaters." www.bartleby.com/42/638.html.

Terada, Rei. *Feeling in Theory: Emotion after the "Death of the Subject."* Cambridge, MA: Harvard University Press, 2003.

Terranova, Tiziana. *Network Culture: Politics for the Information Age*. Ann Arbor, MI: Pluto Press, 2004.

Thomas, Aaron C. "In Search of a Culture that Isn't Appropriate/d." *Tea to Pour*. July 25, 2014. http://teatopour.blogspot.com/2014/07/in-search-of-culture-that-isnt.html. Accessed January 5, 2014.

Thompson, Mary. "'Learn Something from This!' The Problem of Optional Ethnicity on *America's Next Top Model*." *Feminist Media Studies* 10:3 (2010): 335–52.

Tierney, William G., and Estela Mara Bensimon. *Promotion and Tenure: Community and Socialization in Academe*. Albany, NY: SUNY Press, 1996.

Tomlinson, John. *The Culture of Speed: The Coming of Immediacy*. Los Angeles: SAGE Publications, 2007.

Tompkins, Jane. *West of Everything: The Inner Life of Westerns*. New York: Oxford University Press, 1992.

Touré. "The Power and the Passion." *Rolling Stone* 685 (June 30, 1994), 66–68.

"Transcript: Episode #102—'The Invitation.'" *Outpost Daria*. www.outpost-daria.com/ts_ep102.html. Accessed November 29, 2012. This site ceased to exist before publication.

Undank, Jack, and Herbert Josephs, eds. *Diderot, Digression, and Dispersion: A Bicentennial Tribute*. Lexington, KY: French Forum, 1984.

Urban Dictionary. Entry for "what evs." www.urbandictionary.com/define.php?term=what%20evs. Accessed November 26, 2012.

Urgo, Joseph R. *In the Age of Distraction*. Jackson: University Press of Mississippi, 2000.

Urry, John. *Sociology beyond Societies: Mobilities for the Twenty-First Century*. New York: Routledge, 2000.

Vallese, Joe. Email to the author. March 20, 2011.

Van Sant, Gus. "Kelly Reichardt." BOMB *Magazine* 105 (fall 2008). http://bombsite.com/issues/105/articles/3182. Accessed October 5, 2012.

Villarejo, Amy. *Lesbian Rule: Cultural Criticism and the Value of Desire*. Durham, NC: Duke University Press, 2003.

Virilio, Paul. *Speed and Politics: An Essay on Dromology*. Trans. Mark Polizzotti. New York: Semiotext(e), 1986.

Virno, Paolo. *A Grammar of the Multitude: For an Analysis of Contemporary Forms of Life*. Trans. Isabella Bertoletti, James Cascaito, and Andrea Casson. New York: Semiotext(e), 2004.

Warner, Michael. "Whitman's Drunkenness." In *Breaking Bounds: Whitman and American Cultural Studies*, ed. Betsy Erkkila and Jay Grossman, 30–43. New York: Oxford University Press, 1996.

Wasserstein, Wendy. *Sloth*. New York: Oxford University Press, 2005.

Weeks, Kathi. *The Problem with Work: Feminism, Marxism, Antiwork Politics, and Postwork Imaginaries*. Durham, NC: Duke University Press, 2011.

Whiteley, Sheila. *Women and Popular Music: Sexuality, Identity, and Subjectivity*. New York: Routledge, 2001.

Wild, Kara. "Glenn Eichler Interview (Conducted from March 16, 2005 to January 2, 2006)." www.the-wildone.com/dvdaria/glenninterviewsfull.html. Accessed November 29, 2012.

Wilde, Oscar. *The Importance of Being Earnest*. 1895; reprint Buffalo, NY: Broadview Press, 2009.

———. "The True Function and Value of Criticism, with Some Remarks on the Importance of Doing Nothing: A Dialogue." *The Nineteenth Century* (July/September 1890): 123–47, 435–59.

Williams, Jeffrey J. "Deconstructing Academe: The Birth of Critical University Studies." *Chronicle of Higher Education*. February 19, 2012. http://chronicle.com /article/An-Emerging-Field-Deconstructs/130791/#disqus_thread. Accessed February 25, 2012.

Williamson, Eugenia. "Rich Juzwiak, the Superman of Supercuts, Waxes Philosophical about His Métier." *The Phoenix*. May 4, 2012. http://thephoenix.com /boston/life/137997-rich-juzwiak-the-superman-of-supercuts-waxes-phi. Accessed September 23, 2013.

Willmore, Alison. "Interview: Kelly Reichardt on 'Wendy and Lucy.'" *IFC*. December 10, 2008. http://www.ifc.com/fix/2008/12/interview-kelly-reichardt-on-w. Accessed October 5, 2012.

Winter, Gary. "Len Jenkin's *The Dream Express*: The Outlaw Lounge Act Returns." *Brooklyn Rail: Critical Perspectives on Arts, Politics, and Culture*. November 2009. brooklynrail.org/2009/11/theater/len-jenkins-the-dream-express-the-outlaw -lounge-act—returns. Accessed June 9, 2012.

Wood, Michael. "Distraction Theory: How to Read while Thinking of Something Else." *Michigan Quarterly Review* 48:4 (fall 2009): 577–88.

Woubshet, Dag. *Looking for the Dead: Black Queer Mourning in the Early Era of AIDS*. Unpublished manuscript (2012).

Yao, Zhihua. "Four-Dimensional Time in Dzogchen and Heidegger." *Philosophy East and West* 57:4 (October 2007): 512–32.

Yeo, Richard. "Lost Encyclopedias: Before and After the Enlightenment." *Book History* 10 (2007): 47–68.

Young, Damon. *Distraction: A Philosopher's Guide to Being Free*. Melbourne, AU: Melbourne University Press, 2008.

Zimmer, Michael. "*Renvois* of the Past, Present and Future: Hyperlinks and the Structuring of Knowledge from the *Encyclopédie* to Web 2.0." *New Media and Society* 11:1, 2 (2009): 95–114.

Audio Recordings, Films, Performances, and Broadcasts

Amos, Tori. "All Through the Night." Royce Hall Auditorium. Los Angeles, CA. April 25, 2005. *YouTube*. Uploaded September 20, 2010. https://www.youtube .com/watch?v=zangDHSok_Q. Accessed April 27, 2011.

———. "Cooling." Bonnaroo. Manchester, TN. June 11, 2010. *YouTube*. Uploaded June 25, 2010. https://www.youtube.com/watch?v=Z9qc3LwJIsU. Accessed June 15, 2012.

———. "Cooling." QPAC Concert Hall. Brisbane, AU. November 24, 2009.

YouTube. Uploaded November 30, 2009. https://www.youtube.com/watch?v
=wVv8GPPWDN0. Accessed June 15, 2012.
———. "Cooling." *Spark* (UK limited edition). Atlantic Records (1998).
———. "Cornflake Girl." *Under the Pink*. Atlantic Records (1994).
———. "Glory of the 80s." *To Venus and Back*. Atlantic Records (1999).
———. "Liquid Diamonds." *from the choirgirl hotel*. Atlantic Records (1998).
———. "Precious Things." *Little Earthquakes*. Atlantic Records (1992).
———. "Tear in Your Hand." *Little Earthquakes*. Atlantic Records (1992).
———. "When a Star Falls Down." Melbourne, Australia. September 11, 2007.
    YouTube. www.youtube.com/watch?v=YAr7fRgMtZ8. Accessed April 27, 2011.
———. "Your Cloud." *Scarlet's Walk*. Epic Records (2002).
Beeber, Neena. "The Lost Girls." *Daria*. MTV (original air date: March 24, 1999).
———. "Malled." *Daria*. MTV (original air date: March 31, 1997).
———. "Prize Fighters." *Daria*. MTV (original air date: June 11, 2001).
Bernstein, Anne D. "The Invitation." *Daria*. MTV (original air date: March 10,
    1997).
———. "Pinch Sitter." *Daria*. MTV (original air date: June 9, 1997).
———. "Road Worrier." *Daria*. MTV (original air date: July 7, 1997).
———. "That Was Then, This Is Dumb." *Daria*. MTV (original air date: March 16,
    1998).
"Cast and Crew Interviews." *Daria: The Complete Animated Series*. MTV (2010).
Eichler, Glenn. "Arts 'n Crass." *Daria*. MTV (original air date: February 16, 1998).
———. "Boxing Daria." *Daria*. MTV (original air date: June 25, 2001).
———. "Café Disaffecto." *Daria*. MTV (original air date: March 24, 1997).
———. "Dear Beloved Consumer" (liner note). *Daria: The Complete Animated Series*.
    Paramount Pictures (2010).
——— "Esteemsters." *Daria*. MTV (original air date: March 3, 1997).
———. "Fizz Ed." *Daria*. MTV (original air date: February 19, 2001).
———. "The Misery Chick." *Daria*. MTV (original air date: July 21, 1997).
———. "Write Where It Hurts." *Daria*. MTV (original air date: August 3, 1998).
Elwell, Peter. "Legends of the Mall." *Daria*. MTV (original air date: July 12, 2000).
———. "Lucky Strike." *Daria*. MTV (original air date: March 26, 2001).
The Five Obstructions. Dir. Jørgen Leth, Lars von Trier. Zentropa Real ApS (2003).
Gevinson, Tavi. "The Unpredictability of Gen Y." *YouTube*. Uploaded May 27, 2010.
    www.youtube.com/watch?v=1gWxTUBasrU. Accessed December 3, 2012.
Glass, Ira. "Cringe." *This American Life*. National Public Radio (original air date:
    April 13, 2001).
Greenberg, Jonathan. "Groped by an Angel." *Daria*. MTV (original air date: July 19,
    2000).
Jenkin, Len. *The Dream Express: Set I*. November 2004. www.lenjenkin.com/texts
    /The_Dream_Express_Set_I.pdf. Accessed June 9, 2012.
Johnson, Sam, and Chris Marcil. "College Bored." *Daria*. MTV (original air date:
    March 17, 1997).

————. "Depth Takes a Holiday." *Daria*. MTV (original air date: March 10, 1999).

Kightlinger, Laura, and Glenn Eichler. "This Year's Model." *Daria*. MTV (original air date: April 7, 1997).

Old Joy (2006). Dir. Kelly Reichardt. Kino International (2007).

Pride and Prejudice. Dir. Simon Langton. BBC (original air dates: September 24–October 29, 1995).

River of Grass. Dir. Kelly Reichardt. Good Machine (1994).

Romberg, Rachelle. "The F Word." *Daria*. MTV (original air date: March 31, 2000).

ToriAmos.com | Music | Albums. www.toriamos.com/go/music. Accessed March 23, 2011.

12 Years a Slave (2013). Dir. Steve McQueen. 20th Century Fox (2014).

Waters, Derek, and Jeremy Konner. *Drunk History* (2007). www.funnyordie.com/drunkhistory. Accessed October 8, 2013.

Wendy and Lucy (2008). Dir. Kelly Reichardt. Oscilloscope Pictures (2009).

Wynette, Tammy. *Stand By Your Man*. Epic Records (September 1968).

Index

Page numbers in italics refer to figures.

attention: dissipation of, 159–60, 162; fetishization of, 165; lazing and, 69; spectatorship and, 99, 114; techno-genesis and, 166; time and, 102–3

authorial I: as obstruction, 15; embarrassment and, 35–36, 38–40, 57–58; reflexive use of, 14–15, 35, 57. See also subjectivity.

banality: cynicism and 23, 149, 181; ephemerality and, 181, 191; obstruction and 3; shock and 108, 167

Barthes, Roland, 70–71, 72, 79

"Bartleby the Scrivener," 28, 67, 148

Bataille, Georges, 103

Beavis and Butt-head, 127–28, 142

Being and Time, 9, 31

Benjamin, Walter, 163

Berardi, Franco, 74–75, 195–96, 197

Bergson, Henri, 96, 110, 217–18n

Berlant, Lauren: on collective detach-ment, 140; on cruel optimism, 23, 137–38, 203; on hierarchy, 176; on slow death, 3, 123–24

Bieber, Justin, 26

Big Love, 34

"The Big Picture," 52f

Billboard, 50

Birkerts, Sven, 162

Blackout, 34

"Bliss," 54

Bloch, Ernst, 178–79

blogging, 25, 180, 181–92. See also Web.

Blom, Philipp, 174

Bloom, Harold, 195

blush: embarrassment and, 40, 42–43; shame and, 18. See also cringe.

Bolz, Norbert, 178

Bond, Justin Vivian, 64, 92. See also Kiki and Herb

Boondocks, The, 26

Bora, Renu, 188–89

Borges, Jorge Luis, 65

Bourdieu, Pierre, 130

Boys for Pele, 34, 60

Brewer, Daniel, 172

Brinkema, Eugenie, 209–210n

Brooke, Collin Gifford, 179

Brown, Bobby, 192

Buddhism: popularization of, 105; time in, 21, 100, 104–5

Burt, E.S., 48

Bush, George, 118

Butler, Judith, 205n

C.K., Louis, 44

camp, 56, 188, 191, 209n, 210n

capacity: debility and, 205n; digressing and, 158–59, 192, 193; eccentricity and, 3; incapacity and, 13; role segre-gation as, 18

capitalism: academia and, 125–26, 165; afterlife and, 26, 88; contemporane-ity and, 74–75, 87–88; cynicism and, 131, 132, 146–47; disruptions of, 16, 32, 68, 90; extrinsicalness to, 2, 68, 140; fetishism and, 188; history of, 68–69, 124–25; inequities of, 10, 64, 74, 87–88, 116, 118–20, 123–25; infotainment and, 59; realism and, 32; reform of, 74, 88

care, 102, 126, 129, 141, 203

Careless Love, 84

Carey, Mariah, 192

Carr, Nicholas, 162, 165

Carroll, Traci, 127–29

Cera, Michael, 200

Cheadle, Don, 200, 201f

Chekhov, Anton, 23, 149–50

"China," 54

Chun, Wendy Hui Kyong: on enduring ephemerality, 25, 180, 188, 191; on new media, 177–78; on speed, 180, 193

Ciccoricco, Dave, 179

cinema: animation and, 144; camera-work in, 111–12, 114; consciousness and, 100, 108, 114–15, 120–21, 220n;

images in, 110, 112–13, 113*f*, 114; production practices in, 22, 100, 110, 121–22; slowness in, 99, 113–14, 118–20; time and, 108, 109–10, 116

Clark, Andrew H., 170

class: *The Dream Express* on, 83, 90; leisure and, 73, 102; lounge and, 78, 215n; nineteenth-century formations of, 69; obstruction and, 27; working, 116, 120, 123–24

Clerks, 93

Clooney, Rosemary, 61

Cognitive Surplus, 188

Comeback, The, 43

Comedy Central, 202

Como, Perry, 81

Condee, Nancy, 11

Connolly, William E., 101

contemporaneity: asynchronous temporalities of, 11, 14, 93, 101; disorientation and, 101; of *The Five Obstructions*, 10–11; new media and, 24; tyranny and, 33, 74, 101

control: of consciousness, 104–5; coolness and, 61; loss of, 54, 199–200; network protocols and, 179–80; relinquishment of, 7–8, 61, 66–67, 91

"Cooling," 60–61

coolness: cynicism as, 133–34; indifference and, 12–13, 133–34; of The Dream Express, 89; of Jørgen Leth, 7; obverse of, 37, 54, 78–79. *See also* control.

"Cornflake Girl," 53

cosmopolitanism, 23, 85–86, 101, 131–32, 151–52

Cotterill, Anne, 157–58, 167–168

Craig, Geoffrey, 102

Crary, Jonathan, 165

Craven, Wes, 44

Crimp, Douglas, 38

cringe: activity inspiring, 37, 43; blush versus, 18, 43; embarrassment and,

40, 43–44; historicity of, 43–44; as overlooked, 43

cringe comedy, 43–44

critical inquiry: cynicism and, 133–35; digressiveness and, 192; disengagement versus, 21; embarrassment and, 18–19; impediments to, 195; laughter and, 201; laziness and, 65–66; misrecognition and, 29, 40; slowness and, 98, 106, 120–21; sophistication and, 17–18; speed and, 100

Critique of Cynical Reason, 134–35, 147–48

"Crucify," 51

cruelty: embarrassment and, 58; of Lars von Trier, 7; of optimism, 23, 137–38

Csikszentmihalyi, Mihaly, 104–5, 107–8, 125

cultural criticism: American versions of, 17, 33, 35; media and performance studies as, 31; speed as topic in, 100; writing of, 15–16, 49, 121

Cumberbatch, Benjamin, 125

curiosity: contemporaneity and, 17; digressiveness and, 168; disciplinarity and, 31; encyclopedism and, 173

Currid, Brian, 185–86

cynicism: accommodationism and, 22–23, 126, 131, 133–34, 136–37, 140–41, 142, 223n; cinema and, 109; critique and, 22–23, 131, 134, 136–37, 141–42, 142–43, 223n; movement and, 148, 153–54; optimism versus, 23, 136–38; nihilism versus, 23, 132–33; pessimism versus, 23, 132–33, 136; realism and, 130; slogans of, 132, 150; stuckness in, 129; television and, 22, 130, 142–43; tripartite form of, 22–23, 131, 138, 140, 143, 153–55. *See also* Daria *and* Daria.

Cynicism (classical): relationship of cynicism to, 22–23, 128, 132, 136; orthography of, 128; principles of, 131–32, 136, 141; renovated forms of, 131, 132, 134–35, 141, 154

Cyrus, Miley, 58

D'Alembert, Jean le Rond, 171

dance floor: metaphorizing obstruction's embrace, 4; subjectivation and, 185

Darger, Henry, 86

Dargis, Manohla, 109–10, 114–15

Daria (character): affect of, 131; cosmopolitanism of, 151; as Cynical theatricalist, 147–49; gestures of, 148, 149f, 226n; as parrēsiast, 149–50, 153; radical incrementalism of, 150–51; voice of, 147, 153

Daria (series): aesthetics of, 131, 143–44, 146f, 146–47, 149f, 151–52, 152f; "Boxing Daria" episode of, 153; "Café Disaffecto" episode of, 225n, 227n; closing credit sequence of, 151–52, 152f; cosmopolitanism of, 152; development of, 142–43; "Esteemsters" episode of, 148–49; "The Invitation" episode of, 144–47; "The Lost Girls" episode of, 150; opening credit sequence of, 148; "Pinch Sitter" episode of, 153; politics of, 146–47, 151–53; production of, 143; soundtrack of, 153, 154–55; tripartite cynicism of, 23, 26, 131, 143–44, 146–48; "Write Where It Hurts" episode of, 225n

Daria: The Complete Animated Series, 154–55

Darnton, Robert, 171, 173

Davidson, Cathy N., 164–65

Das, Lama Surya, 104–8

daydreaming, 97–98, 163

DeLanda, Manuel, 155, 171, 176

Deleuze, Gilles, 110, 155

Denny, Martin, 79

Derrida, Jacques, 55–56, 95–99, 122, 128, 187, 218n

desire: critical race studies and, 28–29; cynicism and, 22, 142; Cynical evacuation of, 136; role segregation and, 19; unwitting manifestation of, 20; Web innovation and, 59, 183

Desmond, William, 136

Dialectic of Enlightenment, 169–70

Dialogues, 18, 48

Diamond, Cora, 128

Diderot, Denis: contemporaneity of, 161, 179; digressive encyclopedism of, 160, 170, 173–74, 179, 189; as Encyclopédie contributor, 24, 170–75

difficulty, 11, 15, 70

digression: digressiveness versus, 157, 167; as step aside, 157–58, 167

digressiveness: attention and, 24; distraction versus, 24, 160–61; encyclopedism's interplay with, 155, 170, 173–74, 190, 192; metaphors for, 155; movement and, 155, 168; as strategy, 24, 157. See also encyclopedism, Diderot, Denis, fourfour, Juzwiak, Rich, and remixing.

dilation: of time, 96–97, 113–14, 121. See also duration.

Diogenes Laertius, 138–39

Diogenes of Sinope: asceticism of, 131, 135; cosmopolitanism of, 132, 151; mythologization of, 135, 147–48; as parrēsiast, 138–41

disidentification, 183–84, 185–86

disorientation, 101, 116

distraction: attention versus, 159; cinema and, 109, 111; reading and, 162, 166–67; studies of, 24, 166, 162–63; thinking and, 164–66; Web and, 159–60

Distraction, 159–60

Divine, 152

Dōgen, 105–6

15, 131, 195–96; foreclosure through, 27, 197; humility and, 203; impasse versus, 4, 7, 97, 223n; instability and, 202; instruction and, 9; malaise and, 101; movement and, 4, 29, 197; negation and, 197–198; obstacle versus, 5, 7, 97; prefix *ob-* in, 8–9; surprising value of, 1, 97, 99, 130, 198

O'Connell, Deirdre, 64, 84–85, 88–89, 90. *See also* The Dream Express *and* The Dream Express.

O'Connor, Sinéad, 58–60

Office, The, 44

Old Joy: acting in, 115; characterization in, 113, 115; cinematography of, 111–12, 113*f,* 114, 115*f,* 116; direction of, 110–11, 112; pedagogy of, 120; production of, 110–11, 121–22; time in, 110, 116

Oldham, Will, 112, 122

Orientalism, 85–86

Outpost Daria, 144

paranoid criticism, 19, 60

Parkins, Wendy, 102

parrēsia, 23, 131, 138–41, 149–50

pathos: embarrassment versus, 45; subjectivity and, 8, 18, 44–45

pedagogy: archival objects and, 17, 20, 161, 180, 192, 195; critical embarrassment and, 57–58; cynicism and, 153–54; of digressiveness, 192; of Diogenes of Sinope, 147–48; ease and, 81–83; inutility and, 9, 70; laziness and, 90; slowness and, 99–100, 118–19, 121

Perfect Human, The: postmodernity of, 10; remakes of, 6–7, 10

Performing Remains, 200

pleasure: ambition versus, 24, 92; boredom versus, 93, 99, 108–9; cinema and, 108, 114, 118; happiness versus, 135, 221n; slowness and, 20, 22, 99, 114, 118, 123; waywardness as, 24, 80, 168, 192

Plus One Animation, 152, 152*f*

Poor People's Movements, 141

pop music: cultural studies and, 17; in *Daria,* 153, 154–55; embarrassment and, 33–34; identity and, 183; industrial coordinates of, 27, 53; worry and, 194–95

Poor Theatre, 200

poststructuralisms, 15, 18, 44

Potter, Garry, 10–11

Powers, Ann, 36

Pratt, Jane, 150

precarity: Great Recession and, 30, 202; Hurricane Katrina and, 118; markers of identity and, 27, 90; performance of, 91; privilege versus, 17, 27, 31, 87, 117–18, 127. *See also* agency.

"Precious Things," 51–53

"Pretty Good Year," 54

Provenance of Beauty, The, 25–26

psychoanalysis, 27–28

Purshouse, Luke, 37, 41

queer: aesthetics and, 58–59, 64; musical cultures and, 184; race and, 183–86; politics and, 64; self-fashioning and, 185–86; theory and, 3, 16, 37–38, 197, 203; touch and, 190

Rabinow, Paul, 11–12

race: capitalism and, 123–25, 189; musical cultures and, 183; psychoanalysis and, 27–28; Rat Pack and, 83; television and, 58–59, 189; slavery and, 124–25

radical incrementalism, 23–24, 141–42, 143, 150–51, 153–54

Radiohead, 33–34

Rankine, Claudia, 25–27

slowness: animation and, 183; boredom and, 109; cinema of dilation and, 99–100, 109–12, 113–14, 118–20; cinema of duration and, 109; death and, 3, 123–25; dilation as, 96; food and, 102; phenomenality and, 20, 101, 106, 111, 116, 118–19; pleasure and, 101, 114, 118; politics of, 101–2, 116–17; thinking and, 97–98, 114–17, 118–20; space and, 101, 116; travel and, 102, 116; value of, 21, 101. See also Old Joy, Reichardt, Kelly, and Wendy and Lucy.

Smith, Stevie, 66

Smith, Terry, 11–12

snobbery, 32, 35

Sobchack, Vivian, 81–82, 116, 189–90

Sociology beyond Societies, 102

sophistication, 17, 35, 78, 133, 207n, 208n

South Pacific, 60

Spark, 60

Spears, Britney, 34, 55–56

speed: annihilation and, 100–101; blogging and, 181; cinema and, 114–15; modernity and, 100; slowness versus, 101, 219n; television and, 181; Web and, 180

Speed and Politics, 100–101

Spillers, Hortense, 27–29

Split Britches, 27, 64

Springfield, Dusty, 122

Stalnaker, Joanna, 175

Stanley, Sharon, 136–37, 168–69

Stevenson, Robert Louis, 70, 72

Stewart, Susan, 120–21

Stiegler, Bernard, 95, 98, 100–101, 108, 218n

stillness, 22, 67, 110–11, 115

strolling: art of, 24, 168, 178; linguistic resonances of, 168

subjectivation, 76

subjectivity: cinema and, 189–90; contingency of, 8; deformation of, 9,

29, 74, 138; disbursal of, 13, 44–45; embarrassment's contraindication of, 44; faciality and, 43; identity categories and, 185–86

supercut, 181, 183

Swingers, 93

tabloidism, 27

taste: expensive forms of, 35; hierarchies of, 31–32, 64, 187–88; nobrow and, 32

technics: blogging and, 181–82, 188, 190; distraction and, 162; representations of, 190; speed and, 97, 100; writer's block and, 98

Technics and Time, 100–101, 108

television: academe and, 130, 153; advertising in, 152–53; animation in, 143; changing contemporary landscape of, 58–59; cringe genres in, 43–44; cynicism in, 22, 130, 142–43; Dean Martin on, 82, 83f; documentary in, 199–200; recaps of programming in, 25, 183, 184, 190; reflexivity in, 146–47; scale and, 158. See also reality television and Web.

Television without Pity, 181

Terada, Rei, 18, 35, 44–45

Textual Poachers, 35

theatricality: 61, 131, 132, 141, 147, 155

This American Life, 43

Thomas, Aaron C., 185

Thompson, Mary, 184–85

time: acceleration and, 118–19, 125–26; arrests of, 94, 96, 98, 111, 125; capital as, 118; cinema and, 22; deceleration and, 118–19, 125–26; dilating of, 96–97, 99, 107, 114, 123; flows of, 21; experience of, 96–98, 99, 106, 113–14, 118–20; gestation over, 49, 99, 103; length and, 96, 97, 123; lounge and, 81, 85; modernity and, 120; rhythm and, 97, 113–14;

time (continued)
   superannuation of objects over, 182,
   191–92; taking of, 96, 98, 99, 102,
   121–23; tempo and, 100, 102–3;
   thinking in, 97–98, 115–17, 118–19;
   travel and, 102, 112, 116, 118–20;
   space and, 96, 102, 103, 115–16, 120;
   untimeliness of, 14, 32, 92; warping
   of, 96–97; wasting of, 65, 78, 93–94,
   191. See also duration.
To Venus and Back, 34
Tompkins, Jane, 35
Tori Amos: Live from the Artists Den, 36
Tori Amos: Piece by Piece, 36
touch, 186–89, 197–98
traffic, 5–6, 94
12 Years a Slave, 124–25
Tyranny of the Moment, 101

Ugly Feelings, 18
Ultra Lounge, 93
Undank, Jack, 167–68
Under the Pink, 35
undercommons, 29, 90
Undercommons, The, 90
unease: consciousness and, 28–29; as
   keyword, 27; politics and, 83, 123,
   125
Unembarrassed Muse, The, 33
university: corporatization of, 24,
   29–30, 73, 90, 153–54, 165; critical
   studies of, 19, 72–74, 90; teaching
   in, 30–31, 71, 153
Unrepentant Geraldines, 60
Urgo, Joseph R., 164–65, 167
Urry, John, 102

value: capital and, 1, 68, 199–200;
   contemporaneity and, 105; cynicism
   and, 130–31; digressiveness and,
   159–61, 192; of distraction, 163–64;
   eccentricity and, 2, 9, 74, 79, 98, 192,
   194; embarrassment and, 57–58;
   indeterminacies in, 2, 117, 202; lazi-

ness and, 66–67, 74–75; of parrēsia,
   138; recognition of, 74, 75–76, 160,
   203; restructuring of, 20, 68, 80;
   slowness and, 97–98, 218n; specificity of, 17; taste and, 31–32, 35
Vaughan, Vince, 93
Veronica Mars, 25–26
VH1.com, 181
Villarejo, Amy, 5–16, 31, 76–77
Virilio, Paul, 100–101, 218–19n
Virno, Paolo, 74–75
"Vision of Love," 155
von Trier, Lars: contemporaneity of, 11;
   documentary style of, 10–11; sadism
   of, 6–7; subjectivity of, 9

Walt Disney Company, The, 144
Warner, Michael, 198–99
Wasserstein, Wendy, 71, 72, 82
Weaver, Lois, 64, 92. See also Split
   Britches
Web: archiving and, 159, 175–76;
   fandom and, 144, 158–59; history of,
   74, 179–80, 181; Internet versus, 180;
   as medium, 74, 181; metaphor and,
   160, 173, 174, 177–79; navigation of,
   155, 160, 176, 178, 192; networked
   objects in, 80, 176, 178, 192; reading
   and, 162, 166–67, 175–76, 178; tele-
   vision and, 184–85, 202
Weeks, Kathi, 74, 213–14n
Welch, Gillian, 194–95
Wendy and Lucy: aesthetics of: 118–19;
   cynicism and, 128; pedagogy of, 120;
   politics of, 118–20, 123–24; production of, 121–22
West of Everything, 35
"When a Star Falls Down," 55–56
Wilde, Oscar, 67, 69–70, 72, 79, 82
Wilderson, Frank B. III, 197
Williams, Michelle, 118, 119f
Wood, Michael, 163
Wooster Group, The, 200
Wordsworth, William, 3–4

work: academe and, 29–31, 46, 72–74, 122–30, 153–54, 213n; cynicism and, 125–26; embarrassment and, 57; digressiveness and, 24, 158–59; lack of, 87, 118, 125–26; lazing mode of, 19, 66, 74–75; relationship of post-work to, 2, 20, 74, 86, 88; slowness and, 120–23; thinking and, 70; tolls of, 186–87, 188–89, 193; writing as, 19–20, 68, 158–59, 186–187

worry: anxiety versus, 29, 194–95; reading and, 24; rejection of, 194–95; speed and, 21; thinking and, 90–91

Woubshet, Dagmawi, 183–84

Wynette, Tammy, 3

Y Kant Tori Read (album), 49–50, 52f, 54f, 55

Y Kant Tori Read (band), 49–50

Yeo, Richard, 174

"Yes, Anastasia," 54

Young, Damon, 159–60

YouTube, 26, 57, 59

Zeno's paradox, 103

Zimmer, Michael, 178, 180